Pattern Language for Game Design

Pattern Language for Game Design

Chris Barney

CRC Press

Taylor & Francis Group

Boca Raton London New York

CRC Press is an imprint of the
Taylor & Francis Group, an **informa** business

The original illustrations in Section V, "The Fifteen Properties," are by Christopher Totten. The rest of the original illustrations in this book are by Jason Wiser.

First edition published 2021
by CRC Press
6000 Broken Sound Parkway NW, Suite 300, Boca Raton, FL 33487-2742

and by CRC Press
2 Park Square, Milton Park, Abingdon, Oxon, OX14 4RN

© 2021 Taylor & Francis Group, LLC

CRC Press is an imprint of Taylor & Francis Group, LLC

ISBN: 978-0-367-63395-0 (hbk)
ISBN: 978-0-367-36772-5 (pbk)
ISBN: 978-1-003-11902-9 (ebk)

Typeset in Minion
by Deanta Global Publishing Services, Chennai, India

Visit the patternlanguageforgamedesign.com

I want to dedicate this book to the three people in my life who brought me to the place where I had no choice but to write it.

To Jerry Levy, studying under you at Marlboro College set the academic bar that I have strived for throughout my career. You taught me to think deeply and to believe that we must use our understanding to change the world.

To Christopher Alexander, whom I have yet to have the privilege to meet, your words and insight into how we see the soul of the universe inspire me. I hope with all my heart that my work here will help open the doors of Pattern Theory to more designers and help us to all build the strong centers we need to be whole.

To my father, Gary Barney, you are a living example of Alexander's nameless quality. My drive to make the world a better place comes from you, and this book is my attempt to do just that. I hope the pages that follow make you proud.

Contents

Section VII   Building a Language

Chapter 15 ■ Connecting Patterns into a Language   313

Preface

How to Use This Book

M Y GOAL WITH THIS book is to teach you a new way to approach game design. You'll learn how to take the games you've played and the design tools you've already mastered and put them into a framework that you build. That framework will give you access to all of the knowledge you already have in a way that will let you understand when and why each tool is needed.

This book asks you to complete 25 exercises, each of which will help you describe a *pattern* found in game design. These patterns will help you understand or discover the techniques used to design games. Patterns that you produce will be your own, different from those described by other designers. You'll then connect those patterns into a *Pattern Language*. This language serves as the beginning of a framework that you'll use to organize your knowledge of game design so that you can always find the right design tools to solve the design problems you face.

FIGURE 0.1   We all come to game design with the knowledge gained from a lifetime of playing games.

Whoever you are, you already know a lot about game design. If you're a new student, you're coming to your studies with the things you've learned by playing dozens, probably hundreds, of games. But all of that knowledge is buried in your memories and experiences of those games.

FIGURE 0.2 Degree programs hand students so many tools that it becomes hard to know how to organize them.

As a student or beginning designer, your instructors or mentors hand you more tools. But they do it so fast that you don't have time to decide where to put them, and by the time you graduate, you've dropped some of them along the way and forgotten you ever had them.

FIGURE 0.3 Professional designers have accumulated so many tools that choosing the right one can be daunting.

If you're a working designer, you have a vast warehouse of tools and techniques that you've used or seen throughout your career. You have so many options that sometimes it can be hard to decide which ones you should be using or even what some of them do.

The process that this book walks you through will help you look at each tool you have, look at the games you've played, and see the tools used to create it. You'll look at each technique, understand its purpose, and describe that as a pattern, then find its place in your Pattern Language so you can find it again when the time is right to use it.

- Section I of this book looks at what precisely a pattern is. If you don't know, then it's an excellent place to start. If you think you know what a pattern is but you don't know who Christopher Alexander is, then I encourage you to take a look at this section. When I talk about a pattern, I mean something particular, and I promise it'll be worth your time!

- Section II covers the origin of pattern theory and describes how game design and other fields use it already. If you aren't sure about the idea of patterns and want to understand why they're valuable and how the techniques in this book developed, then you want to read this section.

- Section III talks about how a pattern is created or discovered, and shows you how to document your patterns. If you want to jump right in and start digging for patterns, or you want to understand how to get the most out of other people's patterns, then you can jump directly to this section.

- Section IV is where the exercises begin. If you're excited to get started, you can begin here and jump back to the first three sections when you have questions. You'll want to complete each exercise at least once, though each time you complete one, it'll give you a different pattern.

- Section V takes a step back from creating patterns and considers the higher-level properties of game design, which you may have begun to notice appearing again and again in the patterns you've created. Then it moves into more challenging exercises. You may want to skip ahead to this section after creating your first few patterns if you feel ready to add more depth to the patterns you're describing.

- In Section VI, you'll learn to connect your patterns into a language that you can use to design games that work in the way you intend. You'll also learn how to combine your language with those of other designers and adapt patterns that existed long before this book. Next, you'll learn to use your Pattern Language in your studio or classroom with your classmates and colleagues.

- This book also includes an example design produced by students and the patterns that they used to create it.

- Finally, this book includes a comprehensive list of the games used in the example patterns, so you can easily find more information on them to help you understand those examples.

FIGURE 0.4 Creating your own Pattern Language can give the structure you need, whatever your background.

I hope that you find the process of working through these exercises as rewarding as I have found the process of creating them.

Pattern Library Website

THE COMPANION WEBSITE FOR this book is available at patternlanguageforgamedesign.com. The site provides searchable access to all the patterns listed in this book, with more added all the time. It also contains the Games Reference with active links to all the referenced sources for easy access.

The website will allow you to add your patterns to the library and share them with developers all over the world. Over time that functionality will be expanded to allow you to create private languages for your dev team, class, or institution.

Acknowledgments

IT'S TRADITIONAL TO SAY that you could not have written a book alone. Now, at the end of writing one, I finally understand how true that sentiment is! This book may exist because I set out to write it, but if it is readable, comprehensive, rigorous, and beautiful, I have some work to do in providing thanks.

My eternal debt and gratitude to Kamela Dolinova, my life's partner, and to Meadow Osmun, my oldest and dearest friend, both authors in their own right. Your close reading, research, and technical editing allowed me to find the voice to say these words.

Jason Weiser and Christopher Totten have provided beautiful illustrations for this text. Their insight and playfulness may have saved me from producing a humorless impenetrable wall of text. Thank you for giving this book *Lebendigkeit*.

Thank you to Glenna Greer and Carter Seggev for their research work building the Games Reference included at the end of this book.

I must also thank my students at Northeastern University who suffered through and hopefully benefited from the development of the process that this book describes.

Author

Chris Barney is an industry veteran with over a decade of experience designing and engineering games such as *Poptropica* and teaching at Northeastern University. He has spoken at conferences including GDC, DevCom, and PAX on topics from core game design to social justice. Seeking degrees in game design before formal game design programs existed, Chris built his own undergraduate and graduate curricula out of offerings in sociology, computer science, and independent study. In pursuit of a broad understanding of games, he has worked on projects spanning interactive theater, LARP design, board games, and tabletop RPGs. An extensive collection of his essays of game design topics can be found on his development blog at perspectivesingamedesign.com.

I

Introduction

CHAPTER 1

Introduction

WHAT IS THIS BOOK FOR?

This book will not tell you how to design games. This book is not a list of rules you can follow to create games. It will not give you instructions for creating the meaningful games you have inside, the ones that you know will change the world. No list of design principles, methodologies, or even lenses, no matter how insightful, is sufficient for that. Every game is different and unique, and a book of techniques will never quite fit your needs. Memorizing principles and rules of design will never give you the level of mastery you need to shape games out of your passion.

What is this book, then? It's a book of exercises that will help you organize your understanding of design into a language that you can use to create games. If you're a student, this book will help you teach yourself game design. If you're an experienced designer already, this book will help you organize your hard-won understanding and insight. It will help you communicate to your colleagues why the things that you say are true. And if you're an instructor, this book is a new pedagogy. It will let your students derive design principles and rules from their own gaming experience. That process will prepare them to expand their design skills long after they have left the classroom.

What is this magical process? Sadly there is no magic, only hard work. But the short version is that this book will teach you how to apply the ideas of the architect Christopher Alexander, who pioneered the concept of a Pattern Language as the framework for architectural design (Alexander et al. 1977). Computer programmers and, later, game designers took his work and applied it to their fields. At its core, a *pattern*, as defined by

Alexander, is a generalized solution to a design problem found by examining many existing examples. But a Pattern Language is not just a collection of patterns. Those patterns must be linked together so that any designer can select the ones that work together to solve a specific problem. Because patterns are generalized and broadly applicable, any solution that they generate will be unique to the needs of the designer using them.

This book does not provide a Pattern Language for game design. Instead, it offers a series of exercises for you to complete. Each one gives you a different way to create a pattern. Once you've worked your way through this book, you can select the exercise that's best suited for any design problem you face, and complete it again to generate new patterns that fit your design needs. Over time, you'll link all of the patterns you create to build your own Pattern Language. This book contains only 24 exercises, but using them you can discover hundreds of patterns.

I hope that over time we'll share the patterns that we find with one another, combine the ones that are duplicates, and recognize deeper patterns based on the imperfect ones. Slowly, as an industry, we can come to understand the deep structures of our design practice. And that will allow us to create powerful, necessary games with craft, intention, and care.

WHY IS THIS BOOK FOR YOU?

If you already believe that making games is one of the most important things you could do with your life, then you can probably skip the rest of this section. But if you think that game design is just a fun career or a way to make money with your technical or creative skills, then read on. If you know why games must, *must* be carefully and thoughtfully designed, then feel free to skip ahead. But if you think that all you need are your artistic, technical skills and creativity, then this next section is for you too.

I believe that we use stories to tell each other about the world. The idea that early humans used stories to teach each other about the dangers of the world and how to survive them is not new. But the way that we tell stories has changed many times in the thousands of years since we sat in small bands around fires and told each other tales. The world has become more complex, and the number of people in it has increased. As we moved from hunter-gatherers to agricultural societies, the oral tradition became drama and literature. As we moved from agriculture to industry, from cities to nations linked across the globe, theater became cinema and television. As the industrial age gave way to the information age and nations became entwined in a fractally complex global society, theater has given way to tabletop and live-action role-playing games, and then to video games.

Tying those two progressions together into some kind of unified theory of the development of human narrative and its interplay with the development of human society would be a book in itself, but the idea is powerful and useful. It seems to me that as society became more complicated, we needed more robust ways to tell the stories necessary to understand the world around us; to teach ourselves how to survive in our ever more complex societies. Drama allowed us to tell more nuanced, compelling stories to somewhat larger audiences. Literature allowed us to reach thousands and millions with our narratives. Cinema gave us the best of both worlds: the higher fidelity of the image, and the reach and durability of the printed word.

We have reached a place where the world has become so complicated, and the problems we face are changing so rapidly that we manifestly don't know how to solve them, let alone how to craft stories that allow us to share that knowledge. Now we see the rise of interactive narrative. As designers, we use it to tell stories that let the audience become players. We watch players use our narrative frameworks to explore the problem spaces presented by the stories we tell.*

If any of that is even partially true, then it puts a lot of pressure on us as designers. There are still plenty of professional game developers, and even more game players, who will argue that games are "just for fun," and that the games they play and make don't affect their players. Games like Brenda Romero's *Train*† make a strong argument that games are indeed more than just fun and do change the thinking of people who play them. But a few examples are insufficient to prove this point, and it's an important point, so I am going to look at some of the mechanisms by which games influence their players.

First, as narratives, games have the same functional effect as any other form of storytelling: they present a world for us to consider. And as in all types of narrative, they can present information persuasively. As a portion

---

* This theory of the role of narrative in society is just a theory, albeit one I would like to spend a few years of my life rigorously researching. It doesn't have anything to do directly with the development or use of pattern languages, but it provides a good background to understand their importance.

† There are many other examples of profoundly affecting games, such as Lucas Pope's *Papers, Please*, and White Death by Nina Runa Essendrop and Simon Steen Hansen.

of the feast of media we consume, they are part of the cultural rhetoric*
that shapes our view of the world.

Games are unique, however, in that they're defined by mechanics that
players interact with, and those mechanics can reinforce their narrative
and form a type of participatory rhetoric. The player participates in the
demonstration of the validity of the argument. That last sentence was a
bit dense; let me give an example. A player winning a game of Settlers
of Catan has participated in the case that growth is a necessary component of success in a competitive economic environment. A winning player
must expand their settlements to generate a variety of resources in as large
quantities as possible. They are explicitly rewarded for building the longest
road and so on. That argument is not necessarily correct, because the artificial rules that constrain the game create it. Still, it feels very persuasive,
as you experience victory or defeat depending on your ability to play out
that argument.

And last, games are simulations of real-world systems: from a worker-
placement strategy game to a dating sim, from chess to playing house.
Sometimes the simulated systems are literal, and sometimes they're
abstract. Games let you practice interacting with those systems, often in
simplified situations in which it's easier to experiment and come to understand how they work.

If you've been playing games all your life, and if they're so powerful and
capable of influencing and teaching us, then why aren't you a super soldier
or ace pilot or skilled plumber? The answer is that we aren't very good
at using the potential of games. Educational games are mostly ineffective
and not engaging. (I say that having helped make more than a few.) AAA
titles are trying very hard to do a lot of things; however, those things are
all pulling in different directions, implementing systems and executing on
mechanics with high polish and not a lot of intention or understanding.

There are, of course, exceptions—games that make a strong argument
and have a profound impact on their players. If you think back on the
games that matter most to you, you will probably find some of the more
effective ones. For instance, compare the level "No Russian" from *Call of
Duty: Modern Warfare 2* to the white phosphorus scene in *Spec Ops: The
Line*. In *Call of Duty*, the designers put the player into a situation that tells
them to murder civilians. The designers did this for plot reasons, and to

---

* Cultural rhetoric is the idea that everything around us, everything we produce, is influenced by
the culture we live in.

give the player an emotional reason to hate the terrorists they are infiltrating. In some ways it works, but it amounts to the trope of "fridging" (killing a female character to motivate a male protagonist) applied to an airport full of innocents. In *Spec Ops: The Line,* the player is tricked into thinking that the only way past a group of enemy soldiers is to use a drone to target them for a mortar strike. The game hides the nature of the target from players; they see only markers on their radar that they assume are enemy soldiers. To advance in the game, you have to commit an atrocity. After you have located a nearby drone and mortar launcher and used it to fire white phosphorus mortars into the cluster of "enemies," you discover that they were refugees; men, women, and children. To advance to the next level, you walk past their charred bodies, including a mother holding a small child to her chest. Despite the graphic and manipulative nature of the sequence, it doesn't feel like it's using the shock value of the scene to sell copies of the game. It is integral to this game about the horrors of war and the way that interacts with their gamification.

Why did the level in *Call of Duty* feel offensive, but the scene in *Spec Ops* felt like an indictment both of war and of jingoistic shooters like *Call of Duty*? Because *Call of Duty* is a valor fantasy, intended to be fun and competitive and to have a story that makes you feel good about being a soldier fighting for your cause. *Call of Duty* has mechanics, narrative, and art that work to that end. Some aspects of the game, like the killing of civilians or "Press F to Pay Respects" in *Advanced Warfare,** work counter to those goals. The inconsistency in tone and mechanics across those games makes the scenes intended to create emotional motivation seem manipulative and disrespectful of both the player and the subject matter. *Spec Ops*, on the other hand, is entirely focused on its intent of critiquing both warfare and the military shooter genre. In that context, its use of forced moral choice becomes a powerful emotional tool that feels appropriate.†

The Pattern Language you build from the exercises in this book will allow you to design games in a way that aligns all the aspects of your game with the experience you're trying to create through it. Patterns are a neutral tool; games are not. They inherently have meaning, whether you

---

* "Press F to Pay Respects" is an infamous scene where players are attending a military funeral and when they approach the coffin are prompted to press the F key to pay their respects. Many critics found the mechanic shallow and disrespectful of the sacrifice of actual soldiers.

† That is not to say that all players were bothered by "No Russian" or that many players were not angered by *Spec Ops*, just that the reactions of players to that level in *Call of Duty* were unexpected to the developers, and players' outrage at *Spec Ops* was the stated intent of the developers.

intend it or simply echo the culture around you. So you may find patterns to examine the effects of racism and privilege, or you might find ones to help you maximize player retention and monetization. Patterns won't make designers make "games for good," but they will make you aware of what all of the aspects of your game are doing and help you make sure that it's what you intended.

WHY AM I THE PERSON WRITING THIS BOOK?

I've spent around 25 years focused on learning game design. Yet I still often don't feel like a "real" game designer. I certainly never imagined I'd write a textbook about it. But my own long, arduous, and circuitous education in game-making led me to the conclusion that this book was needed. I knew there had to be a better path than the one I had followed.

If you're reading this, you're likely in a class that's part of an educational program in game design or have been through one. Formal games education is a fantastic development, not least because it means I now have a job teaching game design. But it's also still very new. Degree programs in game design didn't exist when I went to college in the late '90s, and so I had to figure out how to learn it on my own.

Coming from a family of teachers, I knew that going to school was how you learn things, so I went to a college that allowed me to design my own program. And I learned a lot. But not enough to think of myself as a game designer.

I knew from reading interviews with "real" designers that the way you learn how to make games is by making them. So I started making games. I'm still proud of many of them, but I knew there were designers out there working far above my ability level. And I hadn't broken into the industry, so I clearly wasn't a game designer yet. I didn't even consider what I was making "real" games, for a number of reasons that seem false and even harmful to me now: I wasn't getting paid for the work, or the games weren't digital, or I was more focused on interactive fiction than mechanics.

Time for more school, I thought, and I got a master's in computer science with a focus on conversational artificial intelligence (AI). I came out of that feeling like I knew some things but still acutely aware of how much I didn't yet know.

Around this time, my good friend Link Hughes, who is currently a game designer at Google, began insisting I come to the Game Developers Conference (GDC) as a conference associate (CA). After three years of applying, the program accepted me. That was probably the best advice anyone ever gave me, not just because of what I learned about making games, but because I met other game developers there. I talked to these people I admired so much and realized they were only human. Some were smarter than I was; some were better game developers. But not all of them. I was new and inexperienced, but not hopelessly out of my depth.

So I made some more games, played more games, and applied for many, many development jobs. And I got no callbacks, so I began to despair. All my studies and practice didn't seem to be worth much to the industry I loved. Maybe I didn't have what it took, and perhaps everyone could see that but me. I hadn't completely given up on my dreams, but I was close.

Then one day, the call came. I was driving, and I pulled over to take it. After my future boss and mentor told me that he was extending an offer to work as a software engineer and game designer on *Poptropica*, I stayed parked on the side of the road for a while to cry. Even after all my work, I don't think that until that moment I had admitted to myself how important I thought games were or how much I needed to be a part of making them.

Let me take a moment here to say that if you don't feel that passion, if you don't *have* to make games, then put this book down and back away slowly. Whatever your skillset, you will almost certainly be paid more for it in another field. Take that job instead, and you won't have to bear the heartbreak that this field generates—and more importantly, you won't have the responsibility for making games. Because make no mistake: creating games is a huge responsibility. If you don't yet understand why that's true, read on, and don't worry, I won't stop harping on it. Kidding aside, the responsibility that game-makers hold is the heart of this book, and you'll need to understand it to understand why patterns are so important.

But let's get back to the path to becoming a game developer and how my journey led me to write this book. The attempt by colleges and universities to design programs that teach game design is admirable, and of course, I'm enthusiastically in support of it. I'm not telling you about my education as a way of griping about how hard I had it back in my day. ("We had to design our levels uphill, both ways! And we didn't even have graphics tighteners!") I'm not even telling you this because I think that the way I had to learn was unfair compared to the programs that exist today.

I'm telling you this because I have become convinced that game design is such a large, broad, delicate, and evolving art that we cannot teach it in the time a degree program gives you to learn it. The gaps that the current system creates in new designers impact the entire industry. Of course, many students go on to become great developers, but even the best of us spend years filling those gaps and learning on the job.

Once I got my first industry job, I recognized that my education was far from over. I began to believe that I was a game designer (maybe), but I didn't fool myself that I knew everything. I learned that the best of my colleagues were driven by passion, too, and while they were skilled and generous, most of them didn't have degrees in game development. They came to their expertise through many different avenues, all driven by that same sense that game-making is a subtle art. No great designer I've met takes their job lightly.

One of my colleagues recommended a book called *A Pattern Language* to the other designers on my team. But since it was the first I'd heard of it, and it was an architecture book, not a game design book, I added it to my endless list without realizing how close I was to a key to solving the problems I was seeing.

Fast-forward a few years, and I was attending the METATOPIA conference, mostly to playtest a board game I was developing. While there, I attended a talk titled "A Pattern Language for Larp Design" (Li and Morningstar 2020). That was my first real exposure to the formal idea of patterns. I loved the idea, but its application was particular to live-action role-playing games (LARPs). While I contemplated the usefulness of having a Pattern Language for general game design, I didn't pursue it then, either.

A year or so after that, I got a job teaching games in the game science and design master's program at Northeastern University. As I prepared to pass on the things that I had learned, I couldn't help but feel that my schooling, and my early experiences adjacent to the industry, had failed to prepare me adequately for the work. I knew that I had wasted years floundering after I graduated. And while my programs had taught me some valuable skills, they hadn't given me a concrete path to move from student to functional game designer.

Game designers often advise hopeful new developers and students that they should play all the games that they can and make games themselves; to learn by observation and practice. It's good advice, but I don't think it's enough. Making games helped, reading about games helped; playing games and thinking hard about them helped a lot. But there had to be a better way. No one had told me what to look for when I played games, or even *how* to look. And I had no way to judge whether the games I was making were good or even improving.

When I started teaching, I read a lot of game design textbooks. Mostly I was excited that such things existed since they hadn't when I was in school. Of course, the most generally useful to me as a designer was *The Art of Game Design* by Jesse Schell (2020). He mentioned the architect Christopher Alexander, who had written the Pattern Language book I had now heard of two times before. He also based several of his "lenses" for game design on Alexander's patterns.

A couple of semesters later, I had the opportunity to teach a graduate-level class with the intimidating name "Spatial and Temporal Design." It turned out to be a course on using architectural theory in game design. At this point, it was clear that it was finally time to read this book that had been chasing me through my career: Christopher Alexander's *A Pattern Language*.

Even with all of the buildup to reading it, I found myself unprepared for the enormity of this book's implications and scope. It's not a book about patterns in architecture. It's a book that proposes a new and powerful way to organize *thought* about a subject—in its case architecture, but with so many other possible applications, about which this book explicitly speculates. These ideas were so clearly crucial to game design that I immediately assumed I had just missed the books and conference talks that explored them.

A little research revealed that several books and doctoral dissertations had indeed been written on the topic by game developers who were as impressed with Alexander's ideas as I was. But when I read what other game designers had done with his work, I saw that all of the previous attempts to apply Alexander's ideas to game design were flawed in one way or another. They were either too narrow in scope or focused on producing one definitive Pattern Language to rule them all. If I wanted to use the idea of Pattern Languages in my teaching, I would have to figure out how to do it on my own.

I made my first attempt in that Spatial and Temporal Design class, and it was relatively successful. My students showed me great patience as I assigned them my early attempts at pattern generation exercises. We worked together to identify 117 patterns. Most of them were obvious things that any game design student would be told in school. At first, I was disappointed, but then I realized something crucial: *I had not told the students those things.* Instead, they had recognized those fundamentals through observation and practice, and I had given them the tools to do it.

At that point, I realized that the true power of Alexander's ideas wasn't in the actual patterns that he identified, but in the way that his Pattern Language *organized learning*. I started talking to my game design and teaching colleagues about my ideas, and one of them, Christopher Totten, became very excited. He asked if I had considered writing a book. I hadn't; on some level, I still wasn't sure that I was a real game designer, even after so many years and games. But I looked at the industry, struggling to mature, and at my students, striving to master the complexities of design. Eventually, I conceded that I needed to write this book: a textbook that doesn't teach game design directly but instead shows a way to use the process of building a Pattern Language to learn game design.

What this book is, then, is the culmination of my attempts to learn game design through the ad hoc processes that currently exist. It is an attempt to put in your hands a set of tools that will allow you not to learn the fundamentals of game design but to derive that knowledge through your lens of experience. It is, I hope, the basis for a new pedagogy, one that allows any aspiring game designer to unlock the principles that drive great games—the kind that changes the world.

PATTERNS, CREATIVITY, AND ART

As I began compiling my work on patterns, I was pleased with what I had. I felt like I had a manageable amount of work to do organizing and structuring the exercises and making sure I was clear about the pattern generation process. I thought I understood pattern theory, and how much or little of it was necessary to share for readers to understand and use these ideas and techniques. It turned out that I was wrong; the scope and significance of creating Pattern Languages far exceeded my initial assumptions.

All that became clear to me as I was speaking with a good friend about my work: I was laying out the plan for this book and all of the theories I just described for you. She nodded, agreeing that I was making a compelling argument, but asked if I saw any place for art and creativity in my theories, a question you may have been asking yourself. If I could look at games and use these techniques to understand the patterns that underpinned their creation, then was I reducing game design to an elaborate form of paint by numbers?

Of course, my immediate response was to say no, of course, not! Even after identifying a large enough group of patterns to use as a primary design method, the very nature of those patterns would be general and flexible. I would still need to apply creativity if I wanted to implement those patterns in my designs in a way that produced unique games that met my design goals. That's all true enough, but knowing that this friend was brilliant and certainly knew all of that, I bit my tongue and asked her what she meant.

She told me the story of an argument she had with a hidebound professor in an undergraduate class. She had written a poem about a flower and thought that it was enough that a poem was about the beauty of that flower and the joy it brought her. Her professor, of course, disagreed. He wanted to know the deeper meaning of the poem and her agenda in writing it. Possibly he wanted her to recognize the role of cultural rhetoric in her art. Maybe he wanted her to look closely at her work to see the craft she was applying to generate the words that had appeared, to her, to flow spontaneously onto the page in an act of pure creativity and art. Or perhaps he was just a jerk. Regardless, the incident stuck with her, and what she was asking me was whether this idea of looking at the product of human effort as being definable through a set of patterns left room for them to be art and not just craft. I said that of course they did. She smiled at me a little skeptically, and our discussion moved on. But she had succeeded in letting some of the wind out of my sails and getting me thinking. I worried about the problem for a while and eventually came to the following conclusions.

Why Are There Patterns?

It's clear that we can find patterns in games as Alexander did in architecture. Patterns seem to exist everywhere in the world around us—in the natural world, but also in everything we create and do as humans. Why? I think that this state is inevitable, given our understanding of the universe. That may seem like a bold claim, but follow along.

The laws of physics govern the universe, and those laws cause it to behave in predictable, repeatable ways that explain the underlying patterns we see around us. From the microscale of electrons orbiting nuclei to the cosmic scale of the earth orbiting the sun, the nature of the universe produces visible patterns. We live our lives dealing with the consequences of those patterns. The turning planet causes day and night, its path around the sun causes seasons, and life has evolved in a world that contains these basic patterns.

The structures of life conform necessarily to those patterns. As life becomes more complex and begins to exhibit behavior, the behaviors that succeed are those that take advantage of the immutable patterns in the universe. What I am describing, of course, is the theory of evolution. Now consider that, as intelligence evolves, not only is it governed by the ability to perceive those behavioral and environmental patterns, but intelligence may well be *defined* as the ability to recognize and regulate behavior to deal with those patterns.

Humans, then, are the most sophisticated pattern recognition machines in existence. They are the inevitable product of an ordered universe. This idea seems to echo Carl Sagan when he said, "We are a way for the cosmos to know itself."

The nascent field of machine learning and neural networks leverages this idea of pattern recognition. While they are still a long way off from consciousness, they lend support to our understanding of pattern recognition as a building block of intelligence in organic brains (Fogel 2001).

If humans are creatures that have evolved to recognize patterns and order their behavior by them, then it seems reasonable that anything we create is going to reflect those patterns that we have perceived. It seems to me that this is why there are patterns—in human behavior, organization, architecture, art, literature, and video games.

All that said, we are imprecise organic machines, and the patterns we perceive and imply are subject to individually limited data sets. There is nothing "true" or "good" about those patterns. The oldest, most persistent patterns would be the ones that had the best outcomes for an individual's or group's survival, not the ones that were true or just. And the existence of a pattern does not mean that it is understood consciously. Similarly, the inclusion of a pattern in a work of art or craft does not imply that the artist used it intentionally. Down that track of reasoning lie stereotypes and tropes, which I will discuss later.

Back to Art

Alexander looks at the world and seeks to identify patterns that architects can use to shape "good" spaces that will enrich the lives of the people who inhabit them. Computer scientists, in a more limited way, try to use patterns to create software that will function better to fulfill its purpose. I am attempting to look at the patterns in games and use them to create more meaningful, useful games that fulfill my intent. We are all turning patterns outward to shape and improve the world around us.

Artists, I think, are examining how the world affects them—seeing patterns in how they feel and using those patterns to make other people feel the things that they do. They are turning patterns inward and using them to understand themselves. That's not to say that artists don't produce art intended to create outward change in the world, or that architects and engineers don't have an inner life! We all combine our self-knowledge and our perception of the world in our work. The tension between the two defines human endeavor, and games sit very much on both sides of that line.

Is There Room for Creativity and Innovation?

Only if we understand what patterns exist can we see the places where we have not defined patterns and explore them. Only by observing the use of patterns in the world can we apply them in original ways or know when replicating the existing implementation of a pattern is all we need.

Different Designers, Different Patterns

Students that are given one of the exercises in this book produce different patterns than professors. Given the same exercise, experienced game designers notice different patterns than professors or students. While some are "better" versions of others, often they differ because they are from and for game designers with different perspectives and needs. A veteran designer's pattern may be profoundly insightful, but useless to a student focusing on the fundamentals. A student's results may be self-evident to a professor, but help the student articulate their understanding of a core concept. That same student might return to the same exercise years later and generate an entirely different but equally valid pattern based on the experience they've had since their first encounter with the exercise.

This book encourages the development of a personal Pattern Language that is what you, as a developer, need. It also promotes the sharing of patterns as a form of communication, with all of the aforementioned in mind. The mutability of pattern exercises also means that the set of exercises in this book can be used by designers from all areas of design to create patterns that are useful to their respective fields. For example, given an exercise based on themes in games,* a technical designer might come up with a pattern describing a mechanic that generates a sense of loss. A sound designer might detail a pattern for using character-based themes to create an attachment to significant non-player characters (NPCs). And an art director might generate a pattern about changing color usage to convey danger in horror games—each of these coming from a single pattern exercise.

---

* See Exercise 10: Theme Patterns.

Forming Patterns vs. Accepting Tropes and Stereotypes

Naively accepting this view of the world as a collection of patterns could lead to thinking that we perceive "truth" in patterns and that using them is "good." I don't believe that's true for several reasons. Patterns, outside of those defined by the physical laws of the universe, are based on human perception. Our ability to perceive and understand those, especially on the unconscious level on which most patterns historically have been formed, is limited and imprecise. The patterns that have persisted are those that give the most advantage to individuals and groups, not those based on "truth" or that produced just outcomes. Thus we have patterns of slavery, oppression, and abuse, things that generated at least a short-term advantage for those implementing the patterns.

While Alexander created the modern conception of a Pattern Language, the idea of patterns in human behavior or art has been around for a long time. Stereotypes are formal patterns, organically developed, and based on limited, reductionist observation. They create an advantage for the in-group and reinforce the maintenance of an insular worldview. The research into their development is extensive. Tropes are a more recent and intentional catalog of functional patterns in media. The patterns identified as tropes are, of course, nothing new, but recognizing them, calling them tropes, and using that knowledge to understand the context and intent, explicit and implicit, of media is relatively new.

In this book I am not using the term "tropes" just to mean an informal description of a pattern in the world or in games. By trope I mean a particular set of formal and functional mechanics that exists across games and other forms of media, and that encapsulates a social context and meaning. The website TV Tropes contains a vast collection of proposed tropes. However, it mixes tropes that fit my description and ones that lack the social context that is relevant to me. For instance, the trope urban ruins (TV Tropes 2020c) is loaded with a social context, while the trope checkpoint is close to a purely functional element (TV Tropes 2020a).

The process of generating patterns through the exercises in this book forces you to think deeply about the mechanics and techniques used in the games you observe. The exercises will help you understand the purpose behind those techniques, to see beyond their surface-level effects.

As you complete the exercises in the sections that follow, pay attention to the kinds of patterns you see. Consider their effect and intent. Some that you uncover will guide you toward creating innovative, compelling games with the potential to change the world for the better. Others that you observe will be recapitulations of the cultural rhetorics of intolerance, misogyny, and fear. Yes, I am saying that those things are present at a deep level in the games we play. I have included an exercise in Chapter 14 to help you look at tropes and understand their effects on games that use them.

Part of the work of developing your own personal Pattern Language is deciding what patterns you want to use to create your art—and to do so with eyes wide open to the effects of those patterns. As an industry, part of the work of converging on a shared Pattern Language will be choosing what patterns we want history to see when it looks back on the world our games are helping to shape. I hope we *all* choose wisely.

II

Background

CHAPTER 2

Background on *A Pattern Language* by Christopher Alexander

C HRISTOPHER ALEXANDER WROTE *A Pattern Language: Towns, Buildings, Construction* in 1977. It represents the most actionable part of his life's work of trying to reform architecture. To understand why he felt that reform was needed and how he thought that his idea of Pattern Languages could help, I need to give some background and then discuss his work itself, both before and after this particular book.

Alexander observed that many modern buildings, from homes to office buildings, were not pleasant places to be. The accuracy of his observation is debatable, but my experience matches his, and I am willing to accept it as sufficient motivation for his work. Alexander cited a disconnect between architects and the people who inhabited the buildings as responsible for the flaws in the buildings, though he did not clearly express the reasons for that disconnect.

He looked at older buildings and saw that they were often more pleasant to be in, both for himself and others he observed in them. He concluded that the construction of these earlier buildings more directly served the needs of their inhabitants. Possibly, this was because people at the time built their own structures, or they were built by people focused on their needs.

From there, he considered the way that buildings are built today. Two factors seem responsible for problems in the modern process. The first is that the technical knowledge required to construct modern houses, not to mention high-rises, is far greater than that needed to build a home a few hundred years ago. Thus, the professionals that design and build homes and larger structures have become more focused on mastering that body of knowledge. This codification of knowledge about building into the field of architecture has led to that field becoming focused on the skills and artistic tastes of architects, rather than the actual needs of people inhabiting their buildings. Not being an architect, I can't speak to how accurate that observation is. It certainly upset many other architects at the time the book was published.

The second factor is more social: modern architecture is almost exclusively driven by capitalism or other institutional forces. Most homes are not built at the request of the people who will live in them. Most high-rises are not constructed at the request of the businesses they will host, let alone by the employees who will work in them. Thus the controlling economic interest for architects is disconnected from the people who will inhabit their buildings.

Given this, it should not be surprising that most office buildings are cubicle-focused or use an even more efficient open floor plan. Thus they can fit as many workers as possible, rather than providing the most comfortable, individually productive workspace possible for however many workers that space can accommodate under optimal conditions. Modern buildings are not failing their owners. They are failing their inhabitants because builders are putting preference on the needs (profit and efficiency) of the building industry, rather than the needs (comfort and happiness) of the inhabitants.

As an architect himself, Alexander didn't think that architects were inherently evil or corrupt. He believed that as a profession, they had the intent to create beauty and to provide the best possible physical space for people to inhabit. But he felt that they were failing because, without the personal or direct connection to the needs of their buildings' inhabitants, they just didn't have a way to facilitate those needs. In the case of public buildings, they focused on the requirements presented to them. In the case of homes, they considered the abstracted needs of individuals.*

---

* For example: "People need kitchens," not "this chief will use his kitchen to enjoy his craft in comfort," or "this working programmer will only cook in an emergency and will be ordering takeout, so his kitchen space should focus on dining rather than cooking."

Alexander arrived at a two-part solution. First, he realized that he could look at existing buildings and derive patterns from the way they functioned. The second was an act of courage. He declared that there was such a thing as a "good" building that "beauty" was more than a subjective personal feeling. He understood a place to be good if it was serving the needs of the inhabitants and beautiful if it was creating a feeling of happiness and contentment in the inhabitants. He let these factors guide his observations of which patterns belonged in his Pattern Language. He referred to this quality of beauty and goodness in his earlier work as the "quality without a name," though in his later book *The Nature of Order* he refers to it simply as "life."

"There is a central quality which is the root criterion of life and spirit in a man, a town, a building, or a wilderness. This quality is objective and precise, but it cannot be named" (Alexander 1979, p. 19). Thus, the "central scientific fact" (Alexander 1979, p. 54) of Alexander's second theory of architecture is that a strong reciprocal relationship exists between environments and their inhabitants (Daws 2017).

> Games and their designers have a strong reciprocal relationship with their players. That might sound obvious, but as in architecture, it is something that we, as professional designers, somehow forget. It's common for designers to believe that mechanics have specific singular effects without consideration of their audience.

In Alexander's conception of traditional architecture, buildings affect the individuals that live there, and they should exist to serve the needs of their occupants. They will function better if their designs are directly dictated by those needs, rather than by an architect's lofty conception of the artistic or philosophical meaning of the building, or worse, by the architect's understanding of the needs of the corporate or institutional owner of the building.

His critique of modern architecture was that when architects looked at the problems that a given structure needed to address and tried to solve those problems based on their education and experience, they simply failed. They created buildings that had all of the parts required but were unpleasant to inhabit.

Of course, as a modern architect, Alexander also understood that the thousands of occupants of a high-rise couldn't directly control its design, and the millions of occupants of a city or region couldn't directly dictate its construction. In his conception of a Pattern Language, he was trying to find a way to capture the need-driven choices of existing architecture and structure them in such a way as to allow architects to create their designs based on the future needs of their buildings' occupants.

He was not arguing that all old buildings have this quality and are thus good, but rather that some few do: those created by builders that understood their own needs and had the skills to actualize them in the structures they built. Further, he argued that by examining those good buildings and searching for patterns in the ways that they solve particular problems, we could come to understand that quality ourselves and capture that understanding in our descriptions of those patterns.

PATTERN THEORY

> Our world can be understood as if it were interwoven by conscious and unconscious patterns, whereby each pattern is linked to other patterns. (Leitner 2020)

There has been an ongoing attempt to understand the work of Alexander and to make it accessible to a broader audience. His life's work, consisting of more than a dozen volumes, is insightful, but its scope and complexity are daunting. The most concise and lucid distillation of this body of work is *Pattern Theory* by Helmut Leitner. His analysis of the value of patterns echoes my own.

> While pattern theory originates in architecture, it is a general the-ory of development (of change, of transformation, of unfolding, of the creative process) and, as such, is relevant to almost every field of application, even for the very complex and for social systems. (Leitner 2015)

If you would like more background on the aforementioned ideas, then I cannot recommend this book highly enough. Reading Leitner's book is not necessary to understand the rest of this one, but taking the time to absorb its slim 156 pages will make the theory here easier to follow.

CRITICISMS

As I mentioned earlier, Alexander upset a significant number of architects. His work continues to generate both praise and criticism more than

40 years after its publication. I want to address a few of the more cogent criticisms before moving on.

Alexander's work is far from perfect, and some of the criticism it generates is merited and requires consideration. However, a surprising amount of it seems to be rooted in misunderstanding or a willful argumentativeness that is difficult to justify. For instance, a meta-analysis of criticisms of *A Pattern Language* lists criticism that physical copies of his work look too much like Bibles and thus suppress criticism (Dawes 2017). I am not even sure how to respond to that.

On the other hand, many critics have pointed out that the examples used by the 253 patterns are primarily from Western architecture. That is demonstrably true. Further, because of that focus, the Pattern Language that they define is focused on creating spaces that will generate comfort and pleasure in Western occupants. I do not agree with some of these critics that this focus invalidates the concepts of *A Pattern Language*. Alexander (1977) addresses this very concern in the book's introduction:

> Every society that is alive and whole will have its own unique and distinct pattern language; and further, that every individual in such a society will have a unique language, shared in part, but which as a totality is unique to the mind of the person who has it. In this sense, in a healthy society there will be as many pattern languages as there are people—even though these languages are shared and similar. (Alexander 1977)

It seems clear that given the imperative to extend the patterns he presents, and the acknowledgment that anyone creating patterns will necessarily define patterns idiosyncratic to themselves, that Alexander did not intend the 253 patterns shown to be applied blindly or universally. Furthermore, he explicitly calls out the uncertain validity of those patterns in a confidence rating assigned to each. The rating ranges from 1 to 5 and indicates whether a pattern is newly documented, seen pervasively, or successfully used in existing projects.

One aspect of Alexander's writing that I find appealing is his willingness to use qualitative language. He describes things that are "good" or "bad" in terms of architecture's effect on people and society. He wrote in this style in the face of the relativist sentiment prevalent in mid-20th-century thought. It was much more acceptable to say that a thing was neither good nor bad and that those kinds of value judgments were only in the perceptions of the observer. While acknowledging that every person will perceive differently and that innumerable factors that shape us and our societies affect those perceptions, Alexander nevertheless says that he believes there are fundamental commonalities between people, whatever their background.

His view fits well with my earlier premise that we are all pattern-recognition machines, and that while many of the patterns we see are social and societal, many are also based in the physical world and thus universal across individuals and cultures. Another way of looking at this would be through the lens of *self-determination theory*, the idea that all individuals desire autonomy, competence, and relatedness. Patterns that increased those feelings in individuals would be perceived by them as possessing "the quality without a name."

Last, some of the resistance to Alexander's ideas comes from the fact that they are openly utopian. He states his desire that architects physically build a better world. His descriptions of what that world would look like, what patterns it would make it up, and what social changes would be necessary to bring it about do not sit well with modern capitalist society. Critics have stated that Alexander's ideas do not leave room for people who have desires that differ from his worldview. This implies that some people want to work as much as possible, discard comfort for efficiency, and so on. That may be true to some degree, at least in the world as it is. Our society is undeniably deeply focused on those kinds of goals. Alexander was unashamed to take the position that those people were being influenced by larger social forces and making decisions against their own best interests. That argument comes down to a philosophical difference even if it's true: isn't it the right of people to behave as they choose? I think that on a moral and philosophical level, Alexander wanted to find a way to push back against those very societal forces, to build a world that didn't drive people into those behavioral patterns.

The tone of this line of criticism leads me to believe that the critics arguing most loudly against his conception of good are the very owners that pay architects to produce buildings based on their desire for profit or efficiency rather than on the happiness of the inhabitants of the buildings.

Regardless of who is in the right in that moral debate, I don't think that it's relevant to the validity of his theory of patterns, only to the types of patterns an individual will consider good and how they will apply them.

IMPLICATIONS FOR GAMES

All of this ties to the exercises in this book, which let you create a Pattern Language for games based on the patterns that you see. How you assess those patterns, which ones you see as "good" and which you see as "bad," will be based on who you are, your experience playing games, your current design skills, and what you want players to get out of the games you design.

One of the most valid points raised against the work in *A Pattern Language* applies strongly to game design: the criticism that Alexander drew entirely from Western architectural tradition as a source for his patterns. The criticism isn't altogether valid, as he did look outside of Western architecture. Still, as a part of Western culture, it is undeniable that his patterns, at least in his early work, had that focus. An example used by one of the critics highlights this problem. Alexander designed a housing project in Lima, Peru, using *A Pattern Language*. The project was not well received. The residents of the new buildings found them uncomfortable in a variety of ways. For example, the homes used a pattern which calls for "bed alcoves." But in Lima, it was quite hot, and the sleeping nooks were stuffy and unpleasant. The critic saw this as evidence that building based on a Pattern Language does not result in buildings that are better to live in than those built with other modern design models. Alexander himself acknowledged the lack of success of this project, and it may have been a factor in his move away from further development of the language that he began.

Yet the problems encountered in this project were not related to the concept or structure of Pattern Languages in general. Alexander fell victim to one of the very issues he was trying to avoid: he did not build for the intended inhabitants of the building. The Pattern Language he developed, and the specific patterns applied to the project, were grounded in a different set of inhabitants. It is critical to understand the people that you are building for and to note as part of your patterns how tied to a specific location or society they are. In game terms, we must be aware of our audience both as we distill patterns and as we apply them. Patterns found in Western shooter games from the 1990s to 2000s are unlikely to apply well to the audience of casual puzzle gamers or Japanese dating sim fans. To some degree, the exercises in this book work to mitigate this problem by asking you to look for as diverse a set of example games as possible. Patterns found in a set of games drawn from across genres and cultures are more likely to be universally applicable. But there will be times when you are specifically interested in patterns that arise in a more narrow set of games. When you generate such patterns, it will be necessary to note their limitations and to take care when applying them beyond the scope of the games that exhibited them.

Implicit in the preceding statement is the need to understand the target audience of a game. This need was articulated by Michela Ott and her colleagues (2011) in their paper on pedagogy in games: "The first basic choice concerns the definition of the target users and the elicitation of their needs." That audience may have been explicit in the game's design, or it may be the unintentional result of the focus of the designers. For example, designers may have created a licensed Barbie game for pre-teen girls from America. Or a game like *Gone Home* may have been organically designed for people who experienced the painful early emergence of queer culture as it played out in the late 1980s and early 1990s. For every game you design and every game you use as a source in the pattern exercises, you must be aware of its intended and actual audience. And in every pattern you generate or use, you must be mindful of the scope of its applicability.

In terms of taking a moral and qualitative stance toward design, I tend to side with Alexander and work to create a Pattern Language for myself that will allow me to make games that will nudge players toward that utopian outcome. Still, there is nothing in the process that necessitates that focus. It is entirely possible to use the exercises to distill patterns that will maximize monetization, encourage toxic behavior, or reinforce hostile worldviews. I intend that statement as a warning and imprecation to use these tools wisely while admitting that there is nothing in them that requires an altruistic moral purpose—beyond our desire to judge the quality of our patterns by their capacity to create Alexander's quality without a name.

CHAPTER 3

Background on the Use of Pattern Languages in Other Fields

COMPUTER SCIENCE

In the early 1990s, as object-oriented programing was becoming a dominant paradigm, several computer scientists took note of Christopher Alexander's work. Their interest stemmed from the fact that to program effectively, in an object-oriented manner, a programmer needs to analyze any problem they are programming a solution for and conceptualize an object-oriented solution. This process is known as object decomposition.

The difficulty is that while some problems suggest a clear object structure, many or even most could either be broken down in near-infinite ways or do not seem to fit an object-based model at all. Any two programmers working at that time could look at a problem and generate entirely divergent object models.

The question of which model for a given problem was better was a common point of contention in programming teams. Was it better to generate a model that most closely reflected the real system or one that was the simplest, or the most computationally efficient, or the easiest for programmers to understand? As computer scientists struggled with these questions, some turned to the concept of patterns for a solution.

Some, like Richard Gabriel, looked closely at the philosophy and purpose of Alexander's work. Gabriel was interested in creating programs that were "beautiful" and that allowed programmers to more intuitively and comfortably construct and maintain code. He saw a similarity with architecture, in that object-oriented design needed guidance and structure to create consistently usable code. Gabriel (1998) quoted Alexander saying:

> It takes away from them the everyday, lower-level aspiration that is purely technical in nature (and which we have come to accept) and replaces it with something deep, which will make a real difference to all of us that inhabit the earth.

But Gabriel saw the users of the code, its "inhabitants," as being the programmers that wrote and maintained it, rather than the computers that executed it or the people that used the programs it produced. In this conception, the users of a program would be the inhabitants of the user experience design of the program and would have little or no stake in the underlying technical structure of the code. The programmers, on the other hand, would have a deep stake in the structure and ordering of that internal logic.

Gabriel (1998) also anticipated problems with the implementation of patterns in an object-oriented design similar to those Alexander faced in architecture:

> The real reason that common patterns are not used rather than tight abstractions is efficiency. It is more efficient to write abstracted, compressed code than uncompressed common patterns, and it is more efficient to execute abstracted code in some cases. For example, if we were to write the two lines that do map-car and length, they would run about twice as slow as some complex compressed version. This wouldn't matter if computers were big enough and fast enough for the programs we need, but right now they aren't. So we continue to pay with the sweat of people so that computers can take it easy and users don't have to be inconvenienced. Perhaps someday the economics of this situation will change. Maybe not.

While I agree with Gabriel's take on the use of patterns in object-oriented programming, his book on the topic doesn't propose a concrete way to create or discover the patterns he calls for, nor does it set forth example patterns. It was a call to action for others in the industry to consider the issues he raised when developing patterns.

———

By far, the most well-known application of patterns in object-oriented design is the much more concrete *Design Patterns: Elements of Reusable Object-Oriented Software* (Gamma et al. 1994.) The authors of this book, often referred to as the "Gang of Four," combined their considerable collective experience and looked at a presumably vast amount of object-oriented code to produce a set of well-defined, useful patterns. A significant segment of the programming industry adopted the patterns in this book. There has been some criticism and pushback, and while many of the patterns do not apply to other styles of programming (such as functional or aspect-oriented programming) that have become more popular over time, it is not a stretch to say that these patterns have been the most influential and popular concepts in programming over the last 20 years.

Frankly, I've always kind of hated these patterns. I have used many of them, and even consider some of them to be fundamental principles of programming or necessary building blocks of any code I write. But they always made me uncomfortable in a way that I was never able to articulate until I began to work toward applying Alexander's idea of patterns to game design. In that light, I see several flaws in the work of the Gang of Four.

The fundamental problem is that they are not design patterns; they are techniques that repeated across many designs. All of the patterns that are listed are indeed found over and over again in object-oriented code. They are useful in understanding how to structure aspects of that code in a functional way, but they lack the two qualities required to be patterns in the Alexandrian sense: they do not address specific design problems, and they do not have the structure of a language needed to produce whole designs. They are useful principles that programmers need to understand to write object-oriented code effectively, but they are not design patterns that a programmer can use to understand how object-oriented structure should be best applied to address the specific needs of any program as a whole.

To give a specific example, one of the patterns is "The Singleton." A singleton is an object that can only exist once in a body of code. You might code a connection to a database as a singleton. In that way, every time you tried to create a new connection, you would be given the same connection object. That would prevent different parts of your code from creating unneeded extra connections, which could impact performance. So it's an excellent technique to use under certain circumstances. But what design problem is it solving? When should it be used? Does it need or assist other patterns?

Additionally, the Gang of Four's book lists 23 patterns. They did admit that other patterns might be discovered, but conceived of the patterns that they were suggesting as fundamentally true and largely complete in terms of providing the structure and guidance needed for writing effective object-oriented code.

Of course, many programmers who adopted the use of those patterns became dogmatic about that use, and labeled any code that did not implement them as having "anti-patterns." In some cases, non-conforming code was flawed, but in others, it was merely solving a specific problem using a pattern that fits that problem rather than forcing the use of one of the canonical patterns.

––––

In short, the potential of a Pattern Language to reshape programming into an engineering discipline that can produce code that is functional, maintainable, and "beautiful" has never manifested, despite the prevalence of the use of "design patterns" in the field. That failure has more to do with the aspects of pattern theory that the authors neglected when producing those commonly used patterns.

SOCIAL AND BEHAVIORAL SCIENCE

The ideas of patterns and Pattern Language have come more recently to the field of social and behavioral science, with active research and development beginning in the early 2000s. This field has stayed closer to Alexander's original ideas than computer science did, the work mainly being a direct implementation of pattern theory to areas such as organizational design, pedagogy, and creative learning.

The most exciting outcome came from a group working on a Pattern Language for creative learning. While they had the goal of producing a Pattern Language, they also documented their process. They published a paper describing their process and how to apply it more generally for creating other languages (Iba et al. 2011). I discovered this work well after developing the methods used here. However, the rigor with which they tested their process helped confirm my observations. Their process consists of five steps: Pattern Mining, Pattern Prototyping, Pattern Writing, Language Organizing, and Catalogue Editing. The process is focused on providing a framework to generate a language needed by a subject area and produces a language document ready for publication.

It is useful to consider the ways that Iba et al.'s process differs from mine and why. They begin with an information discovery phase, in which the group considers their shared knowledge of the topic of the language, then does additional research to gain a broader perspective and makes sure their understanding reflects the needs of those who will be affected by the language. In the case of their example language for creative learning, they were professors at a university focused on creative learning, and their additional research consisted of interviewing other faculty members and students. This choice fits well with Alexander's desire to construct buildings that meet the needs of their occupants in collaboration with those people.

Second, their process included regular "pattern writers workshops" in which in-process patterns were peer-reviewed and revised based on feedback. The construction of their language was a major academic effort that took many hundreds of hours and was the primary focus of the group members during its execution. The finalized document consisted of 42 patterns. It was distributed to more than 4,000 students and was functionally complete on distribution.

The most important difference from this process and what I describe in this book is the focus of a central group on creating a language for broad use by the field. The techniques you will learn in the following sections are focused on the *process* of creating a *personal* language. The language may find broad use, but its intended value is the understanding you gain by creating it.

CHAPTER 4

Background on the Use of Patterns in Game Design

I AM FAR FROM THE first game designer to get excited by the idea of patterns for game design or even a Pattern Language for game design. Before digging into the specifics of the process I have developed, I want to take a look at the previous attempts.

In this section, I am trying to provide a balanced critique of these books, articles, and practical projects. I intend to use them to orient the work of this book and make sure that it is advancing our industry's understanding and ability to use patterns. To that end, I am looking both at what these scholars and designers are doing well and where they seem to be either off track, mistaken, or producing incomplete conceptual work. I compare these works with that done by Christopher Alexander to see whether they fall short of it, meet that standard, or improve on his ideas. I have the utmost respect for the work done by all of these scholars and could not be writing this book without their insight. Please do not confuse my attempt at a rigorous analysis and critique as disrespect or disregard.

BOOKS

Patterns in Game Design

The first of the two major books dealing with game design patterns, and most evident by the title, is *Patterns in Game Design* (Bjoörk and

Holopainen 2006). This book is impressive in its scope and provides a useful catalog of observed patterns. The authors discuss at length the two ways that the patterns in the book were derived:

> Transforming Game Mechanics
> Given this initial conceptual framework, we proceeded by examining game mechanics and converting them to patterns.
>
> Harvesting Patterns by Analyzing Games
> The second approach to create an initial pattern collection was by "brute force" analysis of existing games, concepts and design methods of other fields.
>
> In line with this, we have created a collection of patterns, primarily based on transforming documented game mechanics or well-defined concepts from other research fields.
>
> (Bjoörk et al. 2003)

Patterns in Game Design should be required reading for any new game designer because it succeeds at its primary goal of creating a useful and extensive vocabulary of game mechanics. However, I want to be clear that I would not consider this to be a book of game design patterns in the way that *A Pattern Language* is a book of architectural patterns. As stated by the authors, the patterns listed in the book are simply abstract game mechanics written up in a similar style to that suggested by Alexander. The patterns contained in this book fall short for several reasons.

First, the authors chose to divorce their patterns from the problems they address:

> Unlike most design patterns we have chosen not to define patterns as pure problem/solution pairs. This is due to two observations. First, defining patterns from problems creates a risk of viewing patterns as a method for only removing unwanted effects of a design. In other words, using patterns as a tool for problem-solving only and not as a tool to support creative design work.
> (Bjoörk et al. 2003)

The result of this decision is patterns that don't focus on the reason for their use. I take issue with the idea that understanding the reasons for using a pattern will invalidate its use in creative design work. Perhaps the issue here is misunderstanding what Alexander meant by "problem." Certainly, he saw many problems with the architecture of his day and intended his Pattern Language to help overcome them. However, that was not what he was talking about when he said:

> Each pattern describes a problem which occurs over and over again in our environment, and then describes the core of the solution to that problem, in such a way that you can use this solution a million times over, without ever doing it the same way twice. (Alexander 1977)

The problem he was referring to was not a specific defect in a design that needed a solution, but the desired outcome of the design that needed a solution. While Alexander often started with a literal problem in existing designs as the inspiration for seeking out the pattern that solved them, that is incidental to the nature of the pattern. For example, in Pattern 159: Light on Two Sides of Every Room, the design problem is stated as the following: "When they have a choice, people will always gravitate to those rooms which have light on two sides, and leave the rooms which are lit only from one side unused and empty" (Alexander 1977). This statement addresses the specific problem of rooms with natural light on only one wall being unused, or those rooms feeling unpleasant, dark, or claustrophobic to their users. But it is just as accurate to rephrase the problem to focus on the intended effect, perhaps like this: "To ensure that a room is welcoming and that people gravitate toward its use, place windows on two walls. This will ensure that it is well lit and comfortable for its occupants." The design problem is providing natural light in a space to make it comfortable to occupy as much as it is preventing rooms from being dark and unused.

Looking at a problem from game design will help illustrate this point. An example problem could be negatively stated as "Narrow doors in an first-person shooter (FPS) game cause players to be caught up in the geometry and break the flow of play." Or it could be more usefully stated positively as, "Door size and placement should reflect and support the pace of play." The understanding of the purpose of the pattern is what will allow designers to know if they should be using it. To continue this example, perhaps the first design problem would result in a pattern saying that to promote gameplay flow, doors should be twice the width of the character—a reasonable, if very low-level, pattern. Without a problem statement, I might be designing a horror-themed game and include pleasantly wide doors per the pattern. That could undermine my higher-level goals of creating tension in situations where I want the character to have difficulty navigating to make the player feel the character's sense of panic. However, if the problem is part of the pattern, then I would know that it did not apply to my situation. In fact, it might be a pattern that I would, in the case of a horror game, want to violate explicitly. If I used the second version of the problem, the resulting pattern is more general and applies to both situations: "To create the intended flow and pacing for player movement, designers should place geometry, doorways, obstacles, etc. in ways that facilitate the intended pace of play." In short, clearly stating the problem that a pattern solves—or to phrase it differently, *the effect that the pattern creates*—is one of the critical differences between a well-described mechanic and a pattern suitable for use as part of a Pattern Language.

Despite rejecting problems as part of their "patterns," Bjöörk and Holopainen (2006) continue to acknowledge their importance: "As patterns are general solutions the application of a pattern to any given situation requires a number of design choices specific for the current context." By referring to patterns as "general solutions," they tacitly acknowledge that they must be solving for some problem or providing some effect.

Patterns from this source are heavily mechanics-focused, what I refer to as shallow patterns. They are accurate and useful abstract summaries of mechanics, but they do not provide the context or understanding of when to use the pattern. The template used in *Game Design Patterns* to document the patterns includes a "Consequences" section; this is probably the most useful aspect of this work. However, the consequences are described mainly in terms of the other mechanics-based patterns, so they fail to describe the effects of the patterns fully.

Game Mechanics: Advanced Game Design

The second major work that attempts to incorporate patterns and a pattern language is *Game Mechanics: Advanced Game Design* (Adams and Dormans 2012). This book probably comes the closest to creating the beginnings of a pattern language for game design in the way that Alexander envisioned for architecture. Despite that, I think that it falls short in several ways.

Its first shortcoming is in scope. Adams and Dormans are experts in mechanical game design, so, unsurprisingly, their patterns focus on this strength. That limited scope is not necessarily a problem for a group of patterns intended to be the seed for a much larger language. However, they define only 16 patterns and present them as a nearly complete language, only suggesting that designers should keep their eye out for additional patterns.

In keeping with Alexander, the authors present a format to use in recording a pattern. Their template includes "intent," "motivation," and "applicability" sections that address the question of when to use the pattern. Finally, it includes "implementation" and "examples" sections. Each entry contains most of the information that I would want to see in a pattern. I do think that they take the drive toward abstraction a bit far and that it can be challenging to know how the patterns apply outside of their specific descriptions. This combination of abstraction and specificity makes it hard to understand the full scope and power of the patterns. Usually, a pattern gives only one or two examples of its use, further limiting visibility on the usefulness of the pattern.

The structure and content of these patterns are similar to the computer science pattern collection in *Design Patterns: Elements of Reusable Object-Oriented Software* (Gamma et al. 1994). That book defines useful patterns like "The Factory Method," but does not provide a framework to help programmers understand when or why to use its patterns. Adams and Dormans, like the Gang of Four, clearly understand when and how to use their patterns. But they are so focused on those patterns that they fail to provide the level of context necessary to show other programmers or designers how to use them well as a design language.

I would suggest that patterns like "Static Generator," which details a way to add resources to a game, are more useful when placed into the context of a language. If we provide a parent pattern that makes clear *why* resources are necessary for a game, then it becomes possible to articulate why one type of resource generation is preferable over another. For instance, consider the problem: How can a designer create space in a game for meaningful tactical choices, both providing the player with forward momentum and limiting their progress? You might derive a pattern like: "A designer may wish to limit player progress by introducing a cost for player actions. The resource used to pay this cost can be provided in many ways. See child patterns: Static Generator, etc."

It would then be possible to look at each of the resource generation patterns and understand how their implementation of the parent pattern differs and what more specific problems they each address. I will revisit the idea of improving and adapting patterns from sources like this one in the section on integrating patterns from other sources.

The idea of a Pattern Language is appealing for several reasons. The first that captured my imagination was the promise of having a single complete language, shared between all developers, allowing clear communication without limiting our designs with a rigid set of rules that would sap our designs of creativity. That's a noble goal, and if I knew that I was regarded as one of the leading thinkers in games, as Adams and Dormans are, I might think that I was the person who should or could create such a language. They see the benefits of shouldering that burden for us and putting their hard-won experience to good use: "After all, most of these patterns have evolved in games over a long period. Design patterns allow you to build on that experience without going through a long learning period yourself."

The problem with that goal, though, is that game design is a vast field, so broad that even its best minds focus on particular parts of it; in the case of Adams and Dormans, it's deep systems and mechanics. Those are important aspects of game design, but so are the theme, narrative structure, and art and sound design. I do not mean the implementation of art, narrative, or sound—those are their own distinct disciplines—but the design in each of those areas. Saying that art design is just part of the art department and not part of game design would be like saying that mechanics design is only part of game programming. I am not arguing that an art department can't be responsible for the art design of the assets that they are producing. However, to create assets that are in line with the theme, narrative design, and mechanical design, all disciplines must be engaging with the same design language.

For any Pattern Language to be complete enough to be useful, it must start at a high enough level to encompass each of those areas. Even for a design team divided into those areas, such a language would be necessary for those teams to best work together.

My last criticism of the Pattern Language section of *Game Mechanics: Advanced Game Design* is that the authors do not provide a clear description of the process they used to arrive at the patterns they put forward. The lack of insight into the creation of their patterns limits the reader's ability to extend the Pattern Language they propose.

SCHOLARLY ARTICLES

A large number of scholarly articles and dissertations consider the idea of patterns and a Pattern Language in games. The focus of these is necessarily narrow, but looking at a few provides insight into the ways that patterns are understood and used in the game design field.

"The Case for Game Design Patterns"

The article "The Case for Game Design Patterns," published in 2002, argues that game design needs patterns. It uses the term *Alexandrian patterns*, which I think is a clear way to refer to them and distinguish patterns that conform to all of his theoretical tenets from those that are just inspired by his ideas. The primary reason that the author, Bernd Kreimeier, suggests that patterns are needed is to provide a shared vocabulary for game designers. However, the article also mentions that the connections between patterns could serve to provide a conceptual framework for that vocabulary. The article acknowledges that a shared pattern language would be most useful if it covered the full scope of game design and that the breadth of the field makes that challenging.

Despite calling out the importance of patterns addressing problems, the author states that "pattern methods are simply a successful way to express existing knowledge" and that "patterns are simply conventions for describing and documenting recurring design decisions within a given context" (Kreimeier 2002). This definition results in seeking patterns that are just the elements of design, rather than patterns that suggest ways to solve deeper problems. The first example in the next section exemplifies the difference between Kreimeier's approach and the one used in this book.

Last, this article does not discuss a process for deriving patterns. In the absence of a methodology designed to produce and continually improve upon potential patterns that are likely to be valid, Kreimeier states that the "conventions of any pattern template do not guarantee (or prohibit) that useful patterns will be found and documented." This runs in direct opposition to the purpose of Alexandrian patterns. Alexander did not create his patterns to provide a vocabulary for architecture; it already had that. He created them to help architects understand when to use the techniques that they already understood. In our discipline, we are still struggling to understand the techniques we are using and developing and to understand the formal and functional elements of the field and their effect on the games we are designing. Building a Pattern Language does help you achieve those vital goals. However, its primary purpose is more significant than that. It shows us when elements are needed, why we should be using them, and how we might go about it.

"Developing a Pattern Language for Flow Experiences in Video Games"

The article "Developing a Pattern Language for Flow Experiences in Video Games" (Lemay 2007) attempts to take a conceptual idea from game design and develop a pattern language focused on producing that concept in games. That feels like an important application of Pattern Languages.

For Alexander, the first step in applying his Pattern Language to a project was to identify what design problems the project was trying to solve. He asked what the building was for, how people would use it, and how it should make its occupants feel. He even referred to the subset of patterns chosen for a project as that project's Pattern Language. For instance, the patterns used to build a small country home would be different from those used to erect a barn or a cathedral.

In game design, we are nowhere near having a functionally complete pattern language from which to select smaller project-specific languages. We are still at the point of generating preliminary patterns. We will then have to stitch those together to create a broader language framework defined by their interconnections.

The patterns identified in this article all seem like they will help to produce games that create a flow state, so in that way this work is successful. The author includes a section in each pattern titled "forces"; this is an idea from Alexander's work that is often dropped by groups trying to adapt his work. The forces section provides context for when a pattern is valid and identifies the forces that may help a pattern function, lower its effectiveness, or even prevent its use.

But this project falls short of being an Alexandrian Pattern Language in several ways. First, it is so focused on the purpose of creating flow in games that it does not address the question of when that is desirable. The implication of referring to flow state as "optimal experience" is that it is always beneficial to create it and that any game that does not generate flow in its players is suboptimal.

The process used to derive the patterns also seems to be incompletely described or flawed. The listed patterns are created by using the pattern format to describe theory, rather than by examining existing games that generate a flow state and looking for patterns in how they do that. While the idea may be sound and the pattern-shaped descriptions of the theory may produce the desired results, they are not patterns in the Alexandrian sense. You cannot derive a pattern from observation if you are trying something wholly new, so there may be some value in creating patterns from theory, as I discuss in Exercise 24. However, even in that case, it would be essential to differentiate those patterns from ones with empirical support and to state a low level of confidence in their validity. After a few dozen games implement such a pattern with successful results, a neutral designer should be able to derive the same pattern observationally to validate the theoretical one.

Additionally, this set of patterns lacks a contextual directive. As mentioned earlier, there is no statement of when or why creating a flow state is desirable. The implication that all games should produce this state is demonstrably false. Take the examples of narrative-driven games like *Life is Strange* or sandbox games like *Red Dead Redemption 2*. The slow pace of a narrative game is not conducive to a flow state, and yet the games are immersive, compelling, and successful in their goals as games. The sandbox games may have moments of intense concentration that create a flow state, but they also have long periods of introspective exploration in which flow does not drive the immersiveness of the game. Thus, to be useful as a language, these patterns require that piece of context. I would suggest that these patterns, rather than being a language in and of themselves, are children of a larger pattern that describes the use of flow in games.

Last, the author states that these patterns are interconnected.

> Patterns in these languages are deeply interwoven and form a densely interconnected network, having particular relationships with each other. A particular pattern may be hierarchically connected (either at a superior, identical or inferior level), modulating or modulated by, or conflicting with another pattern. As the complete collection of patterns is still under investigation the exact network of interconnections will be presented later on. (Lemay 2007)

I was, however, unable to find the descriptions of those connections outside the article. The lack of relationships and context diminishes the usefulness of the patterns. It would be relatively easy to address all of my aforementioned concerns and make use of the ideas uncovered by this investigation into the implementation of flow. That project should be within your reach after reading the "Integrating Patterns from Other Sources" section of the book in Chapter 16.

"Design Patterns in Games: The Case for Sound Design"

The fantastic article "Design Patterns in Games: The Case for Sound Design" (Alves and Roque 2013) uses the ideas of a pattern language to help make it possible for sound design to begin during the ideation phase of game design, even when the designers do not have extensive sound design resources. Without question, their project succeeded admirably at their stated purpose.

The most notable thing about this project is the extensive attention that they paid to the connections between patterns. They identify 81 patterns related to sound design. They identified more than 700 relationships between those patterns! For each pattern, they provide multiple in-game examples. The naming convention used for the patterns provides a clear sense of when the pattern should be used, for instance, "Suspicious NPC" or "Imminent Death" (Alves and Roque 2013).

This project generated a printable set of cards and a wiki that includes all of its patterns. The cards allow designers to kinesthetically select and consider the use of the sound patterns easily as they begin their design process.

There are, however, some fundamental problems with their project in terms of generating Alexandrian patterns. The patterns proposed are at best "shallow patterns," situations where games might use sound and why. They are more of a collection of sound use techniques and how they relate to each other.

While the names of these patterns tell you when to use them and their descriptions and examples show you how you might do that, they do not reveal why you need those techniques in a broader sense. As shallow patterns, their logic and justification tend to be circular. The pattern Imminent Death suggests using sounds to indicate that the player's death is imminent so that the player will know that their death is imminent. The presentation on the wiki does, of course, go further and explain that sound should be used for this purpose because the player may be wrapped up in gameplay and miss other visual affordances of health. It also acknowledges the emotional importance of death, in and out of the game. Still, it does not discuss what that emotional impact is or how different implementations of the pattern might affect it. Different effects might indicate imminent death: an alarm sound, a rising heartbeat, or the fading of all audio, for instance. Each would serve a different purpose and be appropriate in a different type of game. The examples given show these different implementations and demonstrate their effects, but recognizing and understanding the differences and their emotional output is left to the designer.

This article does not describe how to choose patterns for your game outside of selecting them based on situations that occur in your game. Understanding the interconnections of the patterns or techniques is important. When there are a daunting number of connections, and using all related patterns is not the intent, it seems necessary to have criteria to help designers understand what patterns to use.

"Patterns and Computer Game Design Innovation"

"Patterns and Computer Game Design Innovation" details the process used by the author, Kevin McGee, for creating Alexandrian patterns as a way to encourage innovation in design. His work developed during the process of teaching several game design courses in which he used pattern creation as a core pedagogical technique. Based on the learning outcomes of those courses, he considered this process to be successful.

There are several aspects to his work that validate my teaching experience and the theoretical framework that I am describing in this book. Specifically, he uses a pattern template as a tool for documenting patterns. Templates are not uncommon among pattern projects. However, in addition to providing a pattern name and pattern description, he cites the importance of including sections for "Feature," "Forces," and "Context." He references Alexander's definitions (McGee 2020):

- **Feature:** What is the "something" we want to build?
- **Forces:** Why is this "something" helping to make the built structure "good"?
- **Context:** When (or, where) will this pattern work?

These definitions differ somewhat from the explicit statements of the problem that a pattern addresses and the description of a solution as I will use them. However, in the examples given, the Forces statement is phrased to include the problem implicitly by stating how the presence or absence of the Feature will affect a game. This format has the benefit of showing a more complex and nuanced understanding of how the problem and pattern interact, but it comes at the cost of some clarity.

McGee's work also proposes a set of characteristics stating what patterns should be:

- **Operational and precise:** We "know what to do" to realize a pattern—and we can clearly confirm the presence or absence of a pattern in a particular built structure.

- **Positive:** They specify something specifically good to achieve, rather than being rules of the form "do not do X."

- **Flexible:** There is more than one solution that satisfies a pattern, e.g., there are a multitude of different ways to attain "natural light on two sides of a room."

- **Debatable:** The pattern is clear enough to criticize.

- **Testable:** We can confirm empirically whether people feel better in structures that contain the pattern versus those that do not.

- **End-user oriented:** That is, not just something good from the perspective of builders/implementers.

These suggestions fit well within my understanding of the needs of a well-formed pattern. The article is critical of the implementation of patterns within the computer science field for reasons similar to those I expressed in the previous section.

In many ways, the process described in this article is closer to my work than any of the previously discussed attempts within game design. However, the patterns it describes only look to a single source to find a pattern. The pattern identified may indeed exist in other games. Still, I have found that only by describing the use of a technique across many games does it become possible to see the generalized pattern and not just describe the method used by one game. The author also does not discuss linking patterns into a language or using more than one pattern in the design of a game.

———

There have been many, many more articles written on the topic of patterns in game design, but they seem to have generally the same strengths and shortcomings in various combinations. Many sources touch on the potential of pattern theory; none fully realize it in terms of game design.

Other articles are referenced and cited throughout the rest of the book as relevant.

OTHER GAME DESIGN PATTERN PROJECTS

In addition to this scholarly work, several practical pattern design projects have been begun and have produced some amount of progress.

LARP Pattern Language

This project details a pattern language built to help with the design of live-action role-playing games (LARPs). It does not describe the process used to create the patterns, and the overall number of patterns is low at only 15 patterns. However, it is one of the better attempts at creating a pattern language outside of Alexander's work.

The project stands out for identifying the "resources" that relate to LARP design. These underlying factors are time, space, energy, memory, and criticality. They are uniquely relevant to this kind of game. They help the patterns focus, and detailing them at the beginning of the language gives the designer context (Li and Morningstar 2020).

The author breaks the patterns into the categories of Setup, Plot, and Interaction. These are analogous to the levels of scale that Alexander uses to structure his language. I think that it's interesting how different this structure is and that it suggests that a language should reflect the nature of the work that it describes rather than merely mimicking Alexander's levels of scale.

This format breaks patterns into two sections. The first is a summary header with the name and relationships to other patterns. A body follows giving the problem, a high-level theoretical solution, an "Instruction," which is a practical application of the pattern, and finally an example.

The project states that its language is incomplete and invites the submission of new patterns. A significant number of patterns would be needed to be added for the language to be functionally complete. Still, it is useful in its current state both as an example language and for practical design use.

Kind Fortress

On the design blog *Kind Fortress*, Isaac Shalev has collected around 20 patterns over the past two and a half years. This collection is ad hoc and seems to simply be driven by the patterns that the author has recently observed. While he cites Alexander as an inspiration, he does not attempt to present his patterns according to a standard pattern template or to relate the patterns to each other in any way (Shalev 2020).

The important takeaway from this pattern collection is the thoughtful analysis of the function of each pattern identified. While it would be difficult to use these patterns in an organized way to create a game design, reading them is informative and suggests that the act of creating them is part of the author's game design learning process.

Interactive Institute Swedish ICT

The Interactive Institute Swedish ICT houses a vast collection of more than 700 game design elements that maps their relationships to each other. This collection includes the patterns in Björk and Holopainen's *Patterns in Game Design* and expands upon them radically. The scope of the project is staggering. The patterns identified vary from incredibly detailed and deeply interconnected to only partially complete "Speculative Patterns" that explicitly call for further development.

The pattern template used to document the patterns is very detailed and provides the pattern name, short and long descriptions, examples, advice on using the pattern, consequences of using the pattern, and relationships to other patterns on a variety of axes. The patterns are presented in a wiki format and linked to each other with such density that half of the words in a given pattern can be links.

As a collection of game design elements and a mapping of their connections, this collection is invaluable. However, as in Björk and Holopainen's published book, the patterns here do not address what problems they exist to solve. As stated earlier, this lack of problem statements makes using the collection as a design tool difficult.

While this collection of patterns does not provide a methodology for deriving patterns, the published book does discuss that process.

One section of the wiki even considers the possibility of using the pattern creation process as a pedagogy:

> Designers and experienced gamers typically have a lot of knowledge about gameplay. This knowledge may, however, not be easily expressible in words, and this may make gamers misjudge how much they actually know about games. We have during several workshops with game students had good experiences letting students identify their own suggestions for gameplay design patterns after presenting the basic idea but not the collection. Armed with

the design pattern concept, the students have easily put words on design choices made in existing games and have then been able to recombine them into new games. Besides showing them practically how patterns can be used for design and analysis this makes them aware of their own knowledge of gameplay and empowers them in the sense that they realize that they can themselves develop descriptions of gameplay concepts when they need them. (Björk 2019)

This analysis matches my experience using patterns in the classroom.

Each of the aforementioned pattern-related projects has strengths and weaknesses. Each of them has contributed to our understanding of game design. Each has shown ways that Alexander's pattern ideas apply to game design. However, none of these projects is perfect, and none of them fully address the needs of the industry or make use of the full potential of creating a Pattern Language for game design.

Read that last sentence again. "The full potential of *creating* a Pattern Language," not the full potential of *having* a Pattern Language. Possibly, given time, I could create a functional Pattern Language. That language would not be as useful to other designers as it would be to me, no matter how clear or insightful the patterns I presented.

I would gain the benefit of having looked at hundreds of games, analyzed them, and discerned the patterns that make them up. That process, more than the Pattern Language it produces, is the secret power whose edge these projects dance around.

By taking the collected work in the preceding books, articles, and projects, refining and reimagining it in the mold of Alexander's original work, this book will build on the work that came before and inspire the creation of individual pattern languages. Eventually, we may combine them into a functionally complete language. It would not be a language written by any one person or even one group of erudite game designers. Instead, it would be a language distilled from the collected games that we have produced over the past decades and millennia.

The rest of this book lays out the process by which you can become one of the designers with the power unlocked by creating a Pattern Language.

III

An Introduction to Patterns in Game Design

CHAPTER 5

An Introduction to Patterns in Game Design

WHAT DOES A PATTERN LOOK LIKE, AND HOW CAN I FIND IT?

This section is the heart of this book. In the following pages, I will explore the process of deriving patterns from your own experience and research. Yes, this book will provide 24 useful patterns, but these are just examples— the by-products of showing you the process that you will use to create patterns yourself.

Earlier I told you that this book wouldn't teach you game design, and it won't. But, the process of creating patterns *will* teach you game design, or it will give you the structure to organize the things you already know. The Pattern Language that you begin with these exercises will turn your learned and intuitive understanding of games into a usable set of patterns that you can share with your colleagues and use together to shape your games.

Christopher Alexander's work is awe-inspiring. The scope of his research and the eccentric detail of his patterns manage to be practical and concrete, while at the same time encouraging designers to apply his ideas in creative ways. His work suggests that designers should expand the Pattern Language he began with his 253 patterns and that designers might even develop entirely separate languages to address their own design needs. His work describes the parts of a pattern and suggests that all patterns should have those parts, but he does not give guidance as to how designers should go about creating patterns that meet his specifications.

I have tried to address this problem by providing a robust set of exercises for pattern generation. These exercises do not generate specific patterns, but rather move to a higher level of abstraction and create either a type of pattern or patterns in a particular area of design. It is beyond the scope of this book to create a comprehensive set of exercises that would build a "complete" Pattern Language. However, I believe this subset is sufficient to teach you the skills necessary to continue expanding your own Pattern Language generated by completing these exercises.

The first sections of this book have presented a lot of background and theory. In the next section, I'll give the template that I recommend using when documenting a pattern. Then I will present a completed pattern and, finally, the exercise that generated it.

The Pattern Template

Following Alexander's lead, I have defined a Pattern Template, very similar to his, to use when documenting my patterns. This template represents a synthesis of the work of other designers in applying patterns to game design and my experience in using patterns to teach design. I strongly recommend using this template until you're very comfortable with the process. Even then, maintaining a consistent format will make it easier for other designers to read and understand your work.

If you'd prefer to see a concrete example of a pattern, feel free to skip to the "Example Pattern" section later in this chapter and refer back to the template if the meaning of any of the parts is not clear.

> **PATTERN TEMPLATE**
>
> **Name:** This should be an easy to remember and evocative name.
> **Confidence:** This number rates the level of certainty you have that a pattern is viable for use in developing games: how sure you are that it will have the indicated effects, and any side effects it might have. See the later section for details on rating your confidence in a pattern.
> **Image:*** An iconic image to represent each pattern. This image can help to convey the essence of the pattern and to serve as a mnemonic anchor for remembering it.
> **Author:** This is the name of the pattern creator or creators.

---

* There is a strong argument for the inclusion of an iconic image to represent each pattern. However, the effort of finding or creating such an image is high, especially for designers who are not artists. If you do not have the means to generate high-quality illustrations, at least describe what you would have illustrated or use images from existing games that demonstrate the pattern. If you do this, make sure to cite your sources and respect copyrighted material.

Design problem: Each pattern exists to solve a problem.* Describe that problem here. If you see a pattern without a problem, look harder. Identifying the problem is critical to knowing when, and if, you want to use the pattern.

Description: Provide a detailed description of the pattern here. This section should go into as much depth as possible. It should be long enough to fully capture your pattern. Do not try to be concise to the point of reducing your description to a single sentence. It can be helpful to start with the following format: In order to [achieve some design effect], a designer may [take some design action, use some mechanic, etc.] because [explanation of how the pattern produces the desired effect].

Games that use this pattern and how:†

1. Game name—Description of how the game applies the pattern. This section should be at least a full sentence, not just two or three keywords, that will make sense to another designer. To help you understand this better, the following two examples illustrate how to do this well, and how I've seen students do it poorly.
2. Good example game—This game uses the pattern in this particular way. By doing this, the game creates these dynamics in the player experience that solve the problem.
3. Not great example game (Don't do this one!)—This game is about these cool things! In it players do these things that do not relate to the pattern. It uses these mechanics [a comprehensive list of the mechanics found in this bad example, many of which are unrelated to the pattern].

Seed: This is the idea that was the starting point for the pattern. For the exercises presented in this book, it will follow the format: Exercise XX: Exercise Name—Game Element. This is important to record, as you will use it in the process of connecting your patterns into a language, as discussed in Section VI of this book. It will also allow your colleagues or instructor to understand what kind of pattern you were trying to create.

---

* What is a design problem? The design problem that is addressed by a pattern should describe a situation you face as a designer. A design problem is not simply the effect of a mechanic stated as a question. It must capture the purpose and intent of the designer not just mechanically but in terms of its effect on the player. In this way, a well-constructed pattern will ensure that you are designing games that intentionally create an experience for the player. If this seems abstract, look over some of the design problems in the example patterns provided for each exercise.

† In the pattern exercises you will in most cases be asked to analyze at least ten games. You do not need to list all of those games here. I recommend citing at least three games that show diverse implementations of your pattern. Having more games is fine if each shows a different use of your pattern.

Related patterns:
Parent patterns: A pattern or several patterns that are required by this pattern for it to function well.
Child patterns:* Patterns that are suggested by this pattern or require it to function well.
Keywords: Keywords that relate to this pattern. Use keywords to link this pattern to others in a non-hierarchical way. The process of choosing keywords is discussed further in steps 2 and 3 of the "Connecting Patterns into a Language" section of Chapter 15 which discuss keywords and pattern categories.

RELATED PATTERNS

This section of the Pattern Template exists to connect this pattern to the others that you will create as part of your Pattern Language. The section of the book that will help you create that language comes much later, after all of the pattern-generation exercises. If you want to wait to complete this part of the Pattern Template until you get to that part of the book, that's okay. If you want to try to fill it in as you go, that's okay too. Either way, you will probably be revisiting all of the patterns you create to fill in or adjust this section.

The Related Patterns section of each example will also suggest other pattern exercises that you can complete to find additional parent or child patterns for the example. These are not part of the Pattern Template, but you may find them useful if you're having a hard time thinking of a starting point when completing the suggested exercise. You may also want to include these kinds of suggestions when writing your patterns to help other developers, or your future self, extend your Pattern Language.

PATTERN CONFIDENCE

It's essential to acknowledge that all patterns aren't equally valid. Different exercises create more or less reliable patterns, and you should carefully consider your confidence in any generated pattern before you use it in your designs. I recommend using this rubric for assessing your confidence in a new pattern, and for updating that confidence as you use the pattern over time. All patterns start with a confidence rating of 0, then add 1 for each of the following items that apply.

---

* As you develop more patterns, other sections like Related Patterns or Alternate Patterns might make sense.

Some of the items are related and "stack." For example, a Common Pattern (+1) would also have to meet the requirements for being a Limited Pattern (+1) and a Singular Pattern (+1) for a total of 3. You should apply all the applicable labels. So if you had used this hypothetical pattern and another developer had independently described the same pattern, you would also apply Demonstrated Pattern" (+1) and Independent Sources (+1) for a total confidence score of 5.

(+0) Theoretical Pattern: The Theoretical Patterns exercise (Exercise 24) generates this type of pattern. You might also create a theoretical pattern by adapting a pattern from an existing repository that doesn't cite example games. This pattern may be valid, but you don't generate it from observation. Instead, you create it by imagining how a theory about game design would fit the pattern format.

(+1) Single Example Pattern: This level of confidence comes from a pattern that was generated based on one example. It's entirely possible to look at a single game and derive a valid pattern from it. However, it can be challenging to determine whether what you see is an actual pattern or just the results of a design technique or element that would yield a different pattern if you looked at its use across many games.

(+1) Limited Pattern: If you've observed the pattern in fewer than ten games, it's a limited pattern. If you have a hard time providing the ten examples in an exercise, this level of confidence may result.

(+1) Common Pattern: The pattern is visible in at least ten games, probably many more. You have found a "common pattern" when you stop recording examples at ten but could go on, and it's a good sign that you've done an excellent job formulating a pattern based on your observations.

(+1) Demonstrated Pattern: A pattern is a demonstrated pattern if you, or another developer, have used it in development, and the effect was as intended.

(+1) Validated Pattern: This confidence level describes a pattern that's in common use among a variety of game developers and has been proven effective through widespread use. At the time of the printing of this book, it's probably not possible to find a pattern validated through use. As you work with patterns throughout your career, it may become more common. A pattern might also be a validated pattern if you conducted empirical user research to show that the pattern was effective.

(+1) Independent Sources: If more than one developer derives a pattern, it has independent sources. In teaching, it's common to discover this kind of pattern as more than one group of students arrives at the same pattern from different starting points. As the community of developers using the exercises in this book increases and shares patterns, this will become more common.

EXAMPLE PATTERN: MYSTERY-DRIVEN EXPLORATION

I have used this example in many classes to teach the concept of patterns and how they apply to game design. It's not the simplest possible example, but it demonstrates the process well. The exercises in the book begin with a slightly more straightforward process and escalate in complexity to a level considerably beyond this example.

Name: Mystery-Driven Exploration
Image:

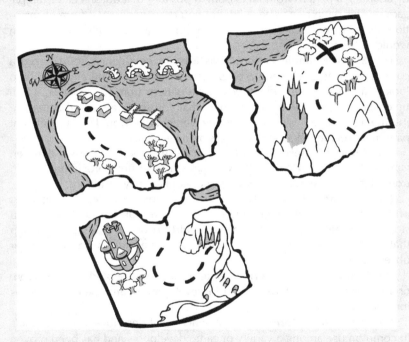

FIGURE 5.1   Interesting but incomplete information can motivate exploration in a variety of ways.

Confidence: 3
Author: Chris Barney
Design problem: Designers need to motivate their players to explore the worlds they create.
Description: To motivate players to explore the worlds they create, a designer may present the player with compelling but incomplete pieces of information, and then give the player gameplay avenues that will allow them to seek out more information and solve the mysteries of the game world.

Games that use this pattern and how:

- *Journey*—*Journey* opens with the view of a bright light shining from a split atop an imposing mountain. The game does not explain the sight, prompting you to investigate. The path in the direction of the mountain is visibly open.

   The second example of this pattern is also from *Journey*. As you play, you regularly encounter small ruins. In the first ruin and many after that, there are murals depicting scenes from the game world. These scenes are usually incomplete and ambiguous, raising as many questions as they answer.
- *Grand Theft Auto*—A map of the game world shows the quests you can do in the area surrounding you at the moment. The rest of the map is visible, but you can't see the available quests in the other areas unless you explore.
- *Skyrim* (and many other *Elder Scrolls* games)—As you move through the world, a horizontal compass in your HUD shows nearby quests and points of interest. Since the indicated locations are nearby, unknown, and often yield mechanical and narrative rewards, they motivate you to divert your travel to seek them out, wandering off of the direct path between primary game objectives.
- *Bastion*—As you explore the levels of *Bastion*, you can only see the world directly around you. The rest of the world literally does not exist yet. As you move forward, the ground rises into existence just in front of the character's feet. On a first playthrough, there's no way to know what will appear as you move forward. That might cause a lack of motivation to explore if you don't have an active imagination! The game avoids that problem by coupling the visual mystery of the missing world with a charismatic and omniscient narrator speaking in a god-like voice-over, always prompting you to act and describing the world as it appears.
- *Dear Esther*—At first glance, this game seems to offer no clear direction. There's no HUD and no obvious path. However, the game presents you with a narrative voice-over that's compelling but vague. The world appears to be open in all directions, but in actuality, the levels give you a limited area to explore. The game avoids feeling on rails by presenting you with a constant stream of visual cues to investigate. Some are small, like a candle or farmhouse in the middle distance; others, like the radio tower, are visible throughout the game. The narrative and visual weight of the clues are generally proportional—things that look more important turn out to be more important.
- *Draugen*—The world of *Draugen* is somewhat similar to *Dear Esther*, except that the game also offers intriguing visual and narrative avenues that are not immediately available to pursue. A sign indicating the entrance to a mine, for example, is blocked by a locked gate. If you

approach, a companion suggests climbing the gate to explore. However, your character only has the option to decline, which primes you to explore in that direction as soon as possible.

Seed: Exercise 2: Higher-Order Patterns—Architectural Weenies*
Parent patterns:
Greater Choice Requires Greater Motivation† (Confidence: 2)—As you apply Mystery-Driven Exploration, you are creating choices for the player. The more mysteries you present the player with, the more important this pattern becomes to maintain the player's motivation to explore.

SUGGESTED EXERCISE

Use **Exercise 6: Emotional Patterns** to generate a pattern based on curiosity.

Child patterns:

SUGGESTED EXERCISE

Use **Exercise 12: Embedded and Environmental Narrative Patterns** to generate a pattern based on a level that presents a mystery through embedded or environmental narrative.

Keywords: Navigation, Motivation, Narrative

The seed of this pattern is "a tall structure visible from many points in the game world," which is a technique known as an "architectural weenie." In case you aren't an architecture student or a theme park designer, an architectural weenie is a tall structure placed in a theme park or even in a city. This technique lets people use it to navigate from a great distance and also draws them to it when they're exploring. The Imagineers coined the term at Disneyland, and the Matterhorn is the archetypical example. However, buildings like the Eiffel Tower or the Dom in Cologne are also great examples that predate Disney by decades or centuries. It would be easy just to use that as a pattern (Kreimeier 2002, p. 9). It certainly sounds like a pattern, a technique that exists to solve a problem. However, it is

---

* Pattern exercises are given in the next two sections of the book. For each exercise I show my work for the exercise and give the pattern that my work produced as an example. The exercise I used to produce this pattern, the Higher-Order Patterns exercise, is a little difficult. When I present that exercise, I give another example.
† Example pattern from Exercise 16: Patterns from Core Mechanics.

missing an essential aspect of a well-formed pattern: being general. "Use architectural weenies to provide wayfinding" is too specific. When you use an architectural weenie to solve the problem of wayfinding, you can spot it a mile off.* The goal of pattern exercises is to get the designer to dig deeper than the immediate technique that inspired the pattern, to ask what problem the technique is solving. Thus architectural weenies become Mystery-Driven Exploration and can be applied in weenie-free ways. If you structure a pattern correctly, you can apply it in many ways outside of those used in the analyzed games.

Initially, when you are creating a pattern, you leave the last three items blank. You may not be able to identify parent and child relationships when you first complete the pattern, because you will have such a small set of patterns. As you develop more patterns, you will add these fields when you recognize that two of your patterns are connected. I cover the process of integrating patterns into a language in the sixth section of this book.

Keywords are also part of that process, and, initially, you may wish to leave that field blank as well. While you can decide on keywords for your first pattern immediately, you will likely find yourself revising them repeatedly as you add more and more patterns and develop a standardized set of descriptors. It's fine to skip them in the beginning, as they have limited utility when you only have a handful of patterns to track. Eventually, though, they will become a critical tool that will let you filter and search your library for patterns on a specific topic. Again, I will cover that process in Chapter 15.

INTRODUCTION TO PATTERN EXERCISES

The following pattern exercises will help you identify useful patterns. Looking randomly at the games you play and trying to find patterns can work sometimes. It might even yield helpful or exciting patterns. However, given that there is an almost infinite number of patterns you could identify (superb pattern recognition machine that you are), it's useful to have tools to focus the patterns you observe toward the specific problems you face. You should also do all you can to make sure that the patterns you recognize are as flexible and insightful as possible.

As you work through this book, I encourage you to do the exercises in order. They build in complexity and specificity, and passing through all of them once will give you the start of a structure for the language you will

---

* See what I did there?

develop from them. Once you have completed the exercises once to build the foundation of your language, you will be comfortable with the process. Then you'll be ready to expand the vocabulary of your language by using it in your daily design work. Your first step when creating patterns will then be to articulate the design problem you're facing and select the exercise that best fits that problem.

Each pattern exercise in this book consists of a set of steps. They begin with a framing task/question: name a functional design element, or pick a mechanic from a boss encounter, or choose an emotional effect.

You are then usually asked to list, through research or experience, a set of games that match the design element you've chosen. So if you picked "jumping," you would then select games that used jumping in as many diverse ways as you could. If you had identified "immortal first boss" as a boss encounter mechanic, you would pick games that had an unkillable first boss.

You then analyze those games and how they achieve the effect you observed in them. You need to describe what you see in some detail, again avoiding using only one or two keywords. It's surprising what insights you can get when you force yourself to describe precisely the thing that seems evident to you.

Next, you will look at the games you've analyzed and see if you observe any patterns. The exercises ask you to find ten games. That number is arbitrary; it is both too large for many new designers and far too small to generate indisputable patterns. However, listing ten games will force you to look at edge cases and pick at least a few games that were not immediately obvious to you. These games will help you understand the scope of your pattern.

These exercises help you find and define *potential* patterns. Don't think that because you were able to complete an exercise that the pattern you have observed is *true* in some fundamental way. The patterns you generate are a good starting point, and you should look for them in games you see going forward. Some you may discard as false starts, some you may adapt many times as your understanding grows as a developer. But even these limited nascent patterns will be useful and allow you to move forward as a designer in a meaningful, practical way.

Here's the exercise I used to create the Mystery-Driven Exploration pattern shown earlier. This exercise is titled "Higher-Order Patterns" and is the second pattern-generation exercise in the book. I will walk through the process of answering each of these questions to create the Mystery-Driven Exploration pattern.

EXERCISE 2: HIGHER-ORDER PATTERNS

Step 1: Name a design element.

Step 2: What problem(s) does that design element solve?

Step 3: Pick one of the problems you identified.

Step 4: List and describe ten games that also solve the same problem in as many diverse ways as possible.

Step 5: Describe the way each game solves the design problem. Focus on each game and try *not* to start looking for patterns as you write.

Step 6: What do those solutions have in common? The solutions may have more than one thing in common. Some games may share one, and other games share another. List and describe each.

Step 7: Is there a pattern? Briefly describe it. Do not create a formal description using the Pattern Template; just make the first attempt to articulate what you see.

Step 8: For each problem you identified in step 2, you may repeat steps 3–7.

The first step, name a design element, is intentionally vague. It will allow you to apply this exercise to virtually any design problem. However, it doesn't give much guidance for you to focus the pattern in any particular way. That makes this a good exercise for creating general, broadly applicable patterns.

Step 1: Name a design element.

A tall structure, visible from many points in the game world.

I was teaching a class on architecture in game design at the time I wrote this pattern, so I chose a design element we'd been discussing in the class.

The next question, What problem(s) does that design element solve?, is intended to get the designer to start thinking about what purposes design elements serve. It's crucial to think carefully and identify actual design problems, rather than just restating the mechanic. For instance, if the design element were "jumping," it would not exist to solve the problem of "letting the player jump." Instead, perhaps "allowing dynamic traversal" or, better yet, "increasing player autonomy by creating more dynamic movement options."*

---

* The first sample for the Basic Pattern Exercise uses this design element, in case you were wondering what design problems jumping does solve.

Step 2: What problem(s) does that design element solve?

A. Architectural weenies help motivate and facilitate the player's exploration of the world. These are two related but distinct functions. I suspect that there are child patterns* related to each.

B. Architectural weenies may create an iconic image or location to set the tone of the game, such as the Great Tree in *Ori and the Blind Forest* or the glowing mountain in *Journey*.

C. They can also create a narrative focus for the game, e.g., Death Mountain in many *Zelda* games or the White-Gold Tower in the Imperial City in *The Elder Scrolls: Oblivion*.

Step 3: Pick one of the problems you identified.

A. Motivating and facilitating the player's exploration of the world.

In this case, I identified three effects that might be created by an architectural weenie. I chose the first one to explore in the rest of the exercise.

The next step asks you to name at least ten games that solve the same problem as the design element you chose rather than ten games that use that same design element. Exercise 1: Basic Pattern Exercise looks at the design element directly; Exercise 2: Higher-Order Patterns looks at the problems solved by the design element. Focusing on the problems allows the exercise to uncover more fundamental patterns by looking at the underlying purpose of the design element rather than the element itself. The phrase "higher-order" here is about zooming out just a little, going from narrower to broader, from specific to more general. So in the case of this example, I was looking for ten games that also solve the problem of motivating player exploration, not ten games that use architectural weenies.

---

* A child pattern is a pattern suggested by another pattern. Usually child patterns require that parent pattern to function well.

Step 4: List and describe ten games that also solve the same problem in as many diverse ways as possible.

Journey, Grand Theft Auto, Assassins Creed, Skyrim, Bastion, Dear Esther, The Secret World, Draugen, Anthem, The Room
Question 4 is relatively simple, but probably requires the most time to complete. You need to articulate as precisely as you can how each game you chose solves the design problem you've identified. In this case, how do *Journey, Grand Theft Auto*, etc. motivate player exploration. If you find that all of your games are solving the problem in precisely the same way, you probably need to think of more games that solve it in different ways. If you don't, you may end up converging back to a pattern that just describes the technique you began with. The goal of this exercise, in terms of the example, is not to describe architectural weenies but to understand the higher-level, more fundamental pattern that they express.

Step 5: Describe the way each game solves the design problem. Focus on each game and try *not* to start looking for patterns as you write.

- *Journey*—The mountain in the distance in *Journey* gives you a sense of direction and has a visually compelling, unexplained light shining from its top.
- *Journey*—The ruins that you can see in the near distance throughout the game stand out from the initial desert landscape, offering direction; when you get close, you can see the embedded narrative of the partial murals on the ruin walls.
- *Grand Theft Auto*—There's a map showing where it's possible to go, but the map is incomplete, which gives you a limited set of short-term goals and teases future quests with the negative space on the map.
- *Assassin's Creed*—The landscape you move through as you play contains many high towers. Given the game's climbing mechanics, they are attractive locations. The quest map is filled in by showing more and more possible quest objectives with each tower you reach.

- *Skyrim* (and many Elder Scrolls games)—The Icons that appear on the compass indicating points of interest provide immediate directions for exploration. They show you what kind of quest you will encounter by going in a direction, but don't give you any details.
- *Bastion*—The world around the character is very limited but forms continuously as you move so that every action results in more of the world's secrets revealing themselves.
- *Dear Esther*—There's no apparent direction or goal at the beginning of the game, but you have only a few paths you can follow. As you move, you hear and see narrative snippets that raise more questions than they answer.
- *The Secret World*—One activity you can do in this massively multiplayer online game (MMO) is collecting "Lore" snippets, which appear as visually distinct hovering items in the game world. Each one contains a bit of a story, but you usually find them out of order.
- *Draugen*—The world constantly presents appealing but inaccessible exploration options; most become available as the game progresses.
- *Anthem*—Much of the drive to explore comes from enticing vistas and collectible narrative items. But you also need resources, and exploring is the best way to get them in the early part of the game.
- *The Room*—This mobile game presents you with one strange puzzle box after another, and you're always given just enough information to open it, but rarely any information about what you'll find when you do. The game narratively implies occult mysteries at every opportunity.

The next question is probably the hardest. Here I ask you to look for patterns. It is entirely possible, though unlikely, that no patterns exist for you to find. It's also possible that several or even many patterns may be present. In this case, I just list a single aspect that the example games share.

Step 6: What do those solutions have in common? The solutions may have more than one thing in common. Some games may share one, and other games share another. List and describe each.

They all provide the player with partial information.

If I had listed more than one property that the games had in common, I would have listed each here and considered whether each was related to the others.

Finally, I ask you to articulate the pattern that you've observed. The response usually comes in the form of a short paragraph. In the next step, you fill out the Pattern Template using the answers you gave in all of the preceding steps.

Step 7: Is there a pattern? Briefly describe it. Do not create a formal description using the Pattern Template; just make the first attempt to articulate what you see.

Yes. More than just providing information, that information is partial and is intriguing, which creates a sense of mystery. Then the developer gives the player a clear path to pursue, gaining more knowledge in the short term and eventually solving the mystery.

It's important to note that the Example Games section of the Pattern Template is not asking for the games from question 4 of the Pattern Exercise, which asked for ten games that solved the design problem in different ways. It's asking for ten games that implement the pattern as you have identified it in question 7 of the exercise where you articulated the pattern. These may or may not be the same games, and, in fact, easily finding additional games that implement the pattern is a sign that the pattern is a good one.

Step 8: For each problem you identified in step 2, you may repeat steps 3–7.

If I wished, I could have returned to step 2 and looked for patterns related to the other two design problems that I listed there.

CHAPTER 6

Common Problems in Proposed Patterns

U NSURPRISINGLY, THE FIRST PATTERNS a designer tries to articulate are often flawed. Here are a few things to look out for as you work through these exercises. I have seen these problems many times as my students struggled with the legitimate difficulty of mastering this process.

PATTERNS SHOULD ADDRESS A DESIGN PROBLEM

This problem is very important—it's the flaw I identified in the book *Game Design Patterns*, and I have seen students and, more commonly, experienced designers produce patterns that do not consider the design problem they address.

Some of the pattern exercises explicitly start with identifying a design problem. Others start with a mechanic, then have the designer identify games that use that mechanic, then look for the problems solved by the mechanic in those games, and then find a pattern. As the process gets more sophisticated, it's easy to lose focus on the step of considering what design problem your new pattern actually addresses. All of the exercise instructions ask the designer to identify the problem. There is a section in the Pattern Template for the design problem, and yet it's common to see patterns that use the format "Many games do x" rather than "In order to y, designers may wish to x."

If you miss the design problem, then it's likely you haven't fully understood the implications of the pattern you've identified. Without a problem statement, it's also harder for you to know when you should be using that pattern. For example, say you observe that in first-person shooters, there's often a mechanic that limits how much you can shoot. Perhaps it's due to scarcity, weapon capacity, or overheating. You might create a pattern like "Developers should limit the amount of damage a player can do by limiting ammo capacity, rate of fire, or ammo availability." That seems reasonable. But why does that mechanic of damage-limiting occur? Is that pattern always true? How much should a developer limit damage?

It would be better if you also noticed that the mechanic of limiting ammo is sometimes used to balance a multiplayer shooter, sometimes used to create situations where the player feels either vulnerable or powerful, and other times used to create strategic choices between weapons. Then you could instead create a pattern saying, "To create a cycle of tension and release in game levels, a designer may limit access to the resources that drive the core gameplay loops." This pattern is far more general. You would then list the example of ammunition in first-person shooters, but also perhaps health in a survival game, or building resources in a real-time strategy (RTS) game. You might even pick one of the other design problems that limited ammunition addresses and come up with an entirely different pattern.

SHALLOW PATTERNS

It's not enough to just look at what a game does. When analyzing a game, that's an example of your pattern; it's essential to look at *why* it's doing what you say it's doing.

For example, when I look at fighting games that clearly communicate the results of combat and damage, I observe that some have destructible armor. Seeing this, I might create a pattern that says, "To make damage feel satisfying in a fighting game, a developer should have armor or character costumes that are destructible."

However, when I think about why these games use destructible armor, I see that, while it's true that destructible armor is a way that those games show damage, that may not be the primary reason they have implemented it. I also see that some developers and publishers have the sexist perception that fighting games have a mainly young male audience. These groups seem to think that young men will like the game better if it presents female characters in an objectifying way, such as making their armor fall off.*

Noting that, I would step back from the already limited pattern mentioned earlier and look more broadly at the ways that fighting games show damage. That perspective results in a pattern more like, "To make damage feel satisfying in a fighting game, it should reflect the results of damage in as many ways as possible. Physical damage to the avatars, health meters, sound effects, animation, or other techniques may be used. Mechanisms that reflect damage should be informative, make the aggressor feel powerful, and make the victim feel vulnerable."

The second pattern is not about what techniques you should use but about what effect that technique should have on the player if you want it to make damage feel satisfying.

CIRCULAR PATTERN

The example I often give of the circular pattern problem is "In order to create a sense of fear, a designer may wish to include elements that generate fear." It may seem like I'm joking, but that was an actual pattern description submitted by a designer new to the process. They had gone through the whole process and distilled their observations carefully and ended up where they started without realizing it. Check to see if your pattern is in the format: "To do x you should create a game that does x." If it is, your pattern is circular.

PATTERNS SHOULD BE PRESCRIPTIVE

Many students are reluctant to state their observations prescriptively. When they observe a pattern, they try to describe it passively as a thing that exists, rather than stating how to use that thing to produce well-designed games. For example, if they have observed that many role-playing games (RPGs) offer the player quests, they will create a pattern with the description, "Many designers, when creating RPGs, design areas that offer players many quests." Of course, this has the circular patterns problem discussed earlier, but it is also just a description. There are several steps necessary to correct this problem. First, ask: If there are quests in RPGs, what design

---

* I will not enter into the argument about whether this is the intent of the developers to be sexist, whether fighting games are guilty of sexism, or whether fighting game players enjoy the way that female characters are portrayed. If you are interested in that argument I recommend the YouTube series *Tropes vs. Women in Video Games* by Anita Sarkeesian (https://www.youtube.com/playlist?list=PLn4ob_5_ttEaA_vc8F3fjzE62esf9yP61).

problem are they addressing?* Then dig deeper by looking at whether quests are the only mechanic that solves that problem, whatever it is. The resulting pattern is most useful if stated prescriptively: "To create situations where players can explore the identities of their characters in an RPG, designers may create situations where the character's actions will have important but easily identified and contained effects on the game world." This pattern, of course, would be supported by examples of quests in RPGs, but also perhaps by dialogue trees, non-player character (NPC) barks that change based on the character's actions, etc.

JUMPING TO CONCLUSIONS

One of the most common and hardest to avoid problems in pattern creation stems from the fact that we are very good at seeing patterns. This becomes a problem as we look over games and try to identify the use of some design element, or in another similar observational step. It is straightforward to look at one or two games, and arrive at a pattern when looking for, say, the different ways that a set of games use jumping. In this case, you might decide that jumping is used to get over obstacles and create a pattern about using jumping to facilitate player navigation. The tricky thing is that that pattern is likely to be valid.

It is then natural to look for that pattern in the rest of the example games. Typically you find it and pat yourself on the back for being so insightful. Unfortunately, when you decided on a pattern, you stopped looking at the remaining games objectively, and you may not have accurately described all of the ways they were using the design element you were considering.

The first exercise in the book uses jumping as its seed element. Pay careful attention to how I describe the use of jumping in each game, then analyze the examples to generate several possible patterns. This process allows me to fully understand the scope of the mechanic's use and pursue the most useful and insightful pattern for the exercise. And, of course, to return to the exercise later and document the remaining patterns.

ANTI-PATTERNS

Some patterns may conflict with others. That does not make either pattern "wrong," it just means that those two patterns are working to either solve different problems or to solve a problem in mutually exclusive ways. When

---

* Of course, it's possible that quests in RPGs may be solving more than one problem … just maybe.

you create a pattern, be aware that it may not always apply to a particular problem, depending on the other patterns at play.

Sometimes you will be able to see this in the games you observe in an exercise. A particular pattern will be apparent in some of those games but not in others. When you see this, look at the sample games that do not implement the pattern and consider what effect it would have on those games. You may find that it would enhance the effectiveness of their solutions to the problem. That's a good indication of the strength of your pattern, though it does not increase the confidence rating of your pattern unless you altered the games to include your pattern and measured the improvement.

On the other hand, you may discover that you can't find a way to use the pattern in the games that don't already include it or that including it seems like it would cause problems. Look at the games that do not use the first pattern you found. How do they still solve the problem you are looking into or use the design element you're considering? If they do, then you can continue the exercise looking for the pattern governing how they address the problem. When you document these new patterns, be sure to mark the first pattern as subtractive or anti-pattern for them.

The term "anti-pattern" is often misused to mean any pattern that is "bad." Here we are using it to mean any pattern that works counter to another pattern. A pattern is only ever an anti-pattern to another specific pattern. I am adopting this arbitrary use of terminology to express the concept that a pattern can be useful in one situation and ineffective or harmful in another, without being inherently flawed.

Consider the following two patterns as an example. The first says that you should increase character abilities in order to give the player a feeling of growing agency and progress. The second suggests limiting player agency to create feelings of helplessness and vulnerability in horror games. The first pattern is not invalid; it just probably shouldn't be used with the second.

In the last section of advanced exercises, there is an exercise for creating "negative patterns." These are not simply anti-patterns, but patterns that actively prevent the solution of a problem.

THE DESIRE TO BE THE AUTHORITY/KILL YOUR BABIES

I have seen the label "anti-pattern" applied to any pattern that is not in an approved canon of patterns produced by a privileged authority. The way I phrased that probably gives away my feelings about that practice. While some patterns are more effective than others, and many potential patterns will prove not to be valid, those are not anti-patterns. Looking at a pattern that someone else has created and disagreeing with it is reasonable. You should take care that you understand the problem that the pattern claims to solve and look at the example games that the author claims use it. If you can find a way to improve, rephrase, or clarify the pattern, then by all means, do so, and keep that improved pattern for yourself. Let the author know about your work; they may appreciate it or reject it, and that's fine.

If you can't find a way to correct the flaws you see in the pattern, and you can clearly state and demonstrate those flaws through observation of the example uses of the pattern, then reject the pattern as invalid. Again, share your conclusions with the author, but recognize that whoever you are, you are not "The Pattern Authority" and do not get to dictate the validity of another designer's understanding of the discipline.

That said, if you are on the other side of this kind of interaction, listen. If another designer has taken the time to read and understand a pattern you have written, you are lucky. If they care enough to dispute it, and form an argument as to why it's flawed, and even suggest improvements or an alternative to it, then you are privileged! Don't hold too tightly to your patterns: defend them vigorously, but be hungry to find solutions that will make you a better designer and improve the overall understanding of the discipline.

IV

Pattern Exercises

CHAPTER 7

Pattern Exercises

T HESE NEXT TWO CHAPTERS are the heart of this book. There are 25 exercises designed to help you create the beginning of your pattern language. You can use each of these exercises to create dozens or even hundreds of patterns, and I've designed each one to guide you toward a specific type of pattern. The first "basic" exercise could generate any pattern, but the more specific exercises will help you focus the process to create patterns in different areas of design.

In this book, I've written exercises that focus on core game design concepts. If this process proves as useful to other game designers and game design instructors as it has to me, developers with more domain knowledge may wish to extend this collection of exercises into other areas of game design, from writing to art to sound design. In Chapter 18, I'll discuss the process of creating new exercises.

Meanwhile, if you want these lessons to be effective:

- *Do not* simply read through all of the exercises and the sample patterns that I've provided. While they're all useful, the example patterns themselves are not the point of this book. They're just that: examples to help you understand and work through each exercise.

- *Do* take the time to read each exercise, the full example of the completed exercise, and the resulting pattern. Once you've finished reading one, stop, go back, and complete the exercise yourself. Only then should you move on and read the next exercise and sample pattern.

After you've completed the first few exercises, feel free to skip around and complete those that match your interests. The exercises in the "Advanced Pattern Exercises" section are challenging. Tackle them whenever you feel ready, but I wouldn't recommend starting with them!

You can jump to the sixth section of the book any time as well. That section talks about how to tie your patterns together into a language that you can use in practical design work. But you should definitely complete at least a few exercises before reading it, so you can relate the section to your work.

EXAMPLE EXERCISES AND PATTERNS

For each exercise, I include an example pattern and show the work of completing the exercise to create that pattern. Because each exercise is subtly or even radically different from the last, it's important to understand how each step of the exercise helps you to uncover and articulate a pattern. I recommend reading the resulting pattern first, then reading through the response to each of the steps above it. Look at how I distill the analysis of each game into possible patterns. Then consider how I describe the chosen pattern in the Pattern Template.

The steps of each exercise are a template to help you move through that process, but I provide the examples to show the subtle function of that process. I did not construct the examples to show an idealized process; they contain the actual intellectual work of searching for and expressing a pattern. They include bits of analysis that turn out not to be important, just as your exercises will. When you're having a tough time completing an exercise, pause and read through the example again and think about how the step responses work to produce the pattern.

CHAPTER 8

Basic Pattern Exercise

BASIC PATTERN EXERCISE
Pattern Purpose

The Basic Pattern Exercise is the most broadly applicable and could probably be used to generate any pattern. I've tailored the exercises that follow to generate specific kinds of patterns, but if you had to use just one exercise, this would be the one! Because this exercise looks at design elements, it has the potential to generate many patterns—more than one for each element. You should focus on one pattern at a time, and complete the first six steps of the exercise before turning your attention to additional patterns.

EXERCISE 1: BASIC PATTERN EXERCISE

Step 1: Name a design element.

Step 2: Name ten games that use that element—the more different ways the games use it, the better.

Step 3: Describe how each of those games uses the element you chose. Try *not* to look for a pattern yet. Focus on accurately describing the way each game uses the element you identified.

Step 4: What design problems do the games use the element to solve? Some games may use the element for one purpose, while others use it for another. Many games use the elements in more than one way. Describe the problems solved by your element for each of the ten games listed in step 2.

Step 5: Look at steps 3 and 4. Are there patterns in the ways the games use the element, and how do those relate to the problems they solve?

Step 6: Pick one of those patterns and describe it using the pattern template.

Step 7: You may repeat step 6 for each pattern you observed.

Example Basic Pattern Exercise
*Exercise**

Step 1: Name a design element.
Jumping

Step 2: Name ten games that use that element—the more different ways the games use it, the better.
*Donkey Kong/Jumpman, Q*bert, Super Mario Bros*[†]. *Mirror's Edge, Gravity Rush/VVVVVV, Alice/Super Mario World/Crackdown, Guild Wars 2, Tomb Raider* (reboot), *Prince of Persia* (second reboot), *Poptropica, Super Meat Boy, Street Fighter/Soulcalibur/Devil May Cry, Doom/Quake/Splosion Man, Tribes, Assassin's Creed, Canabalt, Sonic, Trials HD*

Step 3: Describe how each of those games uses the element you chose. Try *not* to look for a pattern yet. Focus on accurately describing the way each game uses the element you identified.
Jumping is such a fundamental design element that I tried to go back and select games that first used the mechanic in historically significant ways, as well as listing the most modern and innovative uses of the mechanic. Initially, only six examples of significance jumped into my head, so I did a small amount of research to see if there were general opinions on important uses of jumping. The willingness to pause and research a question like this is essential to the pattern development process since we all have played a limited number of games.

- *Donkey Kong/Jumpman, Geometry Dash*—Jumping is used to avoid enemies and traverse the 2D space.

- *Q*bert*—A reflex-based puzzle game made in the wake of Pac-Man, it uses jumping as its only movement mechanic.

- *Super Mario Bros.*—Jumping is used to avoid enemies, traverse 2D/3D space, and as a way to attack enemies.

- *Mirror's Edge*—This game uses first-person jumping as pure traversal.

---

[*] The answers to the questions in the exercises are intended to be a place to show your work and to take notes on your process. What you write here is not part of the pattern you will produce. In the following example, note that I list games in answer to step 2 that I don't use in the final pattern or even in the answer to step 3.

[†] The game *Braid* can be seen as an intentional subversion of the way *Super Mario Bros.* uses jumping.

- *Gravity Rush/VVVVVV*—Jumping combines with control of physics.

- *Alice/Super Mario World/Crackdown*—Jumping with a glide. Also, in-air control?

- *Guild Wars 2*—Jumping for exploration and as a puzzle. There's little need for it in world traversal, and none in combat.

- *Tomb Raider* (reboot)—Your ability to jump in this game is superhuman despite the more realistic tone of the game.

- *Prince of Persia* (second reboot)—This game features assisted jumping where another character helps you jump farther than you can alone. The game is single-player so that may be just a double jump.

- *Doom/Quake/Splosion Man/Tribes*—Jumping for world traversal. Jumping assisted by the physics of unrelated systems (Rocket Jumping, Ski Jumping, Bunny Hopping).

- *Street Fighter/Soulcalibur/Devil May Cry*—Jumping for world traversal, jumping as a combat move.

- *Poptropica, Super Meat Boy*—Jumping for world traversal with very unrealistic physics.

- *Trials HD*—Jumping in unrealistic environments with very realistic physics.

- *Assassin's Creed*—Jumping "on rails" for world traversal, jumping to escape enemies.

Step 4: What design problems do the games use the element to solve? Some games may use the element for one purpose while others use it for another. Many games use the elements in more than one way. Describe the problems solved by your element for each of the ten games listed in step 2.

- Navigation through the world space (all games listed)—All the games I chose used jumping as part of world traversal. At a base level, jumping gives you more movement options as a player.

- Creating a sense of autonomy in the player (all games listed)— Jumping increases a character's mobility in the game world, and that can give you a feeling of greater agency as you play. There's some subtlety in how this works, though. In some games, characters can jump in a way that more closely mirrors the real world, which can make you relate to the character more. In other games, jumping lets the character move through the world in ways you never could in real life, which can still feel empowering because you're controlling the character.

- Creating a sense of danger for the player (*Super Mario Bros.*, *Mirror's Edge*, *Gravity Rush/VVVVVV*, *Super Meat Boy*, *Tomb Raider*, *Prince of Persia*, *Trials HD*)—Jumping can cause death in all of these games. The ratio of how dangerous jumping is to how much it lets you traverse the world directly relates to the amount of power versus fear that you feel when you play. In a game like *Super Mario Bros.*, you may die from jumping incorrectly, but mostly it increases your ability to navigate the world. In a game like *Geometry Dash,* jumping allows you to progress through the world, but it's also the main thing that causes you to die when you do it incorrectly.

- Adding variety to the ways the player can interact with the world— All games listed except *Q*bert* and *Geometry Dash,* in which jumping is the *only* way you move through the world. But this is particularly true in *Guild Wars 2*, where jumping isn't a primary world traversal tool and is mostly used in optional jumping exploration puzzles.

- Enabling player mastery through creating complicated, intricate systems that require player skill growth—All games listed. It seems like this connection is stronger the more central jumping is as a mechanic, and the more complicated and subtle the jump mechanics are.

- Enabling player mastery of game systems by creating opportunities for the player to subvert them (*Doom/Quake, Tribes*)—This is interesting since, in the case of these games, the mechanics were not meant to allow player subversion. Rocket jumping and ski jumping were, on some level, bugs that players found and used to enhance gameplay. The developers, recognizing the value of the bugs, intentionally incorporated them into future games.

- Character building through giving the character abilities the player lacks (*Mirror's Edge, Gravity Rush, Alice, Tomb Raider, Poptropica, Assassin's Creed*)—Superhuman jumping abilities help make the characters seem superhuman, but not inhuman. Improving a character's most basic movement abilities lets you relate to the character—*I can jump, but not like that!*— in a way a completely inhuman ability wouldn't.

- Maintaining immersion in the game world by making character abilities and movement match your understanding of how the real world works—Interestingly none of the example games above use jumping in this way, but other games do (e.g., *Silent Hill 2, Flashback*).

- Enhancing combat by enhancing aggressive player actions (*Street Fighter/Soulcalibur, Super Mario Bros., Devil May Cry*)—The jumping itself may not be aggressive, but it amplifies the character's aggressive action. A jumping punch to the head is just more impactful than a standing punch to the head.

Step 5: Look at steps 3 and 4. Are there patterns in the ways the games use the element, and how do those relate to the problems they solve? *
Yes.

- More complex mechanics provide more opportunities for player skill. This taps into basic player needs like autonomy and mastery.

- When power has a cost, it's frightening to use. This would generate a pattern of dangerous jumping.

- Two great things that go great together, such as jumping and punching. This might be a very specific pattern about those two mechanics, or it might generalize to "movement and attack" or even to pairs of mechanics that create a player experience together that is more than either can produce alone.

- She's just like me! vs. I want to be her when I grow up! This would create a pattern about maintaining immersion by creating realistic character abilities vs. character building through superhuman abilities.

---

* There are clearly more patterns than I have listed. Don't feel like you need to list them all. But listing all the ones that jump out at you will make it easier to go back and flesh out the ones you don't choose later.

Step 6: Pick one of those patterns and describe it using the pattern template.

When power has a cost, it's frightening to use.

Step 7: You may repeat step 6 for each pattern you observed.

For this example, I will only document one pattern. In the next section, I'll show the completed writeup for the pattern I chose. Describing the other three patterns using the Pattern Template is an excellent way to practice before completing the full exercise on your own.

Research:

Creating even simple patterns like this can take a huge amount of both generalized game knowledge and knowledge of specific games. It's easy to feel like the more you know about games and the more games you have played, the better patterns you will see. That's true to a degree, but you shouldn't feel like there's no point in trying to create a pattern because you don't know enough yet. If you're a new designer, the patterns you see may be basic, but they're also probably fundamental. Experienced designers may fail to identify relevant patterns because they're too obvious. That said, when you're constructing a pattern, do try to find at least ten examples. If you can't think of that many games off the top of your head, do some research. The following sources are from the research I did when I was creating this pattern. If you look at the citations, you'll see that I'm referencing a scholarly article, an article on a popular gaming website, a Reddit post, and a fan-made games FAQ website. It's vital to evaluate your research sources and understand how much rigor or opinion there is in what you read. But it's also essential to look beyond academic analysis and consider both media perception and player experience. I do not list the background research for each pattern in the book, but I commonly read a dozen or more sources as I am investigating a possible pattern.

- "The Rise of the Jump" (Butler 2014)

- "What Was the First Game with a Double Jump and Why Was It Implemented?" (reddit 2016)

- "You Say Jump, I Say How High? Operationalising the Game Feel of Jumping" (Fasterholdt, Pichlmair, and Holmgård 2016)

- "What Game Do You Think Has Perfect Jumping Mechanics?" (GameFAQs 2018)

PATTERN NAME

As stated in the Pattern Template, the pattern name should be an "easy to remember and evocative name." There's a fine line between easy to remember and an inside joke or reference to a fleeting meme. Titles should be evocative, but they shouldn't be a reference that only you or your close friends will understand. Think about who will be reading your pattern and make sure that the title, image, and example games are understandable to the developers who will need to use the pattern.

DESCRIPTION AND EXAMPLE GAMES

You may notice that this pattern doesn't have anything specifically to do with jumping. That's not an accident. Many students will see jumping as the pattern itself rather than just a mechanic. Designers tend to want to take the games they've listed in steps 2 and 3 of the exercise and list those as their examples. But it's essential to look at the actual pattern you have generated and find examples of its use that *are not* examples of the functional element from step 1. If you see many natural examples of wildly different implementations of the pattern you've identified, it's a good indication that you've found a viable pattern. If you find examples that only relate to your starting functional element, then make sure that your pattern description reflects that narrow focus.

Pattern

Name: One of These Days That's Going to Get You Killed
Confidence: 2
Images:

FIGURE 8.1 AND 8.2 Jumping over a dangerous pit and suffering from a weapon overheating are both examples of this pattern in action.

Author: Chris Barney

Design problem: How do you maintain game balance and create tension when giving the player greater power in their interactions with the game world?

Description: To maintain balance and create tension when designing character abilities, a designer may introduce consequences resulting from using those abilities. The result may be something natural, like falling into a pit of lava you try to jump over, or it may be something mechanical, like weapon heat build-up or a stamina meter.

Games that use this pattern and how:

- *Super Mario Bros.*—The ability to jump, which increases the character's ability to move through the world and defeat enemies, also puts him in danger. Failing to jump over dangerous obstacles can result in Mario's death. Similarly, failing to jump over an enemy results in the enemy killing Mario.
- *Sekiro: Shadows Die Twice*—Stealth-killing enemies is the easiest way to defeat them, but failing to execute a stealth kill alerts the enemy and nearby enemies and suddenly puts you in a dangerous situation.
- *Anthem*—Firing weapons increases their heat. Failing to manage that resource, to self-limit the damage you are doing, can result in not being able to fire your gun when you most need it.
- *Zelda: Breath of the Wild*—Link can climb almost anything, but he has a stamina meter, so if he tries to climb something too high he will fall. He can jump off things and glide, but if he runs out of stamina, he falls to his death.

Seed: Exercise 1: Basic Pattern Exercise—Jumping

Related patterns:

Parent patterns:

Just Look At What You've Become* (Confidence: 2)—As you apply the pattern One of These Days That's Going to Get You Killed you are introducing consequences for player actions and character advancement. Use this pattern to ensure that character progression is a meaningful transformation. I'm Doing It As Hard As I Can† (Confidence: 3)—The escalating difficulty introduced by this pattern creates the mechanical need for the character progression systems produced by One of These Days That's Going to Get You Killed.

---

* Example pattern from Exercise 25: Creating Patterns from Lenses.

† Example pattern conversion from *Game Mechanics: Advanced Game Design* described in Chapter 16.

SUGGESTED EXERCISES

Use **Exercise 5: Functional Patterns** to generate a pattern based on the functional element of mechanical character progression.

Child patterns:

And Now I Guess We Are Doing This* (Confidence: 3)—When you use One of These Days That's Going to Get You Killed to balance increases in character abilities, you create situations where the character is in peril. You can use these situations to force the player to adjust their playstyle using this pattern.

The Risk of Knowing You† (Confidence: 2)—When you use One of These Days That's Going to Get You Killed to balance increases in character abilities, you both place the character in danger and create a sense of risk for the player. Use this pattern to help you use those two effects to create a stronger bond between player and character.

SUGGESTED EXERCISES

Use **Exercise 4: Formal Patterns** to generate a pattern based on environmental hazards.

Use **Exercise 5: Functional Patterns** to generate a pattern based on character stamina.

Use **Exercise 5: Functional Patterns** to generate a pattern based on limited ammunition.

Keywords: Character Progression, Mechanics, Balance

---

* Example pattern from Exercise 17: Finding Missing Patterns.
† Example pattern from Exercise 7: Player Experience Patterns.

CHAPTER 9

Structural Pattern Exercises

T HIS CHAPTER CONTAINS SEVERAL exercises that produce patterns about aspects of design that affect your whole game. Each exercise creates patterns focused on different aspects of game design. Whatever part of the design process you specialize in, you will benefit from completing all of these exercises.

HIGHER-ORDER PATTERNS

Pattern Purpose

This exercise creates a very broad pattern, one that probably suggests many more detailed or complementary patterns, but is less likely to require other high-level patterns to function.

It's tempting—and reasonable—to start with this pattern-generation exercise. A high-level pattern is easy to find and an excellent introduction to the process. However, because the process of distilling a pattern is a skill and will improve with repetition, you should return to any early patterns you produce with this exercise and refine or replace them with more sophisticated later attempts.

The second and third steps in the exercise cause you to move up a level in abstraction. These steps acknowledge that most design elements can solve many problems, and often, designers use them for multiple purposes simultaneously. When choosing design elements based on a pattern you created with this exercise, you need to look at *all of the effects* that element has, and make sure that you want to introduce those effects into your game. If not, then find a different element that doesn't include the unintended side effects. For this reason, I advise completing step 8 as many times as possible—generate all of the patterns you can, based on the high-level element you choose in step 1.

EXERCISE 2: HIGHER-ORDER PATTERNS

Step 1: Name a design element. For example, camera perspective (first person, isometric, third person, etc.), or levels, or monsters, or non-player characters (NPCs).

Step 2: What problems does that design element solve?

Step 3: Pick one of the problems you identified.

Step 4: List and describe ten games that also solve the same problem in as many diverse ways as possible.

Step 5: Describe the way each game solves the design problem. Focus on each game and try *not* to start looking for patterns as you write.

Step 6: What do those solutions have in common? The answers may have more than one thing in common. Some games may share one and other games another. List and describe each.

Step 7: Is there a pattern? Describe it briefly. Do not create a formal description using the Pattern Template; just make a first attempt to articulate what you see.

Step 8: For each problem you identified in step 2, you may repeat steps 3–7.

Example Higher-Order Pattern

Exercise

Step 1: Name a design element.

Many games have levels. By this, I mean gameplay levels, not character or item levels.

Step 2: What problems does that design element solve?

- Users have a limited time to play a game.

- Player skill level increases throughout a game.

- Designers need to break up complex narratives.

- Players need variety in a gameplay experience, or they may lose engagement.

Step 3: Pick one of the problems you identified.

Users have a limited time to play a game.

Step 4: List and describe ten games that also solve the same problem.

Super Mario Bros., Metroid, Soulcalibur, Rock Band, Tetris, Pokémon Go, Fortnight, Clash Royale, Skyrim, Zelda: Breath of the Wild

Step 5: Describe the way each game solves the design problem. Focus on each game and try *not* to start looking for patterns as you write.

- *Super Mario Bros.*—The game is broken up into many levels in a way that provides discrete chunks of gameplay. However, in the original Nintendo Entertainment System (NES) game, you couldn't save your game, so you had to play from the beginning, meaning the levels alone didn't solve this particular problem. To some degree, it was possible to bypass levels if you knew secret paths, so players could use levels in this game to solve the problem of limited playtime. But the developers hid these shortcuts, so using them to freely access different parts of the game was not their primary purpose in the design. This game may be an early or formative use of the pattern.

- *Doom*—This game is a classic use of levels to create smaller units of gameplay. You can complete each level in minutes, but the overall playtime is much longer than in *Super Mario Bros.* Developers used the discrete gameplay chunks to add additional content in the form of expansions, the most recent of which they released just recently, several decades after the initial launch of the game.

- *Soulcalibur*—Fighting games use the concept of levels in almost the opposite way to the two previous examples. Individual matches, whether against other players or artificial intelligence (AI) opponents, are only a minute or two long. Framing the game as a series of matches against many opponents lets the developers extend the average play session to much longer than the completion of a single fight.

- *Rock Band*—The use of songs as levels works similarly to fighting games, linking together shorter discreet matches into a longer experience. Making the competitive multiplayer elements of the game turn-based breaks up each player's experience, allowing the game to build tension and interest during the downtime while keeping it short enough not to lose the attention of the waiting player(s).

- *Tetris*—Levels in the initial iteration of *Tetris* only partially serve the purpose of breaking up gameplay. The transition to higher levels doesn't interrupt gameplay, and the usual play session ends at failure rather than at the end of a level. In this game, level is almost purely a measure of difficulty. You also can't begin play at a high level. There are only nine levels in the game, with the last continuing indefinitely as your score accumulates. However, in the recent *Tetris Effect*, the game is broken into more distinct levels. Each level is paired with a different song and changes the game's flow in more complicated ways than just increasing the speed with which blocks fall. Again, this more modern approach allows the game to have many more levels and much more diverse gameplay. It's also possible to resume play at any level you've reached.

- *Pokémon Go*—*Pokémon Go* has a complicated use of levels. In one sense, the game is an open world and not broken into gameplay levels. However, any individual encounter in which you engage in the core gameplay loop of capturing a creature by throwing balls at it can be considered a level. These encounters might be too short to be a level or play session, but since this is a mobile game, I think they accurately match a common play session pattern. The game has several other activities that map well to the concept of levels: gym battles, raids, and player versus player (PvP) battles. You can choose to engage with each if you want a slightly longer gameplay experience.

- *Fortnight*—The use of "levels" in *Fortnight* has changed a great deal over the last few years of the game's development. Initially, the game focused on 30–60 minute cooperative levels, and even introduced a very long play mode that often lasted four or more hours—uncommon for non-persistent world multiplayer games. Eventually, the game shifted its focus to the shorter "battle arena" gameplay mode, where the level is static, the playable area shrinks, and there are 100 players. The game ends when only one player remains, and usually lasts 10–20 minutes. The runaway popularity of this gameplay style during the game's development caused part of this shift. However, it also may be a more complicated process—the style and duration of the game shifting to suit the largest audience. The merits of this reactive style of design aside, the result is a playtime tightly coupled with the duration desired by its players.

- *Clash Royale*—This is a mobile game with short PvP matches. The gameplay during a level is very intense and focused, but brief.

- *Summoners War*—This is a more complicated game that has many level types. The length of the levels varies, but ranges from a minute to perhaps 5 minutes. It has both single and multiplayer content and is in the mobile space. It's interesting as an example of the mobile game type that has both interactive play and auto-play modes, where you initiate a level and make starting strategic choices, but then only watch the gameplay out. These levels are part of a slow progression gameplay style, letting you make progress in the game without engaging in its content actively. This passive playstyle becomes necessary as the repetitive play needed to progress exceeds the player's interest in the content.

- *Skyrim*—This is an open-world game without discrete levels. However, you can divide your gameplay into smaller chunks by creating short-term goals that you can achieve in constrained areas. Some of these take the form of dungeons to explore, and others are quests you can focus on within the undifferentiated world. This game uses levels in another interesting way: the creatures and difficulty of the game scale with your character's level. Thus, the gameplay experience of completing a specific quest or exploring a particular dungeon will be different depending on how advanced your character is. In this way, the character's level can be viewed as a game level.

- *Zelda: Breath of the Wild*—In this game, the open world is independent of the character's level, so your geographic location is what determines the challenge level of the game. When combined with your current skill level, this creates de facto playable areas, even though you can access any area at any point in the game. Each area is generally larger than you can cover in a single session, and as you progress your character, the playable area shifts. This gives a sense of progression, but not a sense of discrete levels. A secondary gameplay aspect more closely matches the traditional idea of levels, though. The challenge dungeons in the game provide discrete chunks of content to engage with when playtime is limited. This concept of allowing different gameplay styles that fit the player's needs is indicative of the pattern in all of the preceding examples.

Step 6: What do those solutions have in common? The solutions may have more than one thing in common. Some games may share one, and other games share another. List and describe each.

These games break gameplay into chunks that fit the playtime of the audience/platform.

Step 7: Is there a pattern? Describe it briefly. Do not create a formal description using the Pattern Template; just make a first attempt to articulate what you see.

Yes: Units of design must fit the size of the play, not just the level size, but also the reward frequency, progression rate, difficulty ramp, etc.

Pattern

Name: The Three Bears Theory of Level Size
Confidence: 2
Image:

FIGURE 9.1   Level size should expand or contract to match the desired play style of the game.

Author: Chris Barney
Design problem: Players have a limited time to play a game.
Description: To design games that fit the players' available time, a designer may break up play into chunks. Designers may create this segmentation by building discrete levels that take a set time to complete and sizing the levels to fit the time the designer expects the game's target audience to have available. Alternatively, a designer can provide various activities within an open world that take different lengths of time to complete, so the player may choose how long they want to engage with the game. Or a designer might use short repeatable chunks of play that players combine to build a play session.

Games that use this pattern and how:

- *Doom*—This game is a classic use of levels to create smaller units of gameplay. Each level lasts only minutes, but the overall playtime is often many hours, as players complete multiple levels. These discrete levels are each a part of a larger story.
- *Soulcalibur*—Fighting games use the concept of levels in almost the opposite way. Similar to the levels in *Doom*, individual matches, whether against other players or AI opponents, are only a minute or two long. Fighting games do narratively link multiple matches, but rather than breaking up a longer experience into shorter chunks, they build the longer structure out of the individual matches. Framing the game as a series of matches lets the player extend the playtime to any length they desire.
- *Skyrim*—This is an open-world game without discrete levels. However, designers allow the player to divide gameplay into smaller chunks by creating short-term goals achieved in constrained areas. Some of these take the form of play spaces such as dungeons. Others are quests that give narrative focus within the undifferentiated world. An interesting observation about this game is that the creatures and difficulty of the game scale with the player's level, and so the experience of completing a specific quest or exploring a particular dungeon will be different depending on the character level. Therefore the character's level can be viewed as a game level.

Seed: Exercise 2: Higher Level Patterns—Many games have levels.
Related patterns:
Parent patterns:

SUGGESTED EXERCISES

Use **Exercise 2: Higher-Order Patterns** to generate a pattern based on game level size.*

---

* The parent pattern is suggested by the final conclusion of the exercise. The write up of the pattern in the pattern template focuses on a specific aspect of the larger idea being generated, showing that even a 'high-level pattern' may suggest patterns of higher levels.

Child patterns:

SUGGESTED EXERCISES

Use **Exercise 9: Circulation Patterns** to generate a pattern based on the meta-circulation pattern found in Metroidvania-style games, in which the playable area expands as the character gains new abilities.*
Use **Exercise 13: Breaking Spaces Patterns** to generate a pattern describing how to adjust level size when moving a game's play environment from one venue to another. In step 3 of that exercise focus on elements that change scale when the game is moved.

Keywords: Level Design, Audience, Playtime, Goals, Platform

LOWER-ORDER PATTERNS

Pattern Purpose

This exercise helps you find patterns that are suggested by or depend on a pattern you already understand. Use this exercise when you encounter a pattern that seems particularly complex or that has a lot of implications.

This exercise is challenging because you must recognize problems created by patterns that you've observed or problems that are often paired with a problem your first pattern addresses. You must have a solid understanding of the dynamics that may result from the use of your patterns. If you're an inexperienced designer, this exercise may require research and analysis of the games you used to create the original pattern.

EXERCISE 3: LOWER-ORDER PATTERNS

Step 1: Pick a pattern generated by one of the exercises you have previously completed.
Step 2: If you were making a game with that pattern, what problems/questions would you have? List these problems and describe them.
Step 3: List ten games that have solved one of those problems.
Step 4: Describe the solution used by each game. Try *not* to look for a pattern as you do this and focus on describing each solution individually.

---

* This child pattern is suggested by the analysis of *Zelda: Breath of the Wild*. It is entirely possible for a pattern to have many child patterns and even to have more than one parent pattern. Parent and child patterns should be noted when writing a pattern even if they have not been fully generated. Designers should later pursue defining these patterns completely.

Step 5: What do those solutions have in common? The commonalities in the solutions may exist in all of the games or just some of them, and they may have more than one thing in common. Describe each.

Step 6: List and briefly describe each pattern you see.

Step 7: Pick a pattern and document it in the Pattern Template.

Step 8: You may repeat this exercise for each pattern you observed.

Example Lower-Order Pattern

Exercise

Step 1: Pick a pattern generated by one of the exercises you have previously completed.

Don't Intellectualize My Pain*

Step 2: If you were making a game with that pattern, what problems/ questions would you have? List these problems and describe them.

A. If health increases throughout the game to create progression for the player, the display of the ever-increasing health may become a problem as multiple rows of hearts accumulate and numbers rise to illegible numbers.

B. If health increases throughout the game, then the impact of losing health may decrease as the player's perception of their character progression is at odds with making them feel vulnerable.

C. In a multiplayer game, the display of other players' health may become a problem if players need to monitor the health of multiple other players' characters.

Step 3: Choose a problem and list ten games that have solved it.

Problem A, the formal difficulties of increasing health.

Zelda, Skyrim, Hero Clicker, Dust: An Elysian Tale, Anthem, Last Blade, Dark Souls, The Secret World

---

* Example pattern for Exercise 4. Feel free to skip ahead and look at this pattern. It is a good example of the kind of pattern that you will be using with the lower-order patterns exercise.

Step 4: Describe the solution used by each game. Try *not* to look for a pattern as you do this and focus on describing each solution individually.

- *Zelda*—Larger enemies physically, new enemy attack types, attacks take more hearts. The amount that the character's health can increase during the game is limited by the number of hearts that can be reasonably displayed.*

- *Skyrim*—Enemies scale with player progression, so they don't get easier to kill if you're using the same equipment and tactics, but players gain access to new equipment and special abilities. It's not possible to defeat some enemies with a low-level character but is with a high-level character, even though their difficulty has also scaled up due to the player's increased resources.

- *Hero Clicker*—This idle game has player stats, health included, that increase exponentially and continually. They very quickly become impossible to display visually, and even numeric representations get out of hand, requiring new imaginary units of measure to describe the continuing escalation. The game is, to a degree, a parody, and the nonsensical health display reflects that.

- *Dust: An Elysian Tale*—The character's health increases throughout the game, but the visual display does not change. Enemy difficulty increases as well, keeping you in a similar state of danger throughout the game. The character has other statistics that affect their survivability, defense, armor, and so on. Difficult enemies can kill the character in a few hits even in the late game, so the character's power increase is more focused on the abilities that prevent the character from taking damage, such as ranged attracts.

- *Anthem*—The character's health display size remains constant, but is divided into smaller and smaller sections. The amount of health each section represents remains the same. *Dead Space* uses a similar display technique.

---

* The maximum number of hearts has varied between the games of the series. There were a maximum of 16 in the original game and 30 in *Zelda: Breath of the Wild*. At 30 hearts the legibility of this system has degraded considerably.

- *Last Blade*—Although health does not increase in this old school fighting game, it is one of the earliest examples of a useful technique for displaying large amounts of health in a meaningful way. Your character has a green health bar; when that is depleted it reveals a yellow bar, and then a red one. Only when damage depletes all three does your character die.

- *Dark Souls*—Your character can gain only a limited amount of health in the game, but they gain the ability to carry more and more charges for their Estus Flask, which is essentially a health potion. Having to remember to use the flask means that a character remains vulnerable while still being able to gain a larger and larger pool of health. Abstracting the extra health to an item with multiple charges allows for a simple display.

- *The Secret World*—The size of the character's health display doesn't change as their health pool increases in this massively multiplayer online game (MMO). The amount of damage dealt by creatures at the same power level as the character remains relatively constant, so your perception of the danger to your character is also stable. In the late game, the designers introduced a system called AEGIS. It consisted of different types of damage caused by various enemies and matching shield types that players could activate. This system is similar to the multiple layers of health bar from *Last Blade*, though it's considerably more complicated. These shields also improve in effectiveness over time, but don't change how they're displayed.

Step 5: What do those solutions have in common? The commonalities in the solutions may exist in all of the games or just some of them, and they may have more than one thing in common. Describe each.

1. There are some visual indicators that the character is more powerful.

2. There are some visual indicators that enemies are more powerful and dangerous as the game progresses.

3. There are multiple avenues of power growth available to the player, and health is only one of them.

4. The game abstracts health into multiple layers: health and shield, multiple health bars, health potions, etc.

Step 6: List and briefly describe each pattern you see.

Stronger enemies or other increasing challenges balance the increase in the character's power. This statement combines items 1 and 2. I think that items 3 and 4 are each a pattern, and these three patterns would all support one another.

Step 7: Pick a pattern and document it in the Pattern Template.

I present the pattern combining solutions 1 and 2 from step 5.

Pattern

Name: Old Me Was Afraid of Old You, But New Me Is Stronger! ... And Now I'm Afraid of New You
Confidence: 2
Image:

FIGURE 9.2   Monster facing warrior remembering Facing a recurring enemy can be meaningful if you see them growing more powerful as you progress.

Author: Chris Barney
Design problem: Designers need to give the player a feeling of progress. Many games increase the character's health and power as they progress for this reason. The increase in power and resilience can interfere with the game's sense of tension, danger, or excitement.
Description: To maintain balanced gameplay in the face of a player's power curve, the rest of the game must have a matching power curve. The

designer must raise the stakes in other ways to prevent this from undermining the player's sense of progress. Useful techniques include an increase in the scale of threats faced by the growing character, mounting narrative intensity, or a purely visual and thematic progression, as long as the player feels that their progress is meaningful. (See the child pattern Look at Me Now.)

Games that use this pattern and how:

- *Zelda*—Link gains additional hearts as the game progresses, but faces larger enemies physically, new enemy attack types, and more damaging attacks. The number of hearts that can be reasonably displayed limits how much the character's health can increase during the game, but it is still reasonably large.
- *Skyrim*—Enemies scale with player progression, so they don't get easier to kill if you're using the same equipment and tactics, but you do gain access to new equipment and special abilities. It's not possible to defeat some enemies with a low-level character, but in spite of the parallel health increases of both the character and the enemies, it is possible with a higher-level character due to the player's increased abilities and gear.
- *Dark Souls*—Your character can gain only a limited amount of health in the game, but they gain the ability to carry more and more charges for their Estus Flask, which is essentially a health potion. Having to remember to use the flask means that a character remains vulnerable while still allowing them to gain a larger and larger pool of health. Enemies get progressively more dangerous, but even low-level enemies remain a threat.

Seed: Exercise 3: Lower-Order Patterns—Don't Intellectualize My Pain*
Related patterns:
Parent patterns:
Don't Intellectualize My Pain[†] (Confidence: 3)—If you want to establish power and difficulty curves in your game, you must communicate the power and state of the character. Use this pattern to guide the display of character state.

I'm Doing It As Hard As I Can[‡] (Confidence: 3)—Use this pattern to guide your implementation of the escalating difficulty that you balance character progression against in your game.

---

* Example pattern from Exercise 4: Formal Patterns.
† Example pattern from Exercise 4: Formal Patterns.
‡ Example pattern conversion from *Game Mechanics: Advanced Game Design* described in Chapter 16.

SUGGESTED EXERCISES

Use **Exercise 18: Finding Negative Patterns** to generate a pattern based on poor character progression.

Use **Exercise 19: Finding Positive Patterns from Negative Patterns** to generate one or more patterns that contribute to successful character progression.

Child patterns:

SUGGESTED EXERCISES

Use **Exercise 11: Emergent Narrative Patterns** to generate a pattern by asking yourself the question, "What story do I tell myself when I return to an area that I have already beaten?" This will generate a diverse set of patterns depending on the games you examine.

Keywords: Balance, Character Progression, Damage, Difficulty, Enemy Progression, Health

FORMAL AND FUNCTIONAL DESIGN ELEMENTS

The next two exercises focus on creating patterns that deal with design elements that make up the form and function of the game. For these exercises, I define *formal elements* as the physical or virtual components of a game (its nouns), and *functional elements* as the mechanics or actions of the game (its verbs).

For example, a game described as "a boy and his warrior father explore a hostile world and fight together, combining their abilities to overcome terrifying monsters and dangerous wilderness" would have the formal elements of *a boy*, *his father*, *terrifying monsters*, and *dangerous wilderness*. It would have the functional elements of *exploring*, *fighting*, *having abilities*, and *combining them*. Of course, games are more complicated than the high-level summary of *God of War* (2018), but it's easy to look at the description of any game, or part of a game, and identify the formal and functional elements. Breaking game design elements into formal and functional groups isn't the beginning of some new taxonomy. It's just a practical way to focus on a particular aspect of games and create patterns related to that aspect.

In art and architecture, formal and functional elements have more specific meanings, but fundamentally they're the most basic building blocks of the discipline. The more *elemental* the formal and functional elements you choose for your patterns, the more *fundamental* the patterns you derive from them will be. For instance, you might use the formal element of "characters" to generate a more general pattern, or look at "boy" and "father" to shape a more specific one.

FORMAL PATTERNS

Pattern Purpose

The category of formal game design elements is so broad that it can be challenging to pick one to use in this pattern. I use an exercise in my classes where I have groups of five or so students each individually come up with as many formal elements as they can in five minutes. Then I have the members share their answers with the others in their group. I ask them to pick the elements that either all or most of the group members listed to use in the following exercise. If you're an experienced designer or have done this exercise a few times, try thinking of the most unusual or complex formal elements you've encountered. Those are often more difficult to work with, but also yield exciting patterns.

Sample Formal Elements*			
Ammunition	Target (Goal Post/Hoop)	Maze	Spaceship
Arena	Gun	Mini-map	Sword
Armor	Hallway	Monster	Teleporter Pad
Avatar	Health	Mountains	Tools
Board	Health Bar	Non-Player Character	Town
Car	Health Pack/Potion	Options Menu	Train
Card	Horse	Pit	Treasure
Castle/Fortress	Inventory	Platform	Unit (Controllable)
Companion	Items	Power-Ups	Water
Compass	Ladder	Save Point	Wilderness
Cover	Level	Shield	World Map
Dice	Loot	Ship	
Door	Mana	Shop	

---

* There are literally thousands of formal elements in games! There is nothing special about this list; it is just intended as a prompt to get you thinking about other possibilities. If you find yourself saying "But what about…" The answer is probably "Yes that is a formal element too!"

> **EXERCISE 4: FORMAL PATTERNS**
>
> **Step 1:** Name a formal game design element.
> **Step 2:** Name ten games that use the formal design element you chose in as diverse ways as possible.
> **Step 3:** Describe the way that each game uses the element.
> **Step 4:** What design problems do those games use the element to solve? For each game, describe the way the designers use the element.
> **Step 5:** What do the uses from step 4 have in common?
> **Step 6:** Are there one or more patterns in your observations? If so, describe them.
> **Step 7:** Pick one of the patterns and document it using the Pattern Template.
> **Step 8:** You may repeat step 7 for each pattern you observed.

Example Formal Pattern

In this exercise, I purposely chose a familiar, common formal element to illustrate how a nuanced, insightful pattern can arise from observing the use of even a simple, well-understood formal design element.

Exercise

Step 1: Name a formal game design element.

Health meters

Step 2: Name ten games that use the formal design element you chose in as diverse ways as possible.

The Legend of Zelda, Street Fighter, Dead Space (←Trespasser*), Journey, Final Fantasy 13, The Secret World, Doom (←MidiMaze), Diablo, Silent Hill, Metro 2033/Mirror's Edge, Halo (→Call of Duty/Mass Effect)

Step 3: Describe the way that each game uses the element.

- *The Legend of Zelda*—A user interface (UI) element of hearts represents character health.

- *Street Fighter*—A UI bar-shaped meter represents character health.

---

* Arrows indicate that the use of the pattern evolved from one game to the next, so I am using the game *Dead Space* as the example, but the technique was first seen in *Trespasser*. The implementation in *Trespasser* was poor and I want to use *Dead Space* because its implementation was better and it is more widely known, but I want to show it's debt to the earlier game

- *Dead Space (←Trespasser)*—A diegetic interface represents character health. *Trespasser* uses a heart-shaped tattoo visible in the first-person perspective, and *Dead Space* uses a set of lights along the character's spine, visible in third-person view.

- *Journey*—The character's cape indicates health. *Super Mario Bros.* uses character size in the same way.

- *Final Fantasy 13*—Bar-shaped UI elements represent health and "break."

- *The Secret World*—A bar-shaped UI element representing health overlays a second bar tracking an "AEGIS": shield.

- *Doom (←MidiMaze)*—A UI element in the form of a character portrait reflects the character's health.

- *Diablo*—A UI element in the form of a glass globe holds character health, represented in liquid form.

- *Silent Hill*—The UI menu shows a character portrait that indicates their health. Character behavior also reflects health.

- *Metro 2033/Mirror's Edge*—A camera filter that changes the screen color or focus indicates health.

- *Halo/Call of Duty/Mass Effect*—A bar-shaped UI element indicates health. A second bar-shaped UI element indicates a shield. These differ from the on-screen elements in the previous examples, as one or both return to full over time.

Step 4: What design problems do those games use the element to solve? For each game, describe the way the designers use the element.

- *The Legend of Zelda*—The hearts that indicate health are simple and easy to read. Having low health increases tension in the game. The clear indication of health allows you to adjust gameplay style to minimize death and the frustration of starting over a section of gameplay. As the game progresses, the number of hearts that you have increases, allowing the difficulty of the world to scale as the character's power increases. This shift is independent of your skill as a player increasing, which is less in the control of the developer. The growing row of hearts indicates the character's power to the player, serving a similar role to levels in other games.

- *Street Fighter*—The health bar is a fine-grained way to show health; it's clear and easy to read, allowing for players to adjust strategy as health decreases. The prominent display of the health bar causes it to become a central driver of tension in the game.

- *Dead Space/Trespasser*—Both of these games use a diegetic interface, which is to say an interface integrated into the game world. In *Dead Space*, it's a segmented blue bar on the back of the character's spacesuit. In *Trespasser*, it's a heart tattoo on the character's chest. The health bar/heart serves the previously stated purposes, but also removes a layer of artificial interface between you and the character without eliminating information from your view as you play. The implementation in *Dead Space* works better because it's always visible and because it's diegetic. *Trespasser*'s solution requires you to look down, since the game has a first-person perspective. It's also problematic because it objectifies the character by requiring the player to look down her shirt; this titillation was a little uncomfortable at the time the game was made and has since become more so.

- *Journey*—You can't "die" in *Journey*, so the character's cape is not, strictly speaking, a health indicator. But in the parts of the game where enemies attack the character, their cape becomes shorter when enemies hit them. The cape is a *functional* diegetic interface, because it's both a part of the game world and indicates not just the character's state but the player's gameplay abilities. The length of time a character can fly is indicated by their cape as well. The earliest use of this kind of interface is probably *Super Mario Bros*. In that game, eating a mushroom doubles the size of the character, indicating his increased health. Increasing in size also changes where he can fit and his collision with walls and ceilings.

- *The Secret World*—In the original version of the MMO, health was shown in a standard health bar. When the developers launched a late-game zone set in Tokyo, they added a new health mechanic and display. Called the "Aegis System," mechanically it's just an extra shield you have to break through before you can do damage to creatures. The shield is a different color depending on the type of monster you're facing, and your ability to break through the shields is tracked independently for each type. Mechanically, this allowed the developers to reset the difficulty of enemies in a way that was independent of overall character power, theoretically allowing players to complete areas with different shields in any order. In practice, the interface for using the shields was over-complicated and decreased the fun of playing the game.

- *Doom/MIDI Maze*—In the original *Doom*, a color-coded percentile number indicates health. The condition of the character portrait in the UI also reflects their health. This type of display was technically first used in the game MIDI Maze. More than just indicating the character's health, this display ties the character's health to an emotional state.

- *Ninja Pizza Girl*—The character's "health" is her emotional state. As she becomes sad or discouraged, the color of the game desaturates toward monochrome. When she's defeated, you can click on her repeatedly to generate affirmative statements in her internal monologue until color returns to the world. This system shifts the focus of the game from physical damage to the inner life and emotional state of the main character.

- *Diablo*—The UI shows health and mana levels as globes. This display is functionally just a standard health bar, but is tied thematically to the setting of the game with the intent of increasing immersion, and so this might be considered a semi-diegetic interface.

- *Silent Hill*—The character's health in this survival horror game is indicated diegetically and functionally by auditory cues and by the animations of the character moving. The direct UI indication of health is the color of the character portrait, but the portrait is only visible when the game is paused and in the inventory screen. This inaccessible display creates uncertainty and fear for the player, as it's difficult to know how badly injured you are in the heat of combat.

- *Metro 2033/Mirror's Edge/Call of Duty 2*—A screen effect indicates health in these games that have automatic health regeneration. *Metro 2033* and *Call of Duty 2* apply a red filter to the screen when the character is wounded. In *Metro 2033*, the effect becomes more intense as the character takes more damage. In *Mirror's Edge*, the effect is a blurring of the screen as if the character's vision is tearing up. This more realistic effect is a more diegetic implementation of the design element.

- *Halo/Mass Effect/Call of Duty 2—Halo* was the first major game to use "health regeneration." The character has two bars indicating their health: a health bar and a shield bar. Only the shield bar regenerates, but functionally the shield is just another health pool, one that replenishes over time. *Mass Effect* used this same technique, and it is now common in the genre. *Call of Duty 2* adopted this system, but has only a single regenerating health bar. Subsequent games elaborated on this system by lowering the rate of regeneration as the character's health drops.

- *Final Fantasy 13*—In combat, the health of the characters and enemies are shown in a standard health bar. Additionally, there's a "break" meter. When this meter becomes filled, the character or enemy is vulnerable for a specified period. This system is an inverse of the shield found in *Halo*, which makes the character vulnerable when emptied. This implementation shows up in other games such as later entries in the *Soulcalibur* fighting games. I can't think of an example of treating base health in this way, with a damage meter that fills up rather than a health meter that depletes.

Step 5: What do the uses in step 4 have in common?

- Games add player health to create variable tension based on the perceived likelihood of death.

- Simple, conspicuous health displays make damage and player vulnerability a focus.

- Granular health displays allow strategic shifts based on health in skill-based games.

- Tying health to the character's emotional state through visuals like portraits or animation can increase the player's connection to the character. This technique can fail if the visuals or animation impair gameplay.

- Hiding health indicators is used to increase the player's anxiety. This is effective when paired with a horror setting where the character is supposed to feel fear. The pattern The Risk of Knowing You* would be a parent of a pattern based on this use of health indicators.

---

* Example Pattern for Exercise 7: Player Experience Patterns.

- Removing the micromanagement of health through regeneration is used to focus players toward the emotional effects of high and low health, and away from the strategic and mechanics-based thinking needed to manage health manually.

- Complications to health systems often increase strategic depth.

- Complicated mechanical systems intended to increase player engagement or have a particular effect can often have the opposite effect. This effect is seen here for health systems, but it is true in many areas of design.

Step 6: Are there one or more patterns in your observations? If so, describe them.

- Yes. To create an emotional effect of anxiety or tension in a player, a developer may put the player's character in danger. When this danger is binary, any harm to the character ends the game. Thus the tension is very high, but also mostly static. If the threat is granular and the character can receive some amount of harm before the game ends, then the level of risk needs to be communicated to the player. In these cases, developers may add interface elements to convey the character's state to the player. The effectiveness of these elements is relative to the fidelity of the information displayed. However, the conscious thought required to process complex character state data distances the player from the character and distances the player from the emotional state of the character. To create the intended effect, the developer must balance detail with legibility.

- I think that I could derive several more specific patterns from character health, but this pattern is probably a parent to most or all of them.

Step 7: Pick one of the patterns and document it using the Pattern Template.

I will describe the primary effect discussed in the response to step 6.

Step 8: You may repeat step 6 for each pattern observed.

I identified only one pattern, or rather I generalized many observations into a single pattern. Specific observations may form child patterns.

Pattern

Name: Don't Intellectualize My Pain!
Confidence: 2
Image:

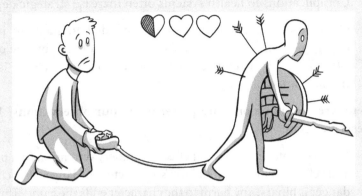

FIGURE 9.3 Player controlling a sad hurt character It is much easier to empathize with a character when their health matches their appearance in the game.

Author: Chris Barney
Design problem: Designers may need to connect players with the physical and emotional state of their characters to increase empathy and immersion.
Description: It's common to see health bars, life counters, shields, break meters, etc. They are used for two related and, to some degree, opposed purposes. First, they connect players emotionally with the state of their characters. Seeing a character with low health evokes anxiety and caution in a player, whereas seeing a character with full health encourages confidence and boldness. Second, clearly understanding the state of a character allows the player to engage strategically with the game. However, the more focused a player is on the character's mechanical state, the further removed they are from a sympathetic emotional response to the character's danger. To create the desired balance between intellectual strategy and emotional reaction, a developer must balance the visible mechanical detail of a character's state and the implied emotional effect of that state on the character and player.

Games that use this pattern and how:

- *The Legend of Zelda*—Hearts clearly indicate the character's health. Though they are non-diegetic, they provide an intuitive framework for the emotional situation of the character. At the beginning of the game, having three hearts means everything's good, and having a quarter of a heart left means things have gone very badly, and the level of drama and tension is high.

- *Street Fighter*—Health bars are the primary formal element driving strategy and drama. Attacks, blocks, etc. are, of course, the primary functional elements. Still, the formal element of the health bar provides feedback that connects gameplay moments and allows both mechanical strategy and emotional narrative.
- *Journey*—The character's cape is a functional diegetic indicator of the character's state. It both indicates how much damage the character has taken and the length of time that they can fly.
- *Final Fantasy 13/The Secret World*—The break meter and the Aegis System, respectively, are complex permutations of character state display. They are used to introduce deep mechanical gameplay, but the heavy mechanical focus shifts gameplay to a more strategic and less emotional mode.
- *Silent Hill 2*—There is no visible interface element indicating character state during play. However, the character's animations and sound reflect his state in a diegetic way; running causes the character to breathe loudly and slow down. Being wounded causes the character to limp and causes the player to feel their heartbeat in the controller (PS2). The uncertainty and lack of precision of these indicators are intentional and increase the player's tension by connecting them to the character's distress.
- *Metro 2033/Mirror's Edge*—The red filter and blurry screen respectively provide legible indicators of the characters' state. The blurry screen is arguably more diegetic, but the effect is similar. These effects would be untenable in a game without health regeneration. Because they do not persist for long, they provide strong stress stimulation in the player as well as useful indicators of the character's danger.

Seed: Exercise 4: Formal Patterns—Health Bars
Related patterns:
Parent patterns:

SUGGESTED EXERCISE

Use **Exercise 2: Higher-Order Patterns** to generate a pattern based on user interface.
Use **Exercise 6: Emotional Patterns** to generate a pattern based on empathy.

Child patterns:
Old Me Was Afraid of Old You, But New Me Is Stronger! ... And Now I'm Afraid of New You* (Confidence: 2)—The techniques described in Don't Intellectualize My Pain are a necessary part of implementing this pattern. You must show the character and enemy states to establish tension and show growth.

---

* Example pattern for Exercise 3: Lower-Order Patterns.

SUGGESTED EXERCISE

Use **Exercise 10: Boss Encounter Patterns** to generate a pattern based on enemy health indicators.
Use **Exercise 17: Finding Missing Patterns** to generate one or more child patterns that contribute help to connect the player to the physical or emotional state of a character.

Keywords: Emotions, Mechanics, Player Feedback, User Interface, Damage, Empathy

Bonus Student Example: Temporally Unavailable Space

A student, Zhihui Chang, generated this pattern in the first semester that I used patterns in my teaching. I have updated the format to match the one used in this book as well as clarifying some English usage. I have also expanded the examples section to reflect the breadth of the application of the pattern. Chang used the Basic Pattern Exercise as applied to mechanics from a group project to generate this pattern.

Pattern

Name: Temporally Unavailable Space
Confidence: 2
Image:

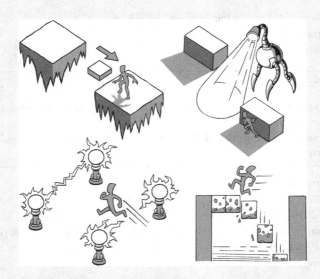

FIGURE 9.4 Temporally Unavailable Space can be created in games using a variety of mechanics creating entirely unique dynamics in the game.

Author: Zhihui Chang (revised and expanded by Chris Barney)

Design problem: While simple static spaces are useful to introduce players to basic movement and the fundamental mechanics of a game, they can become too easy to read, navigate, and understand as player skills advance throughout a game. Designers need to find a way to keep players engaged with the environment.

Description: To create a dynamic and engaging playspace, a designer should consider that the playspace is not just defined by the static architecture of a level but by the space that a player can access at any given time. By employing various techniques to limit and alter that space, a designer can turn the simple traversal of a level into a spatial puzzle.

The pattern of Temporally Available Move Space has several applications. The simplest and most obvious example would be a moving platform—space that is only accessible to a player some of the time.

The temporally available move space has different functionalities. For a moving platform, players have to jump on it within a regular timing period, which increases the difficulty and practices players' skills. For a moving guard with a limited view, a rock that blocks the view is an ideal hidden place for players to avoid detection and allows players to guide their movement path accordingly. Also, as these spaces are temporally available to players, the shift changes players' perception of space, making the gameplay more compelling. Also, there is temporally unavailable move space, which is the opposite side of temporally available move space, like space in front of a moving bullet. It has the same effect to limit players' move space and express useful information.*

Games that use this pattern and how:

- *Assassin's Creed*—Dynamic enemy movement creates a constantly shifting set of available space for undetected character movement.
- *Horizon Zero Dawn*—Enemy movement paths are visible to the player as an ability. Looking at the paths and plotting movement through them to avoid combat seems to be intended as a viable playstyle. The materials and crafting mechanics create tension with this implementation of the pattern, as avoiding conflict starves the player for materials and weakens them when they encounter unavoidable combats.
- *Super Mario Bros.*—Moving platforms create temporary paths for player traversal. Many other platformer games use this technique.
- *The Secret World*—Turret and enemy placements that cause instant death or fail states create complex spaces the player must decode to traverse.

---

* The only difference between available and unavailable space as Chang describes them is which state is the default. I think that the idea of temporally unavailable space is more interesting and evocative so I have used that as the pattern name.

- *Ori and the Will of the Wisps*—This game, and other Metroidvania-style games, use player abilities to shift the temporally available space during play. This application of the pattern allows reuse of gameplay areas in progressively more dynamic areas as the temporally unavailable space decreases.

Seed: Exercise 4: Formal Patterns—Platforms
Related patterns:
Parent patterns:
It All Depends On How You Look At It* (Confidence: 3) — Implement this pattern before considering how you will apply Temporally Unavailable Space. Understanding the experience you want your game to create for your player and how that is affected by the camera perspective will guide your implementation.

SUGGESTED EXERCISES

Use **Exercise 7: Player Experience Patterns** to generate a pattern based on the player's experience of feeling skilled. Look for the pattern that will help you understand how to use temporally unavailable space to control how skilled the player is feeling.

Child patterns:

SUGGESTED EXERCISES

Use **Exercise 16: Patterns from Core Mechanics** to generate a pattern based on *Dishonored* or *Thief*. Either of these games is likely to result in patterns about the use of temporally unavailable space in the context of stealth.

Keywords: Movement, Level Design, Enemies, Platforms, Character Progression, Player Skill

FUNCTIONAL PATTERNS: PATTERNS FROM RULES

Pattern Purpose

Similarly to the Formal Patterns exercise, this exercise encompasses many aspects of game design. This exercise focuses on observing patterns that exist in the actions that you perform in any game.

The subtitle of this exercise stems from the way that I present it to my classes. Most physical games require an explicit statement of the rules for the game. This is true of board games, tabletop role-playing games, and traditional sports. Digital games often have the computer manage the

---

* Example pattern from Exercise 22: The First Choice.

rules and, as much as possible, hide the actual rules of the digital system from the user.

For example, in a board game you might have the movement rule "on your turn you may move up to four spaces," whereas in a digital game the movement rule might be that the player's movement speed is up to ten feet a second, but the game only tells the player to "press w to move forward."

For this reason, it can be easier to apply this exercise to a rule from a physical game the first time you complete it. I often have my students pick a functional design element and then look at the rules that relate to it in physical games. Even if the students haven't played a large number of physical games, it's possible to review the rules of various games as research.

Of course, it's entirely possible to apply the exercise to digital games, and patterns found in physical or digital games may apply more broadly to either type.

Sample Functional Elements*		
Abilities	Dialogue	Learning
Boss Fights	Difficulty Curve	Open/Shut
Breaking	Digging	Push/Pull
Building	Driving	Quests
Buy/Sell	Eat	Racing
Carry	Environmental Effects	Relationship Management
Character Progression	Fast Travel	Resource Gathering
Choice	Flying	Running
Climbing	Healing	Status Effects
Collecting	Healing	Swimming
Combat	Hiding	Take/Put
Crafting	Inventory Management	Time Management
Damage	Jumping	Turns

EXERCISE 5: FUNCTIONAL PATTERNS

Step 1: Name a functional game design element.

Step 2: Name at least ten games that use that element in as many diverse ways as possible.

Step 3: Describe how each game uses the element. Try *not* to think about a pattern while you do this.

Step 4: What design problems do those games use the element to solve?

---

* Again, there are literally thousands of functional elements in games. There is nothing special about this list; use it as inspiration but choose elements that are relevant to your design work.

Example Functional Pattern
Exercise

Step 1: Name a functional game design element.

Combat

Step 2: Name at least ten games that use that element in as many diverse ways as possible.

Space Invaders, Super Mario Bros., Doom, StarCraft, Torment: Tides of Numenera, Street Fighter, Magic: The Gathering, Kingdom Death: Monster, World of Warcraft, Dungeons & Dragons, Life is Strange

Step 3: Describe how each game uses the element. Try *not* to think about a pattern while you do this.

- *Space Invaders*—The primary method of interacting with the world, the combat action of shooting, is the primary mechanic of the game. Combat is real-time and player versus environment (PvE).

- *Super Mario Bros.*—Jumping on enemies and shooting fireballs are methods to get past obstacles. Jumping becomes a combat action, and outside of combat is the core mechanic of the game. The combat action of shooting is not a core mechanic and mostly exists for variety. Combat is real-time and PvE.

- *Doom*—Shooting is the primary mechanic of interacting with the world. Combat is real-time and PvP/PvE.

- *StarCraft*—The combat action here would seem to be shooting, but I think that is cosmetic. The action you're truly performing in combat is "strategic choice": picking a unit to match against another unit. The third-person isometric perspective makes the player's action "directing strategy," and shooting is just the indirect action of the units. Combat is real-time and PvP/PvE. The

player is not playing a unit directly; they are an abstract com-
mander, so their action is directing, not whatever they direct the
units to do.*

- *Torment: Tides of Numenera*—Similarly to *StarCraft*, the player
  is in an isometric third-person view, though closer in this case.
  There is some mechanical combat-related strategy, tied to the
  historical genre of the game, but the combat choices that feel
  most integral to the game, interestingly, are narrative choices.
  The game has normal incidental combats and larger set-piece
  combat/conflict situations called Crises. In a Crisis, the players
  make narratively driven choices with more complex goals than
  "do damage to the enemy." For instance, the player might direct
  a character to turn off a strange device; this might take several
  turns to do, during which time there might be incidental combat
  actions. However, the ability of the player to focus on narrative
  intent seems significant. Combat is turn-based and PvE.

- *Street Fighter*—Punching and kicking are the main combat
  actions. The game is entirely combat-focused, with both offensive
  and defensive moves. The perspective is a third-person, side, or
  isometric view depending on the iteration of the game. I would
  describe the core combat loop as "dynamic strategy." Combat is
  real-time and PvP/PvE.

- *Magic: The Gathering*—In this card game, combat is the primary
  focus. Combat actions involve playing cards, but the focus is strategic player choice. Combat is turn-based and PvP.

- *Kingdom Death: Monster*—In this cooperative board game, combat is the primary focus of the game, but about half the gameplay,
  the other half being base-building and preparing for combat.
  The game overall focuses on emergent narrative driven by randomized narrative events. In combat, strategic player choice is
  important, but both attack and defense player actions have an
  element of randomized narrative events. When you attack, you

---

* This more removed level of interaction is common in strategy-focused video games or in board
games. In this type of game there is usually no avatar and the player is usually an abstract com-
mander. For a concrete example, consider a board game like Risk where you move pieces around
a table to represent armies vying for territory and a physical game like tag where you are trying to
touch another player to win.

draw from a hit location event that drives the narrative effect of your attack. When the monster attacks you, it draws its attack from a deck of narratively driven options.

- *World of Warcraft*—In this MMO, combat is real-time and choice-based. There is some skill in positioning your character, but strategic choice is probably the most important aspect. The group-focused combat, where players take on different combat roles and coordinate to complete encounters, reflects the multiplayer and social focus of the game. The game is in a close third-person perspective. Players commonly modify the game to add more information about the state of other players and monsters, and over time many of these modifications have been adopted by the core game. Combat is PvE/PvP.

- *Dungeons & Dragons*—In this tabletop role-playing game, combat may be more or less of a focus, depending on the players. Combat is turn-based and involves detailed player choices. A dice roll, modified by the character's skills, randomly determines the success or failure of actions. The player running the game decides which actions require dice rolls and which are determined by narrative logic. The mechanics of the game allow for very detailed, mechanically focused combat.

- *Life is Strange*—There is little direct combat in the game, and when it occurs, narrative choices, often made under time pressure, resolve the conflicts.

Step 4: What design problems do those games use the element to solve?

- *Space Invaders* —The simple real-time combat creates tension in the game and allows your direct actions as a player to influence the flow of the game. There's no strategic choice involved in the shooting. Dodging movement and aiming work together to create a flow state, which gives a high level of engagement for short play sessions.

- *Super Mario Bros.*—Combat exists primarily to complicate world traversal and to create dynamic skill-based puzzles to overcome. The combat exists to facilitate the other aspects of the game rather than being the focus. Making jumping the primary combat action helps to keep combat from becoming the focus of the game.

- *Doom*—The game is intensely combat-focused. The application of the shoot combat action has granularity and creates strategic choices. Also, a very tight loop between health and ammunition management, shooting, and movement generates visceral and exciting gameplay. In the initial game, there are very few other systems that would distract you from this loop.

- *StarCraft*—Combat in this real-time strategy game combines long-term planning with short-term tactical choices. This combination creates tension; players limit their future choices with every decision they make. Combat is a feedback loop teaching players whether their strategic decisions are correct or viable in any given situation. This two-stage combat structure of slow preparation followed by short bursts of actual combat allows room for strategic choices in the real-time game.

- *Torment: Tides of Numenera*—Strategic, narratively driven combat in the game aligns with its focus on narrative choice. The mechanics of combat let players use their items and character abilities in meaningful ways. Combat creates tension, helps to pace the game, and resolves conflicts in a way that has narrative weight.

- *Street Fighter*—Even more so than *Doom*, the core gameplay loop of fighting games hangs on the immediacy and strategic choice of the combat. That is to say, your choices as a player aren't limited by what guns you've acquired, how much ammo you have, or whether you've found health recently. Everything outside of your skill in using the character's static abilities is stripped away.

- *Magic: The Gathering*—This is a deck-building and card-based combat game. The core gameplay is turn-based combat driven by tactical choices based on long-term deck-building strategies. Strictly speaking, the deck building is not part of the gameplay as it is with a game like *Dominion*, but it's still an important part of the game structure that takes place between gameplay sessions. This fits the model of *StarCraft* and serves a similar purpose. Since combat is, in this case, turn-based, it's less a source of tension based on time pressure and reflexes, and more purely focused on tactical and strategic choices. Combat is turn-based, so players can administer the rules manually. Still, it also allows for strategic thinking, given the virtually unlimited number of cards and card combinations, in contrast to the ample but finite number of unit types in an real-time strategy (RTS) game like *StarCraft*.

- *Kingdom Death: Monster*—This game contains many systems to generate an emergent narrative. The systems are based on strategic player choices combining with random narrative events that the various card decks generate. Integrating this technique into low-level combat actions fits with the game's overall design. These choices which exist in each of the game's phases make the very different parts, from travel to town building to combat, feel cohesive.

- *World of Warcraft*—The abstracted nature of combat actions (clicking an interface button to do each different combat action) focuses both moment-to-moment combat and progression on the character rather than on player skill. The social and cooperative nature of the dungeon, raid, and PvP combat activities align with or possibly create the massively multiplayer nature of the game.

- *Dungeons & Dragons*—Almost all of the mechanics in tabletop role-playing games are focused on defining the character you're playing. Different games vary in how focused they are on combat, but Dungeons & Dragons falls on the combat-heavy end of that scale. Combat in the game exists for at least two reasons. It's a narrative device to shape the pacing of the story, show the characters' ability to affect the world, and create tension. But it also allows the players to see the effects of the choices they've made in creating and developing their characters.

- *Life is Strange*—The general narrative mechanics of the game almost wholly sublimate combat. The action of shooting someone, when possible, is mechanically indistinguishable from any other choice the player makes. The consequences of combat are likewise entirely narrative, which is to say the player has no health state, and the result of conflict is only to shift the direction of the story.

Step 5: Describe the patterns you see in the ways your example games use the element.

Each of the games I discuss uses combat well. They're all very different games, and the way each implements combat reflects its style or genre. However, many other games across genres include combat and execute it poorly. The pattern here should reflect why combat in each of the example games is "good" despite the games' radical differences.

1. In games that have a simple gameplay loop, the core gameplay action is also usually the combat action.

2. In games where strategy is the most important aspect of play, combat is strategic.

3. In games that focus on narrative, combat has narrative causes and effects, and is often resolved narratively rather than through mechanical action.

Step 6: Pick one of the patterns and document it using the Pattern Template.

I think that the aforementioned three observations generalize into the following pattern: The mechanics and effects of combat in a game reflect that game's core gameplay actions and loops.

Pattern

Name: Fight Like You Live
Confidence: 2
Image:

FIGURE 9.5 Marine shooting giant gun etc. The way you fight in a game should match the rest of the game's core mechanics.

Author: Chris Barney

Design problem: It can be easy for a developer to copy elements from other "good" games when their game is not focused on those elements, and of course, what works well in one game does not necessarily work well in another.

Description: To avoid combat mechanics that don't help or even hinder core gameplay, a developer should make sure that the functional elements of combat align with those of the core gameplay loop. In applying this pattern, it's necessary to understand very clearly what the highest-level functional elements of a game are, and then to understand what the functional element of any combat mechanic is.

This pattern may seem a bit obvious, saying that strategic games should have strategic combat, that action games should have active visceral combat, or that narrative games should have combat driven by narrative meaning. Many games use this pattern well. But a surprising number of games do not, defaulting to shooter combat or combat that mimics the standard for the genre that they fit into, without consideration of the core mechanics that differentiate their game.

Games that use this pattern and how:

- *Doom*—The core gameplay loop of *Doom* is shooting, with very little else in the way. Other elements, such as resource management, serve to tune the tension and excitement of the shooting. So shooting as the functional element of combat for this game is optimal.
- *Silent Hill*—The core gameplay of *Silent Hill* focuses on creating a sense of fear, anxiety, and horror through presenting the player with situations of overwhelming, and often unknown, threats. The intentional use of "awkward combat" as the core action of combat, both in terms of controls and animations, enhances the perceived and actual threat that the player feels.
- *Super Mario Bros.*—The core gameplay loop of *Super Mario Bros.* is skill-based platforming, so its use of jumping as the functional element of combat is optimal.
- *StarCraft*—The multilayered combat systems of this game are created by and reinforce the base-building and resource-gathering systems that make up the remainder of its gameplay. These systems combine to produce combat situations that are the result of strategic choices and that require tactics that match that strategy.
- *Torment: Tides of Numenera*—The complex mechanics of combat in this game reinforce its class-based character building, and the narratively rich Crisis system matches its story-heavy NPC interaction systems.
- *Kingdom Death: Monster*—The AI and Hit Location decks that define combat in this game align with its design goals of creating an emergent narrative in response to character choices.

- *World of Warcraft*—The multiplayer interactions and class-based combinations that this game refined and perfected match the character-driven economy, faction-driven conflicts, and social guild systems that define it as an MMO.
- *Dungeons & Dragons*—The complex, mechanically rich combat choices in this game system contribute to its focus on character development and class differentiation. A character's "class" shapes combat, which furthers role-play.

Seed: Functional Element—Combat
Related patterns:
Parent patterns:
Familiarity Breeds Contempt, or at Least High Expectations* (Confidence: 3)—
As you implement Fight Like You Live to make sure your combat mechanics echo and support the core mechanics of your game, you must use this pattern to ensure that they are the most polished mechanics in your game and live up to player expectations.

SUGGESTED EXERCISE

Use **Exercise 25: Creating Patterns from Lenses** to generate a pattern based on the idea of "unified design" from Lens #11 in *The Art of Game Design* (Schell 2020). In a unified design, all the elements of the game work together to support the theme of the game. The mechanics, sound, visual esthetics, and narrative all contribute to the same design purpose. See how high level you can make this pattern. If you stick to matching the esthetic theme discussed in this lens you may end up with a pattern similar to Bringing About the Apocalypse.† To help with this, look for games that have unified design but have little or no esthetic theme. If you succeed your pattern should fit as a parent of both Fight Like You Live and Bringing About the Apocalypse.

Child patterns:
I Could Be Bounded in a Nutshell and Count Myself a King of Infinite Space‡ (Confidence: 2)—Use this pattern to help create combat within tightly confined spaces when your game focuses on an intimate relationship between the player and the enemy. In terms of the example games, Doom uses this child pattern.

---

* Example pattern from Exercise 19: Finding Positive Patterns from Negative Patterns.
† Example pattern from Exercise 8: Theme Patterns—Post-Apocalyptic.
‡ Example pattern from Exercise 9: Circulation Patterns.

SUGGESTED EXERCISES

Use **Exercise 20: Using Patterns to Understand Techniques** to generate a pattern based on using ineffective combat to cause fear in the player. In this case you will have at least two effects in step 2 of the exercise: games that do create fear with their ineffective combat and games that do not. The pattern you derive will help you understand how this technique functions.

Use **Exercise 20: Using Patterns to Understand Techniques** to generate a pattern based on using slow combat and many player choices. As discussed in the exercise you will have at least the effect of "creating strategy" and failing to in step 2. You may think of games that use this technique to create other effects.

Use **Exercise 20: Using Patterns to Understand Techniques** to generate a pattern based on using fast, simple combat. As discussed in the exercise, one of the effects will be to create a flow state; there may be other effects.

Keywords: Combat, Core Mechanics, Unified Design

EMOTIONAL PATTERNS

Pattern Purpose

This exercise produces patterns that help to create emotional effects in games. As with the other exercises in this section, it produces patterns that span the game design disciplines. It may generate a pattern relating to game art, or mechanics, or sound. It's worth completing this exercise many times for any given emotional effect, since human emotions, and the things that produce them, are quite complex, and you won't capture them with any one pattern. Patterns tend to be additive, and games that produce any given emotion strongly are likely to employ multiple patterns.

EXERCISE 6: EMOTIONAL PATTERNS

Step 1: Describe an emotional effect.
Step 2: List ten games that create this effect.
Step 3: For each game, describe the techniques used to create that effect.
Step 4: List the patterns you observe in the use of these techniques.
Step 5: Pick one pattern and document it using the Pattern Template.
Step 6: You may repeat step 5 for each pattern you observed.

Example Emotional Pattern
Exercise

Step 1: Describe an emotional effect.

Delight

Step 2: List ten games that create this effect.

Monument Valley, Journey, Noita, Beat Saber, The Tetris Effect, Gris, Night in the Woods, Life is Strange

Step 3: For each game, describe each technique that the game uses to create that effect.

- *Monument Valley*—The visual world transforms unexpectedly, revealing beautiful visuals and unexpected gameplay possibilities. There's a strong sense of mystery about the world, and the mysteries unfold as a result of the player solving the game's puzzles. There is an undertone of darkness to the game.*

- *Journey*—Simple controls and low-risk gameplay move you quickly through a beautiful world. There's a strong sense of a mystery that exploring the world slowly reveals. Interactions with other players are unexpected and only ever helpful. There is an undertone of darkness to the game.

- *Noita*—The reactions of the simulated world are very complex, and lead to emergent consequences that can be so unpredictable that they're fun even when the results are catastrophic.

- *Beat Saber*—The direct one-to-one control scheme is responsive and satisfying. The fantasy of swinging a lightsaber, and the satisfaction of the rhythm mechanics, create a sense of power and competence. The game's kinesthetic movement creates an experience of the music that feels like what people have been reaching for when they play air guitar or drums.

- *The Tetris Effect*—The generally pleasurable experience of clearing lines in *Tetris* combines with surprising visuals and

---

* The slight tone of darkness allows a sense of relief, catharsis, or contrast when it is broken by a beautiful moment. That break is a way to tip a merely beautiful moment over into a delightful one. This idea is captured by Alexander in his description of "the nameless quality" as being slightly bitter. I will discuss this in more depth in Chapter 13.

unexpected changes in gameplay intensity, which matches the beautiful musical score of the game.

- *Gris*—The game features simple mechanics, low-risk gameplay, a mysterious story, and beautiful visuals and soundtrack. There is an undertone of darkness to the game.

- *Night in the Woods*—The game has a setting and story full of mysteries. There is an undertone of darkness to the game. The art and music of the game are beautiful. The characters are endearing and relatable.

- *Life is Strange*—Not all of this game is delightful, but in the moments when it evokes delight, there's an unexpected positive event. The art and music are beautiful, the characters are endearing, and the game contains themes of both darkness and hope. While there are occasional moments of stressful gameplay, moments of delight come at low-stress times.

Step 4: List the patterns you observe in the use of these techniques.

- Unexpected events can produce delight.

- Beautiful visuals and audio contribute to delightful experiences.

- Simple mechanics are common, as are intuitive control schemes.

- Games evoking delight are often low stress or low consequences.

- Many of the aspects of delightful games are similar to those that contribute to a flow state.

- The revelation of mysteries can be delightful.

- Delightful games possess either a narrative theme of darkness or place the player in a state of flow with gameplay tension. The result is that there's the possibility of an adverse outcome present in an unstable situation.

Step 5: Pick one pattern and document it using the Pattern Template.

The following pattern combines several of the aforementioned observations.

Step 6: You may repeat step 5 for each pattern you observed.

Pattern

Name: Oh! That Went Unexpectedly Well
Confidence: 2
Image:

FIGURE 9.6   Character looking surprised and happy as they stand over a dead monster and the sun breaks through the clouds Moments of delight can be emphasized by breaking the underlying tension.

Author: Chris Barney
Design problem: Creating a genuine sense of delight in a game is difficult.
Description: To create the sense of surprise necessary to tip the appreciation for a beautiful game or fortunate outcome over into a sense of delight, a developer may need to create a situation where the outcome is uncertain for the player. They might do this by creating a narrative landscape that includes some ominous elements; they can then contrast that implication of danger or negative outcome with positive esthetic elements such as beautiful visual and audio landscapes. These may combine with unexpected and positive mechanical results. The general moment-to-moment gameplay at the point of delight may be relaxed, or if there is tension, the delight may come from an intensified sense of flow.

Games that use this pattern and how:

- *Monument Valley*—This game has simple and intuitive controls. Learning and exploring the control scheme is part of the exploration of the game, and many of the unexpected events in the game relate to the world reacting to your actions in surprising ways. The game has darker undertones to its narrative, showing the past misdeeds of the character or her predecessors. Most of the negative situations that you experience as a player are not the direct result of your actions. The core experience of the game focuses on creating moments of delight by changing the world in unexpected and beautiful ways.

- *Journey*—This game has light gameplay and simple controls. The sound and visual design are simple but beautiful. The game has a strong sense of mystery, and the world unfolds in unexpected ways at many points in the game. These effects are created by changing the color palette, opening or constricting the gameplay space suddenly, adding a helpful player, or in various other ways; the variety of possibilities is important. However, there are darker themes in the game, showing the tragic past of the civilization you explore. The game experience takes a darker turn several times, setting you up to understand that things may not go in a positive direction. However, once the game has established this tone and the player recognizes that possibility, the unexpected events in the game are most often positive and beautiful, creating the desired sense of delight. The darker tone and more frequent negative situations make the game more poignant and less delightful than a game like *Monument Valley*.

- *The Tetris Effect*—This game creates a sense of delight through the same pattern of uncertainty combined with positive outcomes, though it also employs beautiful visual and audio design. The way that this game differs from the previous two is that the sense of tension provided by dark narrative undertones is, in this case, provided by more challenging gameplay. Difficulty in the game ramps up, pushing the players to the edge of their ability to perform. In this game, the player must achieve a flow state, and their sense of momentum and competence contrasts with the increasing feeling that they may fail. Unlike in previous *Tetris* games, the increased tension does not continue until failure, and is relieved by musical shifts, level changes, and completing zones. These points of release coincide with visual and auditory displays.

Seed: Exercise 6: Emotional Patterns—Delight
Related patterns:

Parent patterns:

The Risk of Knowing You* (Confidence: 2)—To implement Oh! That Went Unexpectedly Well you must create some sense of risk for the player. This risk may be mechanical or narrative, and you can use this pattern to guide you in creating it.

Child patterns:

SUGGESTED EXERCISE

Use **Exercise 12: Embedded and Environmental Narrative Patterns** to generate a pattern about creating a sense of threat or impending danger.

Use **Exercise 14: Player Manipulation Patterns** to generate a pattern for creating a player experience of epiphany or unexpected success.

Keywords: Delight, Joy, Emotion, Uncertainty, Slightly Bitter

PLAYER EXPERIENCE PATTERN

Pattern Purpose

One perspective on game design is that its goal is not to produce games but to shape player experience. That is, the games we design are just tools we use to affect players. That's a little unclear, but I think that it highlights an integral part of the design process. Players have an experience when they play a game; that's not in dispute. We can't control that experience directly; we can only use the mechanics, narrative, art, etc. of our game to try to elicit a response from players. Understanding how each aspect of a game may influence a player's experience is key to making games that do what we want them to. Of course, it's also important to understand that any given technique will have different effects on different types of players; that factor is the source of its own set of audience patterns discussed in Exercise 23.

Sample player experiences: tension, release, challenge, reward, effort, uncertainty/risk, balance, oscillation, contrast, variation, rhythm

---

* Example pattern from Exercise 7: Player Experience Patterns.

EXERCISE 7: PLAYER EXPERIENCE PATTERNS

Step 1: Pick a player experience.

Step 2: Name at least ten games that create this experience.

Step 3: Describe *how* each game achieves the intended effect. The more different ways they realize it, the better. Try *not* to think about a pattern while you do this.

Step 4: For each technique, describe *why* the technique has the intended effect. Try *not* to think of a pattern while you do this.

Step 5: Look at the list of techniques you've created. Describe each pattern you see.

Step 6: Pick one pattern and document it using the Pattern Template.

Step 7: You may repeat step 6 for each pattern you observed.

Example Experience Pattern

Exercise

Step 1: Pick a player experience.

Risk, taken from the previous list of player experiences. The functional element of risk is the mechanic of chance or randomness with the presence of significant stakes. I'm basing this exercise on the player's experience of taking a risk—of knowing there are consequences to their actions, but not knowing the outcome. So I'll define risk here as "the experience of uncertainty with consequences."

Step 2: Name at least ten games that create this experience.

Poker, Roulette, *Walking Dead*, *Life is Strange*, *The Binding of Isaac/Don't Starve*, Illimat, *StarCraft*, *Eve Online*, *Tetris*, *Sekiro: Shadows Die Twice*

Step 3: Describe *how* each game achieves the intended effect. The more different ways they realize it, the better. Try *not* to think about a pattern while you do this.

- *Roulette*—This is a straightforward construction of risk, in that the game is not ongoing and the outcome is discrete: you either win or lose. There's some subtlety added by being able to bid on a variety of more or less risky possibilities.

- *Poker*—Several mechanics create the experience of risk in poker: early bidding based on the partial information of the cards you have received so far; late bidding based on your hand without knowing your opponents' hands.

- *Walking Dead*—This is a choice-based narrative game. It creates risk by putting you in situations where the stakes feel very high (and often are), but not providing complete information about the consequences or outcome of any choice you make.

- *Life is Strange*—This game takes the choice-based narrative formula and complicates it by letting you rewind and remake your choices. The game periodically removes the ability to rewind time.

- *The Binding of Isaac/Don't Starve*—These are procedurally generated roguelike games; when you die, you have to start over. Generally, your skill increases between game sessions, and you can make gradual progress as your mastery increases. The procedural nature of the game means that the contents of the next screen are always unknown.

- *Illimat*—In this physical game, each player has several long- and short-term goals that compete with the other players. Players can take only one action each turn, so most plans and strategies need to be executed over multiple turns.

- *StarCraft*—Risk exists in both the short-term tactics the players choose, such as how many troops to commit to a particular attack; and the long-term strategies they pursue, such as what buildings to build in what order, and what kinds of units to produce.

- *Eve Online*—This game, in many ways, is an economic simulation. Much of the risk comes from the game creating opportunities for you to make a profit, and then allowing other players to interfere.

- *The Tetris Effect*—In the base game of *Tetris*, the desire to clear four lines at a time to score the most points creates its sense of risk. *The Tetris Effect* enhances your ability to clear rows of blocks by adding a mode where you can clear more than four lines at a time—up to 16—at proportionately increased risk. The uncertainty comes from not knowing what piece will come next. The game mitigates uncertainty with the ability to set a single piece aside to use later. Also, the speed that pieces fall is variable in this version of the game, increasing uncertainty.

- *Sekiro: Shadows Die Twice*—In this Soulslike game, you're in constant danger of dying if you make a mistake in the combat action gameplay. When your character dies, you lose earned experience that allows progress, and the percent lost increases the more often you die. Three systems reduce risk: the ability to use health items, periodic cave points, and having the ability to resurrect once between each save point.

Step 4: For each technique, describe *why* the technique has the intended effect. Try *not* to think of a pattern while you do this.

- *Roulette*—The player's experience of risk in roulette is very focused and straightforward. There's only one player choice, and the outcome is entirely unknown. This extreme focus creates the intense, concentrated experience of risk that characterizes the game.

- *Poker*—The use of risk in poker is more complicated. The escalating bidding increases the feeling of risk, while the increasing certainty of card reveals mitigates it. Risk spikes at the end of each hand, and stakes build throughout the game until a single player remains. The game stays focused on the risk, but is far more complex and is an excellent example of how varying risk can create modulation in the player experience.

- *Walking Dead*—The sense of risk is combined here with narrative beats and is used to help align you with your character's danger as you play.

- *Life is Strange*—One would think that the ability to rewind time would lower the sense of risk in the narrative choices, except that the game periodically takes the ability to rewind away. At first, you're lulled into taking more significant risks as a player because of the safety net of rewinding time. But as gameplay progresses, you become aware of the possibility that you won't be able to rewind, and this uncertainty enhances the feeling of risk.

- *Binding of Isaac/Don't Starve*—The constant, immediate danger creates a situation where the consequences of your actions are very high. The procedural nature of the game means that the contents of the next screen are always unknown. Game elements like health items and dangerous creatures create a moment-to-moment gameplay loop where you're continually taking actions that feel risky.

- *Illimat*—Because other players have time to observe and counter any strategy between each turn, each player is almost constantly vulnerable to having their plans thwarted. Thus they experience a feeling of risk during much of the playtime.

- *StarCraft*— The risk comes from the fact that your choices as a player may have poor outcomes if the other players don't behave in the ways you expect.

- *EVE Online*—The extreme feelings of risk in this game come from the ability of the players to set the stakes higher and higher as they progress in the game. The real-world value of the in-game stakes enhances the perception of risk.

Step 5: Look at the list of techniques you've created. Describe each pattern you see.

- Higher stakes increase the feeling of risk.

- More unknowns increase the feeling of risk.

- Stakes can be mechanical or narrative.

- Extrinsic stakes can be compelling (gambling and *Eve*).

- Developers can modulate risk by changing stakes or unknowns to create rhythm and pacing.

- A player's risk can simulate their character's danger.

Step 6: Pick one pattern and document it using the Pattern Template.

A player's risk can simulate their character's danger.

Pattern

Name: The Risk of Knowing You
Confidence: 2
Image:

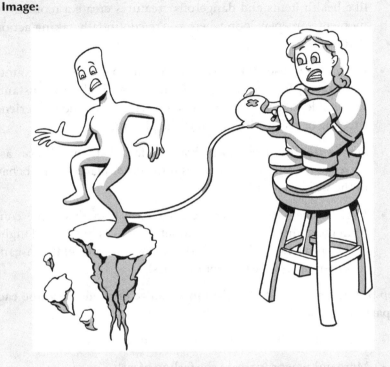

FIGURE 9.7   Player looking fearfully at a controller as the character looks over a cliff Caption: Putting a player's time or success at risk can help them feel the character's peril.

Author: Chris Barney
Design problem: It's hard to make a player feel their character's danger.
Description: To create a feeling of empathy in the player when the character is in danger, the designer may want to put the player in situations where they feel a sense of risk.

Games that use this pattern and how:

- *The Walking Dead*—The characters in this game are in an almost constant state of fear, stress, and danger. Focusing the gameplay around a sequence of meaningful, high-impact choices that the player must make with incomplete information creates an ongoing sense of risk in the player, which allows them to better empathize with the feeling of danger that their character has.

- *Life is Strange*—Similarly to *The Walking Dead*, this game uses high-risk narrative choice to create a connection to the characters' peril. Empowering the character with the ability to rewind time and fix mistakes mirrors the decrease in risk the player feels in their gameplay.
- *Binding of Isaac/Don't Starve*—This high-intensity, high-risk game uses roguelike mechanics to create an intense sense of risk that mirrors the characters desperate, bleak, and unrelenting danger.
- *Tomb Raider* (reboot)—Single-use quick-time events resolve many tense situations. These events are usually not very difficult, and often allow the player to succeed the first time. However, they condition the player to be uncertain of their ability to survive in any given situation, even as the character's power level or the player's skill in the core mechanics increases. This uncertainty helps the player to empathize with the constant fear of danger experienced by the character in this game.

Seed: Exercise 7: Player Experience Patterns—Risk
Related patterns:
Parent patterns:
I'm Doing It As Hard As I Can* (Confidence: 3)—Use this pattern to generate the challenge and tension that you need to create the emotional leverage you will use in The Risk of Knowing You.

One of These Days That's Going to Get You Killed[†] (Confidence: 2)—Use this pattern to balance increases in character abilities and maintain the danger for the character and sense of risk for the player that you need to implement The Risk of Knowing You.

SUGGESTED EXERCISES

Use **Exercise 4: Formal Patterns** to generate a pattern based on the unknown.
Use **Exercise 6: Emotional Patterns** to generate a pattern based on empathy.

Child patterns:
We're Going to a Dark Place Together[‡] (Confidence: 2)—If you have implemented The Risk of Knowing You throughout the game, you may use this pattern to leverage the emotional connection of the player to the character to create more intense and difficult situations without alienating the player.

---

* Example pattern conversion from *Game Mechanics: Advanced Game Design* described in Chapter 16.
† Example pattern from Exercise 1: Basic Patterns.
‡ Example pattern for Exercise 10: Boss Encounter Patterns.

Oh! That Went Unexpectedly Well* (Confidence: 2)—When trying to create a sense of delight for the player, use this pattern to break the tension created by The Risk of Knowing You.

SUGGESTED EXERCISES

Use **Exercise 4: Formal Patterns** to generate patterns based on stakes, that is on the things that a player can lose. Those things could be concrete and intrinsic to the game like gold or items, they could be abstract and intrinsic like progress through a level, or they could be extrinsic like the player's time, or even cash bet on the outcome of a game, or used to purchase in-game effects. Use this pattern to understand what kind of stakes you should use and when to create the tension, pacing, and rhythm you need for your game.

Keywords: Empathy, Risk, Danger

THEME PATTERNS

Pattern Purpose

As with Emotional Patterns, this exercise creates patterns across the spectrum of game design disciplines. However, I've aimed this exercise at a higher level of abstraction. Here I ask you to consider whether there are patterns *across* those disciplines.

In this exercise, I use the word "theme" in the esthetic sense (*Mass Effect* has a sci-fi theme), rather than in a literary sense (*Call of the Wild* contains the theme of man against nature). This exercise is one of the more complex and challenging in the book. Step 5 asks for an in-depth analysis of the effects of the techniques you describe in steps 3 and 4. It's possible to skip step 5 and still produce a functional pattern, but including this step produces far more useful and insightful patterns, so I strongly encourage you to complete it.

If you're looking for low-level, more specific thematic patterns, you can complete the Emotional Patterns exercise using a theme instead of an emotional effect as your starting point. Conversely, if you're looking for higher-order emotional patterns to connect those generated by the earlier exercise, you may complete this exercise using an emotional effect as your starting point rather than a theme.

---

* Example pattern for Exercise 6: Emotional Patterns.

EXERCISE 8: THEME PATTERNS

Step 1: Pick a theme.

Step 2: Select ten games that feature that theme.

Step 3: Describe the techniques that each game uses to support or create the theme. Consider techniques from all aspects of game design, including art design, sound design, narrative design, and mechanics design.

Step 4: Describe how the techniques you listed apply within each discipline across all of the games you cited.

Step 5: Describe how the patterns you describe in step 4 relate to the deeper meaning or literary themes of the games.

Step 6: Select one pattern and document it using the Pattern Template.

Step 7: You may repeat step 5 for each pattern you observed.

Example Pattern

In this exercise, I look at the techniques used to create a cosmetic theme. The process helps to identify many literary themes that result from the mechanical, artistic, and narrative techniques used. Describing these techniques also allows me to explore the structure of the theme, so that the pattern I describe will help me to apply the theme in a way that gives it a deeper meaning.

Exercise

Step 1: Pick a theme.

Post-apocalyptic

Step 2: Select ten games that feature that theme.

- Fall of the Last City*—Board game about the fall of civilization.

- Apocalypse World—Tabletop RPG set after the apocalypse.

- *The Last of Us*—Third-person action game set in a fungus-zombie apocalypse.

- *Fallout 3*—First-person shooter set after a 1950s nuclear apocalypse.

---

* This is an unusual experimental board game I designed. More details can be found in "Games Reference" at the end of the book.

- *Metro 2033*—Russian first-person shooter set after a nuclear apocalypse.

- *The Walking Dead*—Narrative adventure game set after a zombie apocalypse.

- *The Long Dark*—Narrative survival game set after a natural disaster ends civilization.

- *Anthem*—"New style MMO"* shooter set in an apocalyptic sci-fi world.

- *Horizon Zero Dawn*—Third-person action game set in the primitive aftermath of a long-ago apocalypse.

- *They Are Billions*—Strategy survival game set after a zombie apocalypse.

- *Torment: Tides of Numenera*—Isometric RPG set in the fantasy far-future aftermath of many apocalypses.

- *The Flame and the Flood*—Isometric third-person survival game set along a great river in the tradition of *The Adventures of Huckleberry Finn* (Twain 2008).

Step 3: Describe the techniques that each game uses to support or create the theme. Consider techniques from all aspects of game design, including the art, sound, narrative, and mechanics design.

- *Fall of the Last City*—This game is diegetic to its setting; it has a *narrative design* that posits that the game is played in the world in which it is set. The *visual design* of the game reflects the setting, with the game board and pieces made from scrap metal and old canvas. A *limited resources mechanic* reflects the harsh conditions of the setting. A *dwindling resources mechanic* evokes the desperation of the theme. *Social conflict mechanics* help to create a sense of hostility between the players. *Zero-sum competitive mechanics* force the players to make hard strategic and moral choices. *Lethal combat mechanics* create a sense of vulnerability and helplessness in the face of the world. The narrative of the game is a retelling of the fall of civilization, so winning does not

---

* "New style MMO" is a term I have started hearing developers use to describe MMOs with small group co-op play in a persistent world such as *Destiny*, *The Division*, and *Anthem*.

represent saving the world, but instead recognizing your ancestors' part in the apocalypse.

- *Apocalypse World*—The *explicit narrative* of the game sets the theme, including the concepts of loss of mystery, selfishness, and the difficulty of being good in the face of deprivation. The theme is reflected through the *literal and metaphorical visuals* of the game as well. Strict black-and-white art reflect the starkness of the theme. *Transactional social mechanics* focus players on how the theme changes the way the players relate to their humanity and human connections. The *character advancement mechanics* reflect the ease of getting ahead personally and the difficulty of improving the world. The *storytelling rules*, or principles, instruct the narrator to focus on creating a narrative in line with the theme.

- *The Last of Us*—The *explicit narrative* setting reflects the theme. The secondary perspective character highlights the behaviors of the player character and how the theme shapes their behavior. The game's genre-specific functional element, i.e., shooting everyone, is turned from ludonarrative dissonance into a reflection of the theme. Limited resources reflect the scarcity of the setting. The predictable danger of monsters contrasts with the higher threat of human enemies, emphasizing the literary theme that we are the monsters. The brutality of the combat mechanics shows the brutality of characters within the setting. The character's limited and largely realistic combat abilities create feelings of vulnerability. While the game contains hope, saving the world is not a possible outcome within the game.

- *Fallout 3*—The *retro-future visuals and audio* match the *explicit narrative setting* while also giving the game a sense of dark humor. The *character progression* that results in the character becoming powerful matches the focus on the literary theme of might makes right. *Unpleasant narrative choices* for the player present difficult moral questions where the best choice for survival is not the best moral choice. *Environmental storytelling*, showing the world that was lost, is pervasive. Winning the game does not save the world or make it a pleasant place to live.

- *Metro 2033*—*Explicit narrative* and bleak setting are supported by *realistic, bleak visuals*. *Limited resources* create a sense of vulnerability despite standard shooter gameplay. *Winning the game does not end the apocalypse.*

- *The Walking Dead*—The *explicit narrative* is a zombie apocalypse. A *vulnerable secondary perspective character* highlights the horrors of the world. The player faces constant unpleasant moral choices, and w*inning the game does not end the apocalypse. Visual and sound design* reflect the origin of the game as a comic book, but they are consistent with the setting.

- *The Long Dark*—As this is a survival game, resources are limited, and the world is the enemy. Of course, many survival games also have an apocalyptic setting. In this case, humans were not responsible for the apocalypse, which is relatively uncommon. Most of the danger in the game is natural, and the *environment is the biggest enemy.* There is no hope of fixing the central problem of the game. The *stark stylized visuals* reflect the harshness of the world. As befits the genre, crafting is important, but the things crafted match the theme.

- *Anthem*—Though humans aren't responsible for the larger state of the world in this game, they are responsible for the immediate difficulties of the characters in the game. There is no real hope of fixing the world. *Abstracted base building* and *character progression* align with a theme of might makes right.

- *Horizon Zero Dawn*—The setting of the game during the recovery from an apocalypse is an interesting interpretation of the theme. The world is recovering, and the characters are rebuilding. Many of the component themes of the responsibility of humanity for the disaster and the barbarism that deprivation creates are still present. *Environmental storytelling* is pervasive. The robotic *enemies reflect the nature of the apocalypse* in the same way that zombies do in *The Last of Us* or wild animals in *The Long Dark.*

- *They Are Billions*—The setting is explicitly post-apocalyptic. The primary mechanic of base-building reflects the difficulty or futility of trying to survive in the world.

- *Torment: Tides of Numenera*—The setting of the game is not immediately recognizable as post-apocalyptic and appears to be fantasy. The theme is revealed through *difficult moral choices*, the *pervasive environmental storytelling* suggesting the past civilization, and focus on the responsibility of the character for the state of the world.

- *The Flame and the Flood*—The *stylized visuals* reflect the bleak and emotionally harsh nature of the world. *Pervasive environmental storytelling* shows what has been lost. Limited resources reflect the deprivation of the setting. *Constant negative status effects* create a sense of vulnerability. The *awkward rafting mechanic* takes some autonomy away from the character and creates a sense of helplessness. The *danger of combat* reflects the harshness of the world and the vulnerability of the character. The *melancholy sound design* supports a sense of loss in the theme.

Step 4: Describe how the techniques you listed apply within each discipline across all of the games you cited.

- Narrative design:

  - Most games with a post-apocalyptic theme explicitly state that theme in their primary narrative.

  - Environmental storytelling is more prominent than in many other themes, probably due to the need to show the world as it was before the apocalypse.

  - The plot of many games with this theme is often either the survival of a small group or trying to understand how the apocalypse happened. There is usually no hope of fixing the world, nor of reversing, ending, or stopping the disaster.

  - Difficult moral character choices are common, and games with this theme often set the best mechanical choice for the player in opposition to the best moral choice for the character.

- Visual design:

  - The visual design of games with this theme varies from stylized to realistic. The choice seems to directly correlate with whether the game is trying to represent the world realistically or create an emotional experience that captures the feeling of the theme.

- Sound design:
  - Sound design within this theme also varies greatly, from melancholy folk to kitschy 1950s pop to grinding metal. The pattern here is that the music and sound design work together to shape the way the player experiences the apocalypse.

- Mechanical design:
  - Mechanics that model the type of apocalypse the game is representing are common. These games use mechanics that match the theme, such as limited or dwindling resources, lethal combat, and the need to protect a place or person that is more vulnerable than the player character. The mechanical design strongly reflects the theme, creating a play experience that mirrors the difficulties facing the character.

- Social mechanics:
  - While sometimes cooperative, games with this theme usually set players against each other in some way, creating a social experience that mirrors the experience of the characters.

Step 5: Describe how the patterns you list in step 4 relate to the deeper meaning or literary themes of the games.

The specific techniques used in each category in step 4 directly relate to the literary themes each game focuses on within the esthetic theme of the game. Games that have the literary theme man vs. nature, for example, feature a narrative where the apocalypse was either natural or the results of it are confronted through nature. These games also often feature survival mechanics that model the struggle against morally neutral but unstoppable forces, like cold or drought. On the other hand, a game with the theme of we are the real monsters would use techniques such as a narrative design focused on the responsibility of the character—or humans in general—for the disaster, and enemies that are more dangerous the more human they are. The post-apocalyptic esthetic theme is suited to a particular set of literary themes and is usually composed of a number of them.

Step 6: Select one pattern and document it using the Pattern Template.

The preceding analysis suggests a pattern relating the esthetic theme to the literary theme and specific mechanical choices, and thus how those combine to create the player experience of the theme.

Step 7: You may repeat step 6 for each pattern you observed.

Pattern

Name: Bringing About the Apocalypse
Confidence: 1
Image:

FIGURE 9.8 Greek warrior with gun All of the elements of a game must fit its theme.

Author: Chris Barney
Design problem: Designers often need to apply esthetic themes to the game they're creating.
Description: It's often suggested that a game can be "re-skinned" with a different theme, easily changing it from a sci-fi to fantasy to post-apocalyptic by shifting the visual presentation of the game. But for designers to apply an esthetic theme most successfully, all aspects of the game must reflect that theme. The esthetic theme will also reflect the deeper meanings of the game—the literary theme. Examples might be man vs. nature or man vs. man.

To fully realize the potential of a game's esthetic theme, a designer must integrate the thematic choices into all aspects of design, including visual, audio, mechanical, social, and narrative. To do this, the designer must have a deep understanding of the deeper meanings that a given theme will generate within the game. The specific techniques and patterns that the developer uses to integrate their theme should match the meanings the developer wants to create in their game. Only by doing this can the developer be aware of and control the impact of the theme on their game.

Games that use this pattern and how:

- *The Last of Us*—This game uses an explicit narrative to establish its post-apocalyptic theme. It reflects the theme in its visual design and its environmental sound design. It uses a companion mechanic to emphasize the brutality of its setting and to focus on the individual moral cost of the apocalypse. It uses its primary gameplay loop of shooting, which often creates ludonarrative dissonance to create a feeling of extreme violence and its cost. It uses human antagonists that are more dangerous than the monstrous ones to turn the horror of the setting back on humanity. Limited resources force the player to think in the survival-oriented terms experienced by the characters. All of these things combine to reinforce literary themes like we are the monsters and man vs. himself that are common within the post-apocalyptic esthetic theme.
- *Guild Wars 2*—The game explicitly establishes its fantasy theme using a wide variety of narrative tropes, such as many exotic non-human races, a great ancient evil, and heroes to struggle against it. It supports this narrative design with beautiful and fantastical visuals. Complex progression systems for the characters support the idea of a journey to heroic status. Challenges requiring increasingly large cooperative groups support the concept of good banding together to defeat evil. Regenerating health and a low cost for dying take the focus of play away from the player's failures. The place where this game struggles the most is on creating player investment in the scripted narrative of the world. The scripted narratives feel impersonal or focused on characters other than the player's, and don't generate as much investment as they could. The interplayer narratives created by the large-scale cooperative mechanics compensate somewhat for this shortcoming.
- *Red Dead Redemption 2*—The Wild West theme of this game either supports or explains design techniques in all aspects of the game's design. Prominent visual and audio elements evoke the theme. The explicit plot of the game, following an outlaw gang trying to maintain its freedom as the era draws to a close, is deeply thematic. More subtle design choices reflect the role of the outlaw within the setting. For example, a narrative that forces the character to move from location to location takes control away from the player and helps them identify with the role of the outlaw. That lack of control is countered by the general open-world design, which matches the deeper struggle for freedom and autonomy inherent in the setting. Specific mechanics, like the gathering and crafting systems, match the theme far better than they would in a similar game like *Grand Theft Auto*.

Seed: Exercise 8: Theme Patterns—Post-Apocalyptic

Related patterns:
Parent patterns:

SUGGESTED EXERCISE

Use **Exercise 24: Theoretical Patterns** to generate a pattern based on Brenda Romero's talk "The Mechanic is the Message" (Symonds 2013).

Child patterns:

SUGGESTED EXERCISE

Use **Exercise 8: Theme Patterns** to generate child patterns. Focus on techniques that apply to your specific theme and not to others to help generate lower-level patterns that will be children of this pattern.

Keywords: Esthetics, Meaning, Mechanics, Theme

CHAPTER 10

Focused Patterns

THIS CHAPTER CONTAINS PATTERN exercises that are very focused or specific. These exercises will give you examples of how to hone this process to produce patterns that are generally low level and address the specific concerns of a particular domain of game design. These exercises may or may not be directly useful to any given designer, but I do suggest completing them at least once to see how they differ from those in the previous chapter. These exercises will also help you if you want to learn to construct new pattern-generation exercises that focus on your area of expertise.

PATTERNS FROM MICRO, MACRO, AND META CIRCULATION PATTERNS*

A note that this section may get a little confusing, as I'll be discussing a concept with the word "patterns" built into it, with a meaning that's separate from the patterns that are the topic of this entire book. As we go, I'll do my best to be as clear as possible as to when I'm discussing circulation patterns and when I'm discussing patterns such as those we're deriving throughout this text. I'll occasionally refer to the latter as "Alexandrian patterns" to avoid confusion.

Circulation patterns define how a player moves a character through a gamespace and are usually discussed in terms of level design. However, their scope extends beyond the way a character moves through a level (macro circulation patterns) to include how the player moves through the

---

* I use this awkward construction to point out that the circulation patterns used as the starting point for this exercise are not Alexandrian patterns, just repeated techniques. I could have just said "circulation" but the phrase circulation pattern is in common use.

overall game (meta circulation patterns) as well as movement in individual encounters within a level (micro circulation patterns).

A comprehensive discussion of this concept and its usefulness is beyond the scope of this book. However, I can provide a brief description of the three levels of circulation patterns that I've found useful for Alexandrian pattern generation in my classes.

Alexandrian patterns derived from meta-level circulation patterns tend to be high level and address problems that other high-level elements in the game are trying to solve, such as the game's theme, narrative structure, or genre. Some meta-level circulation patterns that have provided good seeds for pattern generation include linear level progression, open world with expanding access, hub-based level access, and temporally progressing open world.

Macro-level circulation patterns are level specific and may repeat in each level of a game, or may shift or complicate as the level changes what problems it's trying to solve. Examples of macro-level circulation patterns include linear progression, hub-based level, ability-gated area access,* or multi-pathed linear levels.† All of these are useful starting points for Alexandrian pattern generation.

Circulation patterns at the micro-level are encounter- or room-scale, and focus on the use of specific game mechanics such as player abilities, monster abilities, room-level architectural design, or a combination of all of these. One good example is the player movement sequences required to defeat specific enemies in *Dark Souls* and how those interact with the locations where the encounters take place. Another is the movement-based puzzles found in the challenge temples in *Zelda: Breath of the Wild* or the *Tomb Raider* reboot trilogy. Looking at the ways these micro circulation patterns solve problems in game design can yield some rich Alexandrian patterns as well.

Pattern Purpose

Like all of the pattern exercises thus far, working through this exercise uncovers game design problems—in this case, problems that developers solve using circulation patterns. But circulation patterns are a particularly useful element to study when constructing a Pattern Language for

---

* This is commonly referred to as "Metroidvania" style level design, especially when this pattern is also used on the meta and micro levels.
† This is often seen in levels trying to provide for several distinct types of gameplay, providing a combat-heavy path and a stealth-heavy path for instance.

your game, because they have three built-in levels of scale to look at: meta, macro, and micro. When designing a game and identifying the highest level problems you're trying to solve, you'll have more success if the patterns you use at all three levels are in alignment. This is of course true across all of game design, but it's more easily visible when looking at this kind of pattern, which maps clearly across these levels of scale.

This exercise, therefore, pays special attention to the problems that circulation patterns solve. It asks you to observe subtle differences in the way circulation patterns are implemented, and the problems that those different implementations solve. The result is that newer designers tend to produce patterns that describe more fundamental uses of circulation patterns, while experienced designers tend to note more abstract or higher-level patterns. Both outcomes are valuable, and this is a good exercise to come back to periodically as it will yield useful patterns many times over your career.

EXERCISE 9: CIRCULATION PATTERNS

Step 1: Pick a meta, macro, or micro circulation pattern. You can choose one you're familiar with or one you observe by looking at a specific game.

Step 2: Name ten other games that use this circulation pattern and describe how they implement it.

Step 3: For each game, list and describe the problems that the circulation pattern solves. Many problems may repeat, so while you should list all of the problems you can identify for each game, you only need to describe them each once unless there are differences.*

Step 4: List and briefly describe how the circulation pattern solves each problem. This list will only describe how each game's implementation of the circulation pattern solves one problem in that game; however, your descriptions should capture the subtle differences you noted in step 3.

Step 5: List and describe any patterns that you see in the way that your circulation pattern solves problems across games.

Step 6: Select one pattern and document it using the Pattern Template.

Step 7: You may repeat step 6 for each pattern you observed.

---

* You do not need to copy–paste problem descriptions for each occurrence of the problem. You *do* need to describe the subtle differences in the problems though. If you only describe a problem once and it's repeated across all of your example games, you're probably missing subtle differences in both the application of the circulation pattern and the details of the problem they solve.

Example Pattern from Micro, Macro, and Meta Circulation Patterns
Exercise

Step 1: Pick a meta, macro, or micro circulation pattern.
Micro-level circulation pattern: circle strafing. This movement pattern involves a character running in a circle around an enemy while facing that enemy and engaging in combat.

Step 2: Name ten other games that use this circulation pattern and describe how they implement it.

- *Quake*—Strafing was a tactic introduced in earlier first-person games by Id Software, but it became more widely used in games based on the *Quake* engine due to a physics bug. Specifically, the maximum run speed of the character was calculated independently on the x- and y-axis, resulting in the ability to move more quickly if you were going both forward and sideways at the same time. Turning while exploiting this bug resulted in circling the enemies at a speed that exceeded the enemies' ability to aim. While the inclusion of this bug was unintentional, the developers later chose to leave the error in the game through its various expansions and to include it in other games that used the engine.

- *The Secret World*—Combat in this game, like in most massively multiplayer online games (MMOs) of its era, involves hitting the tab key to lock onto an enemy target and clicking special ability buttons to perform attacks on that target. Enemies use some special attacks that target areas of the ground around them, called area of effect (AoE) attacks. You can move while performing combat actions, so circling enemies while attacking to avoid their AoE attacks is a common tactic.

- *Legend of Zelda: Ocarina of Time*—To engage in understatement for a moment, the controls for *Ocarina of Time* were awkward and unintuitive by modern standards. Controllers hadn't evolved to handle 3D camera movement well. The ability to lock on to an enemy was an affordance to mitigate the difficulty of the controls.

- *Soulcalibur**—As one of the first fighting games to allow free movement around a fighting arena, *Soulcalibur* makes use of the circle strafing circulation pattern. Interestingly, since it's common for both characters to circle each other and both players to be viewing the same screen, the circular movement doesn't have the same effect as in other games. To some degree, the circles cancel out each other, and combat continues very similarly to how it would if the characters were restricted to a 2D plane of movement. Put another way, the important thing is your distance from the other character, not your combined orientation to the arena.

- *GoldenEye 007*—This game was one of the first attempts at a "serious" or realistic first-person shooter on a game console. The technique was implemented in a similar way to *Quake*, but the use of a GameCube controller made it somewhat more difficult. Both the game's single and multiplayer benefited from the circle strafing circulation pattern.

- *Team Fortress 2*—The implementation in the game was functionally identical to that of *Quake*.

- *Galak-Z* (←*Asteroids* ←*Spacewar!*)—These games are perhaps the most abstract application of this circulation pattern. Moving constantly around a target while facing it is perhaps the primary movement pattern.

- *Monster Hunter World*—This game involves groups of players hunting enormous monsters. You can lock onto a monster in some circumstances, but the implementation has sometimes been buggy, making circle strafing while locked on problematic. It's possible to manually face an enemy whole circling it, as in *Quake*.

- *Battlefield* (helicopter piloting)—Circle strafing is common in this game in the general case of a single soldier, but it has a more interesting case as applied to the vehicles in the game. Specifically,

---

* The skill and strategy involved in the high-level play of fighting games is very high and very specific. Discussing this kind of game is difficult because only a small percentage of players of these games play at the highest levels of skill. In thinking about the use of the circle strafing circulation pattern in this game, I'm focusing on the way it impacts my own play experience and that of other players I've observed.

helicopters can circle a target and do devastating amounts of damage. However, the controls to achieve the maneuver are very difficult.

- *Star Citizen*—This game is still in development, but it's interesting to see the iterative development of its space flight simulator combat. A variety of different circulation patterns are used in the combat of this game. Discussion of their intricacies is out of the scope of this pattern, but the ability to circle an enemy while firing on it is one of the three main patterns.

Step 3: For each game list and describe the problems that the circulation pattern solves.

- *Quake*—Combat for a first-person perspective needs to maintain high speed and frenetic movement while also allowing enclosed level designs and a resource (ammunition pick up) based mechanic.

- *The Secret World*—Movement should feel important to combat, even though it doesn't always increase the level of skill needed to succeed, given a tab-targeted and timed skill activation combat system.

- *Legend of Zelda: Ocarina of Time*—The game needs to provide an exciting and challenging player experience, even given limited controls.

- *Soulcalibur*—When implementing a 3D space in a traditionally 2D genre, you should ensure that it deepens gameplay without alienating players accustomed to the preexisting gameplay.

- *GoldenEye 007*—Provide a way to engage in more advanced movement-based combat in a first-person perspective, given the limitations of early game console controllers.

- *Team Fortress 2*—Circle strafing helps balance different player classes in action combat. (This asymmetrical usefulness of this circulation pattern is one of many techniques that may be applied.)

- *Galak-Z* (←*Spacewar!* ←*Asteroids*)—Creates a constant sense of forward motion when there's limited space, while also allowing for deeper combat options.

- *Monster Hunter World*—Creates movement-based combat for groups of players facing a singular opponent in an open space.

- *Battlefield* (helicopter)—Provides engaging and useful gameplay for vehicles in a game while not unbalancing the gameplay.

- *Star Citizen*—Circle strafing helps resolve the problem that, given the very high speeds of the player's ships in this game, combat can feel removed from the action and enemy ships are barely visible to the attacking player.

Step 4: List and briefly describe how the circulation pattern solves each problem.

- *Quake*—Although the initial bug in the physics implementation of the game was unintentional, it made the circle strafing circulation pattern even more beneficial than it otherwise would have been. This micro-circulation pattern supported the frenetic movement-based combat that these games used as their core gameplay loop.

- *The Secret World*—This MMO focused on creating the feeling of dynamic movement-based combat while still relying on timed attack abilities and hit probabilities/damage rates that were based on character statistics more than player skill. To overcome this, the developers introduced mathematical bases for combat mechanics to encourage player movement. Enemies would attack areas in front of them, and players were informed of this mechanic by visible ground effects. Circling enemies to avoid these attacks became a primary micro-circulation pattern.

- *Legend of Zelda: Ocarina of Time*—When a player was locked on to an enemy, circle strafing became an easy and natural movement pattern. The developers of the game incorporated this movement style into the encounter designs for many of the game's memorable bosses.

- *Soulcalibur*—Free movement adds depth and strategy to the game, but circle strafing actually works to remove some of that effect. What it does add is a great deal of visual variety and interest. It's more fun to watch the characters dancing around each other than just moving back and forth.

- *GoldenEye 007*—Given developers' limited experience creating manageable first-person controls at the time, and the inexperience of players in dealing with that perspective on console controllers, it's interesting to note that circle strafing may be easier on a controller than with a mouse. It gave players a stronger sense of mastery in this game.

- *Team Fortress 2*—In this class-/role-based first-person shooter (FPS), the technique of circle strafing was asymmetrically useful to different character classes. Characters with low health and high mobility were able to use this technique to deal with slower, more durable opponents.

- *Galak-Z* (*Spacewar!*, *Asteroids*)—Circular movement patterns allow the player to be in constant motion without moving off the edge of the screen or requiring levels to be unmanageably large.

- *Monster Hunter World*—Making players face enemies that are always vastly more powerful than they are raises the stakes of avoiding damage. While monsters move freely about the world and chase scenarios are common, circle strafing is also a required circulation pattern for many to most fights.

- *Battlefield* (helicopter)—Flying a helicopter in this game is challenging on its own, but the circle strafing mechanic is vastly more so. The difficulty increases the value of players who have mastered the skill, as well as ensuring that the technique doesn't dominate the gameplay on a regular basis. Helicopters are therefore useful and feared, but don't render the other aspects of the game useless.

- *Star Citizen*—Implementing circle strafing seems to have been effective at bringing space combat into a closer scale and also adding to the variety of viable strategies without becoming dominant.

Step 5: List and describe any patterns that you see in the way that your circulation pattern solves problems across games.

- Accommodation of gameplay space, which is to say level size. This circulation pattern works either to take advantage of limited space available or to keep players closer together through the circular movement.

- Accommodation of controls, to give a sense of movement and provide tactics and strategy given a limited set of controls, or the presence of other mechanics that limit autonomy in other ways.

Step 6: Select one pattern and document it using the pattern template.
Accommodation of gameplay space.

Step 7: You may repeat step 5 for each pattern you observed.

Pattern

Name: I Could Be Bounded in a Nutshell and Count Myself a King of Infinite Space
Confidence: 2
Image:

FIGURE 10.1   Encouraging circular circulation patterns can bring combat into close range while maintaining dynamic movement.

Author: Chris Barney
Design problem: How to bring players into the proper distance from each other to encourage an optimal combat experience.
Description: To bring players close to each other, but not too close, a designer may wish to implement mechanics that support player interactions at the desired distance. The more mechanics that support interaction at a particular distance, the more likely the players will be to engage in play at that distance, and the more natural and rewarding play at that distance will feel.

The circle strafing micro-circulation pattern is a good example of a functional technique that supports player interactions at a close to mid-range. It works particularly well when combat in the game needs to take place in a small space. That space may be small due to level size constraints, in which case the combat design can fit that limitation. Alternately, the available space may be unbounded, and the combat may be designed to bring players into proximity to each other.

The implementation of this circulation pattern has the effect of making the most important spatial factor the distance to the opponent, rather than the scale of the environment.

Clearly, the answers to the aforementioned design problem are as varied as the different kinds of combat found in games. This pattern focuses on the circle strafing circulation pattern and how it can help create a constrained player distance in games where its implementation fits the intended combat style. There are many other circulation patterns, and many other formal and functional techniques that address the design problem in differentially constrained design spaces. However, they should all share the larger pattern described in the first paragraph of this description.

Games that use this pattern and how:

- *Quake*—Strafing was a tactic introduced in earlier first-person games by Id Software, but it became more widely used in games based on the Quake engine due to a physics bug. Specifically, the maximum run speed of the character was calculated independently on the x- and y-axis, resulting in the ability to move more quickly if you were going both forward and sideways at the same time. Turning while exploiting this bug resulted in circling the enemies at a speed that exceeded their ability to aim. Although the inclusion of this bug was unintentional, the developers later chose to leave the error in the game through its various expansions and to include it in other games that used the engine. This micro-circulation pattern supported the frenetic movement-based combat that these games used as their core gameplay loop, and helped to allow this kind of combat within the relatively constrained level spaces that the game engine could support.
- *Galak-Z (Spacewar!, Asteroids)*—These games are perhaps the most abstract application of this circulation pattern. Moving constantly around a target while facing it is perhaps their primary movement pattern. Circular movement patterns allow the player to be in constant motion without moving off the edge of the screen or requiring levels to be unmanageably large.
- *Soulcalibur*—As one of the first fighting games to allow free movement around a fighting arena, *Soulcalibur* makes use of the circle strafing circulation pattern. Interestingly, since it's common for both characters to circle each other and both players to be viewing the same screen, the circular movement doesn't have the same effect as in other games. To some degree, the circles cancel out each other, and combat continues very similarly to how it would if the characters were restricted to a 2D plane of movement. Put another way, the important thing is your distance from the other character, not your combined orientation to the arena. However, the circular movement again allows the characters to be in constant forward motion while remaining in a confined space and maintaining a constant distance from each other.

- *Star Citizen*—This game was still in development at the time of this writing, but it's interesting to see the iterative development of its space flight simulator combat. A variety of different circulation patterns are used in the combat of this game. Discussion of their intricacies is out of the scope of this pattern, but the ability to circle an enemy while firing on it is one of the three main circulation patterns. In the broader scope of this game, the play takes place over extremely large spaces. But in combat situations, limiting the size of the area where a combat encounter happens can make combat feel more immediate and allow the greater visual interest of being able to see your opponent clearly. Because the game takes place in the vastness of space, it's not easily possible to limit the encounter space size through level design. By implementing ship controls that allow circling and firing on a target and weapons that are effective at close range, players are encouraged to engage in combat while remaining close to each other.
- *Zelda: Ocarina of Time*—Effective combat in this game requires that the player use the "Camera Lock-On" feature. This locks the camera onto the enemy and shifts the player's movement to be relative to the enemy, making circle strafing easy and solving some camera control issues on this early 3D console game.

Seed: Exercise 9: Circulation Pattern—Circle Strafing
Related patterns:
Parent patterns:
Fight Like You Live* (Confidence: 3)—For I Could Be Bounded in a Nutshell and Count Myself a King of Infinite Space to function, the combat action of your game must allow this circulation pattern. So, not only is Fight Like You Live a parent, but its implementation must be compatible with this pattern.

SUGGESTED EXERCISE

Use **Exercise 5: Functional Patterns** to generate a high-level pattern based on combat. There should be a number of high-level patterns that you can find by looking broadly at games with very different combat.

Child patterns:

SUGGESTED EXERCISE

Use **Exercise 10: Boss Encounter Patterns** to generate a pattern based on any boss encounter that takes place in a confined space and requires circular movement around the boss.

---

* Example pattern from Exercise 5: Functional Patterns.

Subtractive patterns:

SUGGESTED EXERCISES

Use **Exercise 4: Formal Patterns** to generate a pattern based on environmental hazards. It would seem that environmental hazards would work against this pattern since moving in one direction and attacking in another makes situational awareness more difficult.

Use **Exercise 5: Functional Patterns** to generate a pattern based on long-range combat. By long range I mean sniping or artillery, which would work against the circular movement patterns encouraged by this pattern.

Keywords: Movement, Circulation Patterns, Combat

BOSS ENCOUNTER PATTERNS

Pattern Purpose

This exercise focuses on patterns that relate to boss encounters, and is probably the most specific exercise in this book. This kind of encounter isn't present in every game or even every genre. But there are a lot of design techniques that have developed around this specific type of encounter. This exercise will help you extract patterns from those techniques.

You can use the example of this exercise to generate patterns around most any complex game design aspect. It's similar to the Formal and Functional Game Design Elements exercises (Exercises 4 and 5), except at a higher level of complexity. Boss encounters are made up of many formal and functional elements. Thus, the patterns this exercise produces are also more complex, and observing and articulating them is significantly more difficult and advanced than the earlier exercise.

EXERCISE 10: BOSS ENCOUNTER PATTERNS

Step 1: Pick a boss encounter from a game you know well.

Step 2: Describe the player experience that encounter creates.

Step 3: List up to ten other games that create the same effect using a boss encounter.

Step 4: For each game, describe the techniques those games use to create that effect.

Step 5: List and describe the patterns you observe across all ten games.

Step 6: Select one pattern and document it using the pattern template.

Step 7: You may repeat step 6 for each pattern you observed in step 5.

Example Boss Encounter Pattern
Exercise

Step 1: Pick a boss encounter from a game you know well.
Doctor Klein and The Colossus, Melothat from *The Secret World*

Step 2: Describe the player experience that encounter creates.
This is a difficult encounter in the horror MMO *The Secret World*, which happens at the end of a five-player dungeon called The Ankh. Before it, you have a chance to fight each of the creatures you'll face in the final battle. The player experience is a mix of dread and frustration, evoking empathy for the character's putative emotions of fear and hatred. The game accomplishes this by using several techniques that I'll list here for comparison with the games in step 3:

- The fight is complex and has several phases. You're unlikely to be successful in completing the encounter the first time and are likely to have died a number of times in the preceding encounters.

- The game uses narrative during the lead-up to the boss encounter to support the intended player experience, providing documentation of the atrocities perpetrated by Doctor Klein.

- The monsters have patterns that you need to learn and respond to precisely.

- Mechanically, the fights include instant death mechanics that can be avoided, but are likely to kill the group of players at least a few times as they memorize the monster patterns.

- Enemies have either escaped the characters before (Klein) or have returned when the characters thought they were defeated (The Colossus, Melothat)

- Some of the battles use a timer, meaning that you have to be able to deal with a certain amount of damage in that time to be able to win. For this reason, you might not be able to win no matter how well you play and may need to come back when you're more powerful.

Step 3: List up to ten other games that create the same effect using a boss encounter.

- Pyramid Head from *Silent Hill 2*

- GLaDOS from *Portal*

- The Lich King from *World of Warcraft: Wrath of the Lich King*

- The Final Choice from *Life is Strange*

- *Dear Esther* (Radio Tower)

Step 4: For each game, describe the techniques those games use to create that effect.

- Pyramid Head from *Silent Hill 2*—As the primary boss enemy for the game, Pyramid Head appears several times. Most times you encounter him, he is invulnerable and you must either avoid or bypass him in some way. Figuring out how to survive these encounters results in many character deaths for the player. Background narrative supports the perceived threat of this boss.

- GLaDOS from *Portal*—This boss is built up in narrative throughout the game. When the actual confrontation comes, it requires mastery of the game mechanics while introducing many new elements, which will likely cause you to die many times while you figure them out.

- The Lich King from *World of Warcraft: Wrath of the Lich King*—As the finale of this *WoW* expansion, this fight is extremely difficult. The ten-person fight requires precise play and includes many complex mechanics, including a particular fight phase that results in instant death for all the characters if they do not properly coordinate their movement. Learning how to win this fight can take a group of players weeks of practice, and the scale of the difficulty helps evoke the level of world-saving heroism that the *characters* are experiencing. It also produces catharsis and satisfaction, which is in keeping with the hundreds of hours of gameplay players have invested at that point in the game.

- The Final Choice from *Life is Strange*—This is not a battle, but an encounter where the character faces the storm they have known was coming for the entire game. The content of this encounter is entirely narrative, where the only mechanic is a single binary choice you must make for the character under no time pressure. The character has to decide whether to save their oldest friend and person they have fallen in love with, or to save the entire town from the devastating storm. The experience of the impossibility and unfairness of this choice are conveyed to the player by having them spend 20 hours of gameplay saving the character's friend over and over, and by leading them down a path where the only possibility is this decision point. The frustration and anger the player feels at the unfairness of the game are a good proxy for the character's experience. It's also probably a metaphor for a teenager's fear of coming out.

- The tower at the end of *Dear Esther*—Again, this is not a fight but an encounter. In this case, the player has been wandering alone through a beautiful but desolate island. They have listened to a voice-over that is clearly their character's voice talking about their life. They are at the end of their life and alone, having lost their life partner. In the end, the player is confronted with a tall radio tower, and the only way to end the game is to climb it and jump off, killing their character. The emotional battle that many players experience over whether to "let" the character kill themself mirrors the struggle of the character to let go of their life and find peace.

Step 5: List and describe the patterns you observe across all ten games.

- Players are more tolerant of negative emotions when they are deeply invested in the game and within sight of the end.

- The games do not directly create the emotions of the characters in the players.

- The experience being created has its roots throughout the game, not just in the boss encounter.

- The most powerful and intense character emotions and experiences are reflected in sometimes unpleasant player experiences.

Step 6: Select one pattern and document it using the pattern template.
I think that all of these patterns that may exist across games combine uniquely in the situation of a boss encounter.

Step 7: You may repeat step 6 for each pattern you observed in step 5.

Pattern

Name: We're Going to a Dark Place Together
Confidence: 2
Image:

FIGURE 10.2 The stronger the player's bond with the character the more likely they are to continue playing when the experience is difficult or unpleasant.

Author: Chris Barney
Design problem: It's hard to make the player feel what the character feels, especially when the character's experience is intense or difficult.
Description: To help the player empathize and understand the intense or difficult emotions of a character, the developer may need to create similar but less intense emotions in the player. However, when these emotions are unpleasant by themselves, the developer may want to create them in a focused situation where the player's investment in the game is high.

Games that use this pattern and how:

- *Silent Hill 2*—Creates feelings of dread and powerlessness in the player by confronting them repeatedly with an unkillable monster. Forcing the player to escape and run away many times creates feelings of frustration. These emotions mirror the character's feelings of terror, helplessness, and growing self-loathing. The game subtly tracks the player's reactions to these emotions using various invisible mechanics, such that the ending is satisfying to different player response types.
- *The Secret World*—By the time the player faces Doctor Klein and The Colossus, Melothat at the end of The Ankh dungeon, the narrative has made the player understand that Klein, while human, is a monster. He and his creations have killed the players many times already, raising

their frustration. This helps the players stay invested in both the plot and gameplay of the dungeon, making the experience of killing him viscerally satisfying and allowing easy identification with their character persona.

- *Portal*—Again, the player has been carefully positioned by the narrative and given a high level of mastery over the game mechanics. The introduction of new mechanics and the breaking of the established game conventions enhance the feeling of GLaDOS's omnipotence and make it feel to the player like she is "cheating," mirroring the character's feelings of betrayal.
- *World of Warcraft: Wrath of the Lich King*—The final fight with the Lich King is punishingly difficult. Many players took weeks of play just to defeat this single boss. Players are willing to put in this extreme level of effort because at this point in their play, they have many hundreds of hours invested in the game. The defeat of this boss monster is the result of "heroic" effort on the part of both the characters *and* players.
- *Life is Strange*—Over the course of the 20 or so hours of gameplay, the player uses the character's ability to rewind time to explore the consequences of their actions. The player navigates the character into the situation of being in love with her best friend, and faced with a choice of whether to save her or the town they live in. The time invested and the emotional bond combine with the unfairness of the choice to create feelings of frustration and anger in the player that mirror those in the character.
- *Dear Esther*—At the end of the game, the player makes the choice to end the character's life by jumping from a high tower. This choice is only meaningful because of the environmental and explicit narrative of the game up to this point. If the choice were presented at the beginning of the game, it would either be meaningless or something that the player would be unwilling or unmotivated to do.

Seed: Boss encounters that make you feel like the character feels.
Related patterns:
Parent patterns:

SUGGESTED EXERCISES

Use **Exercise 6: Emotional Patterns** to generate a pattern based on empathy.
Use **Exercise 22: The First Choice** to generate a pattern based on a relatable main character. Start with step 2 and use "create a relatable main character" as your answer.

Child patterns:
The Risk of Knowing You* (Confidence: 3)—Use this pattern to help build the emotional connection between player and character that are needed to support We're Going to a Dark Place Together.

SUGGESTED EXERCISES

Use **Exercise 6: Emotional Patterns** to generate a pattern for a less intense emotion than you will be depicting in your character. The classic emotion wheel is a good place to look for emotions of different valence (Wikipedia 2020).

Keywords: Empathy, Investment, Attachment, Difficulty, Negative Player Experience

EMERGENT NARRATIVE PATTERNS

This next exercise first requires that you understand the concept of emergent narrative—story beats that are created by player interaction with game systems, then joined into a coherent narrative in the player's mind. By its very nature, emergent narrative is difficult to create. Controlling the kinds of narratives that emerge is even harder. Instead of describing a set of techniques for building emergent narratives or a theory of how they work, I've designed a pattern exercise that looks at this narrative form and extracts a set of techniques and theory in the form of patterns. The process asks you to look at the games that produce an emergent narrative and ask creative questions about how that narrative is constructed.

Pattern Purpose

This exercise will help you look at examples of emergent narrative and begin to understand the techniques that make them successful. Step 1 in this exercise is challenging. The old aphorism that there's no such thing as a bad question is not true here. If you find that the question you asked is failing to help you generate a useful pattern, consider asking a different question. Keeping the question simple and empirically answerable will help you successfully complete the exercise the first few times.

---

* Example pattern for Exercise 7: Player Experience Patterns.

EXERCISE 11: EMERGENT NARRATIVE PATTERNS

Step 1: Ask yourself a question about emergent narratives. For instance, how many player choices are needed in a scene, level, or game before emergent narratives occur? Or, how are the kinds of emergent narratives in a game related to the type or diversity of mechanics in a game? Be creative.

Step 2: List and describe ten games that have an emergent narrative.

Step 3: For each game you chose, what is the answer to your question for that specific game?

Step 4: List and generalize your answers from step 3.

Step 5: Do these answers hold up across all of your games, or can you generalize them to do so?

Step 6: List and describe any patterns that your question and answers sound like they're describing.

Step 7: Select one pattern and describe the problem it's solving, then document it using the pattern template.

Step 8: You may repeat step 7 for each pattern you observed in step 6.

Example Emergent Narrative Pattern

Exercise

Step 1: Ask yourself a question about emergent narratives.

When a game makes many choices available to allow a diverse set of narrative options, which choices are perceived by players as having narrative importance?

Step 2: Look at ten games that have an emergent narrative.

- *The Elder Scrolls: Oblivion*—Open-world role-playing game (RPG)

- *The Legend of Zelda: Breath of the Wild*—Open-world RPG

- *Moon Hunters*—Procedurally generated, roguelike RPG

- Apocalypse World—Player-driven, tabletop RPG

- *Fallen London*—Choice-based, text-heavy RPG

- *Susurrus: Season of Tides*—Choice-based, text-heavy massively multiplayer online role-playing game (MMORPG)

- *Anarchy Online*—MMORPG

- *Anthem* (freeplay mode)— Open-world shooter

- *Gloomhaven*—Campaign-based board game

- *Kingdom Death: Monster*—Campaign-based board game

Step 3: For each game you chose, what is the answer to your question for that specific game?

- *The Elder Scrolls: Oblivion*—In this open-world RPG, the player can interact with the world in many ways, exploring the world and the available non-player character (NPC), monster, and quest interactions in almost any order. The primary plot of the game is designed and not emergent, but the actions you take outside of the primary quest are optional. The subset completed by a given player, taken together, builds an emergent narrative. *The interactions that seem most meaningful are those that alter the character in some significant way.*

- *The Legend of Zelda: Breath of the Wild*—This game is also an open-world RPG, but the game structure is subtly different. The overall scripted narrative is much stronger, and the open-world gameplay is structured to generate more cohesive units of narrative organically. Instead of offering scripted side quests, the game allows you to either engage with or avoid open-world encounters like enemy encampments, shrines that you can explore in "any" order, and the eight "divine beasts" to fight. *The narrative significance of these seems to depend on their difficulty, and the degree to which they move the player toward the larger scripted narrative goal.*

- *Moon Hunters*—This is a complex and strange procedural game with a short playthrough time, and is meant to be played many times. Because of the brief playthrough, most events are designed to have narrative significance. *Which events seem most important becomes determined by the intent of the player.* Because a player can quickly get a sense of the overall story, it's common for players to seek out specific randomly available events in pursuit of a particular narrative outcome. *The collection of events the player chooses reinforces the significance of those events.*

- *Apocalypse World*—Unlike most older tabletop RPGs, this game and others that use its base rule set (Powered by the Apocalypse) drive the narrative based on player choices rather than on a plotline prescribed by the game master. Systems exist that allow the game master to introduce or advance narrative elements in the world, but even those systems are driven by player actions. The world the game master creates is therefore focused on the characters' actions and the players' intentions. *Most events that take place feel like they have narrative weight, because the player, game master, and game systems are focused on giving events significance.*

- *Fallen London*—In this choice-based text adventure, the player is faced with a never-ending series of choices as they advance a huge number of scripted plotlines. Some plotlines have many endings, and they follow a variety of narrative structures. The primary mechanic driving narrative advancement is the resource cost of different choices. Given that players have limited resources, *the perceived importance of any choice is derived not just from the player's understanding of the visible narrative but from the cost of the different choices.* Thus, expending a large number of resources on a choice that seems insignificant invests that choice with narrative importance. Of course, the designers use this intentionally, and the payoff for those kinds of choices is carefully maintained.

- *Susurrus: Season of Tides*—This was a choice-driven, massively multiplayer text adventure game that was never fully realized due to the realities of development and the limited resources of the developers. However, the design is still interesting and instructive. In this game, the narrative beats available to any given player were determined by a world state resulting from the actions of all the players. Because the players knew that their actions were altering the overall world, completing and even repeating mundane tasks had the potential to be narratively important, as it might shift and advance the story for all players. *Part of the reason that the play of this game failed was that there was no feedback to the player as to which actions they made affected the world.*

- *Anarchy Online*—Although this MMO had a very complex setting, it didn't have the kind of focused, progressive story found in other genre members such as *World of Warcraft*. Most gameplay was either exploratory, challenge-based, or procedurally generated. Because *most of this gameplay did not have explicit narrative importance*, ridding a dungeon of mutants did not affect the state of the world; the player defined the significance of any action. Some players didn't assign narrative to their actions and simply used the gameplay as a means to mechanically advance their characters. However, more than in any other multiplayer game I have observed, *many players constructed elaborate narratives from these explicitly insignificant events*. The developers facilitated this player habit by including many locations that had no in-game use, but which acted as narrative stages for the role-play of the players.

- *Anthem* (freeplay mode)—In this story-driven open-world multi-player first-person shooter, the freeplay mode provides a space for world exploration and freeform gameplay that also offers character advancement outside of repeatable story-based missions. *Events that occur in this mode have little overall narrative significance, but most of the player stories I hear about the game relate to some situation encountered by a group of players in this mode*. The randomly varied enemy placement and world events that comprise this mode create an opportunity for players to generate small but meaningful emergent narrative experiences: "Do you remember that time when…?"

- *Gloomhaven*—In this campaign-based board game, players progressively unlock chunks of the overall story. Although there's little variation in the final shape of that story, a given group of players may experience it in any order. Additionally, most players will never complete the entirety of the campaign, and thus have very different narrative experiences at the point when they stop playing. *The scriptedness of each unlocked narrative chunk is provided by the designers, but the act of choosing which chunk to experience increases its weight for each group of players.*

- *Kingdom Death: Monster*—Unlike *Gloomhaven*, this game does not have a tightly scripted narrative arc. Each session of this campaign-based board game generates a piece of narrative for the players that is significant, both because of how hard it is to survive in the extremely hostile world, and due to the comedic, horrific, or simply unexpected turns the game can take. *Most choices the players make have significant consequences for the characters, and the overall story and high perceived likelihood of failure make each action memorable.* Additionally, the overall setting is intentionally filled with unexplained elements. Some have explanations that might be uncovered at some point; others invite players to use the actions of their characters to explain the state of the world.

Step 4: List and generalize your answers from step 3.

- The interactions that seem most meaningful are those that alter the character in some significant way.

- The narrative significance of these seems to depend on their difficulty, and the degree to which they move the player toward the larger scripted narrative goal.

- When many events have a narrative payload, which events seem most important becomes determined by the intent of the player.

- When players choose to engage in events, the various events selected reinforce each other's significance.

- When the content of a game is cooperatively generated, most events feel like they have narrative weight because everyone is focused on giving events significance.

- The perceived importance of any choice is derived not just from the player's understanding of the visible narrative, but from the cost of the different choices.

- For players to ascribe meaning to their actions, they need feedback on the effect those actions have on themselves and the world.

- When most gameplay interactions don't have explicit narrative importance, players may construct elaborate narratives from these explicitly insignificant events if they're given a context in which their actions can be meaningful.

- In multiplayer games, shared events that lack larger narrative significance may be translated into meaningful stories by the players that share the experience.

- In games consisting of scripted narrative vignettes, and in which the player controls which subset of narrative components to engage with, the larger narrative that emerges can be perceived by the players as more meaningful due to their active participation in constructing it.

- Players are likely to construct meaningful narratives when most choices they make have significant consequences for their characters, their actions have dramatic consequences, and the overall story and the high perceived likelihood of failure make each action memorable.

Step 5: Do these answers hold up across all of your games, or can you generalize them to do so?

These answers all seem universally true across games that have an emergent narrative. The more of these things that are present, the more meaningful the emergent narrative. These might even be a part of a higher-order interactive narrative pattern.

These qualities increase the meaningfulness of emergent narratives:

- They alter the character in a meaningful way.

- They alter the world in a meaningful way.

- They are difficult.

- They move the player toward a medium- or long-term goal.

- They are chosen by the player.

- They contribute to a narrative goal chosen by the player.

- They connect with other narrative events.

- They are intentionally constructed to have a narrative payload.*

- They have a cost that is proportional to their narrative consequence.

- They make the player aware of their impact on the characters or world.

- The world provides rich narrative hooks to relate emergent events to.

- They are shared with other players.

Step 6: List and describe any patterns that your question and answers sound like they're describing.

"To allow players to construct meaningful emergent narratives, developers should provide players with context, motivation, and consequence for their actions in the game."

I think this is a good parent pattern that addresses the design problem for this exercise. The 12 bullet points from step 5 are probably each a child

---

* While designers cannot construct an emergent narrative for the players, they do have control over the narrative content of the pieces that the players are building their story out of. *Moon Hunters* leans into this and procedurally generates a world littered with mythopoetic puzzle pieces for the player to assemble.

pattern. It's tempting to create a single comprehensive pattern that tells designers to choose as many of the bullet points as possible when creating their game, but that would lose the flexibility and power that breaking them into independent patterns would give. Also, each of those child patterns may apply to other parent patterns outside of emergent narrative.

Step 7: Select one pattern and describe the problem it's solving, then document it using the pattern template.

Step 8: You may repeat step 7 for each pattern you observed in step 6.

Pattern

Name: The Three Pillars of Meaning in Emergent Narrative
Confidence: 2
Image:

FIGURE 10.3   When developers provide context, motivation, and consequence players can construct meaningful narratives.

Author: Chris Barney
Design problem: Given the reality of limited resources, when creating design elements that encourage emergent narratives, designers need to maximize the narrative potential of every element. How can designers know if a given game element will contribute to meaningful emergent narratives?

Description: To allow players to construct meaningful emergent narratives, developers should provide players with *context*, *motivation*, and *consequence* for their actions in the game.

There are many child patterns that contribute to this pattern; two are listed and 12 other possibilities are provided in the suggested exercise, and there may be more. But each one contributes to either the context of, motivation for, or consequences of an event that could be part of an emergent narrative.

Games that use this pattern and how:

- *The Elder Scrolls: Skyrim*—The degree to which the three pillars are present for emergent narrative elements in this game varies. At worst, the events are isolated and unrelated to the player or the world: a group of bandits in a cave with no associated NPCs or consequences for "ridding the countryside" of them. At best, all are present: killing an NPC in town results in the guards becoming hostile, the character attracting the attention of the assassins' guild, and the inability to wear holy armor due to your evil actions.
- *Kingdom Death: Monster*—On a base level, the motivation for most events in this game is either survival or to see what happens. But as the game and the emergent narrative progress, player motivations complicate. Essentially, every event in the game has significant consequences, and most consequences are immediate and clear. The narrative context for actions is always given, and it is additive. Early in the game, you have only the immediately provided context. Yet as the game progresses, the context of the emergent narrative increases and eventually exceeds the designer-provided context of the game world.
- *Apocalypse World*—This is a tabletop role-playing system, so the degree to which these pillars are present in any specific use of the system is dependent on who is running and playing in the game. However, the system itself helps to ensure that these things are present by stating principles like "give everyone and everything a name" (context), "say what happens" (consequence), and "play to see what happens" (motivation).
- *White Death*—This is a live-action role-playing game where the events are largely up to the players, so, as with Apocalypse World, the degree to which the three pillars are present for each is variable. However, the game is designed to help provide context, motivation, and consequence for the actions of the players. A full discussion of the game's nuances is outside of the scope of this example, but the narrative frame of the game provides context and consequence. The characters are endowed with attributes that give motivation and that interact with the attributes of other players to create consequence and motivation. The interaction of the simple mechanics of the game with the role-play of the players produces perhaps the most compelling narrative experience created in any game, ever.

Seed: Exercise 12: Emergent Narrative Patterns—What makes emergent events narratively meaningful
Related patterns:
Parent patterns:

SUGGESTED EXERCISE

Use **Exercise 24: Theoretical Patterns** to generate a pattern based on the theory that The Three Pillars of Meaning in Emergent Narrative is generalizable to narrative in general.

Child patterns:
I Thought You Should Know* (Confidence: 2)—Use this pattern when you need to give context for a piece of emergent narrative.

Greater Choice Requires Greater Motivation† (Confidence: 2)—When you have applied The Three Pillars of Meaning to situations where there are emergent narrative and player choices, then those choices will be meaningful. The more significant you make choices, the more of them your game will be able to support.

SUGGESTED EXERCISE

If narrative meaning is enhanced by adding consequence, context, and motivation, then it would be useful to have patterns describing ways to add those pillars to a game. Here are the qualities I found when creating this pattern. The pillars they relate to are in parentheses.

1. They alter the character in a meaningful way. (consequence)
2. They alter the world in a meaningful way. (consequence, context)
3. They are difficult. (context, motivation)
4. They move the player toward a goal. (consequence, motivation)
5. They are chosen by the player. (context, motivation)
6. They contribute to a narrative goal chosen by the player. (motivation, consequence)
7. They connect with other narrative events. (context, consequence)
8. They are intentionally constructed to have a narrative payload. (context, motivation, consequence)
9. They have a cost that is proportional to their narrative consequence. (context, consequence)
10. They make the player aware of their impact on the characters or world. (context, consequence)

---

* Example pattern from Exercise 12: Embedded and Environmental Narrative Patterns.
† Example pattern from Exercise 16: Patterns from Core Mechanics.

11. The world provides rich narrative hooks to relate emergent events to. (context, motivation)
12. They are shared with other players. (context, consequence)

There are many ways that you can approach generating these patterns.

Use **Exercise 24: Theoretical Patterns** to look at each of these statements as a theory.

Use **Exercise 5: Functional Patterns** to look at statement 3 as the functional element of difficulty.

Use **Exercise 7: Player Experience Patterns** to look at statements 5 or 6 as the experience of choice.

When you have completed all of the exercises in the book, come back to see if you can find other exercises to use to investigate these twelve statements.

Keywords: Emergent Narrative, Meaning, Difficulty, Autonomy, Choice, Cost, Economy

EMBEDDED AND ENVIRONMENTAL NARRATIVE PATTERNS

Pattern Purpose

The ideas of environmental narrative and embedded narrative are related, but slightly different. A designer creates environmental narrative by placing things in the game world such that they tell a story about what has happened before the player's arrival. It might be a trail of blood and a single empty child's shoe in *BioShock*, or a set table in a house with a partially eaten meal and a knocked-over chair. This type of narrative usually gives the player an intriguing mystery or allows them to piece together a coherent story over time. Games like *Gone Home* consist almost entirely of environmental narrative as the core mechanic, while others like *BioShock* use it to reinforce the theme of the primary narrative.

Embedded narrative, on the other hand, is diegetic—narrative that's meant to have been produced and placed into the world by that world's inhabitants.* The murals found in *Journey* or the books found in *The Elder Scrolls* games are embedded narrative.

---

* Of course, in games the developer is adding the narrative in either case, so technically in games all narrative is embedded. But as a designer there is a difference between telling the player and character something by staging a scene for them to observe, and creating a world where the inhabitants have embedded narrative elements into the world to tell each other things.

In the real world, environmental narrative is evidence of events that people have left behind by accident, while embedded narrative is meaning that people have built into the world on purpose. For example, imagine walking into a Catholic church in a poor neighborhood. You see the images in stained glass depicting the life of Christ and the stations of the cross. Those are embedded narrative: they tell you something about the beliefs of the people who created the space, because those people placed them there for you to see. You also see the worn velvet of the pews, the tattered hymnals, and a piece of gum stuck to the cover of a Bible. Those tell you about the people who use that space, about their poverty and piety, not because they wanted to tell you those things, but because you have seen the consequences of their lives.

I ran across an excellent example of environmental vs. embedded narrative in games in an episode of *The Game Maker's Toolkit*. The circular saw blades that you see embedded in the wall in the *Half-Life* level Ravenholm are environmental narrative. They show the player that they can use these blades to cut head-crab zombies in half. In *Dead Space*, on the other hand, the bloody writing on the walls saying "Cut off their limbs" is an embedded narrative. The person who wrote it did so for that as the next person to come along, you would see it and get the message.

The real purpose of this distinction isn't to correctly categorize each piece of narrative in your game; it is to use the difference to help you consider the purpose and execution of each narrative element as you embed it in the environment.

If you consider patterns created by the previous Emergent Patterns exercise, you might imagine emergent game systems that allow players to create environmental narratives through the course of their play. These might be as straightforward as bullet marks and monster or player-character corpses in a first-person shooter, or as complex as the overall world state in a game like *Minecraft*. These systems can also yield interesting patterns.

The patterns created by this next exercise are very focused and are useful for designs that make careful use of narrative technique. Even if this is not your focus as a designer, completing this exercise is useful for developing an appreciation and understanding of these techniques.

**EXERCISE 12: EMBEDDED AND ENVIRONMENTAL
NARRATIVE PATTERNS**

Step 1: Pick a game level.
Step 2: Describe the narrative of that level.
Step 3: List and describe ten techniques used to incorporate that narrative
into the level.
Step 4: Repeat steps 2 and 3 for three to five different games that share a
similar narrative.*
Step 5: Remove techniques that don't apply across games, or generalize
them so that they do.
Step 6: List and briefly describe each pattern you observe.
Step 7: Select one pattern and document it using the pattern template.
Step 8: You may repeat step 7 for each pattern you observed in step 6.

Example Embedded and Environmental Narrative Pattern
Exercise

Step 1: Pick a game level.
The Car Park in *The Secret World*. ("Contract Killers")

Step 2: Describe the narrative of that level.
Your character is sent to investigate a missing team of allies. You enter
an underground parking structure in Tokyo, where you first discover
the bodies of enemies of the team, then the bodies of team members.
Eventually, you find that the whole team has been killed, not by the enemy
but by a mysterious force. As you try to leave the parking structure, that
force attacks you—and it's the ghost of a child. You must avoid confrontation with it as you flee.

Step 3: List and describe ten techniques used to incorporate that narra-
tive into the level.

1. Environmental narrative in the general setting: The lighting and
   sound design use horror techniques to create a sense of danger.

2. Environmental narrative vignettes showing strange behaviors:
   Lights and mechanical devices like gates and car alarms malfunc-
   tion, establishing that things are not normal.

---

* This exercise works well when done in a group. If you are doing this exercise with a class, divide it
into teams of four or five and then combine your work for step 3.

3. Embedded narrative: You can access surveillance camera footage showing some of the things you will encounter, but they are not clear.

4. Embedded narrative: You can find security logs that suggest that something strange was going on here before the events that have brought you here.

5. Environmental narrative showing suggestions of violence: Damage to the environment and blood splatters and trails are introduced.

6. Environmental narrative evidence of violence: Some allies are found dead, killed in a way that suggests a known enemy.

7. Environmental narrative evidence that the obvious is not true: The enemies you suspected of killing your allies are also found dead, killed in the same way as your allies.

8. Glimpse of the true threat: You see the ghost several times in the distance before you reach your target.

9. Environmental narrative vignette, final reveal: A more complicated environmental scene where you discover that all of your allies are dead, all of the expected enemies are dead, and then you are confronted by the ghost and begin to flee the parking structure.

10. The level design is a descent to the truth and an escape back to the surface. The shape of the level is a labyrinth, with only one path in and back out. Areas are gated to make you feel constantly trapped.

Step 4: Repeat steps 2 and 3 for three to five different games that share a similar narrative.

- First level of *BioShock*

  Narrative: Your character's plane crashes, and you're forced to enter the mysterious and dangerous environment of an abandoned undersea city that has suffered a catastrophe. You want to find out what happened, but you're primarily trying to escape. You're quickly given instructions by a distant "ally," and try to follow them in order to survive. The first instructions are to rescue the ally's family.

Techniques:

1. Embedded narrative in the form of inner monologue.

2. Environmental narrative showing immediate plot developments from the plane crash includes items floating down in the water throughout the level and parts of the plane hitting the city.

3. Environmental vignettes showing more distant events: New Years' Eve party in the club, etc.

4. Environmental details showing the decay of the city, faded paint, distressed prop items.

5. Environmental details showing the destruction of the city by its citizens, broken down bathroom.

6. Environmental scenes with NPCs: The death of the person sent to meet you, the woman with a gun in her stroller.

7. Embedded propaganda clip as you descend into the city of Rapture.

8. Embedded narrative in the posters and ads promoting Plasmids.

9. Embedded narrative in the form of the radio broadcasts from "Atlas."

10. Environmental set pieces like the drone killing the first Splicer that attacks you.

- First level of *Dead Space*

   Narrative: Your character is sent to repair a damaged mining space-craft. You become stranded when your small repair ship crashes into the city-sized mining ship. You must survive long enough to repair your ship. The character is personally motivated by a romantic partner who was on the mining ship.

   Techniques:

   1. Embedded narrative of video communication from love interest.

   2. Environmental narrative of debris field around planet.

   3. Environmental narrative of rescue crew's clean ship vs. old mining ship with trash and wear signs.

4. Environmental narrative of ship's damage from crash landing.

5. Embedded narrative of welcome video in landing bay.

6. Environmental narrative of landing bay lobby filled with luggage.

7. Environmental set piece of first Necromorph attack on ally NPCs.

8. Environmental narrative of blood trails and dead crew.

9. Embedded narrative of bloody note on the plasma cutter repair station telling the character to cut off their limbs.

10. Environmental narrative of unseen NPC voice-over cries for help.

11. Sound effects reflecting the malfunctioning equipment and close pairing of sound effects with the musical score.

- Hospital level of *Silent Hill 2*

  Narrative: Your character is following an elusive NPC who enters the hospital in the abandoned town of Silent Hill. You are under constant threat from creatures in the town, where you've become trapped by mysteriously destroyed roads. In the larger game, you're motivated by trying to find your supposedly dead wife who has sent you a message and by trying to understand what's happening in the town.

  Techniques:

  1. Environmental narrative vignette, girl going into the hospital.

  2. Embedded narrative, map of the hospital on the wall.

  3. Embedded narrative, doctor's note about disturbed patients.

  4. Worn, dilapidated textures, overturned furniture.

  5. Doctor's notes from disturbed patient that describe the reality the character is experiencing.

  6. Locked door sounds.

  7. Darkness and no power.

  8. Radio static sounds warning of monsters.

9. Navigational signs (floor levels, room names).

10. Patient props, magazines, and stuffed animals.

Step 5: Remove techniques that don't apply across games, or generalize them so that they do.

1. Embedded narrative normal communications: Logs or notes left by the previous inhabitants of a space, sometimes directed to you, or sometimes justified as communications with bosses or friends, or as personal journals. These may be video, audio, or written communications.

2. Embedded narrative communications: Notes scrawled on walls or paper. These can be found at the player's leisure, but are short and are understood to have been left for whoever came along next.

3. Embedded narrative barks: Shouts from the next room, brief radio messages calling for help. Generally directed at whoever can hear them.

4. Embedded narrative instructions: Signs to help people use the space, from street signs to room name plaques to maps.

5. Embedded narrative exposition: Propaganda/welcome videos, posters, etc. Used to tell the player things about a space that its inhabitants would generally know. Often tightly themed with the rest of the environment.

6. Environmental narrative: General texture, lighting, and audio choices that create the desired environment. These are not telling a specific story but are telling the larger story of the space.

7. Environmental narrative showing what happens here, not a specific event, but the accumulation of evidence of the things that ordinarily occur in this place.

8. Environmental evidence: A single or small set of sounds, textures, or objects, such as a single bullet hole or a lone bloodstain, that don't tell a full story, but point to a specific thing that happened.

9. Environmental vignettes: Larger collections of environmental assets that tell a small, specific story. Usually, these are static; they are

something simple and singular that happened. For example, a dead body and bloody footprints going away down the hall.

10. Environmental set piece: A more complex set of environmental assets and possibly events that happen around the character while they are playing. The character may or may not be able to interact with them, but their interaction can't change the meaning of the events.

Step 6: List and briefly describe each pattern you observe.

1. A wide variety of different embedded and environmental techniques are used in all cases.

2. The use of techniques escalates as the level progresses, reinforcing the gameplay pacing of the level.

3. Embedded narrative exposition is more common at the beginning of levels.

4. Embedded narrative communication is often used as a tutorial or to provide hints.

5. Environmental set pieces are often used as narrative climax beats or to introduce a climactic gameplay moment.

6. General backstory is conveyed by narrative exposition and pervasive texture, lighting, and sound choices.

7. Specific backstory is conveyed through embedded communications and environmental vignettes.

8. Immediate events are shown through embedded barks and environmental set pieces.

Step 7: Select one pattern and document it using the pattern template.
The uses of embedded narrative exposition to give the player context that the character, or the average person in the story, would already possess.

Step 8: You may repeat step 7 for each pattern you observed in step 6.
There is clearly a meta-level pattern here about the density and structure of the embedded and environmental narrative, and how that relates to the intensity of the game experience. All of the games I examined had a very

rapid narrative beat and a high density of embedded and environmental narrative. To fully describe that pattern, it would be necessary to look at games with both slower narrative pacing and less dense embedded and environmental techniques.

Pattern

I have chosen a relatively simple and specific pattern to complete this exercise to show that it can produce both low- and high-level patterns. It's tempting to pursue the highest level, the most "powerful" pattern that you can see. If this is your first time completing this exercise, try to stay specific and return to the exercise later to look for the higher-level patterns that unify the lower-level ones you started with.

Name: I Thought You Should Know
Confidence: 2
Image:

FIGURE 10.4 It's old news to the character, but the player needs to hear it.

Author: Chris Barney
Design problem: Designers often put players into a situation that they know nothing about, but that their character would be familiar with.
Description: To convey commonly known information and still let the character seem like an insider in the situation, the developer may wish

to put the information the player needs to know into embedded narrative aimed at other characters that might be new to the space.

Games that use this pattern and how:

- *BioShock*—When you enter the bathysphere to descend into Rapture, a propaganda video plays that gives the purpose and origin of the city as the player sees it for the first time.
- *Dead Space*—As the player leaves their repair ship and enters the mining ship, a video plays in the landing bay, giving the history of the ship.
- *Call of Duty: Modern Warfare*—In the intro sequence, you ride in a car and listen to a political speech that sets the scene for the game. This speech is overlaid with several other types of environmental narrative; complete the suggested exercise for Child Patterns using this game instead to see if you can find them.

Seed: Exercise 12: Embedded and Environmental Narrative Patterns— Techniques found in the Tokyo Car Park instance in *The Secret World*
Parent patterns:
The Three Pillars of Meaning in Emergent Narrative* (Confidence: 3)—I Thought You Should Know provides context, one of the three pillars described in this pattern.
Child patterns:

SUGGESTED EXERCISES

Use **Exercise 12: Embedded and Environmental Narrative Patterns** to generate a pattern based on the intro sequence of *Half-Life* and that of *The Elder Scrolls: Skyrim*. I might call the pattern this would produce "Where the heck am I?"

Keywords: Narrative, Embedded Narrative, Context

---

* Example pattern from Exercise 11: Emergent Narrative Patterns.

CHAPTER 11

Patterns That Break the Mold

O NE OF THE LEGITIMATE issues I've heard with the idea of documenting patterns and creating a Pattern Language is that using such a creation inherently limits the design space and creativity of designers. With how flexible and abstract patterns can be, and how they can create new, innovative solutions to old design problems, I think this concern is mostly exaggerated.

However, when creating patterns in the observational way that this book describes, we are limited to the set of design problems that we have example solutions for. Game design is becoming more robust as a field, but it's still comparatively new, and I would never say that we've exhausted the set of possible design problems that can be addressed through games! So it stands to reason that we need to be able to create patterns to address new problems and to extend the known design space.

The patterns in this section each try to do that in a different way.

BREAKING SPACES PATTERNS

Pattern Purpose

When we consider a game design, one of the problems we must address is where we intend the game to be played. This question may be influenced by the platform we're aiming for or by the audience. Or it may be one of the primary choices we make, which then affects those other factors.

As games shift with changes in technology, the spaces we can play them in shift as well. Our options for where we might want our game to be played are increasing, but our control over where our game is actually experienced is decreasing.

I conceived this exercise as a way for designers to understand how space affects the play of a game and to consider the effect of moving a game from one targeted space to another.

For this exercise, spaces are defined as the venues of play. You can find a discussion of this concept in Lens #3 of Jessie Schell's *The Art of Game Design* (2020). Schell's venues are evocative and poetic, but essentially break down to the kinds of places you can play a game. These can include private spaces: at your computer, on the couch with friends, or on your phone in private. Public game spaces can happen on your phone while you're doing something like waiting in line, with a group in a game like tag in the park, or even performatively with a sport such as baseball or football.

It would be easy to create an exercise that looked at games that are meant to be played in a particular space and that produced patterns describing how to develop games for that kind of space. Those will be valuable patterns, and I encourage you to do that! However, this exercise focuses on understanding how games can break out of the spaces in which they were originally designed to function.

"Breaking spaces" is defined here as taking a game that would typically be played in one space and moving it into another, usually with affordances and alterations to make the game adapt to the new space.

EXERCISE 13: BREAKING SPACES PATTERNS

Step 1: Pick two venues.
Step 2: Describe ten games that "break spaces" by moving between these two venues.
Step 3: List the elements that those games use to break spaces.
Step 4: List the effects of those elements.
Step 5: List and briefly describe each pattern you observe.
Step 6: Select one pattern and document it using the Pattern Template.*
Step 7: Then think of a game that *does not* break spaces.†
Step 8: Can you apply the pattern to that game?

---

* At this point you may not have the problem that the pattern you have observed solves. That's okay in this case; the problem will be derived in the next steps.
† To put it another way, pick a game that has *not* been adapted to a new space or ported to a new hardware platform.

Step 9: What effect do you think you will create by breaking spaces in the game you chose in step 7? Frame this effect as the problem for your pattern.

Step 10: You may repeat steps 6–9 for each pattern you observed in step 5.

Steps 7 through 9 of this exercise are intended to let you make a preliminary assessment of the viability of your pattern. If you can't imagine how your pattern would apply to the games you select, then it's a good indication that it's not a strong or useful pattern. Being able to imagine applying the pattern is a positive sign, but it doesn't indicate that your pattern is perfect. The only way to build that confidence is through repeated successful application of the pattern.

Example Breaking Spaces Pattern
Exercise

Step 1: Pick two venues.
Tabletop → Tablet

Step 2: Describe ten games that "break spaces" by moving between these two venues.

- *Chess → Battle Chess*—Early digital implementations of chess were very literal adaptations of a traditional chessboard and rules to a digital presentation. *Battle Chess* altered the game by making use of the digital medium to depict each capture as a battle between the pieces. The game didn't provide control in the battles, so the outcome was always the same as in a normal game of chess. An artificial intelligence (AI)-controlled opponent was provided at first, and later versions or clones of this game offered online play. It could be argued that this game was the origin of turn-based strategy games that added gameplay to the battles and less abstract, more representational battlefield maps. Mobile (clone) versions of this game provide a more kinesthetic touch experience.

- *Magic: The Gathering → MTG: Arena*—There have been two significant digital implementations of the collectible card game Magic: The Gathering, i.e., *MTG: Online* and more recently *MTG: Arena*. The digital implementations take advantage of the medium to both manage the mechanics of the game and, in the more recent versions, to provide more engaging play with a thematic playspace and animated card effects and creatures. Both offer online and AI-based play, tutorials, and some thematic story-based elements. A mobile version, *MTG: Duels*, provides a touch-based interface but doesn't alter the gameplay meaningfully.

- *Ticket to Ride*—The digital version of this game is a literal interpretation of the physical game, with AI opponents and computer management of the mechanics. The digital implementation vastly reduces the amount of time it takes to play the game. The mobile version was developed first, though a desktop version is available. The total cost of the game and all expansions is much lower for the digital versions, and they offer tutorials and enhanced visuals.

- *Elder Sign* → *Elder Sign: Omens*—The digital version of this game is mechanically identical to the physical version. Interestingly, the abstract mechanics and the degree to which they were dissonant with the game theme made the physical version one of the less engaging games in this franchise. The digital version, however, makes good use of visuals and sound to create a more horror-focused experience. There is little tutorial scaffolding, but the base gameplay is straightforward in a digital implementation. Again, a tablet version was implemented first, and a desktop port was created later.

- *Carcassonne*—The digital implementation of this board game is perhaps the most literal of all the games discussed here. While it's simple and easy to use, it provides very little digital enhancement. Simple tutorial and multiplayer elements are provided. The mobile version, which was developed first, is designed with the idea of passing a single mobile device among a group of players to be played in a similar venue to the physical game. The desktop version provides significant visual enhancements, along with more focus on online multiplayer.

- *Warhammer* → *Warhammer Quest 2*—There have been a lot of digital adaptations of the Warhammer franchise. These range from close replications of the tabletop war game to real-time action games. They've varied in level of quality, but those that mirror the physical game in a way that provides an intuitive digital experience have been the most successful. In general, the games have provided both single-player modes with AI opponents and multiplayer with online opponents.

- *Clue*—There have been many official and unofficial adaptations of this game in a digital medium. The digital versions provide a gradually increasing level of visual fidelity, and take care of information-hiding and the mechanical management of the game. Interestingly, the games don't add much narrative embellishment and largely reproduce the logic problem that is the core of the game. The most recent implementation supports both local and online multiplayer with global rankings, as well as multiple themes from vampires to the Orient Express.

- *Settlers of Catan* → *Catan Universe*—This implementation is very close to the physical board game, with the computer managing the mechanics of the game. There are some graphical affordances such as visual indicators of who gains resources from which tiles each turn. The game provides AI as well as online multiplayer, and exists on both mobile and desktop platforms, with the mobile platforms developed first.

- *Scrabble* → *Scrabble/Words With Friends*—Digital versions of this game date back as far as 1988. More recent mobile versions are also available. The addition of online play and integration with Facebook made the *Words With Friends* clone vastly popular for several years. One branded mobile version allowed players to play on a tablet and use their phones as their word trays in a way that kinesthetically mirrored physical play. Digital versions provide AI opponents and resolve questions of what words are valid.

- *Labyrinth*—The physical version of this game used knobs to tilt a play board to roll a ball through a maze* while avoiding holes. The digital implementation of this game was first produced for mobile devices and added significant gameplay and control enhancements. The controls used the mobile device's gyroscope to allow the player to tilt the phone.

Step 3: List the techniques that those games use to break spaces.

- *Chess* → *Battle Chess*—Enhanced visuals, gameplay speed

---

* Ironically the game *Labyrinth* is actually a maze. A true labyrinth has only a single winding path that leads inevitably to the center.

- *Magic: The Gathering* → *MTG: Arena*—Tutorial, online matchmaking, enhanced visuals

- *Ticket to Ride*—Reduced playspace size, online matchmaking, asynchronous play, single-player AI

- *Elder Sign* → *Elder Sign: Omens*—Asynchronous play, thematic sound and music, automated management of game systems

- *Carcassonne*—Pass and play, tutorial, online matchmaking, new single-player game modes, automated management of game systems

- *Warhammer* → *Warhammer Quest 2*—Single-player, story focus, microtransactions, tutorial

- *Clue*—Tutorial, automated management of game systems, enhanced visuals, sound, reduced playspace size, online matchmaking, microtransactions

- *Settlers of Catan* → *Catan Universe*—Tutorial, automated management of game systems, enhanced visuals, sound, reduced playspace size, online matchmaking

- *Scrabble* → *Scrabble/Words With Friends*—Tutorial, automated management of game systems, reduced playspace size, online matchmaking, asynchronous play, social integration

- *Labyrinth*—Automated management of game systems, more varied content, difficulty scaling, kinesthetic use of mobile devices

Step 4: List the effects of those techniques.

- Tutorial—An interactive tutorial can make a game more accessible by making the same level of instruction available to all players. In the non-digital versions of a game, superior instruction may be available if an experienced player is present, but that can't be assured and is especially unlikely for a new game.

- Enhanced visuals—Not all digital versions focus on this technique, but it's often seen as important. The games that benefit most use enhanced visuals to increase the amount of information they can convey to the players. For physical games that provide a high-quality kinesthetic experience, providing a high-quality digital presentation can help to match player expectations.

- Reduced playspace size—This is inherent in the tablet medium, but it has the practical effect of allowing more convenient play by freeing it from the table. Essentially, play could take place in any of Schell's venues. The cost of this effect could be the loss of the tactile and kinesthetic elements of play.

- Asynchronous play—The ability to easily preserve the game state allows asynchronous play, where a single game can be stretched over many days. In this way, a play session moves from being a complete game to being a single turn. There's the obvious benefit of allowing multiple simultaneous games and increased accessibility. Reducing the play time also allows much longer games to fit well into the often short mobile play length.

- Single-player/Single-player AI—While some conversions provide local multiplayer gameplay, many do not or don't focus on it. In these cases, it's common to provide AI-controlled opponents to allow for solo play. This can have the benefit of allowing for player learning in a safe environment. It does radically change most games, however, and differs from the fundamentally social nature of board games.

- New single-player game modes—Many multiplayer physical games have solo gameplay rules, but the addition or inclusion of this kind of play is common in digital interpretations. This reflects the more physically solitary nature of playing these game versions.

- Thematic sound and music—It's not unusual for gamers to create soundtracks for playing their favorite board games, but the developer agency in creating this kind of experience is significant. The importance of creating mood varies depending on how thematic a game is, but in almost all cases, it makes the play experience more compelling.

- Automated management of game systems—In recent years, board games have developed more complex systems. Perhaps this is in response to the complexity allowed by digital games, or just an increase in the sophistication of game-makers or the tastes of game players. In any case, it has caused games to become harder to learn, and to consume more time and space. The automation of many of those systems generally has a positive effect, though it's possible to automate things that could be meaningful choices for players.

- Pass and play—Some games that use this technique are trying to replicate the play experience of the physical game as closely as possible. The difficulty is often that the other players are left without anything to look at while others are playing, particularly when there's hidden information and the game device can't be shared. An early version of Scrabble used multiple devices to good effect, but it's no longer available, and this technique is not common in other games.

- Story focus—It's relatively uncommon to see a focus on story added to games, but games that have a significant story focus benefit from the tools that a digital implementation provides.

- Microtransactions—Games with a lot of physical expansions often provide those expansions through microtransactions. Other games, like Magic: The Gathering or other collectible card games, often offer digital packs of cards as microtransactions.

- Online matchmaking—This is also related to accessibility. Allowing for online play of competitive games gives players without access to local opponents the ability to play the game. In the best cases, this play can meet or exceed the standard of local play. The effectiveness of this technique depends on how much fidelity is lost in the translation to a digital game. Usually, what is lost is direct access to the other players. In games with a large social component, this may have a significant negative impact.

- Social network integration—Tapping into a user's existing social network grid allows for both competitive and cooperative play with others that the player knows outside of the game. Unlike some digital games that merely tax a social network, most board games offer meaningful play.

- More varied content—The ease of access allowed by the digital mobile platform can lead to the player exhausting the available gameplay, particularly in more story-driven or cooperative games. Adding new content or extending the scope of the physical game can extend the life of a game somewhat. However, this kind of content delivery can lead to a game that is dependent on it, and that will not live long past the end of active development.

- Difficulty scaling—Variable difficulty has been seen in some board games in the past few years, but it's more common in digital adaptations. Either the difficulty of the game itself may be adjusted or the skill of the AI opponents. This both allows for a more gentle learning curve and extends the life of the game.

- Kinesthetic use of mobile devices—A few games make good kinesthetic use of mobile devices, either by allowing motion controls or using the touch screen to mimic real-world manipulation of game pieces. More often, satisfying physicality is lost in digital adaptations.

Step 5: List and briefly describe each pattern you observe.

1. Loss of physicality is compensated for by enhanced visuals.

2. Loss of in-person social information is compensated for by enhanced information presented in the digital interface.

3. Loss of in-person social information is compensated for by easy access to competitive/cooperative play online.

4. Loss of personal instruction is compensated for by automated tutorials.

5. Loss of opponent skill growth is compensated for by variable AI/ game difficulty.

6. Lower game price is compensated for by microtransactions and paid downloadable content (DLC).

7. Story is introduced where the physical game is very thematic or includes some narrative.

8. Thematic music and sound effects are introduced when the game is heavily themed.

9. Sound effects that mimic physical gameplay (dice rolling, pieces clacking) are used often, but particularly in abstract games.

10. Large-scale social play (leaderboards, tournaments) are introduced in competitive games.

Step 6: Select one pattern and document it using the pattern template.
I think the aforementioned patterns break down into the two pattern seeds. Each can be its own pattern, though they both point to a parent

pattern that probably applies across all games that are moved between mediums or venues.

- Some changes to physical games to adapt them to a digital medium are made to compensate for aspects of a game that are lost when the game is no longer physical. Games that make this transition successfully find ways to maintain the aspects of the game that define it.

- Some changes to physical games to adapt them to a digital medium are made to take advantage of the capabilities of the new medium. Games that are successful in this transition make sure that any new features are aligned with the existing aspects of the game.

Step 7: Then think of a game that *does not* break spaces.
Gloomhaven is a tactical combat adventure board game. It is a long-form campaign-based game played over dozens of two- to four-hour sessions. The game is relatively expensive at $100 plus any expansion content. It supports one to four players and requires a large play area. The game features a persistent world and many complex mechanics.

Step 8: Can you apply the pattern to that game?
Yes. Clearly, the adaptation of this game to a tablet-based or computer-based medium could have many advantages, but would be a complex process. Successfully adapting this game for a digital format would require a deep understanding of the tabletop design space, the intended player experience, and the digital design space.

Step 9: What effect do you think you will create by breaking spaces in that game? Frame this effect as the problem for your pattern.
Adapting this game well could enhance the narrative and world-building aspects of the game and alleviate the difficulty of "getting the game to the table" or finding the time, space, and friends to play with. It could also make the game much easier to learn.

The biggest dangers would be avoiding the temptation to just turn it into a co-op fantasy action-adventure game or even a turn-based strategy game. Part of the adaptation would be looking at all of the systems in the game and seeing what could be automated without eliminating all the interesting player choices.

It would be important to preserve the sense of a persistent world, and to either make the play time of each encounter short enough to fit into a mobile play session or allow the turns of an encounter to be played out asynchronously. You would also want to take advantage of the digital medium to include things like voiced non-player characters (NPCs) and an enhanced visual presentation of the ever-changing world map, while still showing that the players are responsible for the changes to the world.

To frame the way that this pattern informs the design of this kind of adaptation, I would say: "When moving a game from one medium or venue to another, many things about that game will change. While some of those may be obvious, it can be difficult to understand what must and what must not be changed and why."

Step 10: You may repeat steps 6–9 for each pattern you observed in step 5.

Pattern

Name: Know Your Past, Know Your Future, Know Yourself
Confidence: 2
Image:

FIGURE 11.1 What parts of a game do you need to keep when you adapt it, and what parts change or disappear?

Author: Chris Barney

Design problem: When moving a game from one medium or venue to another, many things about a game will change. While some of those may be obvious, it can be difficult to understand what must and what must not be changed and why.

Description: When moving a game from one platform or venue to another, a designer must understand the design of the game, the existing playspace, and the target playspace. Merely understanding the game to be adapted is not sufficient.

Some aspects of the game will exist to serve a particular purpose that's intrinsic to the starting medium and won't function the same way in the new medium, or should be replaced by techniques that serve the same purpose more effectively in the new medium.

For example, in a tactical board game, a player may select a unit to attack with, then choose what ability to use, then roll some dice, count the successes, and calculate damage. That whole process might be replaced by a real-time combat system, where the player presses a button to attack a nearby enemy and damage is dealt automatically. That might seem to achieve the same effect, but several points of player strategy have now been replaced with reflex-based action or moved from player control to game logic. If the purpose of combat in the original game is player tactics and strategy, then any implementation in the new medium should allow the same tactical and strategic choice for the player.

Additionally, the designer must understand the design space of the new medium in order to select techniques from it that preserve the game's intent when implementing that game's mechanics in the new venue. The danger here is the temptation to add unnecessary techniques from the new medium, just because they're expected or common within the target medium.

For example, progression systems are common in tactical games in a digital medium, but it would be a mistake to try to add progression systems to an adaptation of chess. Likewise, a musical score or battle sound effects would add little to that kind of game. More useful would be features that let you explore possible move paths and rewind games to explore and develop your strategic skill, or an AI that could comment on the moves you were making, helping you understand the game more deeply.

To successfully move a game from one medium or venue to another, a designer must consider each element of the game's original design and assess whether it serves a purpose intrinsic to the game or is the result of a context-specific implementation. Then they must consider the target medium and whether the element will function in the same way in the new medium. If it won't, then they must find a new element that will serve the same purpose in the new medium. Even if the existing technique suffices, they must consider whether there's a more effective element in the new medium. Further, a designer must be cautious of adding any new elements to the game, and only do so if those elements strengthen the game.

Games that use this pattern and how:

- *Magic: The Gathering*—There have been several iterations on a digital adaptation for this collectible card game. Each iteration has implemented the basic mechanics of the physical game. All of them use music and sound effects that fit the setting or replicate the sounds of cards in the physical game. The visuals of the earlier games replicate the physical game, and only embellish to indicate information like what cards are playable or are being targeted. All versions include single-player modes that match the player against AI opponents and also contain narrative content; these serve as tutorials and training for new players. The most recent iteration, *Magic: The Gathering Arena*, differs from the physical game more in presentation, though the mechanics are the same. It provides 3D interpretations of creatures and distinct spell effects. This may have been done to compete with other similar digital collectible card games (CCGs) such as Hearthstone. Online multiplayer is the focus of these games, and the business model of selling card packs has been implemented here using microtransactions. Most important, the design focus of card-collecting, deck-building, and competitive play is reflected in most design choices.
- *Labyrinth*—The physical version of this game is focused on creating a challenging, reflex-based puzzle. The digital implementation of this game manages to faithfully capture this experience. The digital version, however, takes advantage of the ability to add many levels, implementing more complicated pinball-like mechanics and puzzles. All of the additions to the game help to create the same kind of kinesthetic puzzle experience as the physical game.
- *Warhammer Quest 2*—There have been many digital adaptations of this franchise of miniatures combat games. This specific implementation focuses on capturing the small-scale strategic combat of the physical game in a single-player context. While this implementation doesn't seek to recreate the totality of what's possible with the physical game, it takes advantage of the ability to automate the bookkeeping aspects of the game and provides enemy AI to make the game accessible to single players. Additionally, the single-player focus allows for more narrative content that draws on the complex world-building of the physical game.

Seed: Breaking Spaces Patterns: Tabletop to Tablet
Related patterns:
Parent patterns: None.*

---

* This may be a top-level pattern. I cannot think of any exercise in this book that would reliably generate a parent for this pattern. Can you?

Child patterns:

SUGGESTED EXERCISES

Use **Exercise 7: Player Experience Patterns** to generate a pattern based on an element from a game that you're considering moving to a new platform. If you were moving chess to a digital form, you might choose turn-based movement. If you were moving *Candy Crush* to a virtual reality (VR) platform, you might choose the top-down camera perspective. When you're done, consider the resulting pattern and see if it applies to your new platform. If the pattern helps you translate the player experience between platforms, then add it as a child here.

Keywords: Venue, Adaptation, Tablet, Board Game

PLAYER MANIPULATION PATTERNS

A word of caution regarding player manipulation: patterns generated by this exercise can go very wrong for a variety of reasons. If we look with clear eyes, we have to admit that almost everything we do as designers is intended to manipulate the player. Mechanics are supposed to make the player feel powerful or vulnerable. Narrative exists to provoke a desire for revenge, or love and sympathy for an NPC. Most of the time, the player goes into the game fully aware of what they're in for. In a sense, this is one of the primary reasons that we consume media, whether it's music that makes us cry, or a book that spurs us to political action, or a movie that makes us believe in heroes and have hope. We line up and consent to be manipulated.

But when we as developers have those tools in our hands, we're often tempted to use them in the most effective way possible, and often that can mean using these patterns and techniques in ways that the player is not expecting. This calls back to the example of *Spec Ops: The Line* from the Introduction. That whole game is based on making the player believe they are playing one sort of game in order to confront them about the experience they have been having. The player is manipulated into enjoying the shooter gameplay, then is gradually made uncomfortable with that enjoyment as the tropes that support it are stripped away. Finally, in the game's big reveal, the developers admit that they have been lying to and manipulating the player the whole time. The moment is effective and powerful, and I fully support the developers' choice to engage in this type of manipulation. That said, there's a legitimate ethical question that you need to ask every time you choose to manipulate the player in a way that they may not be aware of: How are your manipulations going to affect the player? Can they cause harm? As a designer, you have to make the choice as to whether the potential harm your emotional or psychological manipulations might cause is justified and ethical. All I can ask is that you make it openly and intentionally.

Pattern Purpose

Since we're trying to create a player experience with the games we design, the behavior of players in response to our games is a critical component. Player experience can differ from the expected in two main ways: when players behave differently from what the developers expect, and when the developers cause players to behave in ways that they would not have expected to. Looking at these two possibilities leads to two very different sets of patterns. This exercise will focus on distilling patterns that allow the developer to understand what causes these unexpected experiences.

EXERCISE 14: PLAYER MANIPULATION PATTERNS (APPLYING EMOTIONAL PATTERNS)

Step 1: Pick an experience from a game that you weren't expecting. It can be an emotion, like surprise, sadness, regret, or greed. Or it can be a more complex concept, like understanding that teamwork is the only way to win in a game where there is player conflict. To differentiate this exercise from Emotional Patterns (Exercise 6) or Player Experience Patterns (Exercise 7), be sure to choose something that surprised you. Remember, one of the keys to player manipulation is subverting expectations.

Step 2: List and describe ten games that create the same effect, *whether it's unexpected or not.* This process will help you separate patterns of player manipulation from simpler emotional patterns.

Step 3: For each game, describe the techniques that it uses to create that effect, and whether the effect was expected or unexpected.

Step 4: List and describe the patterns you see in the techniques that these games use.

Step 5: Pick one pattern and describe it using the Pattern Template.

Step 6: Think of a game that *does not* produce the effect you chose.

Step 7: If you can imagine how to apply the pattern you identified in step 5, describe that process.

Step 8: If you cannot complete step 7, then pick a different game in step 6.

Step 9: If you fail to complete step 7 several times, discard your pattern from step 5 and proceed to step 6 with the new pattern.

Example Player Manipulation Pattern
Exercise

Step 1: Pick an experience from a game that you weren't expecting.
BioShock. The thirst for revenge. I was not expecting the motivation that the first half of the game set me up to feel when I discovered that I had been manipulated.

Step 2: List ten games that create that effect.

- *BioShock*—First-person shooter.

- *Max Payne*—Third-person shooter.

- *God of War*—Third-person spectacle fighter.

- *Legacy of Kain: Soul Reaver*—Third-person action.

- *Prototype*—Third-person action.

- *Phantasy Star IV* — Turn-based RPG.

- *Red Dead Redemption*—Third-person open world.

- *Soulcalibur*—Fighting game.

- *Werewolf*—Social deduction party game.

- *The Prisoner's Dilemma*—Game theory problem.

Step 3: For each game, describe the ways that it creates that effect.

- *BioShock*—The player is misled by their main contact during the first half of the game and spends the second half trying to get revenge on their betrayer. This is effective, as the player has been misled as much as the character has.

- *Max Payne*—As a player, you're quickly immersed in the character's world, both narratively and through the intro gameplay. Then you're put into a level where you're unable to stop the murder of the character's wife and child. There are significant social problems with this narrative, and a game made today would undoubtedly receive deserved criticism. Nevertheless, the introductory sequence effectively connects your motivations as a player to the character's obsessive drive for revenge by making you feel powerless at the game's start. Of course, sexist if genre-consistent tropes are layered on top of this mechanical motivation. The bullet time effect, where time slows down and you can execute the impossible feats of marksmanship commonly seen in John Woo movies, creates the scenes of slaughter that are in keeping with the character's descent into obsession, madness, and violent revenge. There is some indication that the player should question or object to the actions of the character.

- *God of War*—The character's family is immediately murdered. The plot reasons for this are somewhat convoluted, but the character has an immediate and extreme obsession with vengeance. The player may sympathize with the character, but it's the over-the-top violent gameplay, which is very well-executed, that motivates the player to take the extremely violent actions that the character desires. Ludonarrative dissonance is often cited as an issue with games, i.e., the problem of core gameplay not being congruent with the story a game is telling. In the case of *God of War*, there's a strong sense of what might be called *ludonarrative resonance*. There's little indication that the player should object to the actions of the character in the early parts of the game. The character's actions are called more into question in later installments of the franchise.

- *Legacy of Kain: Soul Reaver*—Early in the game, the character is betrayed and turned into a vampire. The character's quest for revenge frames the early part of the game, until they discover that they have been manipulated and then seek revenge on the person who was manipulating them. Later, the character's motivations shift yet again when they discover the reasons for their manipulation. At the end of the game, the player is given a choice: save the world, or in some sense betray the game and become evil. The constant misdirection in this game sets up the player to want to make this choice—as revenge on the developers for jerking them around for 30 hours! Later games in the series canonize this choice.

- *Prototype*—The character is the product of an experiment that has turned him into a violent killing machine with superpowers. Over the course of the game, he destroys a good portion of the city and kills hundreds of soldiers and bystanders in the pursuit of revenge. Using his destructive powers is core to the gameplay, and is well implemented and intended to be fun. The wanton destruction is in line with the personality of the character. There are strong indications that the character's actions are problematic, but no real option to act differently.

- *Phantasy Star IV*—Although the full plot of this game is not driven by revenge, the first section builds a relationship between the main character and his mentor, and she is later killed at a dramatically appropriate point. The scene is effective because the player has spent a lot of time getting to know the mentor.

- *Red Dead Redemption*—The theme of revenge is realized in a complex way in this game. The character is forced to undertake a series of morally questionable missions by a government agency that's holding his family hostage. This results in a simple quest-giver structure, but also gives time for the player to develop resentment for the agency and watch the character suffer. Eventually, the main character is killed and is unable to enact his revenge, but the player takes control of the character's son and kills those responsible for holding him hostage and killing his father. Essentially, the player gets to directly experience all of the actions that inspire revenge.

- *Soulcalibur*—Revenge is occasionally cited in the backstories of the characters in this game, but for the players, it is one of the primary motivators. As this is primarily a two-player competitive game, half of the players lose each time it's played. Calls for one more game or best two out of three are standard. The thirst for revenge is generated directly in the players, and the game strives to make the player feel like next time they might win.

- *Werewolf*—The primary driver of this game is social deception. There's little explicit call for revenge in the setting of the game, but in repeated play, characters who are killed by "the werewolves" (or "the mafia" or "the witches") typically seek revenge on the players they were betrayed by in the previous game.

- *The Prisoner's Dilemma* (iterative)—In the iterative version of this classic game theory construct, a player is influenced in their choices by the past actions of the other player. With no outside influences on the players' choices, their distrust and the logic governing their actions very closely resemble a thirst for revenge. When this element is introduced into a game with outside factors that should influence the player *not* to pursue revenge, this becomes even more evident as players pursue their desire for revenge even against the logical factors that make it a suboptimal choice.

Step 4: List and describe the patterns you see in the techniques that these games use.

- Coercive Ludonarrative Resonance—I use this term to mean the case when the gameplay and the narrative are in alignment, but the experience of the character and player are not in alignment. In this scenario, the character's narrative forces the player to recontextualize their experience of the gameplay.

- I'll Miss Our Time Together—The player is given time to bond with an NPC so that they will have a stronger emotional reaction to the loss of that NPC.

- Next Time, Gadget!—A primarily multiplayer pattern where the loss of a game is the primary motivation for playing again.

Step 5: Pick one pattern and describe it using the pattern template.
Coercive Ludonarrative Resonance

Step 6: Think of a game that *does not* produce that effect.
Super Mario Bros.

Step 7: If you can imagine how to apply the pattern you identified in step 5, describe that process.
In this game, Mario is motivated by a damsel in distress trope, but Mario shows little reaction to either the enemies that are responsible for kidnapping the princess or the non-diegetic message that she's in another castle at the end of each level. A few simple changes to the game's sound design, such as sounds of disgust when he crushes Goombas or sounds of frustration when the princess is yet again not where he expected to find her, could show Mario's emotional reactions.

I think these kinds of changes would probably give Mario more depth of character, but they would also undermine the game's light tone. For any game, it's worth considering whether the game's themes would make it a darker and less fun experience. If so, you should think about whether those themes and tropes are the best choices.

Step 8: If you cannot complete step 7, pick a different game in step 6.

Step 9: If you fail to complete step 7 several times, discard your pattern from step 5 and proceed to step 6 with the new pattern.

Pattern

Name: Coercive Ludonarrative Resonance
Confidence: 3
Image:

FIGURE 11.2   When gameplay and narrative are aligned the player may find themself pulled into an experience they didn't expect.

Author: Chris Barney
Design problem: Sometimes as a designer, you want to give the player a sense of empathy for a character's experience that the player may not be familiar with or predisposed to. For example, a player may not know what it's like to have a murderous thirst for vengeance, or a suicidal sense of despair and loneliness.
Description: To help align the experience of the player with the experience of the character, a designer may wish to create gameplay that is enjoyable for the player, but that also aligns with the experience of the character. By performing the gameplay actions required to complete the game and watching the consequences of those actions play out for the character, the player can get a sense of responsibility for, and participation in, the state of the character.

As with all patterns that manipulate a player, this is a delicate technique. It's very easy to create situations where the player will become uncomfortable, and either not wish to continue the game or become genuinely upset with the game and the developer. If the designer is not always aware of the potential experiences of the player, it's possible to unintentionally use this pattern in cases where the developer is aligning the mechanics of the game and its narrative. This may be the case in the example of *God of War* (see later).

As the example games show, the more aware of and prepared for the narrative and mechanical experience of the game that players are, the more comfortable they will be with having their experience shaped by the ludonarrative resonance.

Games that use this pattern and how:

- *Max Payne*—The game uses various techniques to create a situation where the character is seeking revenge and willing to kill anyone and do anything to get it. The smooth shooting mechanics and satisfying bullet-time mechanics make the process of enacting the character's revenge "fun" for the player. But the scale and intensity of the violence become uncomfortable for the player, highlighting the character's instability and obsession—an effect the narrative intends.
- *God of War*—Again using some pretty heavy-handed tropes about violence against women and children and the expected masculine response, the first *God of War* game places the character on a path of bloody vengeance. The combat gameplay is extremely well implemented and satisfying, allowing the player to guide the character along an ever-escalating path of violence. This is in keeping with the narrative, and for many players is a satisfying and cathartic experience. However, players who enjoy the action gameplay but are uncomfortable with the depicted actions and motivations of the character find themselves increasingly caught between having fun and causing actions through their gameplay that they find unacceptable, even in a fictional narrative.
- *Spec Ops: The Line*—This game sets up a military first-person shooter experience narratively and mechanically. As the game progresses, it shifts the narrative to call the mechanics of the game into question. There are many mechanics in the game, and the character who is in alignment with them performs them unselfconsciously. The player may or may not be comfortable with these mechanics or the narrative. Late in the game, the character's perspective shifts, and he becomes aware of the horror of his actions. This either releases the player from the tension they had been feeling between their objection to the narrative and mechanics, or explicitly shows them that they should have been experiencing this kind of discomfort.

- *Dear Esther*—The slow, meditative gameplay, linear-level progress, and pacing of narrative exposition work together to give the player the experience of a sad and tired man at the end of his life. The game's unavoidable conclusion in the suicide of the character confronts the player with the choice of accepting or rejecting the narrative and gameplay experience they have had.
- *Virginia*—The experience of this game is created by unifying the difficult and limiting experience of being a professional woman working in a male-dominated world in the 1970s with gameplay that limits the player's control over their experience of the game. I found this extremely effective after recognizing what was happening during the first scene of the game. Other players who did not recognize the reasons for the gameplay limitations did not understand that their frustration with the game was intended to mirror the frustration of the character.
- *Hellblade: Senua's Sacrifice*—The narrative of this game focuses on mental illness and the pain it can cause in someone's life. The mechanics of the game create an ongoing dread of dying using a threat that the player may lose all progress if they die too often. It creates a sense of obsessive searching for imaginary signs in the world around you by asking the player to line up objects in perspective to form arbitrary symbols. And it creates a sense of panic by periodically plunging the character into a world on fire and forcing them to escape by running blindly through the flames. The game is explicit about the kind of experience it's seeking to create, and players who engage with the game get what they signed up for.

Seed: Exercise 14: Player Manipulation Patterns—The Thirst for Revenge
Related patterns:
Parent patterns:

SUGGESTED EXERCISE

Use **Exercise 24: Theoretical Patterns** to generate a pattern based on Brenda Romero's talk "The Mechanic is the Message" (Symonds 2013).

Child patterns:
We're Going To A Dark Place Together* (Confidence: 2)—The sense of investment in the character that Coercive Ludonarrative Resonance produces is necessary or very helpful when implementing this pattern.

Just Look At What You've Become† (Confidence: 3)—For character progression to be believable as transformation, the mechanical and narrative changes must be aligned as described in Coercive Ludonarrative Resonance.

---

* Example pattern for Exercise 10: Boss Encounter Patterns.
† Example pattern for Exercise 25: Creating Patterns from Lenses.

SUGGESTED EXERCISES

Use **Exercise 6: Emotional Patterns** to generate a pattern based on shame.

Use **Exercise 6: Emotional Patterns** to generate a pattern based on schadenfreude.

Keywords: Player Manipulation, Mechanics, Narrative

PATTERNS IN INNOVATION

Pattern Purpose

This exercise looks at the ways that games are innovative and uncovers the patterns they use to create that innovation. As always with these exercises, the purpose is not merely to identify the innovative elements in specific games, but rather to see what underlies them. Noticing an innovative game and replicating that successful innovation has a higher chance of producing a viable game than simply trying something completely new and untested. Applying this process may seem counterintuitive here, and indeed, it won't inherently create innovation—it may only ever make your game be the second to do something. That may be preferable to true innovation if you're concerned with the viability of your game. The real purpose of this exercise, though, is to look deeper than a specific mechanic or technique and discover how that technique produced innovation.

I've designed this exercise to help developers understand what things allow some innovations to be more successful than others. By completing this exercise, and applying the patterns you uncover, you will increase the chances that the innovations you devise will succeed in producing the effects you intend. These patterns will not hand you new techniques that are magically guaranteed to produce successful innovative games, but they will help you choose and assess the innovations you're considering.

EXERCISE 15: PATTERNS IN INNOVATION

Step 1: Make a list of at least ten of the most unusual games you can think of.
Step 2: List the things that those games have in common.*
Step 3: Pick and describe one item from your list in step 2.

---

* The similarity doesn't necessarily have to be in the thing that is unusual about the games. Noting a mundane thing that is shared by many innovative games may still lead to a pattern that will help you be innovative.

Step 4: For each game you listed in step 1, list and describe the techniques that game uses to achieve the effect you picked in step 3.
Step 5: List and describe the patterns that you see in the use of those techniques.
Step 6: Pick one of these patterns and document it using the Pattern Template.
Step 7: You may repeat step 6 for each pattern you identified.

Example pattern
Exercise

Step 1: Make a list of the ten most unusual games you can think of.

I arrived at a list of 17 games to start with. Since they are very different, I decided to list commonalities from as many games as possible and then eliminate the games that seem to be unusual for different reasons.

White Death, Death Stranding, ~~Beat Saber,~~ *Disco Elysium,* ~~Johann Sebastian Joust,~~ *Persona 5, Kingdom Death: Monster,* ~~Starwhal,~~ ~~Katamari Damacy,~~ *The Stanley Parable, The Path, Pathologic, Virginia, Catherine, The Void, Dear Esther, Nier: Automata*

Step 2: List the things that those games have in common.

Unusual story (narrative premise), unusual core mechanic, combination of genres, unusual control scheme, abstract or intellectual meaning

Step 3: Pick and describe one item from your list.

Abstract or intellectual meaning—Many games that are *not* innovative have abstract or intellectual meanings. *BioShock* and *Torment: Tides of Numenera,* for instance, are wonderful games with deep themes, but they are simply exceptional instances of established game forms. There are certainly also games that are innovative that either have little narrative coherence or are concerned with more common themes. However, of the 17 games I listed, 13 have abstract or intellectual meanings. I was trying to list games that are both unusual and to some degree "good games,"* which is to say that they at least have good gameplay and aren't just strange for the sake of being strange. Those with any narrative coherence exhibit

---

* See the fifteen fundamental properties of wholeness in Chapter 13 for more detail on what might be objectively considered a "good game."

abstract or intellectual meanings. The others focus on gameplay to the almost complete exclusion of narrative.

Step 4: For each game you listed in step 1, list and describe the techniques that game uses to achieve the effect you picked in step 3.

- *White Death*—This live-action game uses the combination of several mechanics to cause players to behave in strange ways that are emotionally evocative. These mechanics are a pairing of an emotional state and a physical limitation, such as "you feel superior to everyone taller than you" and "you must keep your hands on the floor." In addition, the game is played in a small, lit area in a dark room, and features melancholy vocal music by artists such as Nick Cave and Johnny Cash. The narrative premise is that the characters are trapped in a cold place and slowly freezing to death. As the game progresses, they are "freed" from their bodies by the players who have already died. What emerges from this set of mechanics and this theming is a harrowing game about letting go of the things that cause us pain. The narrative is tightly coupled to, and supportive of, the mechanics in producing the meaning.

- *Death Stranding*—Mechanically, this game is a literal walking simulator. Narratively, it is a story about uniting a post-apocalyptic America by traveling across it on foot, and physically and socially connecting the survivors. The meaning of the game is conveyed both through its mechanics and through somewhat heavy-handed narrative exposition.

- *Disco Elysium*—This game is perhaps about the psychological origins of self-destructive behavior, the potential for redemption, and the process of putting yourself back together after hitting rock bottom. The core gameplay loop seems not to be particularly innovative. Still, the way that the game validates the player making strange character choices that they might avoid in other games is unique and creates a narrative that is among the strangest that I have seen.

- *Persona 5*—Each game in the *Persona* series explores different aspects of the self through the lens of characters that manifest the archetypes of those aspects to battle evil. The games include mechanics that define those aspects through the social relationships of the characters. In this way, the mechanics are tightly coupled with the visual and narrative metaphors. *Persona 5* is the most polished and sophisticated example and the most easily available now.

- *Kingdom Death: Monster*—This board game combines a city-building mechanic, monsters with complex behaviors, and characters that both become important to the players and die often to create an emergent narrative that explores the search for meaning in a nihilistic universe. The AI systems for the creatures are revolutionary, but they stand out even more here because they help create the emergent narrative that builds player connection to the characters.

- *The Stanley Parable*—This game starts with the mechanical tropes of the first-person shooter genre and extrapolates the meanings those mechanics have, then walks the player through the absurdist results.

- *The Path*—This is a short game with the mechanic of walking down the path "to grandmother's house" from the story of *Little Red Riding Hood*. The player may either stay on the path or explore the woods as each of seven young girls that represent different archetypes. The storytelling is done exclusively through environmental narrative and a brief, cryptic cutscene at the end of each girl's journey. The slow pace of the game serves to give the player time to think about the meaning of the things they see. Much of the meaning is metaphorical.

- *Pathologic*—This complex Russian game focuses on themes of the nature of evil, the price of totalitarianism, and the search for self-worth, among others. The gameplay has a survival horror feel, with a focus on managing scarce resources and iterative play. Those mechanics reinforce both explicit and environmental narrative. It uses visual and narrative metaphor, and is symbolism heavily.

- *The Void*—This game is also by IcePick Lodge, the creators of *Pathologic*. Both the theme and gameplay are intentionally opaque, and the game is designed as a method for contemplating its own meaning, and perhaps the meaning of a poem by the Russian poet Maximilian Voloshin. Again, limited resources and repetitive gameplay expose the player to symbolic imagery and events over and over.

- *Virginia*—The themes of this game arise from the experience of being a marginalized person in a position of responsibility. The mechanics of the game are subtractive, which is to say that they start with mechanics that are common and expected, then strip them away to create feelings of limitation in the player that mirror those of the character.

- *Catherine**—The narrative and meaning of this game focus on masculine fragility, and present a reductive and negative view of women driven by the main character's fear. The platforming mechanics of the game create a tense environment where these themes play out. The character/player's actions are also tracked in a second, dating-sim-like portion of the game, and a variety of endings are possible based on the player's choices. However, those choices seem to reflect the real-life actuality of the fears depicted in the game.

- *Dear Esther*—The gameplay is simple exploration in a covertly linear world, exposing the player to narrative and visual beats in the form of voice-over and environmental narrative. Eventually, the player enacts the character's suicide and watches as his soul soars free of the pain that was his solitude at the end of his life.

- *Nier: Automata*—Intense action gameplay engages the player in combat and destruction against a robotic enemy, while the environmental and explicit narrative delve into the futility of war and the nature of being human. The game is also iterative, and different meanings are revealed each time a section of the game is repeated.

Step 5: List and describe the patterns that you see in the use of those techniques.

Games that have an innovative mechanic often use it to emphasize a deeper meaning that is created by the narrative framing of the game. This suggests that the innovative mechanics may have been conceived to support the deeper meaning. Or, that successfully creating deeper meaning in a game requires mechanics that go beyond those that are common in games that don't share that meaning.

Step 6: Pick one of these patterns and document it using the Pattern Template.

I only synthesized a single pattern out of this portion of the exercise.

---

* To say that *Cathrine* is problematic is an understatement; see this article from *Slate* (Auerbach 2014). However, it is an innovative game that uses its narrative and mechanics together to make a statement (Rochefort 2017). Understanding how it does that is valuable, regardless of the problematic nature of its meaning.

Step 7: You may repeat step 6 for each pattern you identified.
While I only arrived at one pattern, it would be worth considering these games in the light of the other commonalities listed in step 2: unusual story (narrative premise), unusual core mechanic, combination of genres, unusual control scheme

Pattern

Name: There Had Better Be a Very Good Explanation for This
Confidence: 2
Image:

FIGURE 11.3 When a crafting mechanic is tied to themes of survival it becomes a compelling part of the game's core purpose.

Author: Chris Barney
Design problem: As gamers and game designers mature, the desire to create and experience more meaningful games increases, but the existing vocabulary of mechanics and narrative structures seems to impose limitations.
Description: To support deeper and more complex narrative meaning, designers may need to devise new mechanics that support the meanings they wish to create. Many games that succeed at creating a deeper meaning also introduce innovative mechanics to support that meaning.

If you're attempting to build a game around an innovative mechanic, it's useful to think about what meanings that mechanic might support. The new mechanic may seem strange and unapproachable on its own, but when seen in the context of a supporting narrative, it can create a powerful experience for the player.

If you're designing a game that has a deeper meaning, think about whether established mechanics are sufficient to support it. If they are not, then explore new mechanics. If you create those mechanics in support of the understood narrative and user experience, they're more likely to succeed.

In either case, any new mechanics or narrative structures you conceive of should be carefully playtested as early and as often as possible, as our conception of a new mechanic's effect often does not survive its first contact with a player.

Games that use this pattern and how:

- *Death Stranding*—Narratively, this is a story about connecting a post-apocalyptic America by traveling across it on foot and socially connecting the survivors. The meaning of the game is conveyed both through its mechanics and through somewhat heavy-handed narrative exposition. Mechanically, this game is a literal walking simulator, but the mechanics of walking and carrying supplies have been built out to a degree never seen in a game before. The moment-to-moment gameplay loop is just managing your ability to walk. The consequences of carrying and delivering goods are also extremely robust, from the detailed reports you see of every delivery you make, to the development of routes that you travel, to the social responses of the characters receiving your deliveries.
- *Virginia*—The themes of this game arise from the experience of being a marginalized person in a position of responsibility. The mechanics of the game are subtractive, which is to say that they start with mechanics that are common and expected and then strip them away to create feelings of limitation in the player that mirror those of the character. When players experience the game, they are expecting a particular set of mechanics and the effects those mechanics have. Taking away the mechanic has the result of taking away the expected effect.
- *Dear Esther*—The gameplay is simple exploration in a covertly linear world, exposing the player to narrative and visual beats in the form of voice-over and environmental narrative. Eventually, the player enacts the character's suicide and watches as his soul soars free of the pain that was his solitude at the end of his life. The innovation in this game was in removing the common gameplay elements of a first-person game and leaving only the exploration, environmental narrative, and voiced exposition. The player has only the choice of whether to complete the game: that this is the only choice is the very point of the narrative.

Seed: Exercise 15: Patterns in Innovation—Abstract or intellectual meaning
Related patterns:
Parent patterns:

SUGGESTED EXERCISE

Use **Exercise 25: Creating Patterns from Lenses** to generate a pattern based on the idea of "unified design" from Lens #11 in *The Art of Game Design* (Schell 2020). I suggested this exercise in Exercise 5; if you completed it there, then look to see if the pattern you generated fits as a parent here. If you did not take on the suggested exercise at that point, take the pattern you produced by completing it now and see if it fits as a parent to *Fight Like You Live** and *Bringing About the Apocalypse†*.

Child pattern:
I See Where You Are Going With This‡ (Confidence: 2)—Use this pattern when trying to create context and supporting mechanics for innovative mechanics that you have created by implementing There Had Better Be a Very Good Explanation for This.

SUGGESTED EXERCISE

Use **Exercise 7: Player Experience Patterns** to generate a pattern for learning new mechanics. Pick games that are teaching new or unusual mechanics well. Use this pattern to guide your introduction of the mechanics called for by There Had Better Be a Very Good Explanation for This.

Keywords: Narrative, Meaning, Mechanics, Innovation

---

* Example pattern from Exercise 5: Functional Patterns.
† Example pattern from Exercise 8: Theme Patterns.
‡ Example pattern from Exercise 24: Theoretical Patterns.

V

The Fifteen Properties

CHAPTER 12

Taking a Step Back

What We Have Learned So Far

O VER THE COURSE OF the previous 15 exercises, you should have had a chance to apply much of the theory presented in the first sections of this book. You should have, at this point, completed each of those exercises at least once. You have seen at least my 15 example patterns, and if you're working in a class or with a group of other developers, you will have seen many more.

It's likely that you've noticed things that these patterns have in common. Some of those things are higher-level patterns. You may eventually choose to document those patterns: that is an important part of the process of converting your patterns into a Pattern Language and is covered in detail in a later section of the book.

Beyond those directly implied parent patterns, you may be seeing properties that various patterns have in common even when they seem to be in no way related. In my experience of developing and writing the patterns I've used in my teaching, and of writing this book, I began to feel the need to find a consistent language to use when expressing these shared properties.

Frankly, I found this irritating, as I have worked very hard *not* to invent and promote new jargon and terminology. The industry might benefit from a shared vocabulary, but the way to get there is not for me to become yet another developer insisting that my words are the best words.

Nevertheless, I found myself wanting to clearly express these properties that were becoming evident. At this point you may be feeling the same, or if not, you should at least be comfortable enough with the process to be ready to look at these properties.

Turning once again to the work of Christopher Alexander, I found the concepts that I was struggling with clearly articulated. The following chapter discusses them in detail.

CHAPTER 13

The "Fifteen Fundamental Properties of Wholeness" in Game Design

A s a game designer, I find it very appealing to center my work and my understanding of design on the precept that design can be "good." To do that, and not have it just be a matter of opinion or esthetic preference, there must be a rubric by which I can evaluate the design and know, not only whether it's valid or functional, but whether it is good.

In *A Pattern Language*, Christopher Alexander describes good architecture as having what he calls "the nameless quality." He sometimes refers to this quality as "wholeness," and later in his work as "life." In English, this sounds a bit strange, but in German, the word *lebendig* is used to describe the "aliveness" of nonliving things (Leitner 2020).*

Alexander continued to work and evolve his theories about design long after completing his work from *A Pattern Language*. In his later work, *The Nature of Order: The Phenomenon of Life* (Alexander 2004), he proposes "fifteen fundamental properties of wholeness." The website of the TKWA

---

* German is a bit complicated in the way that words can change to be different parts of speech and the word *leben*, or "life," can become *lebendig*, or "lively," or become the noun *Lebendigkeit*, which can be used to describe inanimate things.

Urban Lab has an excellent discussion of these properties (Kubala 2020a). In this book, Alexander lists these properties as

> levels of scale—strong centers—boundaries—alternating repetition—positive space—good shape—local symmetries—deep interlock—contrast—graded variation—roughness—echoes—the void—inner calm—not separateness

These properties are all rather abstract concepts, but they are powerful, and after spending the time to understand them, you will begin to see them everywhere. At this point, late in Alexander's career, his concern was exploring the ways that different aspects of the universe embody the property of life. By "life," he does not mean the biological processes of being alive, but something closer to the German word *Lebendigkeit*. This is the nameless quality that he describes in *A Pattern Language*—the quality that makes spaces or things whole. By his definition, something that has that nameless quality is

> alive—whole—eternal—comfortable—free—exact—egoless—not simply beauty—not only fitness for purpose—slightly bitter

Those ten words or phrases, ultimately, are Alexander's rubric for judging whether a design is good. Designs that contain a high density of the fifteen fundamental properties of wholeness embody the words that make up the nameless quality.

Again, all of that can seem very abstract, subjective, and perhaps even spiritual, but I don't think that's the case. Assessing design to determine whether it is good is, and should be, difficult. But I agree with Alexander that it is something you must do deliberately and precisely. I do not know if Alexander's fifteen properties are a sufficient vocabulary to describe the kind of dynamic, interactive design that we do as game designers. But I do think that it is an excellent place to start.

Jesse Schell gave a talk about Alexander's fifteen properties, titled "The Nature of Order in Game Narrative" (Schell 2018), at the Game Developers Conference in 2018. In this talk, he applies the fifteen fundamental properties to narrative design in games. I recommend listening to it; his analysis is excellent, and the conference session is available for free. Listening to his talk made it clear to me that there is value in trying to understand how the fundamental properties apply not just to narrative but to games in general.

Later, I'll describe Alexander's properties and the nameless quality as they apply to game design. But before I can do that, I must explain those words he uses to describe the nameless quality and describe them in game design terms:

- Alive—The game is complex and dynamic. It doesn't feel static or fixed. The act of playing the game is one of discovery and meaning.

- Whole—All of the parts of a game, i.e., its mechanics and its visual and narrative elements, work together to create a unified experience for the player.

- Comfortable—It feels good to play the game. The subject matter is not necessarily pleasant, but the act of playing the game feels like something you should do and want to do.

- Free—All aspects of the game are there because they are an intrinsic part of the game, not because other games have them. Players can play the game without feeling hampered by mechanics or tropes that act against the intent of the game.

- Exact—Every aspect of the game serves the designer's intended purpose, and the player understands that purpose.

- Egoless—The game does the things necessary to serve its purpose, to have its intended effect. It does not include esthetics or systems to make itself more appealing to an audience if those systems hinder its core design.

- Eternal—The game will continue to serve its purpose beyond the current technology cycle. The success of the game at achieving its design goals is not dependent on any current fad in mechanics, genre, or visuals.

- Not simply beauty—The game has substance beyond the appeal of its presentation. Playing the game makes an impression on the player.

- Not only fitness for purpose—The game has a depth of intent; its designers realized that it's not "just for fun." It accepts that all games have meaning, and the game acknowledges and embraces the depth of its meaning.

- Slightly bitter—Playing the game has weight; the actions of the player and the character feel like they have consequences. The game leaves the player thinking about the experience long after they have stopped playing.

Keep the understanding of these terms in mind as we move on to discussing the fifteen fundamental properties of wholeness as they apply to games. As we progress, you'll notice that the properties have strong relationships with one another and, in fact, are interdependent with each other. It might be possible to describe them in isolation, but that misses the point and the power of this set of concepts.

FIGURE 13.1 Not just ships, but the flying mechanic existing at three levels of scale.

LEVELS OF SCALE

Since elements of the game vary in size and scope, they should exist at multiple levels of scale. In architecture, and thus in the level design of games, the elements are spatial; they may exist in the foreground, middle distance, or on the horizon. Having levels of scale gives a sense of detail, context, and potential. It allows the inhabitant to be grounded, understand where they are, and feel a part of something larger. In the interactive context of game design, levels of scale also apply to mechanics, sound design, narrative, social design, and so on.

A game might exhibit levels of scale when placing a character next to a much larger creature, and then putting them both in the courtyard of a soaring castle that sits at the foot of a forbidding mountain. But it might also show levels of scale when a player crafts a potion, and later crafts a fortress, and still later orders the building of cities across a continent. Or it might incorporate them in allowing a player to join a party with other players to slay a monster, and also to join a guild to hold territory or support a chosen group of players in long-term play, and then thrust all of the players on a server into conflict with those on other instances of the game world.

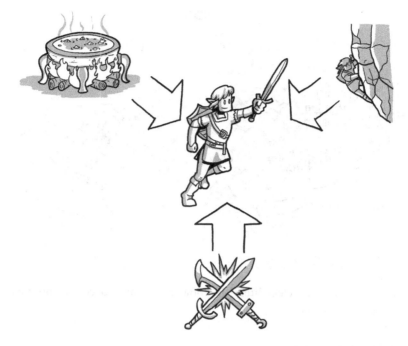

FIGURE 13.2   Each system is complete in itself and also contributes to the overall game.

STRONG CENTERS

For spaces or games to function, the elements that make them up must work together. But that statement alone is not sufficient to help designers organize their designs effectively. The idea of strong centers is that the elements of a game that interact directly should relate strongly and reinforce each other. Different groups of related systems should collectively support each other at a higher level of scale. The need for strong centers is present for the physical elements as in architecture, but it is also necessary for mechanical and narrative elements.

Strong centers can be seen in level design when the spaces a player moves through have a clear purpose both in gameplay and within the fiction of the world: a town that huddles at the edge of a desert, fully a believable town but also a place for the character to prepare for the challenges ahead. The mechanics of a game show strong centers when each mechanic is rewarding to interact with and also combines with the other mechanics of the game naturally to create an experience that feels whole, as shown in the illustration of the systems in *Zelda: Breath of the Wild*.

FIGURE 13.3 Not just clear literal boundaries in gamespace, but boundaries between game systems.

BOUNDARIES

Games consist of multiple elements of any given type: spatial, mechanical, narrative, or esthetic. The boundaries between these components or groups of components should help define and focus attention on their purpose or center.

This dynamic is analogous to architecture in the case of spatial elements, like the boundary between levels, or between desert and forest. It is equally valid for more abstract elements like narrative or mechanics. In terms of mechanics, a boundary might exist between resource gathering and spending, or between traversal and combat. Narrative boundaries might exist as plotlines, or more concretely as quests or cutscenes.

Additionally, the boundaries of one type of element are often related to those of another when they share a purpose. For instance, an environmental damage mechanic, a desert location, and the narrative beat of a character suffering regret for his past actions might all work together in a game. The boundaries of these elements, in terms of the player's experience, should also be related. Aligning these boundaries creates stronger centers.

FIGURE 13.4   Alternating repetition in the flow of gameplay.

ALTERNATING REPETITION

Repetition is frequent in games for a variety of reasons, from building player mastery to creating a rational development pipeline to the reuse of assets. By creating a pattern of alternating repetition, the designer can create rhythms in the game.

These rhythms can be visual as they are in architecture, for example, the pattern created by the repetition of window–door–window, window–door–window on a block of row houses in Baltimore. But they can also be narrative, creating story beats, or even mechanical. Consider the difference between a long string of combats and the pattern of conflict, reward, recovery. As earlier, the patterns of alternating repetition span the different elements of a game and must support each other for the best effect.

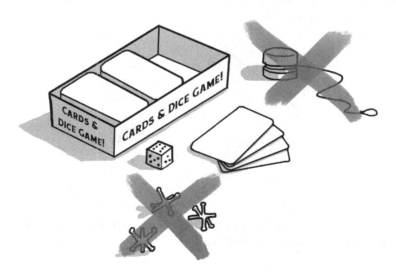

FIGURE 13.5   All the elements the game needs and only the elements that are needed.

POSITIVE SPACE

To apply the idea of positive space to games in a general way, consider "space" as a concept rather than a literal volume. The existence or presence of any element in a game takes up space within that game. Every element added to a game has positive space; all of the elements of the game together should define that game's positive space. The positive space of one element contributes to another's if they, together, support the purpose of the game at higher levels of scale.

This is true for the geometry within a level, or on a larger scale for levels within a game. The climbable buildings in *Assassin's Creed: Black Flag* create a cohesive dynamic play environment. The game's islands group those spaces into cohesive chunks, and travel between them on various ships presents a different, alternately repeating visual and spatial experience. But both the islands and the ships are part of the pirate esthetic that the game is presenting.

Positive space can also be seen in mechanics or in narrative. Looking at *Black Flag* again, the game's divergent systems of traversal, stealth, sailing, and ship-based combat all are necessary parts of the experience of the game. The most evident flaws are when there are parts of the game that do not feel necessary, such as collectibles with no narrative justification. In Alexander's words, there can be "no leftovers." If some aspect of the game is not part of the positive space of a larger level of scale, then it cannot be part of the wholeness of the game.

FIGURE 13.6 Each "shape" in the game is pleasing and fits the whole, whether it is a space, a mechanic, or a piece of the story.

GOOD SHAPE

Alexander also uses the term "adaptation" to describe good shape, such as a house that fits well into its environment. Does it serve its intended purposes, to shelter the family that lives there, act as a strong center for their lives, and situate them within their neighborhood and city? Good shape is situational. A home might have good shape for a family, but not for a lone person. Or it might have a good shape if found in one country, but poor shape in another. Centers that have the nameless quality display this "fitness for purpose," but go beyond it when they contain other properties.

At a low level of scale, understanding good shape in terms of games is easy: a space with a strong center, well-defined edges, local symmetries, and so on. Or a mechanic that is simple to use and understand, that serves a clear purpose and creates gameplay intentionally and legibly. Good shape is harder to see when the level of scale is more substantial. A game level, for example, has good shape when it has good shape as a whole and when all of its components also have good shape. A piece of the story has good shape when it is meaningful, discrete, and fits well within the larger narrative, but also contains characters that have good shape themselves.

This is the place where it is most valuable and necessary to apply the terms that Alexander uses to describe his nameless quality. Look at any element of a game and ask yourself if it is alive, whole, comfortable, and so on. Then step back and look at the systems and levels of the game, then at it in its entirety. Are all of those things still true?

Striking a block in *Beat Saber* has good shape. It's visually satisfying, the sound it makes, the slight vibration of the controller, movement of your arm, the trajectory of the sliced parts as they respond to your blow, the knowledge that your strike was not perfect. They are whole, comfortable, exact, slightly bitter. Those things are as true for a full song level in the game as they are for the single strike; both have good shape.

FIGURE 13.7 Two asymmetrical armies in asymmetrical siege warfare, but with symmetry between some units.

LOCAL SYMMETRIES

Symmetry is defined as "the balanced distribution of equivalent forms or spaces about a common line or point" (Kubala 2020b). It applies at different levels of scale.

When applied to the entirety of a thing, symmetry can cause that thing to seem lifeless or mechanical. Imagine a castle where each room on the right of the castle has a mirror on the left side. The castle sits in a clearing next to a river, and on the other side of the river is an identical clearing and identical castle.

This problem with global symmetry applies to aspects of a game outside of its physical layout, such as a story where every character has an evil counterpart, or a war game where all sides have identical units and resources.

When only individual aspects of a thing are symmetrical at lower levels of scale, symmetry is local. In contrast to the earlier negative example is a story where both the hero and villain have a best friend but otherwise dissimilar lives. Or a war game where both sides have similar units but face each other in an asymmetrical siege.

Local symmetries have the effect of creating strong centers that create order out of the overall chaos without feeling artificial. In these examples, you can see this idea applies to all aspects of game design, from the narrative structure to multiplayer combat mechanics.

FIGURE 13.8   The deep interlock of the traditional holy trinity of classes in massively multiplayer online games.

DEEP INTERLOCK

A game's components must interconnect; they must have boundaries, form positive space together, and support each other's strong centers. This property is about *how* they should be connected. These connections should be deep and meaningful, but they should also create ambiguity.

In spatial terms, the boundaries between spaces should often be soft, making it unclear which space one is in at each moment as you pass from one to another. Stepping from the desert zone to the forest zone in a game with only the separation of a loading screen is not deep interlock. Watching the trees become smaller and be replaced by scrub and then cactus as you walk is better. Helping the farmer at the edge of the forest fend off the desert cats while he repairs his irrigation systems that have become clogged with sand is better yet.

In mechanical terms, aspects of one mechanic should be part of another, improving the function of both. A simple example would be the ability to run in a game being connected to the ability to jump. The mechanics are distinct, but the interlock between them is deep.

FIGURE 13.9 The contrasting game spaces of open fields and a maze.

CONTRAST

The idea of contrast is understood and applied across most of the disciplines of game design. Contrast is present in open and cramped spaces, light and dark rooms, music and silence, and combat and respite. What is less obvious is how the rest of the properties inform the application of contrast. The two things that are contrasting both need to be strong centers. It is not enough to have a strong center juxtaposed against a meaningless contrasting element; the second element must also be part of the positive space created by the whole. There must be a reason for both the element and its contrasting element.

If combat contrasts with moments of tranquility, those quiet moments must have a purpose in the game, or they will just be boring dead space. Perhaps tranquility exists in the space of time that it takes a player's health to refill. Perhaps those moments allow the player to absorb the damage that the combat has done to the world or give room to strategize about the next conflict. All of these things might even be true, providing deep interlock between the contrasting elements. That contrast could then be the building block for the alternating repetition that structures the flow of combat and recovery in the game.

FIGURE 13.10   The gradual shift from the darkness of a dungeon to the light of day.

GRADED VARIATION

Graded variation describes another way that elements connect. Any time two elements are present, the transition between them may be sudden or gradual, forming a gradient between them.

In physical space, that gradient might be the change between grassy areas and patches of dirt, or a dark room and the daylight outside. Either could happen suddenly or gradually; generally gradually is better.

In a mechanical sense, it might be an increase in characters' abilities throughout the game. Transforming a weak character into an unstoppable juggernaut halfway through a game is not as effective at giving a player a sense of growth by breaking that transition into a set of levels or power unlocks. In many cases, moving from discrete levels to skills that improve over time or abilities a player can acquire and then develop can be even more effective.

In a narrative context, you might see an opportunity to incorporate graded variation in showing a character's descent into madness. Suddenly declaring the character to be unhinged is both narratively jarring and likely to be an offensive portrayal of mental illness. Slowly introducing inconsistencies in the character's behavior or perceptions and showing the consequences of those would allow the player to notice the changes organically, and allow the developer more subtlety in their portrayal.

All of these things—space, mechanics, and narrative—are stronger centers when they change from one state to another gradually, allowing for subtlety in the players' experience.

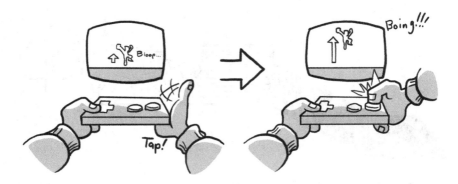

FIGURE 13.11   Roughness in input mechanics as well as in textures or plot.

ROUGHNESS

While simple to understand as a concept, roughness can be hard to apply to games. For Alexander, imperfections and complexities in space allow for better contrast, deeper interlock, and even strong centers at lower levels of scale.

In games, it can be technically challenging to create a sense of roughness. Creating a street that doesn't feel antiseptic was a challenge, and remains so even as graphical fidelity increases. Roughness might take the form of textures showing surfaces with imperfections or pieces of geometry that don't line up with the grid you're placing them on. In games with roughness, similar things aren't identical; houses or non-player characters don't endlessly reuse the same model with no variation.

GrungyBrick.png

FIGURE 13.12   A distressed texture might be the most literal example of roughness in a game.

Mechanically, roughness is difficult because mechanics are, well, mechanical. To create "rough" jumping physics requires more work than using the simplest mathematical calculations, perhaps introducing analog variables that rely on player controls or dynamic interactions with surface materials. When systems have that sense of detail and complexity, they are also likely exhibiting good shape and deep interlock with other systems. The game *Ori and the Will of the Wisps* is an example of this kind of roughness. Character movement is complex and often unexpected, but never feels random or imprecise.

Narrative roughness can come from details that are unexpected or not fully resolved. It's not an excuse for carelessness though, and too much roughness could make the story seem poorly thought out or hard to understand. But there is still room for details that leave the player wondering. The unexplained embedded narratives found in *BioShock* are a good example, as is the mysterious man with the briefcase in *Half-Life*.

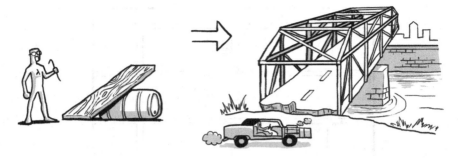

FIGURE 13.13   Echoes occurring in spaces but also in mechanics and narrative.

ECHOES

This property relates closely to levels of scale, as the presence of two similar things at different levels of scale can create echoes. However, echoes can exist across all aspects of a design. The choice of architectural style might echo in the selection of instruments for the soundtrack. The theme of the dangers of power in the narrative might echo in the splash damage of weapons. These kinds of echoes, of course, result in deep interlock and make the centers of each element stronger.

In *Assassin's Creed*, for instance, you see echoes in the shape of the character's hood and the physical eagle that is used to indicate places that the player can climb to unlock new areas of the map, and the player constantly looking down on the world from a great height.

THE VOID

The void property is about the use of negative space. In architecture, negative space is defined by the places that the building is not, such as the emptiness of a courtyard, the spaces between buildings or a green belt of trees between housing developments.

Again in games, space must be taken conceptually. In a physical sense, it is about creating spaces that have strong centers that are supported by negative space, whether it is a castle surrounding a quiet courtyard or an empty bowl. Negative space can be found in the ocean between the continents in *World of Warcraft* or the cliffs that form the edges of the open world of *Anthem*.

Narratively, it is about the pauses in the narrative in which nothing happens, the story beats that provide contrast to the action. This is

FIGURE 13.14 Sometimes the experience of space and gameplay is defined by the things that are absent from it.

exemplified by the moments in *Life is Strange* when the character can sit down and the player can watch the camera slowly pan around the environment.

Mechanically, the void might be the things a player can't do: the fact that the lack of the ability to jump creates interesting circulation patterns, or that the lack of ranged weapons creates natural melee combat or stealth gameplay. The game *Virginia* relies very heavily on mechanical negative space, removing mechanics that the player expects to encounter to create the experience of a character who does not have access to the personal agency that those mechanics represent.

INNER CALM

In architecture, inner calm is about removing the unnecessary parts of a building or space, this helps to create simple spaces that serve their purpose. This is not to say that spaces with inner calm must be plain or even uncluttered, just that everything in the space serves a purpose and does not distract from the intent of the space.

FIGURE 13.15 Fighting the constant drive to add features to meet genre and audience expectations.

In games, this property is similarly about focus and simplicity. It is about the removal of unnecessary elements from a game. Inner calm is not merely functionalism, which states that there should be no element not necessary for the function of the thing being designed. It is instead more inclusive, stating that all the factors that are present should contribute to the strong centers and good shape of the game. These contributions might be spatial, mechanical, or esthetic. There should be no elements that detract or distract from the wholeness of the game.

This property can be hard to notice in a game that possesses it, but its lack is easy to see in a game full of one-off mechanics or systems that make you grit your teeth every time you have to interact with them. A game like *Monument Valley* possesses inner calm not just because of its beauty and meditative gameplay, but because it contains no elements or systems that are unnecessary. Conversely, a game like the 2016 reboot of *Doom* fails to produce a sense of inner calm, not because it is a violent and frenetic game, but because it includes systems, like suit upgrading, that distract from its elegant core gameplay loop.

FIGURE 13.16   Each part of the game connected meaningfully to the next.

NOT SEPARATENESS

Similar to inner calm, this property states that all the elements of a design should be part of that design and share its intent.

In architecture, not separateness means that the elements of a structure do not exist in isolation. Each room in a house supports the function of the rooms it touches; houses work together to form cohesive neighborhoods, towns, and cities.

In games, that might mean that each scene in a level works to create the experience of that level, and that levels feel connected by theme and narrative. The areas you explore in a Metroidvania-style game have a strong sense of not separateness; those in *Super Mario Bros.* do not.

But not separateness also exists through a game's levels of scale, in its alternating repetition, its local symmetries, deep interlock, graded variation, and echoes. There is nothing leftover in a design that has not separateness, because every part of the game is connected and integral to the whole. This property shows in the relationships between the fifteen principles—when you notice that every mechanical system supports another. When jumping encourages dynamic exploration, exploration results in a sense of discovery. Art and theme create a sense of wonder and joy. That joy shows in the spirit of freedom and autonomy that the character is shown to experience when they jump.

———

This is my application of one of the most insightful conceptual frameworks I have ever encountered to game design. The ideas in this section are very large, and my exploration of them is just the beginning of understanding the ways they can inform our designs. Each of you reading this has a different set of skills that span the breadth of the industry. Once you have a grasp of the fifteen fundamental properties, you can begin to apply them to your specialties. Our work as designers must fully embody these properties if we want our games to have strong centers, inner calm, positive space, and not separateness—if we're going to make games that are fundamentally whole.

APPLYING THE FIFTEEN PROPERTIES OF WHOLENESS TO YOUR PATTERN LANGUAGE

Now that you have added these concepts and terms to your vocabulary you can start considering them as you document patterns. Going forward I have added the properties to the keywords sections of the example patterns; they are listed in italics at the end of the keywords. I find that I am easily able to list three or more properties that are enhanced by each pattern I document.

When you are using your Pattern Language to drive or assess your design, keep a tally of how many patterns in your design support each of the properties. If you find that one or more of the properties are unsupported by your patterns, consider whether your design should have those properties. If you think that they are necessary, then you should consider additional patterns that will help you incorporate those properties into your game.

VI

Advanced Pattern-Generation Exercises

CHAPTER 14

Advanced Pattern-Generation Exercises

THIS NEXT SET OF exercises is united by the fact that they're all quite difficult; they require that you understand the pattern creation process well. Each exercise has a basic premise that's more complex than just picking an aspect of game design. The introductions to these patterns will be a bit longer and include a more complete discussion of the premise of the exercise.

PATTERNS FROM CORE MECHANICS

Core Mechanics

Before engaging with this exercise, I want to clarify what I mean by "core mechanics." I covered the idea of looking at the most basic building blocks of a game in the exercises about formal and functional design elements. Core mechanics, then, are simply the set of basic mechanics that form the core gameplay loop.

To identify the core mechanics of a game, I like to imagine how a non-designer might describe the thing that makes a game awesome to a friend. For *Overwatch*, they might say, "There are all of these awesome characters with cool abilities," or for *Assassin's Creed*, "You get to parkour all over the city and kill people like a badass ninja." A *Doom* enthusiast might describe it as "an over-the-top run-and-gun killing spree."

You then need to take those descriptions and think about what mechanics they're actually talking about, and how those mechanics facilitate the experience the gamer describes. Here's how I'd do that for the aforementioned examples:

Overwatch → cool characters! → asymmetrical roles → complex metagame

Assassin's Creed: parkour! → dynamic traversal → exploration/stealth

Doom: run and gun! → dynamic enemies/static resources → movement-based combat

Sometimes it can be hard to decide which mechanics are core to a game. Many elements may be necessary to a game without being core to its identity. For instance, you couldn't have *Skyrim* without inventory management or a crafting system. But those systems, while an important part of the game, are not what defines it. You could make the argument that in a game as large as *Skyrim*, different styles of play even have different sets of core mechanics. In which case, any subset of players could give very different descriptions of what makes the game great. One player might say, "You get to be a master thief or assassin, and you can steal anything and kill anyone," while another might say, "You get to find dragons everywhere and slay them." I'd argue that the elements of gameplay that are *consistent across all play styles* constitute the actual core mechanics. In the case of *Skyrim*, I'd suggest that those are exploration and the constant potential for heroic action. The specifics of what constitutes "heroic action" varies across players: it might be fighting dragons or pulling off a difficult assassination. The commonality is that at any point, you feel like you're moments from a situation where you get to embody the kind of character you are playing in a meaningful way.

Pattern Purpose

Understanding how sets of mechanics combine to create singular user experiences is essential. This exercise will help you to see and articulate these combinations of mechanics, and produce the patterns that govern how to create groupings like this effectively.

EXERCISE 16: PATTERNS FROM CORE MECHANICS

Step 1: Pick a game.
Step 2: Write down how a non-designer would describe what makes that game awesome.

Step 3: Figure out what they're actually describing. Use your understanding as a designer to translate for them; don't describe what you understand as an expert to be the important gameplay features.

Step 4: Describe the consequences of the mechanic you described in step 3. How does the mechanic you identified create the experience the player described?

Step 5: Name and describe the way that ten other games use that mechanic to create the same experience.

Step 6: List any patterns you see.

Step 7: Choose one pattern and document it using the Pattern Template.

Step 8: You may repeat step 7 for each pattern you observed.

Example: Pattern from Core Mechanics
Exercise

Step 1: Pick a game.
Anthem

Step 2: Write down how a non-designer would describe what makes that game awesome.

You have an Ironman suit and you can fly anywhere in this whole crazy world and blow things up with your friends!

Step 3: Figure out what they're actually describing.

- High levels of player mobility.

- Wide choice of activities or objectives.

- Cooperative asymmetrical combat.

- Level/world design that takes advantage of player movement abilities.

- Beautiful space to explore.

So, which of these mechanics are core? I would say that high levels of player mobility and the choice of activity or objectives are the core mechanics. Multiplayer supports the fun of the core mechanics. Good level and world design make the core mechanics challenging and rewarding. And the beautiful world helps drive the exploration. This is a complex game, and there are many patterns that work to support the core mechanics, including a loot-based progression system and a mysterious setting. Still, the strongest center is the ability to go anywhere and do anything.

Step 4: Describe the consequences of the mechanic you described in step 3. How does the mechanic you identified create the experience the player described?

From the very beginning of the game, the player has almost unparalleled mobility. The ability to fly and travel at speed through a large world creates a sense of freedom and empowerment. The game drives exploration through assigned plot missions early in the game, but play is intended to extend beyond the completion of the plot. Motivation is extended somewhat by the inclusion of collectibles and lots of long-term objective-completion goals. However, these alone would be insufficient to maintain long-term interest in the game. Character power progression and challenges of escalating difficulty are the primary drivers of play at this point. The activities that players continue to engage in are the ones that allow them to make meaningful progress on this axis.

Where the game fails is in the places where activities that are intrinsically enjoyable become meaningless on the axis of character progression.* So, world exploration and engaging in emergent play lose focus, even though they are intrinsically enjoyable elements. Completing linear, instanced scenarios gains focus, and while it's an enjoyable aspect of play for many players, it deviates from the core gameplay loop of exploration and discovering unexpected challenges and events.

Step 5: Name and describe the way that ten other games use that mechanic to create the same experience.

- *Assassin's Creed: Black Flag*—This franchise in general uses free movement and diverse goals in an open world as its core gameplay loop. This general design choice is bolstered by the addition of an

---

* There has been a great deal of criticism for *Anthem* due to the imperfections in its loot progression and lack of endgame content. Those are valid critiques; however, there has been some correction in these areas and I do not feel that the faults in the early implementation of this system impact this analysis of its core mechanics.

island-based map that lets you sail to any island at almost any time. The overall progress of this single-player game is more limited, so there is less of an issue of motivating long-term play. Moving through the game world freely, in this case by climbing or sailing, is similarly gratifying. This core mechanic is hindered by the fact that many of the activities that you can pursue—collectibles in particular—feel artificial, and are neither intrinsically fun or extrinsically rewarded by progression systems. As a result, they don't drive the core gameplay loop effectively.

- *The Elder Scrolls*—This game may only partially fit this mold, in that the nature of the physical movement through the game world is not a focus of the game. It does fit in the sense that it's an open-world game, and provides a wide variety of activities to engage in during play. The mechanics of player progression are tied to every activity you can perform, and so whatever activity you pursue, your character advances in power. If there's a weakness in the implementation of these core mechanics, it's that the activities you can engage in don't always tie strongly into an overarching narrative.

- *Ori and the Blind Forest*—In contrast to the preceding game, movement is the primary focus of this game. Your ability to explore the world is limited by the skills and movement abilities you have access to. In this way, this game doesn't fit the pattern, in that exploration is gated by movement. However, the very limiting of movement allows the game to maintain a relatively constant level of difficulty, even as the abilities available to the character grow. The further you progress in the game, the more open the world becomes, and the closer it gets to the core mechanic of *Anthem*.

- *Minecraft*—As with the graphical presentation, movement in this game is primitive. But because of your ability to alter the world, you're able to move freely throughout the world. The developers haven't done much to structure player behavior in this game in terms of setting specific goals. But the crafting progression and resource distribution systems make the game's player movement abilities— that is, world-altering abilities—a perfect embodiment of the "go anywhere, do anything" core mechanic.

- *Eve Online*—In this massively multiplayer game, which simulates vast sprawling space empires struggling for profit and dominance, the individual players have free movement in a local sense. You can move anywhere in the larger conceptual space of the universe, though that's mitigated by the danger posed by other players and enemies present in those locations. The game is overall very skill-based, and it takes a long time to acquire many of those skills. However, since the game has existed for well over a decade, a large percentage of players are able to engage in virtually any activity that's possible within the game. While player progression is a major driver of player activity for the game's long, leveling-up period, the core gameplay is also driven by the complex oppositional activities of other players. Which is to say, you can go anywhere and do anything, but many of the things you might do either oppose the activities of other players or will be opposed by them. This creates sustainable long-term play for players that find the available activities compelling.

- *Horizon Zero Dawn*—While the spatial movement in this game is more dynamic than in a game like *Skyrim*, it's not as free as in a game like *Anthem* or *Assassin's Creed*. Character abilities like climbing and rappelling are limited to areas designated by the developers. There's a strong linear story progression that gates access to the different areas of the map, but once areas become accessible, they are freely explorable. As in the *Assassin's Creed* games, there are collectible systems present in the game, though here there's at least some narrative and mechanical justification for them. The emergent challenge of fighting the large-scale monsters in this game provides perhaps the most intrinsically compelling "do anything" gameplay out of these example games.

- *Dungeons & Dragons*—As a tabletop role-playing game with a human game master, this game truly allows players to go anywhere and do anything. Complex and fine-grained character progression provides long-term mechanical motivation for player exploration and activities. The game master provides narrative motivation, so the degree to which it's compelling is tied to the game master's storytelling ability.

- *Pokémon Go*—In this geolocated augmented reality game, the character's ability to go anywhere is limited by where the player can physically go. At release, the options available for player interaction were very limited, allowing only for capturing new Pokémon and collecting resources at geolocated points. In the three-plus years since the game's release, the diversity of gameplay available has increased dramatically and is comparable to that available in the console versions of the franchise.

Step 6: List any patterns you see.

1. The degree to which dynamic spatial movement (flying and climbing in most cases) is compelling is tied to how meaningful the character/player reasons are for going to places accessible through that movement.

2. How compelling optional (or required) player activities are is determined by a number of factors including:

   a. Narrative relevance

   b. Intrinsic activity fun

   c. Contribution to character progression

3. The greater the degree of character freedom (of movement or choice), the stronger the motivation required to make players feel like the choices they make are enjoyable and rewarding.

4. As player movement options increase, players have more choices of where they can go at any given moment. When combined with many activity options in open-world games, this freedom can create decision paralysis and flat-seeming gameplay.

Step 7: Choose one pattern and document it using the Pattern Template.

3. Greater choice requires greater motivation.

Step 8: You may repeat step 7 for each pattern you observed.

Pattern

Name: Greater Choice Requires Greater Motivation
Confidence: 2
Image:

FIGURE 14.1   Too many quests can be overwhelming, but seeing a burning building makes the choice clear.

Author: Chris Barney
Design problem: How do you keep players motivated to explore and interact with systems as the scale of the game world and available activities increase?
Description: The greater the degree of character freedom (of movement or choice), the stronger the motivation required to make players feel like the choices they make are enjoyable and rewarding.

In a very linear game, every player action visibly leads to progress, and the player is unlikely to feel that their actions aren't meaningful. When games are nonlinear, allow a lot of player exploration, or give constant action options, players might not be sure which actions are optimal, i.e., whether they're generating meaningful progress or are just a waste of time.

Players thus require more and more motivation to feel confident in their choice to pursue a particular action. There are many patterns that suggest how to generate player motivation; they tend to indicate that any possible activities in the game should provide either meaningful narrative or mechanical progress, and ensure the player understands the nature of that progress.

Games that use this pattern and how:

- *Horizon Zero Dawn*—The spatial movement in this game is dynamic and includes character abilities such as climbing and rappelling, though these are limited to areas intended by the developers. There is a strong linear story progression that gates access to the different areas of the map, but once areas become accessible, they are freely explorable. The collectible systems present in the game include at least some narrative and mechanical justification. They also are diegetic to the game, since you sell the collectibles to non-player characters (NPCs) who ask you to collect them for currency, which you can then use for character progression. The emergent challenge of fighting the large-scale monsters in this game provides perhaps the most intrinsically compelling "do anything" gameplay of any of these example digital games. These battles, which are the most iconic activity the players engage in, generate resources you can use both for progression and as consumables. The overall narrative and quest-giving NPCs encourage you to explore the map, but the nature of the incidental activities you engage in creates a world where you can see the positive results of any action you choose.
- *Ori and the Blind Forest*—In contrast to the preceding game, movement is the primary focus here. Your ability to explore the world is limited by the skills and movement abilities you have access to. While you can't initially go anywhere you want, the eventual goal is to go everywhere. Unlike in a linear game where you move through the game space sequentially, this game uses a nonlinear space that you move through cyclically. As your increasing freedom of movement gives you access to more and more of the space, you return to areas of the game over and over. This very limitation of movement allows the game to maintain a relatively constant level of difficulty, even as the abilities available to the character grow.
- The game is essentially over once the world is completely open, so in that sense, this game might be seen as falling outside of this pattern. However, there's motivation to return to previously visited spaces to collect resources you need to continue character progression. This progression, of course, unlocks further movement options, and the cycle repeats. In terms of story, a strong overarching narrative motivates the player, but short-term motivation is generally very simple and disconnected from the larger meaning of the game.
- *Pokémon Go**—As a geolocated augmented reality game, *Pokémon Go* limits the character's ability to go anywhere using the player's ability to move through non-digital space. It's likely that no other game has

---

* As a mobile title with continuous updates, the gameplay has changed radically over the course of the game. The changes made to the game reflect the consistent design methodology of iterative incremental improvement. The game is discussed here as it was in the spring of 2020.

as large and dense a playspace, with the exceptions of Niantic's other games that use the same dataset of interaction locations. As a player in this game, you can literally go anywhere. In keeping with this pattern, each activity the player may engage in must provide the player with a strong sense of motivation. The game achieves this through the deep interlock of all its systems. Each system provides the resources for interacting with the other systems, and every system is resourced by multiple other systems. This allows players to engage only with activities they also find intrinsically rewarding.

Seed: Exercise 16: Patterns from Core Mechanics—Go anywhere, do anything
Related patterns:
Parent patterns:
The Three Pillars of Meaning* (Confidence: 2)—When trying to apply Greater Choice Requires Greater Motivation, this pattern describes the way that motivation can combine with context and consequence to create meaning. (At least in the context of emergent narrative as described in this pattern.)

SUGGESTED EXERCISE

Use **Exercise 9: Circulation Patterns** to generate a pattern about circulation systems for exploration in open world games.

Child patterns:
Mystery-Driven Exploration[†] (Confidence: 2)—Navigation and exploration are one set of choices that Greater Choice Requires Greater Motivation can help players to make. The more options for exploration a player faces, the more compelling a mystery will need to be to drive the player.

SUGGESTED EXERCISE

Use **Exercise 5: Functional Patterns** to generate a pattern about player choice.

Keywords: Autonomy, Choice, Meaning, Motivation, Open World, *Deep Interlock, Inner Calm*

---

* Example pattern from Exercise 11: Emergent Narrative Patterns.
[†] Example pattern from Chapter 5.

FINDING MISSING PATTERNS

Pattern Purpose

This exercise looks at an existing pattern and asks whether it's effective in isolation. The answer to this question is almost always no, or if it is yes, then it could solve the problem more effectively if it was supported by parent and child patterns that reinforced its effect. I include the question here to give you a chance to think about how this pattern would function in isolation. When you looked at it during the exercise that you used to create it, you were looking at real games in which the pattern was working in concert with many others. Consider it now all on its own, trying to solve its problem, and compare that with how effective it was in the example games you cited. This exercise will help you make sure it's that effective when you use it.

EXERCISE 17: FINDING MISSING PATTERNS

Step 1: Choose a pattern you've created that has no parent or child patterns listed. Look at the design problem it solves.

Step 2: Can this pattern best solve its design problem alone?

Step 3: If not, then look at ten games that implement this pattern and also solve the problem well. Some of these games can be the example games you initially cited, but it's good to look for other games now that you have some distance from the seed pattern.

Step 4: For each game, list and describe the design elements that support or enhance the effect of the pattern. At this point, try not to look for fully formed patterns in these elements.

Step 5: List and describe any patterns you see in your response to step 4.

Step 6: Pick one pattern and document it using the Pattern Template.

Step 7: Does this pattern require your seed pattern? It might, if this pattern is more specific or lower level than the seed pattern. If so, list the new pattern as a child of the seed pattern and the seed pattern as a parent of this one.

Step 8: Is this pattern enhanced by the seed pattern? This may be the case if the pattern is higher level or more fundamental to solving the problem than the seed. If so, then list the seed pattern as a child of the new pattern. List the new pattern as a parent of the seed pattern.

Step 9: You may repeat steps 6 to 8 for each pattern observed in step 5.

Example Finding Missing Pattern
Exercise

Step 1: Choose a pattern you've created that has no parent or child patterns listed. Look at the design problem it solves.

Pattern: One of These Days That's Going to Get You Killed

Pattern problem: How do you maintain game balance and create tension when giving the player greater power in their interactions with the game world?

Step 2: Can this pattern best solve its design problem alone?
This pattern is general and high level, and it's tempting to say that an adequate implementation of the pattern will address its design problem. However, it will be stronger if it has the context of a parent pattern that addresses *why* the player is given the particular power over the environment. Depending on how the increase in ability is meant to make the player feel—more powerful, out of control, the best hope against impossible odds, or whatever—there are also likely to be child patterns that modify the pattern's effect.

Step 3: If not, then look at ten games that implement this pattern and also solve the problem well.

- *Super Mario Bros.*—From the origin pattern: "The ability to jump, which increases the character's ability to move through the world and defeat enemies, also puts him in danger. Failing to jump over dangerous obstacles can result in Mario's death. Similarly, failing to jump over an enemy results in the enemy killing Mario."

- *Sekiro: Shadows Die Twice*—From the origin pattern: "Stealth killing enemies is the easiest way to defeat them, but failing to execute a stealth kill alerts the enemy and nearby enemies and suddenly puts the player in a dangerous situation."

- *Anthem*—From the origin pattern: "Firing weapons increases their heat. Failing to manage that resource, to self-limit the damage you are doing, can result in not being able to fire your gun when you most need it."

- *Zelda: Breath of the Wild*—From the origin pattern: "Link can climb almost ANYTHING, but he has a stamina meter, so if he tries to climb something too high, he will fall. He can jump off of things and glide, but if he runs out of stamina, he falls to his death."

- *Quake*—Some of the most powerful weapons in the game have splash damage that can easily hurt or kill the character, which makes them feel dangerous to use.

- *Star Wars Roleplaying Game*—A Jedi player can at any point boost their powers by tapping into the "dark side of the force," but doing so builds up "dark side points" that can cause dramatic negative mechanical and narrative effects.

- *The Elder Scrolls: Morrowind*—It's possible to create magical effects that are very powerful, like jumping for miles or flying, but these effects don't include affordances to protect you. Jumping for a mile can end by crashing into the ground and dying, or a flying potion will end, dropping the character from their current height to their death. As a player, you can mitigate these effects with careful planning, but they help make magic feel like it has consequences in a very natural way.

- *Life is Strange*—The main character has the ability to rewind time. At first, it feels like it gives you unlimited do-overs, and it's used to construct puzzles that can only be solved with repetition. But the power doesn't work in all circumstances, and sometimes using it causes you (and the character) to learn things they would rather not know.

- *Torment: Tides of Numenera*—Magic items give the character powerful effects, but using too many at one time (or even having them on your person) causes negative side effects.

Step 4: For each game, list and describe the design elements that support or enhance the effect of the pattern.[*]

- *Super Mario Bros.*—The *narrative and gameplay progression* that your jumping enables takes you into more and more *dangerous situations*.

- *Sekiro: Shadows Die Twice*—To take advantage of stealth kills, you have to *engage in risky behavior*; getting close to enemies puts you in danger. When you alert an enemy, the gameplay changes from stealth to action.

- *Anthem*—Gameplay is frenetic, so you're commonly in situations where you've *failed* to watch your heat gauge, and your weapon goes into cooldown. This situation leads to *alternate gameplay*. Extreme

---

[*] For each game I list the design element in italics for clarity.

mobility and the need to move to collect health and ammo often puts you in sudden and unexpected gameplay situations.

- *Zelda: Breath of the Wild*—*Weapon breaking* also puts you in situations where you suddenly lose power, a weapon in this case, and where you have to *self-limit the use of your powers.* Having open-world traversal abilities, but a world where certain areas are more dangerous than others, lets you get into dangerous situations that you have to *alter your gameplay style to survive.*

- *Quake*—The need to constantly move to avoid damage, and collect weapons and health often puts you in dangerous situations.

- *Star Wars Roleplaying Game*—The combination of mechanical drive to power and consequences of power is bolstered by the conflicting narrative desires to be the hero and to create dramatic situations by following a darker narrative path.

- *The Elder Scrolls: Morrowind*—The open world and interaction of large numbers of systems empower you as a player, but also create emergent consequences to chaotic player behaviors. Most of the systems are meant to be used in moderation and produce reasonable results when used that way, but they also allow you to take them to an extreme and reward you with chaotic outcomes.

- *Life is Strange*—The linear narrative and gameplay path force you to use your rewind powers in a particular way. The game manipulates you into thinking it's a choice-based game, but the time-rewinding power turns those choices into iterative steps in pursuing the linear outcome.

- *Torment: Tides of Numenera*—Narrative choice in this game is real, but narrative choice is very mechanics heavy, in that the choices available are statistics dependent. This makes the magic items/side effects mechanic effective both for players pursuing a combat-mechanic-heavy path and for those following a more narrative-choice-driven gameplay style.

Step 5: List and describe any patterns you see in your response to step 4.

1. Using an ability leads to situations where you need to use the ability more.

2. Triggering the consequences of the player's power instigates new gameplay styles.

3. Reinforcing the mechanical limit-pushing with narrative context is common and effective.

Step 6: Pick one pattern and document it using the Pattern Template.
Triggering the consequences of the character's powers instigates new gameplay styles for the player.

Step 7: Does this pattern require the seed pattern?
Yes. The new pattern is a child pattern that enhances the effect of the parent.

Step 8: Is this pattern enhanced by the seed pattern?
No. In this case, the child pattern identified requires the parent pattern rather than just being enhanced by it.

Step 9: You may repeat steps 6 to 8 for each pattern observed in step 5.

Pattern

Name: And Now I Guess We're Doing This
Confidence: 2
Image:

FIGURE 14.2 Unexpected events can force players to transition between gameplay styles, in this case between stealth and combat.

Author: Chris Barney

Design problem: Players can get trapped in comfortable gameplay loops, which can both bore them and keep them from taking advantage of all the gameplay possibilities of your game.

Description: To get players to transition from one gameplay type to another, developers can take advantage of players' tendencies to push their characters' limits and abilities. When you build in lethal consequences to overextending character abilities, you create a situation where the player has to change their way of playing to survive.

Games that use this pattern and how:

- *Sekiro: Shadows Die Twice*—To take advantage of stealth kills, you have to *get close to the enemy.* If you fail to kill the enemy, the gameplay changes from stealth to combat action or to traversal as you flee.
- *Zelda: Breath of the Wild*—Weapon breaking also puts you in situations where you suddenly lose power, a weapon in this case, and must either flee or change to a different weapon and fighting style. Having open world traversal abilities that depend on stamina, and a world where certain areas are more dangerous than others, often drops you into dangerous situations where your stamina runs out, and you have to alter your gameplay style to survive.
- *Anthem*—The character has very powerful abilities and weapons, but the abilities have cooldowns, and the weapons can overheat and can't be fired. Gameplay is frenetic, so you're commonly in situations where you've failed to watch your heat gauge or your abilities are on cooldown. This forces you to transition from offensive combat to traversal. While the general focus is still fast-paced action revolving around combat, the use of this pattern creates changes in pacing and a chaotic rhythm to the action.

Seed: Exercise 17: Finding Missing Patterns—One of These Days That's Going to Get You Killed

Related patterns:

Parent patterns:

SUGGESTED EXERCISE

Use **Exercise 5: Functional Patterns** to generate a pattern based on the functional element of gameplay rhythm.

Child patterns:

One of These Days That's Going to Get You Killed* (Confidence: 3)—The consequences suggested by this pattern are an excellent way for developers to implement And Now I Guess We Are Doing This.

---

* Example pattern from Exercise 1: Basic Patterns.

SUGGESTED EXERCISE

Use **Exercise 9: Circulation Patterns** to generate a pattern about how the circulation pattern changes when a player shifts from combat to stealth-focused gameplay. Look at games that contain both of these gameplay types in step 2.

Other related patterns:

SUGGESTED EXERCISE

Use **Exercise 24: Theoretical Patterns** to generate the pattern I Could Get Used to This based on the theory "using an ability leads to new situations where you need to use the ability again." I think there is a pattern about designing situations that use a new ability after you introduce it. Games that do this well add new abilities that support the core gameplay and continue to provide situations that use those abilities for the rest of the game. What will the relationship between these two patterns be?

Keywords: Abilities, Consequences, Mechanics, Player Motivation, *Alternating Repetition, Deep Interlock, Contrast*

FINDING NEGATIVE PATTERNS

Negative patterns are related to the anti-patterns discussed in earlier in the book in Chapter 6. Negative patterns cause a problem in a game or actively prevent its solution by other patterns. You can usually state them in the form, "To avoid [problem], a designer should avoid [pattern description]."

Pattern Purpose

These patterns have some utility in terms of avoiding bad design. But they're also useful as a way to understand a given problem. Mapping out negative patterns around a problem can make it clearer where to look for the patterns that solve it. Additionally, in games we often want to create negative situations, environments, or experiences for dramatic or gameplay purposes. As a designer, you might use a negative pattern intentionally. A negative pattern like "to avoid causing the player too much stress, the designer should avoid putting their character in a constant state of danger" is useful if your goal is to create an unpleasantly stressful situation.

EXERCISE 18: FINDING NEGATIVE PATTERNS

Step 1: Pick a game with a design flaw.
Step 2: Describe that flaw.
Step 3: List ten games that have the same flaw. The more different the games are, the better.*
Step 4: List and describe the elements that contribute to the flaw in each game.†
Step 5: Describe the patterns you see in how the listed elements produce the design flaw you described in step 2.
Step 6: Pick one pattern and document it using the Pattern Template.
Step 7: You may repeat step 6 for each pattern you observed.
Step 8: Consider a game that does not have the design flaw from step 2. Would applying your pattern in that game cause the flaw?

Example Negative Pattern
Exercise

Step 1: Pick a game with a design flaw.
Dreamfall: The Longest Journey

Step 2: Describe that flaw.
Combat. Pretty much everything about this game's combat is a negative experience for the player, but I think the combat is just a symptom of the flaw. Bad combat stems from implementing a feature that's core to the perceived game type (in this case action-adventure) but is not core to the actual experience of the game. So I'll call the underlying flaw "false core mechanics."

Step 3: List ten games that have the same flaw. The more different the games are, the better.

- *Dreamfall: The Longest Journey* (combat)

- *Dreamfall: The Longest Journey* (stealth)

- *Silent Hill 2* (combat)

---

* The problem should be a real design flaw, not just something you don't like. Do not list ten first-person shooters because you don't like that kind of game.
† Describing first-person shooter games and saying their problem is having a first-person perspective and shooting is not what you are being asked to do!

- *The Secret World* (stealth)

- *Doom 2016* (progression systems)

- *Pokémon Sword* and *Pokémon Shield* (cooking)

- *Mass Effect 1, 2,* and *3* (Planetary Interaction Systems)

Step 4: List and describe the elements that contribute to the flaw in each game.

- *Dreamfall: The Longest Journey* (combat)—The focus of this game is story and exploration, with light puzzle-solving elements added for pacing and to provide challenge. The combat systems of this game are not well-implemented; they're buggy and have awkward controls. As a result, the outcome of any combat encounter is somewhat arbitrary, and even when you succeed, the experience is frustrating and unsatisfying. I think a lack of time, budget, and expertise in implementing 3D action combat all contributed to the combat feeling tacked on.

- *Dreamfall: The Longest Journey* (stealth)—The implementation of the stealth elements of the game are independent of the combat in terms of gameplay and mechanics. But they suffer from the same problems and detract from the overall game experience for the same reasons. I've included them as a separate entry because they show that this problem is not about combat per se, but about including a poorly implemented system in core gameplay.

- *Silent Hill 2* (combat)—This is a counterexample, since while the combat in this game has the same flaws as the combat in *Dreamfall*, in this instance the poorly implemented combat systems enhance the game rather than weaken it. The core gameplay loop of fearful exploration requires that there be the possibility of combat, but that combat should be something to avoid and fear. The awkward combat system helps the player feel the same fear of combat that the character does.

- *The Secret World* (stealth)—The core gameplay loops of this game are exploration and character progression, with puzzle-solving and combat used to create difficulty and provide pacing. The game also features many stealth missions that the player base generally finds either frustrating and difficult, or pointlessly easy. The stealth mechanics of the game aren't clearly implemented, and they often fail to create the intended experience. Sometimes, however, they work wonderfully and create the tense, exciting experience intended. Again, I think a lack of time and budget to polish the mechanics and a lack of developer experience in implementing these mechanics is likely the cause of the poor implementation.

- *Doom 2016* (progression systems)—This run-and-gun first-person shooter includes several character progression systems that involve upgrading the character's weapons, armor, and skills. The systems are competently implemented, but I list them as a flaw because I felt annoyance every time I was prompted to engage with those systems. They felt external to the core gameplay loop of grabbing weapons and armor, and killing monsters.

- *Pokémon Sword* and *Pokémon Shield* (cooking)—There are many merits and flaws of this game, but I'm considering the cooking systems, which I see as a flaw because I was able to complete the game without ever engaging in them beyond the required tutorial. Perhaps they contribute to making the world feel more alive or complex, but given the low difficulty of the storyline game experience, they seem an unnecessary use of developer resources. Maybe they become relevant in the post-game play, but even if so, it doesn't justify their inclusion in the earlier parts of the game if they don't contribute meaningfully to the player's experience.

- *Mass Effect 1, 2,* and *3* (planetary interaction systems)—The *Mass Effect* games are huge and complex, skillfully blending exploration, combat, and narrative choice. But each game included a system for gathering resources from and interacting with planets, meant to connect you with the scale and scope of the galaxy, and make you feel that the locations outside the main story matter. The Mako ground vehicle used in the first game is difficult to control, and the procedurally generated missions using it lack polish and interest. The second game includes a planet-scanning mini-game interface, which seems like it might fit with the game's fiction. However, using it is unlike other interactions in the game, and it's mostly dull and interrupts the game's flow. The final game lets you fly your ship around planetary systems from an isometric third-person perspective and search for resources. But the control system doesn't reflect the ship's movement in the rest of the game, which can take you out of the feeling that you're playing the role of Shepard.

Step 5: Describe the patterns you see in how the listed elements produce the design flaw you described in step 2.

- Gameplay systems that aren't well implemented, or where the level of polish is below that of the rest of the game, stand out, and their shortcomings are evident.

- Gameplay systems that don't enhance or complement the core gameplay loop distract from that loop, and can reduce a game's overall effectiveness.

Step 6: Pick one pattern and document it using the Pattern Template.
Gameplay systems that aren't well implemented, or where the level of polish is below that of the rest of the game, stand out, and their shortcomings are evident.

Step 7: You may repeat step 6 for each pattern you observed.

Step 8: Consider a game that does not have the design flaw from step 2. Would applying your pattern in that game cause the flaw?
Yes, this seems very evident. It's tempting to say that this pattern is so apparent that it isn't worth articulating; however, the repeated occurrence of poorly implemented systems in games seems to justify the pattern. Additionally, the occasional use of poorly implemented systems to positive effect makes it worth noting. A good example of a game with many well-designed systems that all contribute to the core gameplay experience is *Stardew Valley*. This game, which at first seems like a farming simulator, includes seemingly tangential systems such as mining, fishing, and socializing in town. All of the systems, while simple, are implemented with the same level of depth and polish as the farming mechanics. Collectively, these systems create a complicated gameplay rhythm that changes the game from a farming simulation to an exploration of the rhythms of rural life. Each system, while different, was added and integrated into the others to create a game that possesses Alexander's quality without a name.

Pattern

Name: Game, Know Thyself
Confidence: 2
Image:

FIGURE 14.3   Just because you have built a cooking system doesn't mean it belongs in your action game. I know you worked hard on it, and it looked good on paper, but it just didn't turn out very well and it is getting in the way of the parts of the game that are good.

Author: Chris Barney
Design problem:* Several design problems may lead to the attempt to add additional systems to a game, including but not limited to:

- Broad game scope—The game world you are trying to create is complex, and you want the player's experience of it to be as complex as the character's.
- Need for pacing—Core gameplay moves along at a rapid pace and will create a game experience that's either too short or too homogeneous.

---

* In the context of this pattern, the design problem is very interesting. What problem was the poorly implemented system supposed to solve? Could the system have solved that problem if it had been well implemented? Would solving that problem have made the game better? Were there other ways to solve the problem that should have been considered instead?

- Genre expectations—The game fits into a well-known genre, whether it be first-person shooter (FPS), role-playing game (RPG), multiplayer online battle arena (MOBA), etc., and other games in this genre have a particular mechanic.
- Sunk cost fallacy—Sometimes, developers spend a lot of time on a system, and it either doesn't turn out as expected or doesn't reflect the way the rest of the game turned out. But at that point, it represents too significant a time investment to discard.

Description: To solve any of the preceding problems, a developer may decide to include additional mechanics in a game that aren't well implemented or that don't match the tone or quality of the rest of the game.

Even if these systems are designed to serve a constructive purpose in the game, they won't perform as intended under these circumstances. It's easy for logistical, financial, or design conditions to favor the inclusion of suboptimal systems in a game, but the negative consequences can be seen in the following example games.

Games that use this pattern and how:

- *Mass Effect*—The *Mass Effect* games are huge and complex, skillfully blending exploration, combat, and narrative choice. But each game included a system for gathering resources from and interacting with planets, meant to connect you with the scale and scope of the galaxy, and to make you feel that the locations outside the main story matter. The Mako ground vehicle used in the first game is difficult to control, and the procedurally generated missions using it lack polish and interest. Despite the size and experience of the teams at BioWare, they lacked either the time or resources to build both a carefully designed story-driven action RPG and procedurally generated mission-driven one. Because the missions on the procedural planets are optional and don't contribute to the core story-driven gameplay, and the resources gathered are not necessary for advancement, they created only a weak link between the core and supporting systems.
- *Dreamfall: The Longest Journey*—This is the second in a series of story-driven adventure games. The first game was a classic 2D point-and-click adventure. This game moved to a third-person 3D presentation. The expectation for 3D adventure games to be in the action-adventure genre seems to have guided the developers to incorporate systems for combat and stealth into the game. Unfortunately, neither set of systems was well implemented, and while the game's story is remarkable, it is almost painful to play through the forced combat and stealth portions of the game. It would be the best part of a decade after this game's release

before walking simulator games like *Gone Home* or choice-driven games like *The Walking Dead* would show that story and exploration alone are enough to sustain a satisfying game experience.

Seed: Exercise 18: Finding Negative Patterns—Games with poorly implemented combat
Related patterns:*
Parent patterns:

SUGGESTED EXERCISE

Use **Exercise 24: Theoretical Patterns** to generate a pattern based on Christopher Alexander's conception of *positive space* as described in Chapter 13 about the fifteen fundamental properties of wholeness.

Child patterns:
Familiarity Breeds Contempt, or at Least High Expectations[†] (Confidence: 3)—In games that poorly implement this pattern, the root cause is often described by Game, Know Thyself.

SUGGESTED EXERCISE

Complete the documentation of the second pattern suggested in step 5 of the example for Exercise 18: "Gameplay systems that do not enhance or complement the core gameplay loop of a game distract from that loop and can reduce the overall effectiveness of a game."

Keywords: Combat, Stealth, Game Systems, Development Resources, Game Genre, *Positive Space*, *Deep Interlock*, *Inner Calm*[‡]

FINDING POSITIVE PATTERNS FROM NEGATIVE ONES

Some negative patterns can be easily turned into positive ones. However, you can't just reverse the wording and assume you'll be able to create an opposite effect. It's essential to walk through the steps of pattern creation

---

* Related patterns are a little different for negative patterns are a little different. Parent patterns are higher-level patterns that can contribute to this negative pattern existing. Those parents might be negative patterns themselves or positive patterns that can have negative side effects. Likewise child patterns may be other negative patterns that can be caused by this pattern, or they might be positive patterns that are often introduced to deal with the negative effects of this pattern.
† Example pattern from Exercise 19: Finding Positive Patterns from Negative Patterns.
‡ Because this is a negative pattern it inhibits these three fundamental properties in games that exhibit it.

to assess whether the changes you want to make to the negative pattern can be observed to have the effect you'd like them to.

Pattern Purpose

This exercise is intended to help you observe any possible patterns that are the obverse of negative patterns found using the previous exercise. In plain English, this exercise will help you check to see if reversing a negative pattern is likely to reverse the effect of that pattern.

EXERCISE 19: FINDING POSITIVE PATTERNS FROM NEGATIVE PATTERNS

Step 1: Pick a negative pattern.
Step 2: For each game listed as an example, think of a similar game that doesn't have the problem that the negative pattern produces.
Step 3: For each game, list and describe the elements in that better game that differ from its flawed counterpart.
Step 4: Describe the patterns you see in how the listed elements address the design flaw you described in the seed negative pattern.
Step 5: Pick one pattern and document it using the Pattern Template.
Step 6: You may repeat step 5 for each pattern observed in step 4.

Example Positive Pattern
Exercise

Step 1: Pick a negative pattern.
Game Know Thyself (Exercise 18)

Step 2: For each game listed as an example, think of a similar game that doesn't have the problem that the negative pattern produces.
This step can go two ways:

- Games that do implement additional systems, but in a way that's successful at achieving the intended effect. As seen in *Mass Effect* compared to *Dragon Age: Inquisition*.

- Games that avoid adding unneeded mechanics in similar situations to the initial example games. As seen in *Dreamfall: The Longest Journey* compared to *Life is Strange*.

Step 3: For each game, list and describe the elements in that better game that differ from its flawed counterpart.

- *Mass Effect*—These games demonstrate a mechanic with strong positive intent that was not well-integrated into core gameplay. As stated earlier in the negative pattern, these games added planet exploration mechanics, intended to both generate resources in the game and to create a sense of galactic scale. Each iteration of the game implemented a different mechanic to solve this design problem, and each failed for the same reasons.

  Interestingly *Dragon Age: Inquisition*, another game by BioWare, solves a similar design problem with similar mechanics, but in its case, they're successful. In the case of *Dragon Age*, the developers succeeded in showing the size of the world outside of playable areas and creating a sense of the political and strategic complexity of a kingdom-spanning war. The mechanic is a "War Table," which allows you to fast-travel around the game world, and, in your role as a general, to assign agents to various missions. Unlike the first *Mass Effect*, these missions don't involve any gameplay, and they progress the primary narrative of the game. Additionally, completing some of these War Table missions unlocks new areas to explore in the primary action-adventure gameplay mode. It seems that the systems in this game work well because they are tightly coupled with the core elements of the game.

- *Dreamfall: The Longest Journey*—This game includes stealth and combat mechanics that were thought of as necessary to the genre, but were not important to the core exploration and puzzle gameplay of the particular game.

  Life is Strange has a very similar core gameplay loop to *Dreamfall*, though its secondary mechanics are very different. The game contains no combat or stealth, and instead introduces choice-based narrative branching and a time-rewind mechanic that allows you to explore the consequences of different choices.

  So how are these two mechanics different than those implemented in *Dreamfall*? Both combat and stealth are mechanics that were genre expectations, but they are also mechanics that have been iterated on and perfected in thousands of other games. The presumption was that players would expect to see them in a game billed as an action-adventure or that the game would be action-adventure by virtue of their inclusion. The game's reception suggests that players had specific expectations for the quality of the implementation. Everyone understood what good combat or stealth felt like, and that those elements in *Dreamfall* were lacking. At the time of *Life is Strange*'s release, its time-rewinding mechanic was uncommon and unique in narrative games. The focus on choice-based narrative in games like *Life is Strange* was somewhat more common given the popularity of games by Telltale Games, but its implementation met those heightened expectations.

Step 4: Describe the patterns you see in how the listed elements address the design flaw you described in the seed negative pattern.

- Deep interlock: This is one of the fifteen fundamental properties of wholeness that Christopher Alexander wrote about later in his career, and I have discussed it in detail in Chapter 13 of this book. But briefly, elements of a thing that is "good" or works well are deeply interconnected and support each other. A game design pattern based on this property might look like this: "To make sure that the mechanics you add to a game perform as intended, and feel to players like they belong there, you as a designer should make sure that those mechanics support the primary gameplay loop as much as possible."

- Familiarity breeds contempt, or at least high expectations: The more common a mechanic is and the more excellent implementations of that mechanic there are, the higher players' standards will be for that mechanic. The pattern might look like this: "When allocating resources in development, the resources allocated to perfecting a particular mechanic should be proportional not only to the prominence of that mechanic in the game, but the prominence of that mechanic in the industry in general. This practice will help meet players' expectations for the quality of that implementation."

Step 5: Pick one pattern and document it using the Pattern Template.
Familiarity breeds contempt, or at least high expectations.

Step 6: You may repeat step 5 for each pattern observed in step 4.

Pattern

Name: Familiarity Breeds Contempt, or at Least High Expectations
Confidence: 2
Image:

FIGURE 14.4   When your players know what a dragon (or any formal or functional element) looks like it will be very obvious to them when yours isn't what it should be.

Author: Chris Barney

Design problem: Resources are often limited in game development, and there may not be enough resources to implement all aspects of the game with equal polish.

Description: When allocating resources in development, the resources allocated to perfecting a particular mechanic should be proportional not only to the prominence of that mechanic in the game, but the prominence of that mechanic in the industry in general. Players' expectations for the quality of a mechanic grow as they become more familiar with it and have seen it implemented well in many games. Player's will compare the mechanic in your game to the same mechanic in other games and compare it to the other mechanics in your game.

Games that use this pattern and how:

- *Dragon Age: Inquisition*—The War Table mechanic, in which the player's character deploys agents to pursue their goals and engages in travel over the continent, stands in contrast to the previous BioWare games in the *Mass Effect* franchise. In both cases, the mechanic is meant to create a sense of scale and solve fast travel and resource-gathering design problems. In the case of *Dragon Age*, this mechanic succeeds and adds to the game experience, while in the *Mass Effect* franchise, it feels underdeveloped and distracts from the core gameplay loop. The difference is in the level of polish and the degree to which all aspects of the mechanic contribute to the core design of the overall game.

- *Stardew Valley*—This game is chock-full of mechanics that simulate different parts of rural life (admittedly rural life full of mine monsters), from farming, to mining, to fishing, to going to town to socialize. These could easily make the game feel unfocused or distract from the core gameplay in a different game. In this case, every mechanic fits into the fictional frame of the game, each is equally well implemented and necessary for success, and each intrinsically supports the core gameplay. That core gameplay, in this case, is time management, so having a variety of possible actions at all points is critical. The way that each is implemented creates a rhythm for the gameplay that mirrors the rhythm of rural life.

- *Pokémon Go*—The initial design of this game was done on a minimal timeframe and with limited resources. It wasn't possible to implement all the mechanics that players would expect. Instead of cramming in as many mechanics as possible at the cost of quality, only a few mechanics were implemented at launch. They were very polished, though they made up a barely minimally viable product. The game received some criticism for not having richer gameplay. But soon after launch, Niantic began adding new mechanics, which has continued throughout the ongoing lifespan of the game. Each mechanic contributes to the existing game and moves toward a long-term goal of deeper gameplay; it is released only when its quality meets player expectations. In the cases where expectations are not met, player response is actively addressed before more mechanics are introduced.

Seed: Finding Positive Patterns from Negative Patterns: Negative Pattern—Game, Know Thyself
Related patterns:
Parent patterns:
I See Where You Are Going with This* (Confidence: 1)—As you use the pattern Familiarity Breeds Contempt, or at Least High Expectations to allocate your development resources, you must make sure that the mechanics you prioritize are legible to your players by giving sufficient resources to their supporting mechanics.

---

* Example pattern for Exercise 24: Theoretical Patterns.

SUGGESTED EXERCISE

Use **Exercise 1: Basic Pattern Exercise** to generate a pattern looking at developer resource allocation. This is intended to produce a pattern to guide business-related resource allocation for developers. The basic pattern exercise will work for this, but it would be a good place to develop a more targeted exercise. Look at a broad selection of games that prioritize different aspects of their designs when searching for this pattern.

Child patterns:

SUGGESTED EXERCISE

Use **Exercise 5: Functional Patterns** to generate patterns about how different functional elements should be implemented in order to meet player expectations.

Keywords: Development Resources, Core Mechanics, Secondary Mechanics, Player Expectations, *Strong Centers, Good Shape, Not Separateness*

USING PATTERNS FOR UNDERSTANDING

All the exercises up to this point have focused on creating patterns meant to be used in design and as part of a growing Pattern Language. The next two exercises are different. They may produce patterns that will become part of your language, but that is not their primary purpose.

One way you can use the exercises in this book is to help you understand how and why game design techniques work the way they do, and how those techniques fit into the larger design process. The patterns you produce are an expression of that understanding, but even in cases where an exercise fails to produce a usable pattern, it may generate valuable understanding of the design process, the nature of a technique, or an aspect of design.

These exercises focus on that property. They explore how and why aspects of design function in the way they do. They may or may not produce useful patterns; the most valuable output of the exercise may be the response to the exercise itself.

UNDERSTANDING TECHNIQUES

Pattern Purpose

This exercise looks at the effects of a technique. It might be formal or functional; it might be from any game design discipline. When looking at a technique in previous exercises, you may have noted that a technique has several different effects under different conditions. In those exercises, you were asked to choose an effect and focus your pattern on how it's created. This developed your understanding of how to control the effects of a technique in various specific ways.

Now you'll look at all of those effects, focusing on the differences and on the conditions that cause the effects to vary. It's challenging to distill a pattern from this process; you may end up instead with a list of variables and how they affect your technique. These variables will be other techniques, not patterns. And while you can pursue this process recursively, it's easy for that process to lose value and become circular.

Why pursue it then? Because the first level of understanding is advantageous to a designer. It's valuable to understand, for instance, how other aspects of a design can make the functional element of jumping create a sense of empowerment and agency in *Super Mario Bros.* or *Devil May Cry*, but a sense of vulnerability in *The Last of Us*. And of course, it's sometimes possible to distill a useful meta-level pattern from this exercise. This kind of pattern, describing ways that the effects of a technique change, is incredibly valuable. It can allow you to use the technique in an entirely new way, while understanding how your design choices are likely to impact the player experience.

EXERCISE 20: USING PATTERNS TO UNDERSTAND TECHNIQUES

Step 1: Pick a design technique that has different effects in different games.

Step 2: Pick and describe ten games that use that technique to create different effects. (You may not find ten different effects, but you still need ten games.) List the games and the effects.

Step 3: How does the technique create each effect? Here you may have fewer than ten examples—one for each effect, not one for each game.

Step 4: Are there patterns in the way the techniques create the different effects? What you're looking for here is why the effects are different in each game.

Step 5: Take one pattern and expand it using the Pattern Template.

Step 6: You may repeat step 5 for each pattern you noted in step 4.

Example Pattern
Exercise

Step 1: Pick a design technique that has different effects in different games.
Running

Step 2: Pick and describe ten games that use that technique to create different effects. (You may not find ten different effects, but you still need ten games.) List the games and the effects.

- *Silent Hill 2*—Vulnerability and character limitation.

- *Silent Hill: Shattered Memories*—Vulnerability.

- *The Secret World*—Growth and increasing character power.

- *Canabalt*—Character power and agency, vulnerability, player limitation.

- *The Sinking City*—Character vulnerability.

- *Anthem*— Convenience of mobility, character limitation.

- *Mirror's Edge*—Character power, player agency.

- *Summer Games* — Player limitation.

- *Tag*—Player limitation.

- *Legend of Zelda: Breath of the Wild*—Character limitation, character growth, player agency.

Step 3: How does the technique create each effect? Here you may have fewer than ten examples—one for each effect, not one for each game.

- Vulnerability—Characters are often made vulnerable when they can run, but not enough to escape monsters, or when they can't attack and have to deal with threats by running. Not being able to stop and running into danger creates a similar effect in *Canabalt*.

- Character power—Running can let you avoid combat, particularly when the character can move quickly through areas that they've completed or that contain enemies that have become trivial to defeat, as in *Secret World*. Running can also let the character traverse the world in ways that the other entities in the game can't, as in *Mirror's Edge*. In these cases, the character's ability to run is generally far greater than yours or than a normal human's.

- Player limitation—The physical action required to run can focus you on your limitations, whether you have to strike alternating keys at top speed to represent your left and right feet as in *Summer Games*, or literally run as in tag. Success or failure in the game mean more, as they relate more directly to you as the player than to a character.

- Character growth—The character's ability to run grows throughout the game. This is an obvious and powerful way to show the character's increasing power in the game world, as in most games where you can run, you spend a lot of your time running.

- Character limitation—This is related to vulnerability but also to character growth. Games that use this technique either limit the ability to run or take it away. In the case of *Anthem*, although the character can run, and quickly, running is far more limited than the ability to fly, which is core to the gameplay. When you lose your flying ability, even the ability to run very well is limiting. In these cases, the character's ability to run is usually similar to or worse than yours.

- Convenience—This is the effect created by using running to allow you to compress the less exciting parts of gameplay—like moving from place to place—by increasing the character's speed.

Step 4: Are there patterns in the way the techniques create the different effects? What you're looking for here is why the effects are different in each game.

- If the character's ability to run increases throughout the game and allows them to avoid or overcome the threats they face, it gives the player a sense of agency and the character a sense of power.

- If the character's ability to run is lowered or is insufficient to bypass or overcome the threats they face, it makes the character more vulnerable. It may also make the player feel a loss of agency, which may cause frustration.

- If the ability to move in the game is tied to the player's ability, it may create a feeling of close parity with the character, if the character is not in fact the player (as is the case in physical games like tag).

Step 5: Choose one pattern to document using the Pattern Template.

Pattern

Name: More or Less Running Away
Confidence: 2
Image:

FIGURE 14.5 The effect of running in a game changes dramatically depending on whether it is slower or faster than enemies.

Author: Chris Barney
Design problem: Introducing running into a game to solve the practical problem of getting a character quickly from one place to another can have a variety of different impacts on the player experience, depending on the details of the implementation.
Description: To control the effect of adding the functional element of running to a game, the developer must decide how they want running to affect the character and the player. The ability to outrun opponents will give the character a sense of power and give the player more agency, while running slower than opponents will make the character seem vulnerable. Increasing a character's speed over the course of the game will emphasize the growth of the character's power, whereas lowering or removing their ability to run will focus the player on the character's limitations. And tying the character's ability to run to the player's abilities can cause the player to relate closely to the character, but it is difficult to implement if there is any significant amount of running in the game.

Games that use this pattern and how:

- *Silent Hill 2*—In this survival horror game, you move at a walk by default. You have the ability to run, but doing so depletes the character's stamina. There's no display for stamina, but there are visual and audio cues, and when the character becomes tired, they double over when they stop running. It's possible for the character to escape enemies by running, but it's not certain. The limits to running create feelings of vulnerability while still allowing you to traverse the larger open spaces in the game more quickly.
- *Mirror's Edge*—This first-person action game focuses on running. As such, the character's ability to run is one of the primary ways that the character expresses their nature and personality. It's also the primary way for both the player and the character to express their autonomy. The tone of this game is tense action rather than horror, so running gives the character greater ability to avoid and deal with danger than the previous game.
- *The Legend of Zelda: Breath of the Wild*—The use of running in this game is very complex. It uses a similar stamina mechanic to *Silent Hill 2*, but as a heroic RPG, it reinforces the nature of the character by allowing you to use running to escape most combat as you traverse the open world. As the game progresses and enemies become more dangerous, your ability to run scales up as well, providing a sense of character growth. The complex interplay of these and other systems, such as crafting, complement the game's focus on character development.

Seed: Exercise 20: Using Patterns to Understand Techniques—Running
Related patterns:
Parent patterns: [This pattern probably generalizes to movement within a game.]

SUGGESTED EXERCISE

Use **Exercise 20: Using Patterns to Understand Techniques** to duplicate the work for this pattern, but use movement as the seed instead of running. Do you find that movement is used in the same way as running? If so, then consider eliminating this pattern and replacing it with yours. If you find differences in the effects and uses of general movement compared to the specific movement of running, then consider whether your pattern is a parent to this one.

Child patterns:

SUGGESTED EXERCISE

Use **Exercise 6: Emotional Patterns** to generate a pattern based on vulnerability.

Use **Exercise 7: Player Experience Patterns** to generate a pattern based on character power, control, or autonomy.

Keywords: Movement, Running, Mechanics, Empathy, *Deep Interlock*, *Graded Variation, Roughness*

UNDERSTANDING TROPES

Pattern Purpose

This exercise can help a developer assess the effects of a trope on their game. It's not an exercise intended to convert a trope into a pattern. Although it may be possible to make that kind of conversion or to break a trope down into its formal and functional elements and create patterns around them, this exercise is focused on understanding the effects of the trope as it exists.*

To complete this exercise, you must understand the cultural meanings the trope carries. Understanding the mechanical definition of the trope is not enough, and attempting to complete this exercise without understanding the trope's context can result in a pattern that will cause you to imply meanings in your game that you may not be aware of. Therefore, you'll need to research the trope that you choose as part of step 1 of the exercise. Take care in this research, pursue multiple sources, and discuss the things you find with your development colleagues and classmates.

Do not shy away from the negative aspects or implications of the trope, because they are as crucial to this exercise as the useful narrative or mechanical effects. I recommend looking at the video series "Tropes vs. Women in Video Games" by Anita Sarkeesian for an example of the kind of analysis that you need to be performing for this exercise. If you're not comfortable or able to do this kind of research and analysis on your own, I would even recommend picking a trope covered in that series and using it for your first attempt at this exercise.

---

* See the section "Forming Patterns vs. Accepting Tropes and Stereotypes" in Chapter 1 for more details on how the term "trope" is being used in the context of this book.

You may find it difficult or impossible to determine whether the use of the trope is intentional on the part of the developers or if it's just present because of the cultural rhetoric the developers were working within. But that isn't as much of a problem as it might seem. The developers don't need to have intended a meaning for that meaning to be present in a game. Often in seeking examples, you'll see a trope interfering with other aspects of the game. These are likely cases where the use of the trope was not intentional. Other times, the mechanical effects of the trope will be in line with the other mechanics of the game, but the connotations of the trope's meaning will be at odds with the other meanings in the game. These may be cases where the trope was used intentionally, but without a deep understanding of its cultural baggage. And, of course, you'll find cases where the meanings of a trope are clearly in line with the mechanics and broader meanings of the game, indicating use that's intentional and well-considered.

EXERCISE 21: USING PATTERNS TO UNDERSTAND TROPES

Step 1: Describe the meaning and context of the trope. This step may require research.

Step 2: Pick and describe ten games that use that trope. If you can't think of ten games, pick a different trope.

Step 3: For each game, describe how that trope shapes the meaning of the game.

Step 4: For each game, describe how the game would change if it didn't use that trope.

Step 5: For each game, state whether you think the designer intended the meanings of the trope to shape the meaning of their game.

Step 6: Pick one effect of the trope and articulate it as a pattern using the template. The pattern you generate in this way may be a positive or negative pattern, depending on the trope and the effect you chose.

Example Pattern

Exercise

Step 1: Describe the meaning and context of the trope. This step may require research.

The lone warrior. This trope portrays a single hero taking on the forces of evil. It goes so deep that it's implicit in the Western mainstream understanding of what it means to be a hero. In Western media, the lone warrior is almost always male, white, and heteronormative. These things are not important to the basic function of the trope, but they're often defaulted to when the trope is present. This trope serves a variety of purposes, which can be summarized by the following three points:

- It's easier to tell a story with a single protagonist.

- It's easier to make a game with a single-player character.

- A whole scaffolding of other tropes falls into place when this one is adopted.

Step 2: Pick and describe ten games that use that trope. If you can't think of ten games, pick a different trope.

- *Doom*—Soldier takes on the forces of hell alone.

- *Ninja Gaiden*—Ninja seeks revenge for his father's murder and saves the world.

- *God of War*—Spartan warrior seeks revenge for his family's death and kills the gods.

- *Horizon Zero Dawn*—Rejected girl seeks to find her place in the world and save her tribe.

- *Zelda*—Chosen warrior must defeat evil to save the princess and save the world.

- *Super Mario Bros.*—Plumber must rescue the princess.

- *The Elder Scrolls*—Prisoner must gain enough power to face the forces that threaten the world.

- *Dark Souls*—Undead warrior must survive the horrors of the world they are trapped in.

- *Myst*—The player must explore the world alone and solve puzzles to decide the fate of the other characters in the game.

Step 3: For each game, describe how that trope shapes the meaning of the game.

- *Doom*—The almost complete lack of context for the playable character creates a sense of isolation. The core gameplay loop is simple, as is the overall game design, and doesn't require the kind of narrative scaffolding that a more complex premise would provide. The level of hyperviolence in the game, which is used to some comedic effect, matches the more negative connotations of the trope's typically male hero. While there are simple key-based puzzles in the game, you mostly make progress by moving through the levels, which require a high level of carnage and reflect the behavior of a lone warrior using force or violence to solve every problem. In this case, the choice of trope reflects the design intent.

- *Ninja Gaiden*—In this classic side-scrolling beat-'em-up game, which has been remade as many times as *Doom*, the straightforward narrative that this trope generates fits well with its simple gameplay.* In this case, however, there's more characterization and motivation, and in turn, additional tropes. In a revenge-based narrative, the lone warrior trope's effectiveness is weakened by the fact that lone warriors often refuse to express their emotional distress, or have no one to express it to, making it hard for the player to be aware of their deep and compelling inner life, or lack of one. It's also harder to show the impact of the character's loss, due to his loner tendencies. This trope also models a strong sense of masculine self-reliance and fear of showing weakness or seeking help.

- *God of War*—This game is another revenge narrative. The aforementioned effects of the lone warrior trope are on display here, but here the game leans into these negative character traits and creates a story about an unlikable antihero. The game produced by these design choices appealed to a significant audience, but also alienated other players.

- *Horizon Zero Dawn*—The use of the lone warrior trope in this game is interesting. In this case, the protagonist is female. She begins the game not alone, but with her father figure. Although his loss is one of her motivators, she is primarily driven by trying to save her adoptive tribe, who have rejected her. Her goal is both understanding and gaining acceptance within her tribe. In this way, her status as a lone warrior is externally imposed, which gives the trope negative consequences. This subversion of the trope reinforces the game's themes of community and interdependence, even while allowing mechanical

---

* Simple, not easy. *Ninja Gaiden* has a well-deserved reputation for significant levels of difficulty.

game design that takes advantage of the simplicity of single-character gameplay.

- *Zelda*—Although this game's tone is lighter, the lone warrior trope is still in evidence. Link's status as a loner is also externally imposed: he's given the status of the chosen hero and sent out on that path. He gets some support from the world he's been sent out to save, as seen in the iconic dialogue, "It's dangerous to go alone. Take this!" There are still sexist overtones here, as Link has the personal motivation of saving the princess, who's presented as a potential love interest. The main character's quest in the original iteration of this franchise works well with the lone warrior trope. Some of the later games, which rely more on side quests, suffer from the issue of the world-saving hero being asked to solve every trivial problem anyone faces.

- *Super Mario Bros.*—The narrative of the first iteration of this game was very light, providing a premise and motivation for the mostly nonsensical plot. However, the basic lone warrior trope is present, again reinforced by the damsel in distress trope. In later games in this series, the narrative becomes somewhat more complicated, if not more sensical. Regardless of the tone or complexity, the structure of this game series became an iconic model for what was expected and acceptable in games.

- *The Elder Scrolls*—In each of this series of role-playing games, the player creates a character, which elides some of the gender-related aspects of this trope. The mechanical benefits of simpler single-player combat are present, though there are sometimes companions present in later iterations of the franchise. The close-mouthed, mysterious nature of the lone warrior is leveraged here to allow NPCs to give generic responses that are appropriate to any character the player creates. Later iterations of the game customize responses somewhat based on the race and gender of the player character.

- *Dark Souls*—The grimdark and obscure esthetic of this game works very well with the lone warrior trope. The isolation of the character is in keeping with the esthetic and narrative of the game. Because of the strangeness of the world and the lack of additional motivating tropes, the game mostly avoids the trope's negative connotations. It's possible for other players to aid or hinder the player in these games, but their presence is ghostly and not core to the primary gameplay.

- *Myst*—In this puzzle-based game, the player character is trapped inside a book written by another character in the world. There are no other characters in the game, and you're left to unravel the mystery in isolation. The identity of the character is unknown, and their behavior is not governed by other tropes, which avoids negative connotations. The character's solitude reinforces the themes of the game.

Step 4: For each game, describe how the game would change if it didn't use that trope.

- *Doom*—Interestingly, both movie versions of *Doom* have featured a squad-based narrative. This choice reflects the different requirements of games versus film. However, if you replace the single-player components of *Doom* with a squad-based narrative frame, the game might look something like *Destiny* or *Anthem* or *Left 4 Dead*. If you replace the deathmatch or competitive multiplayer elements with a squad-based premise, you would end up with a game like *Team Fortress*. In both cases, the games become about the group of players and about the fiction that binds them together.

- *Ninja Gaiden*—A variety of four-player arcade games, such as *Teenage Mutant Ninja Turtles*, could be argued to be similar to this game without the lone warrior trope. However, those games simply add additional players without altering the gameplay or story in any meaningful way. Games like *Child of Light* or even *Little Big Planet* give some insight into what this game might become in the absence of this trope. Allowing for interaction between players, or between a single player and meaningful NPCs, could distract from the tightly focused action of the game. But it could also add the possibility of combat mechanics that require player cooperation. As discussed earlier, letting the main character have meaningful interaction would allow more narrative exploration of the revenge narrative premise.

- *God of War*—The clear example of what this game becomes without the lone warrior trope is the 2018 *God of War* release, in which the main character has aged and has a son. As suggested with regard to *Ninja Gaiden*, this allowed both more complex combat and an exploration of the main characters through their interactions during gameplay.

- *Horizon Zero Dawn*—The complex combat, battles against huge enemies, and tribe-focused narrative of this game seem like they would benefit from abandoning this trope. I do think that the lone warrior trope fits well with the narrative themes of rejection and seeking group membership. However, shifting to a more group-focused theme might better fit the game's narrative progression.

- *Zelda*—Removing this trope from an action RPG like *Zelda* might allow for the character to complete quests with various NPCs, allowing for both satisfying cooperative combat and time to flesh out the character's relationships with others in the world. Narratively, there is not a strong reason for this trope. To some degree, massively multiplayer online games (MMOs) are examples of what *Zelda* might be without a focus on a lone warrior protagonist. However, even most MMOs regularly fall back to this trope, primarily sending players' characters out alone.

- *Super Mario Bros.*—I don't think the answer here differs much from that for *Ninja Gaiden*, though the example of *Little Big Planet* fits better in this case.

- *The Elder Scrolls*—All social interaction in the *Elder Scrolls* games is a little stiff and stilted. Later games do introduce companion characters, but those companions don't alter the gameplay much. But even this slight deviation from the lone warrior trope allowed some players to bond with these companions and to become more emotionally invested in their characters. A game like *Dragon Age* shows the potential of this type of game without this trope.

- *Dark Souls*—The grim solitude of this trope strengthens the intentional isolation of the player and character in this game. The game *Ashen* is a good example of the changes that removing this trope would cause. In *Ashen*, the player is almost always accompanied by a companion character when they leave their settlement to complete a quest. The constant interaction with these NPCs allows players to form stronger bonds with them and with the settlement they're building together.

Ashen also incorporates a multiplayer component, which replaces the optional and elusive ghosts of *Dark Souls* with players being placed into each other's companion NPCs. This is mostly transparent to the players involved, each seeing themselves as the main character and the other player as the companion NPC. At its best, this allows for realistic NPC behavior and dynamic combat. At its worst, it enables player trolling that can prevent progress in the game.

- *Myst*—Although it was a niche game that never found its full expression, *Uru: Ages Beyond Myst* was an exploration of how the world and gameplay of *Myst* would change with the introduction of multiplayer gameplay and a focus on community. At its best, forming a community and exploring this world was thrilling, but the nature of puzzles that need only be solved once did not fit well with the amount of time players needed to form social bonds, and the game soon ran out of content.

Step 5: For each game, state whether you think the designer intended the meanings of the trope to shape the meaning of their game.

- *Doom*—Yes

- *Ninja Gaiden*—No

- *God of War*—Yes

- *Horizon Zero Dawn*—Yes

- *Zelda*—No

- *Super Mario Bros.*—No

- *The Elder Scrolls*—Yes

- *Dark Souls*—Yes

- *Myst-*—No

Step 6: Pick one effect of the trope and articulate it as a pattern using the template. The pattern you generate in this way may be a positive or negative pattern, depending on the trope and the effect you chose.
Using the lone warrior trope creates a sense of isolation for the player and character.

Pattern

Name: Can I Do This Alone?
Confidence: 2
Image:

FIGURE 14.6 When you use a trope you inherit a whole host of meanings and follow-on problems that you must consider very carefully.

Author: Chris Barney
Design problems: The following design problems may result in the inclusion of the lone warrior trope. The trope does address these problems, but when used carelessly without consideration of this or other related patterns, it may have unintended side effects.

- Multiplayer gameplay is complex to produce.
- Cooperative NPCs are complicated to implement.
- Many common video game character motivational tropes are closely coupled with the lone warrior trope.
- The intended gameplay requires a single character and is combat-focused.
- The designer wants to create a sense of isolation in the character and/or the player.
- The designer wants to afflict the character with the negative social connotations of the lone warrior trope.
- The designer wants to confront the player with the negative social connotations of the lone warrior trope.

Description: When seeking a narrative premise that will create a sense of isolation in the player and character, a designer may wish to make use of the lone warrior trope. This trope can have significant cultural baggage, however, and developers must carefully consider how it is implemented to achieve the intended effects without unintended connotations.

In its most basic form, the trope is that a lone warrior must confront the forces arrayed against them. The negative connotations of this trope arise from the fact that traditionally this warrior is male and often exhibits the behavioral patterns of toxic masculinity. These behaviors can range from a refusal to accept help, to an inability to communicate their needs, to actively hostile behavior towards anyone they encounter as no one can understand their pain, and so on.

Other problematic tropes such as the damsel in distress (Sarkeesian 2016a), what these people need is a honky (TV Tropes 2020b), or stuffed into the fridge (Sarkeesian 2016b) are often associated with the lone warrior. When employing the lone warrior trope, designers must be aware of other tropes that they may include without explicit intent.

Of course, not all instances of this trope include all or any of these negative aspects. But due to the nature of tropes, even instances free from these negative aspects may still be implied by players familiar with the trope. This is of course projection on the part of the players, but no less real for that.

When using this trope, the designer must be aware of these connotations and either actively subvert them or make use of them intentionally. Otherwise, they run the risk of having their narrative intent colored.

Games that use this pattern and how:

- *Doom*—As the player, you begin, play, and end the game alone. You are told that only you stand between the forces of hell and earth. This game does partake of some of the trope's negative aspects via the angry expressions of the character portrait. The trope, however, fits very well with the simple gameplay and the desired sense of desperation, isolation, and eventual heroic victory that it intends.
- *Dark Souls*—The implementation of this trope in this game is much more nuanced. The ability to choose your gender, along with the game's melancholy atmosphere, removes much of the hypermasculinity associated with this trope. The game also uses that expectation to emphasize that in this world, there's little glory in this lonely struggle. However, the antagonistic nature of the multiplayer components brings back some of the trope's more negative connotations.
- *Horizon Zero Dawn*—The lone warrior trope is used skillfully in this game, subverting its negative aspects with the use of an explicit female character, and by making one of the character's main goals to escape her isolation and gain acceptance in her tribe.

Seed: Using Patterns to Understand Tropes—The Lone Warrior

Related patterns:
Parent patterns:

SUGGESTED EXERCISE

Use **Exercise 24: Theoretical Patterns** to generate a pattern based on the idea that cultural rhetoric influences a developer's design choices.
Use **Exercise 24: Theoretical Patterns** to generate a pattern based on the idea that cultural rhetoric influences the player's interpretation of the elements in the game.

Child patterns:

SUGGESTED EXERCISE

Use **Exercise 21: Using Patterns to Understand Tropes** to generate a pattern based on the trope *damsel in distress*.
Use **Exercise 21: Using Patterns to Understand Tropes** to generate a pattern based on the trope *what these people need is a honkey*.
Use **Exercise 21: Using Patterns to Understand Tropes** to generate a pattern based on the trope *stuffed into the fridge*.

Keywords: Tropes, Isolation, Single Player, Motivation, *Strong Centers*, *Deep Interlock*, *Echoes**

THE FIRST CHOICE

Pattern Purpose

This exercise is meant to produce very high-level patterns. It asks the designer to pick the first question they ask themselves when they're asked to make a game. These questions can be all over the map: How much money do I have to invest? What is the story? What is the camera perspective? What is the game genre? Or any of a thousand considerations. The point is to ask a big question, one that will define the shape of the game at the highest level.

This is a strange exercise, and it may say as much about the designer completing it as it does about the importance or validity of any initial game design question. But it does tend to produce interesting patterns. While your choice of starting question may be idiosyncratic, it will provide

---

* These three fundamental properties are enhanced by the use of tropes. However, the centers they create, interlock with, and echo may not be ones you intend!

a top-level pattern. It will not be *the* top-level pattern, but when combined with the results of this exercise from other developers it will help to provide a healthy variety of these top-level patterns for your language.

EXERCISE 22: THE FIRST CHOICE

Step 1: Pretend you have been asked to make a game.*
Step 2: What is the first question you ask yourself?
Step 3: Name ten games that you think asked this question first.†
Step 4: Describe them. What kind of games are they?
Step 5: List and describe any patterns you see.
Step 6: Pick one pattern and document it using the Pattern Template.
Step 7: Repeat step 6 for each pattern you observed in step 5.

Example Pattern
Exercise

Step 1: Pretend you have been asked to make a game.
Okay, I'm pretending. For this exercise, I imagine needing to decide what game to make and think about the different things that factor into that decision. I need to be able to determine things like how to pick a story, select a team size, or design my core mechanics. I select a first question that will help me work through these problems.

Step 2: What is the first question you ask yourself?
I'm cheating a little bit here as I've done this exercise several times, and I'm going to pick the question that yielded my favorite pattern. But each time I've completed the exercise, it's generated a useful high-level pattern.

In this case, my question is, What perspective am I going to use for this game?

---

* In my classes I usually give students a little context here. I might say, "Imagine that you have been put in charge of your first game at the company you work at. Your boss gives you the assignment. What is the first question that pops into your head?" It would be just as valid to imagine that you were setting out on your dream indie project and trying to think of the most important decision you would have to make, or if you are a student, to imagine that you're starting the design of your final senior project or thesis project.

† Not games that answered the question the same way that you would, just games for which the answer to the question is the defining aspect of the game. If the question was about budget, then games for which budget defined the rest of the design choices, or for which story defined the design, or perspective, etc.

Step 3: Name ten games that you think asked this question first.

It is, of course, effectively impossible to know whether most games asked your question "first." For the purposes of this exercise, it's sufficient to select games that are defined by your question.

Tomb Raider, Gears of War, Monument Valley, Beat Saber, The Room, Silent Hill, Nier: Automata, Echochrome, Among the Sleep, Black & White

Step 4: Describe them. What kind of games are they?

- *Tomb Raider* (1996)—The choice of camera in this game is perhaps the strongest element in establishing its identity. The close third-person perspective allows the traversal and platforming puzzles that make the game distinct from the first-person 3D games that came before it. This camera allows the character to be your primary focus as the player. This had both positive and negative effects, in that it allows more opportunity to define the character by her appearance and to connect you emotionally with the character by showing her reactions to events. But it also allows for the sexual objectification of the character and the fetishization of the character's death sequences. Both of these effects were intentional, and were possible and effective because of the camera choice.

- *Gears of War*—The choice of an over-the-shoulder third-person camera for this game helped it define the cover-based shooter genre. The perspective also helped with the game's greater focus on character and story.

- *Monument Valley*—The fixed isometric camera allows the optical illusions and visual surprise that define the game.

- *Beat Saber*—Giving this game a first-person fixed-location virtual reality (VR) camera creates the feeling of being present in the game like no other. Additionally, it allows the one-to-one control scheme that makes the experience of the game possible.

- *The Room*—The first-person camera is set a little unusually, as the player cannot move freely.* The game focuses on the manipulation of puzzle items in the world, and in many ways the camera

---

* This "fixed" first-person perspective was used in the early puzzle game *Myst*, though the later version of that game, *Real Myst*, allowed free character movement. In *Myst* the perspective was used largely due to technical limitations; in this game it is used intentionally to facilitate perspective-dependent puzzles.

functions more like a third-person camera. However, it enables an almost one-to-one interaction mapping that allows you to feel like you're moving things around in the game world with the touch controls as you play.

- *Silent Hill*—The third-person camera, which is sometimes trailing and sometimes fixed, facilitates the character's limited perspective. The game uses other affordances, such as fog and darkness, to create the same effect when the camera is trailing. The limitations of this camera view make the controls less intuitive to use, which furthers the character's (and the player's!) awkward panic and fear of the unknown.

- *Nier: Automata*—This game uses a wider variety of perspectives than is typical. It includes a side-scrolling 2D camera, an over-the-shoulder third-person camera, and a top-down isometric scrolling camera. The switches between these are all done in the same engine, which adjusts the camera to whatever style of gameplay the designer desires at a given point. The constant shifting may unsettle you as a player, but it also intrigues, keeping you guessing as to what kind of game you're playing.

- *Echochrome*—This game is similar to *Monument Valley*, if much simpler in presentation. The fixed third-person camera allows gameplay that's heavily based on the optical illusions and impossible spaces of M.C. Escher. There's more freedom in this game to rotate the game world, allowing for somewhat different puzzles but resulting in less intuitive gameplay.

- *Among the Sleep*—This game has a first-person perspective, but adjusts the camera height to match that of its two-year-old protagonist. The result is startlingly effective in creating a sense of vulnerability in this horror-themed game.

- *Black & White*—The free-flying distant third-person perspective reflects the disembodied omnipotence of the "god game" genre, of which this game is probably the best example.

Step 5: List and describe any patterns you see.

1. Games that are defined by their choice of perspective use that perspective to enable or emphasize a core mechanic.

2. The closer the perspective of the camera to the character, the more the player identifies as that character. That's true enough in a literary sense, but adding both the ability to control the character's actions, and a visual sense of being either distant from, close to, or inside of the character makes it even more powerful in games.

3. Different perspectives are useful for different kinds of gameplay, specifically:

   • Isometric perspectives support exploration and high levels of player information.

   • A 2D side and fixed perspective make spatial awareness easier by limiting it to two axes, which can facilitate puzzles (*Tetris*) and platforming (*Super Mario Bros.*).

   • Third-person perspective can be easier to control (console games) and can provide visibility for a character when character identity is an important narrative element.

   • First-person perspective can make aiming and shooting easier, it can increase a player's ability to project themselves into the character, and it can provide a more immersive window into the game world.

   • VR perspective can allow intuitive one-to-one physical/game controls and an unparalleled sense of presence in the game world.

Step 6: Pick one pattern and document it using the Pattern Template.
Because I'm looking for a good high-level pattern, I'm going to document my first answer to step 5: "Games that are defined by their choice of perspective use that perspective to enable or emphasize a core mechanic."

I think that the pattern I noted in answer 2 is interesting, but it may be more of an emotional pattern. It does seem worth documenting later, though.

The set-off patterns would clearly be children of the first, so I will leave them for another time.

Step 7: Repeat step 6 for each pattern you observed in step 5.

Pattern

Name: It All Depends on How You Look at It
Confidence: 2
Image:

FIGURE 14.7 When the camera perspective doesn't match the core mechanic it can become hard for the player to engage with the experience you are trying to create.

Author: Chris Barney
Design problem: When beginning to make a game, the camera perspective is often one of the first choices a designer has to make. Many factors go into this choice, and the best option is often unclear.
Description: To design a game that creates a particular experience as effectively as possible, the designer should first understand the experience they want to create, and then the techniques, both mechanical and esthetic, that they'll use to create that experience. Only then should they consider which camera perspective to choose.

Different camera perspectives are better at supporting some mechanical and esthetic choices than others. The child patterns listed here go into detail about which camera perspectives support which techniques, but the following observations can serve as basic guidelines:

- Isometric perspectives support exploration and high levels of player information, as in *The Legend of Zelda* or *League of Legends*.
- A 2D side and fixed perspective make spatial awareness easier by limiting it to two axes, which can facilitate puzzles, as in *Tetris* or *Bejeweled*, and platforming, as in *Super Mario Bros.* or *Ori and the Blind Forest*.
- Third-person perspective can be easier to control, particularly on game controllers used by console games. It can also provide visibility for a character when character identity is an important narrative element.

- First-person perspective can make aiming and shooting easier, it can increase a player's ability to project themselves into the character, and it can provide a more immersive window into the game world as seen in games like *Doom* or *The Elder Scrolls V: Skyrim*.
- VR perspective can allow intuitive one-to-one physical/game controls and an unparalleled sense of presence in the game world, as seen in games like *Beat Saber* or *Resident Evil 7*.

Games that use this pattern and how:

- ***Tomb Raider***—The choice of camera in this game is perhaps the strongest element in establishing its identity. The close third-person perspective allows the traversal and platforming puzzles that make the game distinct from the first-person 3D games that came before it. This camera allows the character to be your primary focus as the player. This has both positive and negative effects, in that it allows more opportunity to define the character by her appearance and to connect you emotionally with the character by showing her reactions to events. But it also allows for the sexual objectification of the character and the fetishization of the character's death sequences. Both of these effects were intentional, and were possible and effective because of the camera choice.
- ***Among the Sleep***—This game has a first-person perspective, but adjusts the camera height to match that of its two-year-old protagonist. The result is startlingly effective in creating a sense of vulnerability in this horror-themed game.
- ***Beat Saber***—Giving this game a first-person fixed-location VR camera creates the feeling of being present in the game like no other. Additionally, it allows the one-to-one control scheme that makes the experience of the game possible.

Seed: Exercise 22: The First Choice—Camera Perspective
Related patterns:
Parent patterns:

SUGGESTED EXERCISE

Use **Exercise 22: The First Choice** to generate a pattern based on the choice of core mechanic.
Use **Exercise 22: The First Choice** to generate a pattern based on the choice of narrative.
Use **Exercise 22: The First Choice** to generate a pattern based on the choice of hardware platform.
How are these patterns related? Do they drive the choice of camera perspective or are they driven by it? Are they parents or children of this pattern?

Child patterns:

Temporally Unavailable Space* (Confidence: 2)—The implementation of this pattern depends on the choice made in applying It All Depends on How You Look at It. Once you have made that choice, use this pattern if you want to make your levels more dynamic.

Fight Like You Live† (Confidence: 2)—Once you have decided on player experience and chosen camera perspective, you may use this pattern to guide your combat design if your game includes combat.

I Could Be Bounded in a Nutshell and Still Count Myself a King of Infinite Space‡ (Confidence: 3)—The way that you implement this pattern is determined by the choice you make when applying It All Depends on How You Look at It. Use this pattern if your camera perspective and player experience demand that you confine combat to limited space.

SUGGESTED EXERCISES§

Use **Exercise 4: Formal Patterns** to generate patterns based on isometric perspective, 2D side-scrolling perspective, third-person perspective, first-person perspective, or VR first-person perspective.

Use **Exercise 5: Functional Patterns** to generate patterns based on isometric perspective, 2D side-scrolling perspective, third-person perspective, first-person perspective, or VR first-person perspective . How do the patterns generated by Exercise 4 differ from those generated by Exercise 5?

Keywords: Perspective, Camera, Mechanics, *Boundaries, The Void, Not Separateness*

AUDIENCE PATTERNS

Pattern Purpose

As we've discussed in a previous exercise, games have different effects on different players. On one level, no game will have the same impact on any two people. That observation, while technically true, is not all that helpful to us as designers. It's more useful to examine the effects of games on different people and observe patterns.

---

* Example pattern for Exercise 4: Formal Patterns.
† Example pattern for Exercise 5: Functional Patterns.
‡ Example pattern for Exercise 9: Circulation Patterns.
§ You may have noticed that Exercises 4 and 5 are essentially the same. The only real difference is in whether you are looking at a formal or functional element. As you can see here, something like perspective could be looked at either way. The perspective could be part of the shape of the game or part of how you interact with it. When you can't decide whether you should use Exercise 4 or 5 to generate a pattern for a particular design element, try using both and look at how the patterns you find differ.

This, however, is extremely difficult for several reasons. First, looking at the effects of games on diverse audiences requires a degree of research and social sciences training that's not feasible for most designers. And second, most games are still made for very limited audiences.

We still consider ourselves lucky to find a single game that masterfully creates a strong experience, whether it's an emotion like joy or grief, or an abstract concept like the futility of war or the catharsis of violence. Few designers could call to mind ten games that created that kind of experience across ten different audiences! So in this section, I will propose a more modest exercise and then present two more robust versions for those with the resources to pursue them.

It's vital when making observations to be aware of your own implicit and explicit biases. Try to observe the effect of a game or technique, and not assume based on your own internal stereotypes of different kinds of gamers based on race, gender, age, or economic factors. You may or may not have the ability to observe or discuss games with diverse audiences, but at a minimum, read the firsthand accounts of marginalized gamers when completing this exercise.

Additionally, be aware that the stereotypes, tropes, and assumptions you're trying to avoid have been embraced by the marketing apparatus of companies around the world over the last 40 years of game design. Those marketing messages, reinforced by ambient cultural racism, sexism, and other systemic prejudices, have shaped the expectations of many of the more privileged audiences that you may be designing games for. Take that into account when researching your audience and their reactions to games that may have been subject to those forces.

EXERCISE 23: AUDIENCE PATTERNS

Step 1: Think of a particular effect that a game has had on you personally, that you know it had because of who you are.

Step 2: Identify the aspect of yourself that allowed the game to have the effect on you that it did. (This might be your gender, race, sexuality, nationality, economic background, age, level of education, or some other quality.)

Step 3: Look at the effect the same game had on someone who's different from you in that particular way.*

---

* In the later versions of this exercise you will look primarily at other players' responses to games. Here you're just using another player's response to the game to help you define your own and to see what parts of your response may be tied to the audience that you are part of.

Step 4: List as many games as you can that are targeted toward an audience that has the quality you identified in step 2.

Step 5: List the things those games have in common.

Step 6: List the patterns you see in the items you listed in step 5.

Step 7: Select a pattern and document it using the Pattern Template.

Step 8: Share your pattern with a designer who doesn't share the quality you identified in step 2.

Step 9: Seek out a pattern from another designer who doesn't share the quality you identified in step 2.

Exercise 23 will allow you to produce a pattern based on an audience that you are part of. This will help you understand your own audience segment, and the biases and narrow perspective that may come along with it. It will also produce a pattern that helps describe effective design for your audience. The last two steps of this pattern are unusual, because the utility of this pattern comes from sharing it with developers who are part of a different audience than you, and reviewing patterns that describe their own audience segments, which will be different than yours. Through this process, we can all develop a more robust understanding of the patterns around audiences, even if we don't each have the broad perspective and deep insight to create those patterns on our own.

Example Audience Patterns
Exercise

Step 1: Think of a particular effect that a game has had on you personally, that you know it had because of who you are. Describe the game and its effect.

Virginia. Playing this game put me firmly into the role of the main character: a woman of color in the 1990s in the male-dominated field of an FBI field agent. I'm not saying that this was an accurate representation of the profession or that the depiction of the experience of being a woman of color was accurate. But the mechanics and narrative content of the game made me feel the role I was being asked to play in a way that felt distinct from my own experience of life. It also felt different from games where I'm expected to project myself onto the character I'm playing.

Step 2: Identify the aspect of yourself that allowed the game to have the effect on you that it did. (This might be your gender, race, sexuality, nationality, economic background, age, level of education, or some other quality.)

I think my role as a game developer is partially responsible for the game's effectiveness. I was seeking out and trying to embrace the effect of the game. I also think my desire to be an ally to the represented group contributed. The game provided an environment where I could explore my understanding and empathy without inserting myself into a conversation that was outside of my lived experience.

I don't know if I'm the primary intended audience for this game. I can imagine that playing this game might make players that more closely match the demographic profile of the main character feel seen and represented. However, I do feel that the experience of playing the game is meant to be more educational than representational.

Step 3: Look at the effect the same game had on at least one person who is different from you in that particular way.
M.O., female, age 43, gamer, gaming style: action/FPS. She found some character moments effective, but not enough to connect emotionally with the character or experience empathy. Some moments that I found compelling because they differed from my lived experience just seemed unremarkable to her. Things like seeing how small my character's hand was when being shaken by a man or being harassed by teens at a gas station. She found the mechanical restrictions frustrating and "claustrophobic," but mostly didn't connect that feeling to the experience of the character. She thought the minimalist art style made the world feel less meaningful overall. She remarked on the jump cuts and sometimes found them disorienting, but also felt that they took away what might have been meaningful choices, rather than removing meaningless filler choices.

Step 4: List and briefly describe as many games as you can that are targeted toward an audience that has the quality you identified in step 2.

- *Virginia*—You could describe this game as an adventure game where you play an FBI agent investigating a possibly supernatural disappearance in a small town. But this hides the fact that this is a game with no dialogue, extremely minimalist visual style, very intentionally limited player choice, and scenes/levels that jump forward in time unexpectedly and only allow you to see or participate in scenes that matter to the narrative.

- *Spec Ops: The Line*—This game is an indictment of gamer culture around military FPS games like *Call of Duty* or *Battlefield*. Ostensibly the audience for this game would be the players of that genre who unselfconsciously enjoy the violence and virtue fantasy. I am not sure that the game is effective for that audience, but it was effective for me as a developer and a gamer critical of that genre. It showed me why such games are enjoyable, and then made me uncomfortable with having enjoyed those aspects of the game.

- *Loneliness*—This simple game is intended to show the emotional landscape of loneliness. It uses a simple black and white palette and the behavior or small black squares toward the player's small black square, set against melancholy music to achieve its effect. I think that this game would be universally effective, but I also imagine that my designer's mindset and openness to art games made it more so.

- *Gone Home*—This game is set in the early 1990s and evokes a sense of nostalgia, while also conveying the experience of discovering that someone you know very well is gay. The strong sense of nostalgia the game evoked in me, as someone who grew up in the period it depicts, made me connect with the character and personally relate to her experience of discovering her sister's sexual orientation.

- *This War of Mine*—This game uses survival mechanics to present the impossible choices people are forced to make as civilians in times of war. By offering clear strategic choices that violate clear moral norms, the game drives its point home. The game was created by survivors of the siege of Sarajevo.

- *Night in the Woods*—Similarly to *Gone Home,* this game creates a sense of nostalgia and explores the story of a college-age girl trying to come to terms with life in her home town after an abortive stint in college. I completed my course of study, but the game successfully connected with my fears of failure in life to create empathy in me for the character.

- *Hellblade: Senua's Sacrifice*—This game uses a variety of esthetic and mechanical techniques to try to create the experience of mental illness. That's not the plot of the game, but it is the emotional payload. I found it somewhat uncomfortable, as I wasn't sure whether the developers were sufficiently respectful in their design choices. Still, I did find that the mechanics made me behave in ways that are typically associated with the psychological challenges it was depicting.

- *Dear Esther*—The minimal mechanics and limited choice in this game are overlaid with a narrative of sadness at the end of a lonely man's life and his eventual suicide. It's debatable whether the game is about literally choosing to kill yourself or rather about letting go at the end of life. I was conflicted at the end of the game, but found the freeing of the man's spirit touching and beautiful. I would say that it went so far as to help me understand and respect his choice.

Step 5: List the things that those games have in common.

- They depict emotional landscapes that are painful or difficult.

- They are effective for players who have not experienced or don't deeply identify with the characters or situations they depict.

- Many of these games were made by developers with lived or first-hand experience of the situations they depict.

- These games rely on mechanics to reinforce their emotional statements in ways that could be seen as coercive to the player.

- Most of the time, the critical success of these games directly relates to the degree to which they are explicit in their intent.

Step 6: List the patterns you see in the items you listed in step 5.

1. To make your emotional reactions to a game make sense, you need to understand the game's intent. That is to say, if the mechanics of a game are making you the player feel things, then it'll be more effective if you can also see that the character is feeling those same things. If the player has a strong emotional reaction, but doesn't empathize with the character, then the player is likely to feel that emotion toward the game itself. In games where that emotion is negative, it leaves the player with a negative experience of the game.

2. Games that are about a particular lived experience may read more clearly or have more impact on players outside of that lived experience. *Virginia* might be an example of this kind of game, as I feel like it was trying to show the experience of the character to a player that had not had that experience.

The effect I'm describing is different from other games that provide representation for particular groups, but treat a subject that's more accessible and universal. *Papo Y Yo* might be a good example of this type of game, as the setting is steeped in the esthetics of Brazilian culture, but the subject matter involves coming to terms with alcoholism. The fact that I'm not like the character in this game but found its message very effective suggests that this may be true.

3. The aforementioned pattern may also be different from games that are about subject matter specific to an audience but assume the lived experience of the audience. *Gone Home* would be an example of that last statement for me, as it assumes the lived experience of growing up in a suburban nuclear family in the 1980s and '90s.

Step 7: Select a pattern and document it using the pattern template.
The first pattern in step 6 is interesting and I think very valuable, but I believe it will end up being a pattern about player manipulation. There is nothing wrong with deriving that kind of pattern from this exercise, but for the sake of clarity in this example, I am going to document the second pattern as it more closely relates to audiences.

Step 8: Share your pattern with a designer who does not share the quality you identified in step 2.

Step 9: Seek out a pattern from another designer who does not share the quality you identified in step 2.

AUDIENCE AND INTERSECTIONAL IDENTITY

Audience may be a relatively neutral choice for your game, such as "kids from 8 to 12 years old" or "North America." Or it may be related to questions of gender, race, sexuality, and other cultural factors that our industry has struggled with since its inception.

I strongly believe that we need more diverse characters in our games, we need more diverse game designers, and we need games that deal with the issues that we face in our real lives related to the diverse, problematic, and complex world we live in.

Being part of making that happen is challenging, whether you're one of the growing number of diverse developers entering the industry every day, or an old cis white guy like me trying to help our industry change and live up to its potential.

Asking what diversity in a game looks like is a legitimate question. I think there are, unsurprisingly, a diverse set of answers. As I discuss in step 6 of this pattern, there are at least three ways that a game might be diverse. A game may be about a group and have that group as its audience. A game may be about a group and have a different group as its audience. Or a game may not present characters that are like its audience but may still be targeted toward that group.

Regardless of whether you're making a game about one audience for another or making a game about an audience for that audience, you must have deep, preferably lived experience of the groups you're representing.

Ideally, if you're making a game about a group, then your design team should be led by, or at the very least contain, members of that group. If not, ask yourself why. Making a game about a group that you and your team are not part of is an uphill battle. Doing research and hiring consultants to review your work can help. But before you take on that kind of task, be very sure that you are the right team to make the game you're considering.

Pattern

Name: This Game Isn't about You ... But It Is *for* You
Confidence: 1
Image:

FIGURE 14.8 Elements that are noticed or understood by one audience may not be noticed or understood by another.

Author: Chris Barney

Design problem: When beginning the design of a game, the developer must decide on the audience for the game. Determining the audience for a game can be difficult, but it's usually vital for the success of the game— from the start of design, to marketing, and through to critical reception and sales.

Description: Sometimes a game's purpose is to create the experience of a group and make it accessible to an audience made up of members of a different group. In this case, it's important to recognize that your audience may notice, and attribute to the depicted group's experience, things that you as a member of that group aren't even aware of. To represent these aspects of the group's experience, you must break down and articulate that experience. Only when you have a concrete list of distinct experiential aspects can you begin to construct the mechanics and narrative that will read as intended to the non-group members.

Games that use this pattern and how:

- *Virginia*—This game uses a variety of techniques to suggest the experience of being a marginalized woman in a male bureaucracy. Player choice is very limited, sometimes to a single axis of visual movement and a single choice, to show you how limited the character feels her options are. The game also uses cinematic jump cuts to move from one significant character moment to the next, without allowing you to explore the environment and experience it on your own terms. The design subtly uses elements of scale to make you feel small in comparison to the men in the game.
- *Hellblade: Senua's Sacrifice*—This game tries to convey the experience of mental illness through both mechanical and esthetic techniques. For example, as you play, you must create symbols and meaning out of things that only exist in the character's mind. By lining up various objects in the environment, you can form runes that unlock the next area in the game. Instead of a helpful tutorial voice-over, you get a multitude of voices whispering suggestions to the character—voices that are often lying.
- *Loneliness*—This simple game is intended to show the emotional landscape of loneliness. It uses a simple black and white palette, melancholy music, and the behavior of small black squares toward your small black square to achieve its effect. While this game is mainly communicating through metaphor, it's also clearly using mechanical and esthetic techniques to show you what the experience of loneliness can feel like.

Seed: Exercise 23: Audience Patterns—*Virginia*

Related patterns:
Parent patterns:

SUGGESTED EXERCISES

Use **Exercise 2: Higher-Order Patterns** to look for a pattern based on audience. Pick games that you feel were designed for a specific audience. The audience should be different for each game. This will help you find a higher-order pattern that guides games that focus on a specific audience.

Child patterns:

SUGGESTED EXERCISES

Use **Exercise 7: Player Experience Patterns** to generate a pattern about a specific player experience you are trying to create. Be specific. Don't use the experience of "being a soldier"; instead look for patterns about specific experiences a soldier might have such as being told to kill, or facing separation from loved ones, or knowing your choices are protecting something you believe in. Use the pattern to guide your implementation of the details you are trying to convey to your audience.

Keywords: Audience, Player Experience, Mechanics, Esthetics, *Strong Centers, Good Shape, Roughness, Echoes*

The following two proposed exercises are intended for developers with the resources to engage in research. The first looks at how a particular effect is created across different games and audiences. The second shows how a specific game can affect different audiences. These exercises would be appropriate as a research project for an entire class for a semester or as thesis projects. In a professional setting, they might be relevant at the beginning of a large-scale project where audience is a significant concern.

EXERCISE 23A: AUDIENCE PATTERNS

Step 1: Pick a game that you have observed having some specific effect on its audience.
Step 2: Name and describe that effect.

Step 3: Research what games have had a similar effect on a different audience.*

Step 4: Describe the techniques in your original game and in the games you found through research that created the effect from your initial game.

Step 5: List and describe any patterns that you observe in your response to step 4.

Step 6: Pick one pattern and document it using the Pattern Template.

Step 7: You may repeat step 6 for each pattern you observed.

EXERCISE 23B: AUDIENCE PATTERNS

Step 1: Pick a game that you have observed having some specific effect on its audience.

Step 2: Name and describe that effect.

Step 3: Research how ten different audiences experience that game.†

Step 4: Describe the experiences of those audiences.

Step 5: Describe each pattern you observed.

Step 6: Select a pattern and document it using the Pattern Template.

Step 7: You may repeat step 6 for each pattern you observed.

THEORETICAL PATTERNS

I've left this exercise to last for a reason: because it's the path to the dark side. We're all very good at coming up with theories about game design. Sometimes these ideas are insightful and represent cognitive leaps based on the patterns we don't even realize we've been observing. It's very tempting to believe that every theory of yours is like this, that you are the brilliant innovator that will change game design forever with your blinding creativity and insight. The thing is, you're probably not—and you don't need to be. You have the privilege of being part of a field of brilliant, skilled colleagues who are all, like you, working to make games better. It is implicit in every exercise in this book that the ideas of the game designers of today are the best platform, grounding the ideas you'll use to build the games of tomorrow.

---

* Ideally you would look for ten different audience groups that have had a game targeted for them to achieve a particular effect.

† Again, this is difficult, sensitive work. Be respectful in your research and interactions with different communities of gamers.

Understanding the patterns that exist in the games that have been made and proven is far more valuable to you as a tool than any theory you may have about how you can build a better game.

All of that said, sometimes we have ideas. And it's useful to state those ideas as patterns. When we do that, we must give those patterns a low confidence rating, no matter how good we think they are. By taking that low confidence into account, you can responsibly implement those patterns in your games. Over time, they can earn a higher confidence rating, and other developers may adopt them. Eventually, they might even be derived by future readers of this book!

Pattern Purpose

This exercise will allow you to propose a pattern without examples, a pattern that you think should exist based on a theory in game design. Patterns produced in this way will have a very low level of confidence since they will have no examples of successful use. These patterns can only be validated by building games with them and observing how successful they are.

EXERCISE 24: THEORETICAL PATTERNS

Step 1: Articulate the game design theory that you want to express as a pattern. You are not stating it as a pattern here, just describing the theory.

Step 2: Identify and describe the game design elements that are part of the theory.

Step 3: Identify the purpose of the theory. Describe what the application of the theory accomplishes.

Step 4: Restate your answer to step 3 as a game design problem.

Step 5: Use the elements that you identified in step 2 to form the description of a pattern that solves the problem you stated in step 4.

Step 6: If possible, name ten games that implement the pattern you've created to solve the problem you stated.

Step 7: Document your work using the Pattern Template.

Step 8: Set your confidence level to 0 if you can't cite examples of games using the pattern, to 1 if you can find one instance, and to 2 if you find many instances.

Step 9: Try to think of games that follow your theoretical pattern, but do not solve the problem it addresses. If you find examples, ask yourself why the pattern is not effective in these cases. Adjust the pattern to take these factors into account. If you cannot adjust the pattern, then discard it.

Example Theoretical Patterns
Exercise

Step 1: Articulate the game design theory that you want to express as a pattern. You are not stating it as a pattern here, just describing the theory.
Theory: A game's ability to create its intended effect in a player is directly related to how prepared the player is to have the experience the game provides. Games that aren't innovative but that are well-executed are successful because they deliver a polished experience that players are already primed to understand. Games that are very innovative without regard to player expectations have difficulty finding a large audience. Games that innovate successfully introduce the player to familiar concepts and only gradually introduce their innovative gameplay, allowing the user to acclimate.

Step 2: Identify and describe the game design elements that are part of the theory.

- Player expectations—A player's understanding of existing game design techniques. This understanding may be at an unconscious level, just experiential familiarity rather than explicit recognition of specific techniques.

- Innovative techniques—Mechanics, modes of play, themes, etc. that the player has not experienced before, or that the player has not seen used in the ways the developer is employing them.

Step 3: Identify the purpose of the theory. Describe what the application of the theory accomplishes.
Developers should understand what techniques are innovative in their designs and how they relate to aspects of the game that will be familiar to players. Developers need to balance the level of innovation in their games if they're going to maintain financial and critical viability. The application of this theory would allow developers to introduce innovation more carefully, in ways that players will accept.

Step 4: Restate your answer to step 3 as a game design problem.
As designers seek to advance the art of game design and create ever more effective and diverse games, they often alienate players who don't have the context to understand a rapidly expanding design vocabulary.

It can be very frustrating for a clever designer, who has devised a complex system of innovative mechanics that work in support of each other. The temptation is to unveil a new game that fully utilizes all of the new techniques at once, showing how well they function as a whole. However, if players can't understand what the game is supposed to be, what it's about, what it's doing, or why, then it's unlikely they'll engage with it for long enough to understand its value.

Step 5: Use the elements that you identified in step 2 to form the description of a pattern that solves the problem you stated in step 4.
To allow players to understand new design techniques, designers may wish to introduce those new techniques gradually and in situations that provide enough familiar gameplay to give a context for understanding.

To give a language analogy: It's not that difficult to read a sentence with one strange word in it, especially if that word appears several times so that its context provides clarity. But a sentence made up of mostly unfamiliar words is hard to understand, and you're likely to lose your reader.

Step 6: If possible, name ten games that implement the pattern you've created to solve the problem you stated.
Popular non-innovative games—*Call of Duty, Battlefield, Assassin's Creed, Elder Scrolls, Madden, FIFA*, annualized AAA titles and pervasive sequels

Innovative games that had poor critical reception—*Dear Esther, Virginia, Ingress, Echochrome*

Innovative games with positive reception—*Portal, Pokémon Go, Dead Space, Monument Valley, Gone Home*

Step 7: Document your work using the Pattern Template.
See following pattern.

Step 8: Set your confidence level to 0 if you cannot cite examples of games using the pattern, to 1 if you can find one instance, and to 2 if you find many instances.
Confidence: 1. I see examples of games without this pattern failing, and games that don't require this pattern due to lack of innovation succeeding. I can name a few successful innovative games with this pattern, but fewer than ten, so I'm giving it a low confidence number.

Pattern

Name: I See Where You Are Going with This
Confidence: 1
Image:

FIGURE 14.9   To much change all at once can make even good things unpleasant.

Author: Chris Barney
Design problem: As designers seek to advance the art of game design and create ever more effective and diverse games, they often alienate players who don't have the context to understand a rapidly expanding design vocabulary.

Trying to connect with players can be very frustrating for a clever designer, who has devised a complex system of innovative mechanics that work in support of each other. The temptation is to unveil a new game that fully utilizes all of the new techniques at once, showing how well they function as a whole. However, if players can't understand what the game is supposed to be, what it's about, what it's doing, or why, then it's unlikely they'll engage with it for long enough to understand its value.

Description: To allow players to understand new design techniques, designers may wish to introduce those new techniques gradually and in situations that provide enough familiar gameplay to give a context for understanding.

To give a language analogy: It's not that difficult to read a sentence with one strange word in it, especially if that word appears several times so that its context provides clarity. But a sentence made up of mostly unfamiliar words is hard to understand, and you're likely to lose your reader.

Games that use this pattern and how:

- *Portal*—This is a perfect example of the use of this pattern. The game's movement mechanics are very innovative. The main focus of the game as a kinesthetic puzzle-solving game is innovative. However, the game begins in a standard first-person mode, familiar to anyone who has played FPS games. It introduces new mechanics one at a time, and the fact that it's a puzzle game is hidden behind the familiar tutorial style of the levels. By the end of the game, when gameplay shifts to a more freeform use of the mechanics, players are prepared for the experience.
- *Pokémon Go*—It's helpful to consider this game in the context of the previous game by the developer, *Ingress*. *Ingress* was a very innovative game that introduced the concept of mapping a game world to real-world locations, using a digital map and geospatial coordinates provided by cellphones. The game was compelling to a niche group of players, but it lacked gameplay elements familiar to most players and found a relatively small audience. *Pokémon Go,* as the second game by this developer, included catching and collecting mechanics familiar to the large audience of players of that intellectual property (IP), and even to a large segment of new players due to the IP's cultural pervasiveness. This second game was vastly more accessible and successful.
- *Dead Space*—This game introduces the single innovative mechanic of needing to dismember enemies to defeat them. The rest of the game has standard third-person gameplay with a polished horror theme. The game was very successful as an AAA title and established a franchise.
- *Monument Valley*—This game is interesting when compared to a similar, much more obscure game called *Echochrome*. Both games use perspective in a similarly innovative way to create puzzles. *Monument Valley* has been far more successful. It uses the familiar idea of characters navigating a space, rather than abstract shapes. It also uses comfortable control affordances that cause discrete changes in the game world. These affordances are both more like controls in other puzzle games like sliding block puzzles and provide a clearer understanding of the puzzles themselves.
- *Gone Home*—This walking-simulator-style game is interesting when compared to the game that founded the genre, *Dear Esther*. The earlier game introduced the idea of simply moving through a space and discovering the story that's happened there. The gameplay is almost all in the mind of the player as they piece together the narrative. The game was critically well-received but only found a small audience. It was actively rejected by many mainstream gamers, who questioned whether it was even a game. *Gone Home* had a more familiar setting and a more relatable narrative. It also included an interactive environment and light puzzle structure that felt more like nostalgic point-and-click adventure games. *Gone Home* was far more financially successful and generated little negative feedback from mainstream gamers.

Seed: Exercise 24: Theoretical Patterns—Personal game design theory
Related patterns:
Parent patterns:
There Had Better Be a Very Good Explanation for This* (Confidence: 2)—
To provide context and supporting mechanics using I See Where You Are
Going with This, you must first have an innovative mechanic. Use this pattern to help you choose one.

SUGGESTED EXERCISES

Use **Exercise 23: Audience Patterns** to generate a pattern about how
you, as a player, learn a new skill in a game. I mean "learn a new
skill" in general, not how you learn some specific skill.
Use **Exercise 23A: Audience Patterns** to generate a pattern about
how different audiences learn a new gaming skill.
Use **Exercise 23B: Audience Patterns** to generate a pattern about
how the techniques used to teach new skills in one particular game
affect different audiences.
Do these three exercises generate the same pattern? If they generate three distinct patterns, is there an even higher level pattern that
governs all three?

Child patterns:
Familiarity Breeds Contempt, or at Least High Expectations† (Confidence: 3)—
When picking supporting mechanics using I See Where You Are Going
with This, you must be sure that you implement those mechanics well and
meet player expectations.

SUGGESTED EXERCISES

Use **Exercise 4: Formal Patterns** to generate a pattern based on *learning affordances*, or elements of the game that help you to understand
the functional elements of the game. For example, non-diegetic on-screen prompts such as "Press Space to Jump" or diegetic instructions from NPCs.
Use **Exercise 5: Functional Patterns** to generate a pattern based on
tutorials.

Keywords: Mechanics, Innovation, Business, Player Experience, *Deep
Interlock, Positive Space, Local Symmetries, Echoes*

---

* Example pattern for Exercise 15: Patterns in Innovation.
† Example pattern for Exercise 19: Finding Positive Patterns from Negative Patterns.

VII

Building a Language

CHAPTER 15

Connecting Patterns into a Language

INTRODUCTION TO PATTERN LANGUAGE CONSTRUCTION

Hopefully, I've convinced you that patterns are useful in and of themselves, and also that the process of deriving patterns is an excellent way to develop a deeper understanding of game design. However, patterns in isolation aren't all that Christopher Alexander has to offer to game design. In terms of learning game design, we still need a larger conceptual framework to structure the specific insights created by deriving individual patterns. Only with that can we use them as a primary tool for game design. We must make the jump from patterns to a Pattern Language.

In Section II, I discussed the previous attempts to use patterns for game design. Linking patterns together into a language is not something game designers have accomplished before. That's not surprising given how difficult that process is, relative to the difficulty of creating a single pattern or even a large group of patterns.

Here are the basic steps you will follow to turn your collection of patterns into a functional Pattern Language.

BUILDING A PATTERN LANGUAGE

Building a Pattern Language

1. Make sure that you have enough patterns.
2. Add keywords to all of your existing patterns.
3. Understand the scope of your language.
4. Fill in the parent patterns field for as many of your existing patterns as possible.
5. Fill in the child patterns field for as many of your existing patterns as possible.
6. Add other related patterns as needed.
7. Suggest possible parent and child patterns where you see them.
8. Complete Exercise 24: Theoretical Patterns to create these possible patterns.
9. Add link confidence and descriptions to your linked patterns.

1. Make Sure You Have Enough Patterns

To create a language, you first need to have a reasonably large number of patterns. You don't need to have identified "all" patterns; I don't even think that's possible given the mutability of our field. Still, a large group, maybe 50 or a 100 patterns, would be needed to shape the beginnings of a language.

The patterns that you've derived from the exercises in this book are where you'll start; when you have completed them all you will have at least 25 patterns. To reach the 50 or more patterns required, you may need to complete the exercises again. Or you may combine the patterns that you've found with those derived by your colleagues or fellow students.

Additionally, in many of the exercises, you may have seen several possible patterns in the games you were looking at and have chosen one to write up for the exercise. I encourage you to go back and write up the others, but more important, whenever you see many possible patterns that are related but distinct, they may share a higher-order parent pattern.

The lower-level specific patterns are still important; don't discard them in pursuit of a unifying higher-order pattern. Passing over specific low-level patterns in favor of documenting higher-order unifying patterns too aggressively results in the same overly abstract Pattern Language as applying the higher-order patterns exercise recursively.

In these cases, you should look at each of the possible patterns the exercise generated, and write up the ones that are just notes from your exercises if you can. What do these patterns that all solve the same problem (or result from the same design element, or create the same theme, etc.) have in common? Use the Finding Missing Patterns exercise (Exercise 17) to document this new pattern.

The resulting collection of patterns should be somewhat related to each other. It is likely that as you worked through the exercises, you noticed these connections and began to tentatively fill in their parent and child pattern fields as instructed, which is excellent. If you have not noticed any connections, you may want to go back and do the higher-level and lower-level exercises starting with some of your existing patterns.

If you iteratively apply the higher-order pattern exercise, you will eventually be *unable* to derive a higher-order pattern that is meaningful or useful. The highest level patterns often begin to resemble the basic descriptions of what constitutes a game. If you iterate on the lower level exercise, you will eventually reach a minimum level of useful granularity. If you find yourself in either of those places, stop.

For each pattern in your language:

1. Complete any Suggested Exercises you may have added when writing the pattern.
2. Look back at your answers to the exercise questions for the pattern. If you found other patterns with the exercise, finish documenting them as instructed by that exercise.

WORKING ON A PATTERN LANGUAGE WITH A TEAM

If you are building a Pattern Language with a team of other developers or students, then it is important to work collaboratively. Complete each of the steps in the process for the patterns that you authored. Where those steps involve another pattern, be sure to consult with the author of that pattern. Ask whether they think that your pattern fits as a parent or child of theirs before adding it.

If you aren't sure you understand someone else's pattern, ask. Your questions will help them improve their pattern. When other developers ask you about your pattern, take the time to explain, but make sure you update your pattern to make it clearer so next time they won't have to bother you!

This period of reading other's patterns and discussing how they connect to yours is where the patterns start to become a language that your team shares.

2. Add Keywords

To effectively use the patterns in your language, you need to be able to pick a useful subset of patterns to apply to the design problems that define your game. Choosing your patterns may not be difficult when you have a dozen or so. However, it becomes more challenging as your language grows or as your design team develops a significant library of patterns. In a language with hundreds of patterns, it becomes impossible, or at least prohibitively time-consuming, to read through every problem entry in search of problems that are similar to your own. If you don't address this difficulty and create affordances to increase the usability of your language, then you and the teams you work on will not make use of it.

One useful approach to solving this problem is to make your language more easily searchable. It is, of course, possible to simply search the full text of your patterns for words or phrases from the problem you are facing. That is a reasonable technique and one that you will likely use. However, you will find it more useful if you include a section of explicit keywords. This section will allow you to concisely call out all of the aspects of game design that your pattern impacts. It is also useful to think of your keywords as part of an enumerated value rather than an ad hoc collection of words. You should maintain a list of all of the keywords you have used and make sure that you consistently use the same words to mean the same thing. For example, if you have a pattern that relates to a third-person isometric camera perspective and you tag it with the keyword "third-person," do not later tag a pattern as "3rd Person" and another as simply "Isometric."*

The following table contains all of the keywords that I've used to tag patterns in this book. I do not intend it to be an exhaustive list. Perhaps it's useful to readers of the book to use these keywords to increase the interoperability of the patterns you produce. However, it's more important to use words that match the vocabulary you use and that of your design colleagues.

As you adopt keywords from this list or decide on words of your own, add them to a keywords list. Refer to that list every time you add keywords to a pattern. Your list will grow, but make sure that you reuse keywords consistently so that you can search your library for those words later.

---

* Isometric would be a good tag, but since all isometric cameras are also third person but all third-person cameras are not isometric, you would want to add both tags.

Sample Keywords List

Keywords		
Abilities	Evolution	**Player Expectations**
Action	Exploration	**Player Experience**
Adaptation	Exposition	**Player Feedback**
Adventure	Failure	**Player Manipulation**
Aesthetic	Fear	**Player Motivation**
AI	Feedback	**Player Skill**
Aiming	Fire	**Player**
Anticipation	Flaw	**Playtime**
Architecture	Flow	Portals/Thresholds
Audience	Freedom	Practice
Audio	**Game Systems**	Predictability
Autonomy	Gameplay	Problem Solving
Balance	**Genre**	Progression
Board Game	**Goals**	Puzzle
Boredom	Gravity	PvE
Boss	Guidance	PvP
Budget	**Health**	Quest
Building	Hidden Objects	Randomness
Business	Hiding	Realistic
Camera	Horror	Replayability
Challenge	Humor	Resource Priority
Character	Immersion	Rest
Character Progression	Incentive	Rewards
Choice	**Information**	Rhythm
Circulation Patterns	Interaction	**Risk**
Combat	Interest	Randomness
Communication	Intrigue	Roleplay
Companion	**Isolation**	**Running**
Complexity	Items	Scale
Consequences	Knowledge	**Secondary Mechanics**
Contrast	Learning	Setup
Control	**Level Design**	Shadows
Core Mechanics	Lighting	Shooting
Costs	Locks and Keys	Short Term
Crafting	Long Term	**Single Player**
Cues	Management	Skills
Customization	Mastery	Social/Fellowship
Damage	**Meaning**	Spawn
Danger	**Mechanics**	Speed
Decisions	Meta	**Stealth**
Delayed Gratification	**Motivation**	Strategy

(Continued)

Keywords		
Detail	**Movement**	Supply
Development Resources	Mystery	**Tablet**
Dialogue	**Narrative**	Tactics
Difficulty	Narrow Space	Tension
Economy	**Navigation**	**Theme**
Effects	NPCs	Throwing
Elevation	Objective	Tradeoff
Embedded Narrative	Obscuring	**Tropes**
Emergent Gameplay	**Obstacles**	Tutorial
Emergent Narrative	Online	**Unified Design**
Emotion	**Open-World**	**User Interface**
Emotions	Options	Variation
Empathy	Pacing	**Venue**
Empowering	Partner	Verb
Enemies	Personalization	Visuals
Enemy Progression	**Perspective**	Weapons
Environmental Narrative	Physics	
Environments	**Platform (Hardware)**	
Esthetics	**Platforms (Formal Element)**	

Note: Keywords used in this book are listed in bold.

Create a master Keywords List for your language.
For each pattern in your language:

1. If you have listed keywords, add them to your master Keywords List.
2. If a similar word is already in the master list, choose the best word and update all other patterns that list the older word.
3. For patterns that do not have keywords, add them, making sure to use words from the master list and add any new words to that list as well.

3. Understand the Scope of Your Language

The scope of a Pattern Language exists on at least three axes. I will refer to them as breadth, depth, and density. The breadth of your language deals with how many aspects of game design it covers. In this book, I am helping you to build a broad language. However, there is nothing wrong with a language that is more focused as long as you understand its limits. The depth of a language is bounded by how abstract and specific its patterns are. If your language has only abstract (high-level) or only specific (low-level) patterns, then it does not have much depth. Again, the process we are working through is helping you to develop a language with significant depth. But a very abstract language, like the mechanics-focused language in *Game Mechanics: Advanced Game*

Design (Adams and Dormans 2012), or a very focused language, like Alves and Roque's (2013) sound design language, can be valid and useful as well. The last axis, density, measures the number of patterns in your language and how interconnected they are. A deeply interconnected language is always richer and more potent than a sparse language. The variety of pattern relationships and the use of keywords and diverse pattern creation exercises in this book will help you make sure that you produce a dense language.

Pattern Categories

You must have patterns from across disciplines to generate a well-rounded language that covers all of the different aspects of game design. On your own, you will naturally focus on your strengths as a designer because it is easiest for you to find patterns in that design space. If you are a student or new designer, you will be even more limited in the breadth of patterns that you have the perspective to see. The exercises in this book try to address this problem by helping you focus on different aspects of design, but I chose them, and my areas of expertise are limited.

It's useful to look at which categories of design your patterns fall under to help you see your blind spots as a designer. This next section suggests several sets of categories that you can apply to game design.

When building your language, consider adding the relevant categories from the following lists to the Keywords section of each pattern. When you have finished, look to see what areas of design are missing and which are pervasive. These will likely mirror your areas of understanding. Seek other designers who have different areas of focus and expertise, and work to combine your language with theirs. That process will strengthen and add context to both your combined language and your understanding of the larger field.

The first list is my own, but I've also included the categories that other pattern language projects have used. While I have found fault with many previous efforts, the thought that they have given to the ways that a pattern language should be structured is useful in understanding how the patterns that you create fit into the larger structure of the field.

Categories from Disciplines

When creating the example patterns, I based the primary categorization that I considered on the disciplines that become departments in larger game companies. I believe that patterns from all of these categories are necessary to create effective games. Thus, I think it's vital that patterns from all of them should exist in a language, and further, that the best patterns will bring together elements from several disciplines or solve the same problem as it applies to multiple disciplines.

Categories from Disciplines	
• Art	• Mechanics/Gameplay
• Architecture (Spatial Design)	• Sound
• Writing/Narrative	• Business

Categories from Game Mechanics

These categories taken from *Game Mechanics: Advanced Game Design* (Adams and Dormans 2012) are all, like the book, focused on game mechanics. It is reasonable to include one or more of these categories if you are tagging a pattern with the Game Mechanics keyword.

Categories from Game Mechanics	
• Physics	• Social Interaction
• Tactical Maneuvering	• Progression Mechanisms
• Internal Economy	

Categories from Genre

Gameplay genre, as found in *Game Mechanics: Advanced Game Design* (Adams and Dormans 2012), is also a useful categorization to apply to your patterns. The nine high-level genres from that book are a reasonable way to begin, although you may want to apply more specific genre categorizations as they apply to your patterns.

Categories from Genre	
• Action	• Management Simulation
• Puzzle	• Sports
• Strategy	• Social Games
• Vehicle Simulation	• Adventure
• Role-Playing	

Categories from Patterns in Game Design

The following categories are drawn directly from *Patterns in Game Design* (Björk and Holopainen 2006). They break up their patterns into 14 or so categories. Within each, they define 10 or more patterns. All of these categories are well suited for use as keywords. Going even deeper and looking at the actual patterns defined in their book yields more useful keywords, because the "patterns" described in that book are techniques in this book's terms, and each of them would yield any number of patterns. Thus, if your pattern is using one of their patterns as a technique, then tagging it with that keyword will be useful.

Categories from Patterns in Game Design	
• Game Elements	• Game Sessions (Time)
• Immersion	• Narrative
• Resources	• Mastery and Balance
• Social Interaction	• Predictability
• Information	• Replayability
• Goals	• Learning
• Events	• Metagames

Categories from Pedagogy

The categories used in this application of pattern languages can at first seem very esoteric and only relevant to serious or educational games (Ott et al. 2011). However, after some consideration, I think that they are more broadly applicable. It's useful to restate them without using the domain-specific language of that area of academia. I will take a little more time to explain each and propose an alternative keyword.

- Integration patterns—These are patterns dealing with the techniques used to embed things to learn into the game. In a broader sense, they are about explicitly embedding meaning in a game. I would use the term *Embedded Meaning* to tag related patterns.

- Cognition patterns—These are patterns that relate to causing the player to think about the game content and use it in the process of playing the game. I would use the term *Problem Solving* to tag related patterns.

- Presentation patterns—These are patterns concerning the need to communicate the state of the game as it relates to their learning and gameplay goals. Outside of the educational context, I think it would be useful to tag games with the *Feedback* keyword when they relate to this kind of technique.

- Social interaction and teaching patterns—These patterns are relatively specific to educational games in that they describe techniques used to give the player feedback showing their success in the learning task. This category could be referred to as *Player Feedback* and used to tag games that use patterns like providing scores or ranks for given tasks.

- Engagement patterns—These patterns relate to getting players to engage with the game and its learning material. Engagement has historically been a struggle for educational and serious games. However, the problem of generating player engagement is in no way limited to these kinds of games. I think that in this case, using the keyword *Engagement* or *Player Motivation* to tag related patterns is useful.

Categories from Live-Action Role-Playing Game (LARP) Design
The categories proposed in this partial language (Li and Morningstar 2020) are specific to the domain of live-action games, but they map to broader categories.

- Setup—This maps to patterns relating to spatial design.

- Plot—The mapping to narrative design is direct.

- Interaction—This maps to social design.

Categories Master List			
Action	Goals	Physics	Social Games
Adventure	Immersion	Player Feedback	Social Interaction
Architecture	Information	Plot	Social Interaction
Art	Interaction	Predictability	Sound
Business	Internal Economy	Problem Solving	Sports
Embedded Meaning	Learning	Progression	Strategy
Engagement	Management Simulation	Puzzle	Tactical Maneuvering
Events	Mastery and Balance	Replayability	Vehicle Simulation
Feedback	Mechanics/Gameplay	Resources	Writing/Narrative
Game Elements	Metagames	Role-Playing	
Game Sessions	Narrative	Setup	

For each pattern in your language:

1. Look at the preceding Categories Master List and add any applicable categories to the pattern.
2. Remember to include any categories you adopt in your master Keywords List.

Meta-, Macro-, and Micro-Level Patterns

Part of understanding the scope of your language is knowing how specific, or abstract, your patterns are. There's nothing wrong with a very abstract language or one that is very specific. However, what problems your language can solve is bounded by where your patterns fall in this range. If you would like to create a language that's capable of solving a broad range of design problems, then you need to have patterns from the full range of the axis. To reach this understanding, you must divide your language into sections that contain patterns dealing with different levels of abstraction or scope. I built the idea of this type of hierarchy into the process you used to create patterns with the higher-order and lower-order pattern exercises, as well as by including explicit parent and child sections in the pattern template.

In this section, I describe three general levels of design in games. I don't think they actually exist; the level of abstractness or specificity of a pattern is analog and likely exists on a spectrum. Still, this distinction is useful to create order in your collection of patterns.

Meta-level patterns deal with decisions at the whole-game level, like what is the camera perspective, what genre is the game trying to fit into, or what is the target audience.

Macro-level patterns deal with more specific design decisions, choices that relate to one particular level, or an individual system in the game. Elements like the theme of a level, or the mechanics and interface that create the game's stealth system, are addressed by macro-level patterns.

Micro-level patterns deal with the lowest-level design decisions, such as the kind of feedback to give the player for melee hits in an role-playing game (RPG) or how armor should affect the jumping mechanics.

As you go through the process of assigning your patterns to these categories, you may notice that a micro-level pattern you have identified, say the one relating to armor and jumping mechanics, only applies in certain circumstances. For instance, if the pattern was "a character's abilities should have drawbacks that reflect the real-world systems they represent to *create a sense of realism, provide meaningful strategic choice,* and *maintain gameplay balance,*" then it might only apply in a game where you were trying to create a sense of realism and also create strategic choices based on character power-ups. So the use of this pattern should depend on higher-order patterns about those things.

Look at your existing patterns. If you have created a pattern that addresses that need, then add the parent–child relationship. If you have not, then use the Higher-Order Patterns exercise (Exercise 2) to generate the missing pattern. Then fill in the parent/child relationship.

This categorized list of your patterns will be useful in the next sections, when you have to decide the relationship between two related patterns. Sometimes that relationship will be clear: pattern A is the parent of pattern B. But often you could make a logical argument for either relationship. When you are unclear, you should refer to the list you are creating now. If pattern A is a higher level then pattern B, then it's likely to be the parent rather than the child.

META, MACRO, MICRO PATTERNS LIST

1. Create a document with the sections Meta, Macro, Micro.
2. Add each pattern in your language to the most appropriate section.

---

4. Adding Existing Parent Patterns

A NOTE ON ADDING PARENTS AND CHILDREN

I have found it useful to create an index document that has only the names of all patterns in my collection, and then list the parents and children under each. It can be easier to see which patterns are missing a parent or child in the condensed list.

In the Pattern Template, I describe a *parent pattern* as "a pattern or several patterns that are needed by this pattern for it to function well." If you have completed all the exercises in this book more than once, or you are working with colleagues or classmates, you may have a large enough collection of patterns that you can find parent patterns in your existing collection. Unfortunately, if your collection is large enough to contain the parents you're looking for, then it is large enough to make them hard to find. While you should read through your library and add parents as you discover them, there is another technique you should employ. Search your library using the keywords of a pattern. Other patterns that share the same keyword may be related. Do not just add any keyword match as a parent! Each time you find a match, read the pattern carefully, and decide if it is *necessary* for your pattern to function.

If one pattern assumes that the problem of a second pattern is solved, then that second pattern is a parent of the first. For example, say you were looking at a pattern that described how to increase player movement abilities to create a sense of autonomy for the player. If you saw another pattern that explained how to increase player autonomy through progression systems, then that second pattern would be a parent to the first. The progression systems pattern is more general, and for the second pattern to make sense, progression systems must already be present in a game for player movement to be increased by them.

If you are working to build a pattern library as a group, you must consult with the authors of each pattern before using it as a parent. When you find a prospective parent, contact the author of that pattern and find out whether they agree with your idea. You may discover that you did not understand their pattern correctly. Additionally, you may discover that their pattern almost fits as a parent of yours, but not quite. At that point, either you or the other author may want to update one of the patterns so that the relationship is valid. This revision should be carefully considered, and only done if it makes the pattern that you're changing clearer and more flexible.

1. For each pattern you contributed to, find all of the patterns in your collection that you think are parents. If your language is large, remember to use keywords to help you search for parents.
2. If you did not write both patterns, then consult with the other author.
3. Add each pattern you find to the parent patterns field of your pattern.
4. Look at the parent pattern and confirm that your pattern fits as a child. If it does, then go ahead and add your pattern to the child patterns field there. Remember to look at your Meta, Macro, Micro list if you are unsure of the hierarchy.
5. If your pattern does not fit as a child, consider whether that pattern is actually a parent, or whether it is perhaps an additive or subtractive pattern as discussed in the next section.

5. Adding Existing Child Patterns

In the Pattern Template, I describe *child patterns* as "patterns that are suggested by this pattern or require it to function well." Child patterns are reciprocal with parent patterns. So you can look at patterns that have parents, then add those patterns to the child patterns field of their parents. You shouldn't stop there, though. Sometimes it is easier to see child relationships than parent ones, so you should again use keywords to search through your patterns looking for existing children.

Remember that a child pattern *requires* its parent to function well. So if you see a low-level pattern that works well with another pattern but understand that the pattern can perform well on its own in other circumstances, then the higher-order pattern is not a parent, just a related pattern that is additive. You should still record the relationship, just not as a child. There may be cases where a child pattern has several parents. In that case, it might not need a particular higher-order pattern to function, but it does need one of its parents to be present to succeed.

You might think this step wouldn't be necessary, given that you've been adding the child side of connections while looking for parent patterns. However, it's my experience that you often see a different set of connections when you're looking from this perspective.

1. For each pattern you contributed to, find all of the patterns in your collection that you think are children. If your language is large, remember to use keywords to help you search for children.
2. If you did not write both patterns, then consult with the other author.
3. Add each pattern you find to the child patterns field of your pattern.
4. Look at the child pattern and confirm that your pattern fits as a parent. If it does, then go ahead and add your pattern to the parent patterns field there. Remember to look at your Meta, Macro, Micro list if you're unsure of the hierarchy.
5. If your pattern does not fit as a parent, consider whether that pattern is actually a child or whether it is perhaps an additive or subtractive pattern.

6. Linking Other Related Patterns

In the Pattern Template, I list parent and child patterns; these are the most necessary to identify to construct a functional Pattern Language. However, patterns may have a variety of other relationships with each other. As you complete more patterns, you should try to see these other relationships. You can add any of the following relationships to your patterns. The more of these you identify, the more robust and useful your Pattern Language will be.

- Additive patterns—Patterns that work well together and improve each other, but where one does not require the other to function.

- Alternative patterns—Patterns that solve the same problem, but where one should probably replace the other rather than combine with it.

- Subtractive or "anti-patterns"—Patterns where one reduces the effectiveness of another.

Making a note of subtractive patterns is very important in creating a useful Pattern Language. It can be tempting to avoid calling attention to "flaws" in your patterns by pointing out that other patterns "undermine" their effectiveness. But that is the wrong way to think about subtractive patterns! Many patterns have a limited scope, whether they just apply to action games, or horror games, or games with a first-person perspective. Identifying the limitations of a pattern makes it more, not less, valuable. As an example of additive and subtractive pattern relationships, consider these three patterns. The first is a jumping pattern describing limited jumping used to create a sense of vulnerability in horror games. The second is a pattern about using jumping to create a sense of mobility and autonomy in the player. The third pattern relates to falling damage creating a sense of realism, immersion, and believability. The falling damage pattern is likely additive to the limited jumping pattern, but subtractive to the jumping for autonomy and empowerment pattern. You might intentionally incorporate the falling damage pattern into a game with the extreme jumping pattern to limit or balance the power you were giving the player. Still, it would be important to be aware of that subtractive effect.

Likewise, it's important to identify alternate patterns because often, a developer will need to choose between several alternate patterns when having more than one will cause the patterns to interfere with each other and reduce the effectiveness of both. For instance, consider the aforementioned two patterns relating to jumping. The first described the ways that limited and realistic jumping can create a sense of vulnerability and tension for a player, and the second described how increasing a character's ability to jump great distances can increase the player's sense of autonomy and empowerment. These two are alternate patterns.

For each pattern you have contributed to:

1. Consider whether any of the other patterns in your collection, that aren't parents or children, make it stronger or weaker. Record those patterns as additive or subtractive in the related patterns section of your pattern.
2. Consider whether any of the other patterns in your group solve the same problem as your pattern, but in a different and mutually exclusive way. Record those as alternate patterns in the related patterns section of your pattern.

7. Suggest New Parents and Children

Suggesting new parents and children is a dangerous step. You need to look at an existing pattern and speculate about what patterns might be necessary for it to function or might need it to function. Often, there are several very obvious-seeming patterns just sitting there waiting for you to document them. *Do not* jump directly to the Pattern Template and write down your blind guesses. If you do, the result will, at best, be a theoretical pattern with very low confidence; at worst, it will be your unsupported opinion disguised as a validated pattern.

How do you create reasonable patterns out of the possible parent and child patterns you can see? First, ask yourself what problem your imagined pattern would exist to solve. Then if you think that it's a parent pattern, begin the Higher-Order Patterns exercise (Exercise 2) starting on the third step. If you're trying to create a child pattern, go to the Lower-Order Patterns exercise (Exercise 3). Do your best to set aside the pattern that you think exists and complete the exercise with an open mind. By examining games as part of the exercise, you will generate a pattern supported by evidence rather than one based on your intuition.

You may also consider using a different exercise from the book if you think it's more appropriate than the higher/lower pattern exercises. This is a more subjective approach, but if you have worked through all of the exercises by this point, you may be comfortable investigating new parents and children in this way. The suggested exercises that I've included with each pattern often use this method.

For each pattern you have contributed to:

1. Consider whether the listed parents and children are sufficient for you to use the pattern in design.

2. If they aren't, then use one of the preceding methods to create a new pattern.
3. When that pattern is complete, evaluate whether it meets your needs. If it does, add it to the appropriate related patterns section.
4. Return to step 1 and repeat this process until your pattern has the connections that it needs to be used in practical design.

8. Use Exercise 24: Theoretical Patterns to Find Related Patterns

If the pattern produced by step 7 doesn't turn out to be the one you were imagining when you started the exercise, and you still think that the pattern you imagined would be valuable, then you may take that pattern idea and complete the Theoretical Patterns exercise (Exercise 24) to document it. Theoretical patterns are more prone to bias than patterns produced by the other exercises in this book, so be very clear in your pattern description that you're basing a pattern on your guesswork. That doesn't mean that it's not valid, but as stated in that exercise, only successfully implementing the pattern in games can demonstrate its efficacy.

THERE IS NO SPOON

All patterns that we create are on some level based on our opinion and on our theoretical understanding of game design. Don't delude yourself into thinking that the process of building a Pattern Language is an exact science or that the patterns you derive are "truth." Always question your patterns, and be ready to discard or revise them when you see evidence that they don't function in the way you thought they did.

---

1. Use Exercise 24: Theoretical Patterns to generate a pattern based on an idea sparked by any previous pattern exercise.
2. Look at the completed pattern and consider whether it's related to the pattern that sparked the idea, whether as a parent, child, or other related pattern.
3. Add the needed keywords, categories, and related patterns to your new theoretical pattern.

9. Link Confidence

In addition to providing a confidence rating for your patterns themselves, you should rate your confidence in the links you propose between patterns. Expressing your confidence in the links between your patterns will become critical when you want to apply a pattern to solve a design problem you're facing. If you see a link to a parent pattern with a high confidence rating, it's a strong recommendation that you also apply the parent pattern. If the confidence is low, then you should be more cautious about complicating your solution by applying the additional pattern.

As with patterns, your confidence in links is affected by observation, understanding, and demonstration. Begin by looking at all of the example games in both the parent and child patterns. Your confidence may rise because you've observed that many of the example games exhibit both patterns. However, even if you don't see the patterns used together in the example games, you may still see logical connections between your patterns. That inconsistency might be due to flaws in the design of the games you're observing. In other words, they would be better games if they had adopted the related patterns as your links suggest. Those logical connections cause your confidence to rise as well. You may even be suggesting links with theoretical patterns that do not yet exist in any game. It's useful to suggest these kinds of links, but when you do, it's important to be clear about your confidence in those links so that you don't mislead yourself or other developers. Following is the proposed rubric. Links can only reach the highest levels of confidence when designers use the linked patterns together as part of a new design, and then only when you observe the success of the pairing.

LINK CONFIDENCE RUBRIC

OBSERVATION

Observed Link (+1): You see this link in at least one example game.
Common Link (+1): You see this link in many instances of these patterns.
Ubiquitous Link (+1): This link is always or almost always present when these patterns are present.

UNDERSTANDING

Theoretical Link (+1): A link that you think should logically exist, but which you have not observed.
Functional Link (+1): This link may not always be present in example games, but when it's not, its absence negatively impacts the game in an observable way.

DEMONSTRATION

Demonstrated Link (+1): You have successfully used the linked patterns to create their intended effects.

"Proven" Link (+1): The linked patterns are in common use in the manner suggested by their link.

1. For each pattern you have contributed to, look at each related pattern you have listed.
2. Write a short, one-sentence description of that link.
3. List up to ten example games that use your pattern and the linked pattern.
4. List up to ten example games that use your pattern but not the linked pattern.
5. List up to ten example games that use the linked pattern but not your pattern.
6. Use the Link Confidence Rubric to assign the link a confidence rating.
7. Apply that rating to the link in both patterns.

CHAPTER 16

Organizing and Maintaining a Pattern Language

INTEGRATING PATTERNS FROM OTHER SOURCES

Given the large number of pattern-related projects that exist, it seems useful to look at the possibility of integrating patterns from other projects into the pattern languages that you're developing based on the exercises in this book. But don't just adopt a pattern from another language uncritically. First, you must look at the existing pattern to see if there are parts of the Pattern Template that it is missing. Then decide whether you can produce those parts of the pattern yourself. As an example, I'll complete this process for a pattern from three major pattern-related projects.

Each of these projects is a significant achievement. This book would not be possible without the work of the game designers and scholars who built them. Adapting the patterns from these projects is in no way intended to reduce the work done to create them, or suggest that they're not useful or complete within their context. However, these patterns need adaptation to work in the context of this book and of your language. I believe that applying the techniques that you've learned here will add utility to these existing patterns.

Game Mechanics: Advanced Game Design

Patterns from the book *Game Mechanics: Advanced Game Design* (Adams and Dormans 2012) are quite close to following the Alexandrian form that this book has been using. I will look at each of the sections of the pattern provided by Adams and note how they correspond to the pattern template from this book. Then I'll rewrite the pattern using our template. I will list the fields used by *Game Mechanics*, followed by a description of how they relate to the Pattern Template used in this book.

- **Name:** This is identical to the pattern name.

- **Type:** This is a keyword that describes the fundamental mechanic that the pattern implements.

- **Intent:** This is a short description of the intended effect of the pattern. It seems like it might be part of the "pattern description" in this book's pattern template, but it tends to be more abstract and not relate to why that effect would be wanted.

- **Motivation:** This is a more elaborate statement of the intent above. Again it doesn't address the why of the pattern. It may give abstract examples of the effect, but doesn't provide concrete examples.

- **Applicability:** This section comes close to being the problem field found in the Pattern Template in this book. However, it doesn't frame the effects of a pattern as the solution to a problem or consistently articulate why a developer would want to create the described effect. This section does describe the mechanical context that the pattern is applicable in, often more clearly than in the example patterns in this book. You should strive for this level of clarity when writing your patterns.

- **Participants:** This describes the game design elements that are part of the pattern. This section is not formally present in the Pattern Template in this book. I am of two minds about it; I think it can help improve the clarity of a pattern, but it also encourages the creation of proprietary and idiosyncratic language around games. That kind of language could be useful if everyone agreed on it, but that's not a hill I want to die on, so I try to avoid creating this kind of jargon.

- **Collaborations:** This section emphasizes the difference between patterns in *Game Mechanics* and those in this book. It describes the pattern in terms of the relationships of the elements described in the participants section. This structure limits the nature of the patterns it describes, though it makes sense for the kind of mechanics-focused patterns found in *Game Mechanics*.

- **Consequences:** This section describes the mechanical results of the pattern. It also discusses some of the player-focused consequences, as they directly relate to interacting with these mechanics in terms of strategy and the player's mechanical goals.

- **Implementation:** This section discusses different implementations for the pattern; where there are choices, it describes the requirements and consequences of those options. Again, this section is very focused on the mechanical execution of the pattern in terms of the elements, or participants, that make it up.

- **Examples:** This section provides specific examples of the pattern in games. It sometimes uses the *Machinations* visual language to diagram these implementations. Machinations is very useful and powerful for this kind of mechanics-focused pattern. I recommend reading *Game Mechanics* to learn more about Machinations.

- **Related Patterns:** This section has four subsections: *elaborates, is elaborated by, combined with,* and *balanced by.* These sections very clearly describe the relationships between the pattern and the others defined in the book. This level of interconnection is to be desired, but becomes increasingly difficult to produce as the number of patterns in a language increases.

Next is the original pattern from *Game Mechanics* in italics, with my comments on each field in normal text.

- *Name: Escalating Challenge* This name is descriptive but not particularly evocative. The abstract, high-level name may be a symptom that the pattern of Escalating Challenge is closer to a complex functional element than an Alexandrian pattern.

- *Type: Escalation* The language defined in *Game Mechanics* has 12 patterns, 3 of which have the type of escalation. Creating categories is useful; however, in a larger language, this would probably be a keyword.

- **Intent:** *Progress toward a goal increases the difficulty of further progression.*

   This intent description seems a bit circular, and I am not sure that it adds anything that is not conveyed by the name escalating challenge. It does clearly state the mechanical identity of the pattern.

- **Motivation:** *A positive feedback loop between player progress and the game's difficulty makes the game increasingly harder for players as they get closer to achieving their goals. This way, the game quickly adapts to the player's skill level, especially when the good performance allows a player to progress more quickly.*

   This more elaborate restating of the intent does add a description of the consequence applying the pattern to the player experience. It causes the game to quickly adapt to the player's skill level. The description in "Motivation" is close to what is needed for the pattern to fit into our Pattern Template.

- **Applicability:** *Use escalating challenge when:*

   - *You want to create a fast-paced game focused on player skill (usually physical skill) in which the game gets harder as the player advances; his ability to complete tasks is inhibited as he goes.*

   - *You want to create emergent mechanics that (partially) replace predesigned level progression.*

   The applicability section seems close to the Problem field in the Pattern Template. In this case, Adams and Dormans cite two applications, which may indicate that the set of functional elements that make up the Escalating Difficulty pattern in the *Game Mechanics* book would produce two patterns when converted to our Pattern Template, one for each problem. However, the second application, to "create emergent game mechanics," while interesting is not explained in the following sections of the pattern. I will focus on the first application, "creating a fast-paced game focused on player skill,": when I adapt it to the Pattern Template.

Structure: *<Structural Diagram>*

   The diagram in the Machinations format shown for the original pattern is a precise representation of the mechanics of the pattern. However, it's very abstract, and for a pattern as intuitive as this, I'm not sure it adds a great deal of value. This structure diagram isn't the same as the illustration field in the Pattern Template. For patterns that you can diagram with Machinations, I would recommend adding a diagram in addition to an illustration.

- *Participants:*

  - *Targets represent unresolved tasks.*

  - *Progress represents the player's progress toward a goal.*

  - *A task either reduces the number of targets or produces progress.*

  - *A feedback mechanism makes the game more difficult as the player progresses toward the goal or reduces the number of targets.*

Breaking down a pattern into the elements that compose it is useful. Where those elements are unclear, defining them is worthwhile. However, in this case, the definitions largely make a simple concept more complex. To be specific, defining a participant as "targets represent unresolved tasks" rather than naming "goals" or "player goals" as a participant seems like an instance of introducing the jargon of "targets" from Machinations, when commonly understood words would be more transparent. Defining "progress" as "the player's progress toward a goal" seems redundant, when the term "targets" was just defined instead of using the word "goals." Saying that tasks reduce the number of targets after defining targets as the number of unresolved tasks seems circular. The definition of a feedback mechanism as a mechanic that makes it more difficult for a player to complete tasks is useful. Still, it adds confusion, as a feedback mechanism might represent different mechanics in other patterns.

While defining the "participants" in a pattern seems like a valuable part of a pattern, in this case, the simple description of escalating difficulty as "functional elements that progressively make it more difficult for a player to achieve their goals" would have been clearer.

- *Collaborations: The task reduces targets, produces progress, or does both. The feedback mechanic increases the difficulty of the task as the player gets closer to achieving the goal.*

  Given the earlier definition of the participants, this is an accurate description of escalating difficulty. I can see that the process of clearly defining a set of participating elements and then describing them in terms of their interactions could be the best way to describe a pattern. I endorse following this process if a simple description of the pattern produces ambiguity. For low-level patterns, however, it seems that this format reduces clarity.

- **Consequences:** *Escalating challenge is based on a simple positive feedback loop affecting the difficulty of the game. Its mechanism quickly adjusts the difficulty of the game to the skill level of the player. If failure at the task ends the game, escalating challenge ensures a very quick game.*

  This consequences section is accurate as far as it goes, but states the most apparent literal results of the pattern. Escalating Challenge that is triggered by player skill will indeed adjust the difficulty of the game to the skill level of the player. However, this section does not discuss the consequences of different ways that a game could increase difficulty. Deeper analysis and description should be present in patterns, as described in this book. For instance, if a game gradually increases difficulty throughout, it forces a matching increase in player skill to complete the game. Depending on this difficulty curve, the audience of the game may be limited. Still, the developer may be able to shift the experience of playing the game toward a focus on achieving a sense of mastery. On the other hand, quick spikes in difficulty can cause frustration in the player. A developer could create this effect intentionally, to help the player empathize with the anger felt by their character.

- **Implementation:** *The task in a game that implements the escalating challenge pattern is typically affected by player skill, especially when the escalating challenge pattern makes up most of the game's core mechanics. When the task is a random or deterministic mechanic, players will have no control over the game's progress. Only when the escalating challenge pattern is part of a more complex game system and players have some sort of indirect control over the chance of success does a random or deterministic mechanic become viable. Using multiplayer dynamic mechanisms is an option but probably works better in a more complex game system as well.*

  The implementation section is interesting. It points out several valid issues you should consider when implementing escalating difficulty. The consequences section pointed out that escalating difficulty "quickly adjusts the difficulty of the game to the skill level of the player." And, that escalating difficulty reduces the length of the game if failure ends the game. Given those two observations, this section correctly points out that the systems that have Escalating Difficulty need to have direct skill-based player interaction. For instance, targets in a shooter that move more and more quickly would be an example of escalating difficulty applied to a skill-based mechanic. Adding a chance that a weapon would fail in that same shooter and then increasing that chance throughout the game would be a bad example. Because while the increasing weapon failures would increase the difficulty of the game, the player does not have any skill-based interaction with that system.

However, the implementation section does not describe other factors that you need to consider when implementing escalating difficulty, such as how quickly the difficulty should increase or whether the increase should continue past the point of player skill. The implication is that the difficulty increase should be static and continue throughout the game. It seems that other possibilities might yield a richer pattern. When incorporating patterns from external sources like this, it's important to look for this kind of omission and try to improve upon the pattern as you incorporate it.

- *Examples:* Space Invaders *is a classic example of the escalating challenge pattern. In* Space Invaders, *the player needs to destroy all the invading aliens before they can reach the bottom of the screen. Every time the player destroys an alien, all other aliens speed up a little, making it more difficult for the player to shoot them.*

  Pac-Man *is another example. In* Pac-Man, *the task is to eat all the dots in a level, while the chasing ghosts make it more and more difficult to get to the last remaining dots.*

  These examples are clear and show two different implementations of increasing difficulty. *Space Invaders* is the simplest, in that the increase in difficulty is linear, and the feedback loop governs player progress. It's the same for players of any skill level at a given point in the game. The example of *Pac-Man* is a bit more complicated, but this section does not describe that complexity. The element that has the escalating difficulty is the speed of the ghosts, which is analogous to *Space Invaders.* However, the feedback loop is more complicated, in that it's driven forward by the player completing levels. But it's also mitigated by the player's skill in deciding the pattern of movement that they will use to consume the dots in the level. The player's skill in constructing these patterns increases as they progress through the levels, allowing them to compensate for the escalating ghost speed on both strategic and reflex-based axes.

In adapting this pattern, it's important to include additional examples that have more diverse implementations of escalating difficulty to help designers apply the pattern in creative ways that fit their games, rather than duplicating existing implementations.

- **Related Patterns:** *By combining escalating challenge with static friction or dynamic friction, a game can be created that quickly matches its difficulty to the ability of the player.*

  This section introduces the essential information that matching difficulty to a player's skill is not achieved solely through the application of this pattern, but by combining it with a pattern of the "friction" type, which *Game Mechanics: Advanced Game Design* describes as patterns that consume resources.

- **Additional analysis:** This pattern, and most of the patterns from this source, suffer from an interesting problem. In some ways, they resemble what I would refer to as "shallow patterns" in my students' work. In this case, though, I don't think this quality comes from a lack of deep analysis or understanding. I think that the opposite is the case. The authors have distilled such deep fundamental patterns that they approach being functional elements. They are not simply basic functional elements, though; they are compound elements. Calling more complex sets of elements patterns makes sense, and I think that this is common in pattern collections in general. However, the patterns and Pattern Language this book generates focus on how the pattern relates to a design problem, and how implementing a pattern through a set of game elements creates different effects in the game to solve the problem. The patterns described in *Game Mechanics: Advanced Game Design* are not wrong or lacking; they are just not the same thing as the patterns generated by the exercises in this book.

———

Here is the revised pattern documented using the Pattern Template.

Pattern

Name: I'm Doing It As Hard As I Can
Confidence: 3
Image:

FIGURE 16.1   Escalating difficulty can create engagement as a player's skill increases, and allow players of different skill levels to enjoy your game.

Author: Chris Barney, derived from "Escalating Difficulty" by Ernest Adams and Joris Dormans
Design problem: Skill level varies between players, and an individual player's skill level changes throughout play. Additionally, narrative and mechanical progression both benefit from an increase in the challenge for a player.
Description: To create a feeling of challenge and escalating tension in the player, a developer may want to gradually increase the difficulty of one or more mechanics throughout the game.

This increase in difficulty may be static and tied to the player only through their linear progression through the game, thus requiring that the player's skill increase by a fixed amount in order to progress. When this is the case, this pattern may be combined with *a pattern based on the functional element of Levels of Difficulty** to account for varying skill levels between players.

---

* To pursue this pattern, complete Exercise 5: Functional Patterns using levels of difficulty as your response to step 1.

The *rate of change* in the difficulty may be tied adaptively to the player's performance, increasing more rapidly for skilled players and levelling off as player skill plateaus. This effect creates a more consistent player experience, but may allow players to avoid increasing difficulty by not overperforming. That effect may be desirable if a more relaxed experience is desired or in the case where the developer is trying to create a flow state in the player.

Games that use this pattern and how:

- *Space Invaders*—This game uses a simple linear difficulty adjustment that is independent of player performance, increasing difficulty as the player progresses through the game on a per-enemy-killed basis.
- *Gradius*—This is an early use of dynamic difficulty adjustment (DDA) from 1985. The game defines several difficulty settings, and shifts the player between them based on the formula $\left(\text{Time since last death} + \text{Level number} + \text{Power} - \text{ups collected} + \text{Lives remaining} + \text{Difficulty level}\right) / 2$
- This formula is applied in addition to the game's gradual increase in difficulty.
- *Teenage Mutant Ninja Turtles: The Arcade Game*—This is an interesting case, as the developers may not have included dynamic difficulty and challenge increase to improve the player's experience. The difficulty is adjusted based on several factors, such as the number of players and the number of player deaths per level. As an arcade game, the implication is that the developers may have tuned the game to maximize the number of quarters per play rather than for the optimal player experience.
- *Candy Crush*—This is a more modern implementation driven by the same optimization target as *Teenage Mutant Ninja Turtles*. While the specific DDA algorithms are not public, developers have discussed the fact that they introduce "pinch" levels that are very difficult to complete. These levels encourage microtransactions and are placed based on player investment, as determined by length of play and levels completed.
- *Snatcher*—In this early game by Hideo Kojima, the player is given a shooting tutorial and practice in a shooting gallery. The game measures the player's skill in this section, and the difficulty of shooting sequences later in the game is adjusted to provide the intended level of challenge.
- *Mario Kart*—In this well-known example, the multiplayer difficulty is adjusted using various rubber banding techniques that help losing players and make the game harder for winning players.
- *Crash Bandicoot* (series)—Dynamic difficulty was refined throughout these games to create the difficulty curve the developer intended. This example is significant because difficulty adjustments include level design elements like obstacle placement that are more complex than simply increasing enemy health or character attack damage.

- *Left 4 Dead*—One of the advertised features of this game is an "AI Director" that dynamically adjusts elements in the level to create a cinematic experience for the players. This open announcement is interesting because developers often hide dynamic difficulty from players. Acknowledging and advertising its presence allows some of the adjustments to be more overt without alienating the player.
- *Final Fantasy VIII*—Games in the RPG and, in particular, the JRPG genre often use the functional mechanic of "grinding" or repeating content to advance character progression. This game tried to remove the value of this behavior by introducing dynamic difficulty escalation based on player level.
- *Elder Scrolls* (*Oblivion* and *Skyrim*)—Challenge escalation has been present in the *Elder Scrolls* games for most of the title's iterations. In *Oblivion*, the difficulty increase existed across most of the game's systems and generally matched the character's increase in power. This parallel scaling created a static level of perceived difficulty throughout the game. In *Skyrim*, a more complex system created areas of the game with enemies that were consistently stronger or weaker than the character, allowing the player to feel both challenge and mastery depending on where they were in the game world, while maintaining a general sense of balance in the game world.

Seed: Escalating Difficulty from the book *Game Mechanics: Advanced Game Design*
Related patterns:
Parent patterns:

SUGGESTED EXERCISE

Use **Exercise 2: Higher-Order Patterns** to generate a pattern based on difficulty.

Child patterns:
The Risk of Knowing You* (Confidence: 2)—When you use I'm Doing It As Hard As I Can to create challenge and tension for the player, you are also putting the character (if your game has one) in danger. Use this pattern to take advantage of the emotional leverage you have created.

Just Look At What You've Become† (Confidence: 3)—When you use I'm Doing It As Hard As I Can to escalate the difficulty throughout a game, you may also add character progression to help the player deal with the challenge. Use this pattern to turn progression into transformation and add a more profound sense of meaning to your game.

---

* Example pattern from Exercise 7: Player Experience Patterns.
† Example pattern from Exercise 25: Creating Patterns from Lenses.

Old Me Was Afraid of Old You, But New Me Is Stronger! ... And Now I'm Afraid of New You* (Confidence: 3)—There is an arms race between escalating challenge and character progression. Use this pattern to take advantage of this dynamic, create pacing and rhythm in your game, and avoid having one system cancel out the other.

One of These Days That's Going To Get You Killed[†] (Confidence: 2)— Use this pattern to help you add progression systems for the character without undermining I'm Doing It As Hard As I Can.

SUGGESTED EXERCISE

Use **Exercise 5: Functional Patterns** to generate a pattern based on handicapping. This practice is common in competitive sports like golf or bowling, but is relatively uncommon in competitive multiplayer games. Use this pattern to understand why, and whether there are ways to incorporate this technique into your games using escalating difficulty.

Additive patterns:

SUGGESTED EXERCISE

Use **Exercise7: Player Experience Patterns** to generate a pattern based on immersion. When picking the ten games in step 2, pick games that have a well implemented difficulty curve as well as maintain player immersion.

Keywords: Mechanics, Difficulty, Skill, Progression, *Levels of Scale*, *Graded Variation*, *Not Separateness*

CHALLENGE

Pick a pattern from *Game Mechanics: Advanced Game Design* and use it to generate an Alexandrian pattern using the example of converting Escalating Difficulty to I'm Doing It As Hard As I Can.

Patterns in Game Design

Staffan Björk and others have expanded the pattern library established in the book *Patterns in Game Design* (Björk and Holopainen 2006) in an online repository, which contains 607 entries at the time of this writing

---

* Example pattern from Exercise 3: Lower-Order Patterns.
[†] Example pattern from Exercise 1: Basic Pattern Exercise.

(Björk 2019). As noted in Chapter 4, the patterns from this source are not the same as patterns in this book. Yet the value of the patterns listed in this repository is immense, because each is a well-defined formal or functional design element as described in Chapter 9. For clarity, I will refer to the "patterns" from *Patterns in Game Design* as "elements" for the rest of this chapter. You can use any item from this source as a seed for Exercise 4: Formal Patterns or Exercise 5: Functional Patterns.

When using the repository in this way, it's useful to read the full entry for the element there. In the complete online collection, each entry links to all related entries and contains an in-depth analysis of how those game design elements interact on a basic level. These entries are structured similarly to the Pattern Template that you're familiar with from this book. I will outline the best way to make use of these sections next.

Each entry begins with the element name, followed by a brief literal description of the element, then a longer description of the way that games use the element.

Next, this format provides as many as ten examples, but discussion of each is minimal, often a sentence or less. These examples are a useful place to start in selecting the ten games required by Exercises 4 or 5. Though you would, of course, need to describe each game and its use of the element in more detail. You should not blindly use these games for examples in the Pattern Template, as they may not be good examples of the pattern that you derive from looking at the elements from this repository.

A section titled "Using the pattern" follows the examples. This section is usually much more extensive, and discusses how the element relates to other elements to create different effects. Often this analysis considers the interplay of dozens of different elements. Each of these interactions may suggest a possible pattern or patterns. To take these abstract interactions or elements and turn them into patterns as defined in *Patterns in Game Design*, you can consider each interaction of a set of *formal elements* as a *functional element*, and complete Exercise 5 by looking at games that contain an example of that kind of interaction. For example, the entry for the element "Penalties" states that failing to achieve "Committed Goals" is a reason that penalties are applied. Committed Goals is another element that you can click through to, to make sure you understand what it means. So, in Exercise 5, you would look for ten games that use the functional element of applying penalties for goal failure. Perhaps looking at a player versus player (PvP) first-person shooter that has a delay on player respawn on death, or a dating sim where choosing the wrong dialogue option causes a potential match to reject you, and so on. You would continue the exercise and look for patterns in the way that those games apply the technique.

Next, this format presents the "Consequences" section. This section may contain statements that come close to being patterns, as defined in this book. For example, again looking at the Penalties element, it states both that penalties can create tension and that they can promote role-playing. To begin validating these assertions and converting them to patterns, you must look at games that have penalties and see if some, many, or all of them exhibit these effects. You then need to assess the degree to which the effects exist, and see if there are patterns that govern penalties producing the effects of either tension, role-playing, or both.

There is then an extensive section detailing the "Relations" of each entry with many other entries. Just considering these relations can be useful. It would be possible to devise exercises aimed at generating patterns by looking at how those relations functioned. This section breaks down the Relations into the following categories:

- **Can Instantiate**—These are other elements that may be created by the current element. For instance, a developer may "instantiate destructible objects" to use the loss of an object as a penalty.

- **Can Modulate**—The presence of the current element can change the effectiveness of other elements. For instance, penalties can increase "attention demanding gameplay" by punishing inattention. Or it can decrease "player killing" if the designer applies a penalty for such behavior.

- **Can Be Instantiated By**—These elements may cause the current element to exist by their presence. For example, adding "ability loss" to a game is likely to apply as a penalty.

- **Can Be Modulated By**—These are elements that are additive or subtractive to the current element. For example, penalties could be made more manageable by having "predictable consequences" or made more detrimental by having "geometric progression."

- **Potentially Conflicting With**—The elements listed here are just ones that have strong negative modulation, or to use our terminology, strongly subtractive patterns.

As you can see, the amount of information contained in this repository is a tremendous resource for creating patterns. While the entries, as listed, may not be fully functional patterns on their own, applying the appropriate exercises to any of them will generate multiple patterns.

1. Select an entry from the *Patterns in Game Design* repository website, listed in the bibliography (Björk 2019).
2. Decide whether the entry is a functional or formal element.
3. Use the entry with Exercise 4 or 5 to generate a pattern.
4. Integrate the pattern with your language adding keywords and related patterns as needed.

The Art of Game Design: A Book of Lenses

The widely known book *The Art of Game Design: A Book of* Lenses, by Jesse Schell (2020), presents a series of essays that cover the breadth of the game design discipline. Schell follows each topical section with an insightful but commonsense assertion and a set of questions. These questions help designers apply the assertions to their games. The third edition of the book contains an awe-inspiring 116 of these sections, which he refers to as "lenses," named for the different ways they let you look at your game design.

This collection of lenses is not a collection of patterns, though in some ways the lenses it presents have a similar feel and utility to a Pattern Language. Most game design students or working developers will have already read this book. If you have not, then I cannot recommend it strongly enough. Reading the book will help you understand game design better, no matter your current level of skill. *The Art of Game Design* is as useful to master designers as to students. Through the questions that allow the designer to apply each concept, it reflects their varied skill and experience.

For example, in Lens #74: The Lens of the Obstacle, Schell provides some supporting context in the form of a rule of thumb from cinema: that a good story requires a character with goals and obstacles to stand in their way. Some precise commonsense analysis follows, suggesting that this concept also applies to games. Then he states that "a goal with no obstacles is not worth pursuing," and that you should "use this lens to make sure your obstacles are ones that your players will want to overcome." These statements seem to be good advice. Schell then poses these questions for the reader to answer about the obstacles in their game:

- What is the relationship between the main character and the goal? Why does the character care about it?

- What are the obstacles between the character and the goal?

- Is there an antagonist who is behind the obstacles? What is the relationship between the protagonist and the antagonist?

- Do the obstacles gradually increase in difficulty?

- Some say "the bigger the obstacle, the better the story." Are your obstacles big enough? Can they be bigger?

- Great stories often involve the protagonist transforming in order to overcome the obstacle. How does your protagonist transform?

Answering these questions is useful and prompts you to consider your game from the perspective of the lens. The carefully constructed questions help the reader to consider both the problems that using the lens will solve and the problems with using the lens.

Often, it's clear how you can change your answers to the questions and thus change your game for the better. However, the lenses don't always provide the guidance you might need to understand what specific changes you would need to make to benefit from their perspective or even *if* your particular game will benefit from addressing the view of a particular lens. That is where I think that pattern analysis can provide some value.

How can pattern theory be applied to the framework of lenses? Looking carefully at the structure of the lenses provides some clues:

$$\text{Evidence} \rightarrow \text{Declaration} \rightarrow \text{Questions}$$

This format is similar to parts of the process we go through to create a pattern:

$$\text{List 10 games (evidence)} \rightarrow \text{Pattern problem (declaration)} \rightarrow$$

$$\text{Exercise questions (questions)}$$

The typical pattern exercise step of listing ten games maps to Schell's essays that provide evidence for the lenses. His declaration within each lens seems like it might map to the pattern problem section within the Pattern Template. And it seems evident that the questions from the lens would map to the questions of a pattern exercise.

But that's not quite right: the declaration that Schell makes is closer to the actual pattern that we derive, and each of the questions is more like the problem section of a pattern than the exercise questions. So the lens format would map this way:

Evidence = List ten games step

Declaration = Pattern description

Questions = Pattern problem statement

Given that mapping, it becomes possible to construct an exercise that will generate a large number of patterns from each lens. The exercise will also help us understand how to apply the pattern in more specific circumstances to solve the problems that exist in our games or avoid using the lens if our game does not address those problems.

Exercise 25: Creating Patterns from Lenses
When you are looking at a game through one of Schell's lenses and either you do not know how you should adapt it to address the perspective of the lens or are not sure how making those changes will affect your game, consider the following exercise:

Step 1: Consider the assertion of the lens.
Step 2: Look for at least ten games that exemplify that assertion.
Step 3: Answer each of the questions listed in the lens as it applies to each of those games.
Step 4: For each question, consider your ten responses and look for patterns.
Step 5: Look across all of your responses for all ten games for high-level patterns.
Step 6: Document each pattern using the Pattern Template.
Step 7: Consider whether your game needs to solve any of the problems that those patterns address.

I will work through this process to demonstrate using Lens #74 that I discussed earlier.

Example Pattern from Lenses
Exercise

Step 1: Consider the assertion of the lens.
"A goal with no obstacles is not worth pursuing" and "use this lens to make sure your obstacles are ones that your players will want to overcome."

Again, this statement part of the lens maps to a pattern description in the Pattern Template. You can convert this statement to a pattern description by rephrasing it in this way: "To make sure that players find the goals of your game satisfying, you need to place obstacles that make achieving the goal a challenge for the player."

Step 2: Look for ten games that exemplify that assertion.
In looking for example games for a lens, which tends to be a very high-level pattern, it is more important than usual to try to think of a wide variety of games that seem to apply the lens. It also may be useful to consider "good" and "bad" games that do not seem to apply the lens at all, and understand why they do or do not need it. For example, the following games seem to apply the lens strongly, as we'll see when we look at their answers to the questions in the next step: *Dark Souls, Borderlands 3, Pokémon Go, The Witness/Myst, Warcraft/World of Warcraft*, Kingdom Death: Monster.

The following games make sense to view through the lens, but their answers are more mixed: *Tetris, Vikings: War of Clans, Journey, Virginia*.

And this last set of games don't seem to apply the lens at all, but still have a strong goal and experience of trying to reach that goal: *Dear Esther, Loneliness*.

Step 3: Answer each of the questions listed in the lens as it applies to each of those games.
As you will see, the process of addressing a set of questions from a lens for ten games is no small task. However, answering these questions for your set of games is likely to create many patterns. The actual work-to-pattern ratio for this exercise is probably higher than any other in this book because of the rich nature of Schell's lenses.

Here are the questions posed in Lens #74:

1. What is the relationship between the main character and the goal? Why does the character care about it?

- *Dark Souls*—The goal is survival and escape, at least initially. The character wants to survive, but the motivation provided isn't especially strong. For the player, curiosity and the drive to achieve mastery over challenging gameplay are the reasons they care or their motivation.

- *Borderlands 3*—The goal is to open a treasure vault. The character is motivated by helping a legendary hero and seeking personal wealth and fame.

- *Tetris*—The goal is to clear rows of blocks. There is no character, but the player's motivation is seeking a high score. This kind of goal might be referred to as "player achievement," as it's not a goal for the character achieved through the player's control, but a goal of the player achieved by the character's actions.

- *Vikings: War of Clans*—The goal is to dominate other players. Player achievement and supporting members of your clan are the primary motivations.

- *Pokémon Go*—There are multiple long-term goals: collecting all the Pokémon, completing research quests, and competing in PvP competitions. Player achievement is the primary motivation.

- *The Witness/Myst*—Solving the mystery of the island is the goal in both of these games. There is some narrative motivation, but the player's curiosity is probably the main reason for engaging with the game.

- *Warcraft/World of Warcraft*—Both of these games have a strong narrative motivation, but player achievement is at least equally as strong.

- *Kingdom Death: Monster*—Surviving the campaign is the primary goal; it is easy to assume that the character cares about this out of a sense of self-preservation. The player, on the other hand, is motivated by player achievement and curiosity about the game's mysterious narrative.

- *Journey*—The primary goal is to reach the mountain; for the character, this is a culturally driven spiritual quest. The motivation for the player is mostly narrative curiosity.

- *Virginia*—The stated goal of the game is to help the character "solve" the mysterious disappearance of a child. For the player, the goal is to understand the narrative. The character has the motivation of proving themself; for the player, curiosity is the motivation.

- *Dear Esther*—The goal is to reach the radio tower. The character is motivated by the drive to reach the end of their life. The player is motivated by curiosity.

- *Loneliness*—The goal is to find dots that will accept you. The motivation is "to not be alone."

2. What are the obstacles between the character and the goal?

- *Dark Souls*—Enemies of varying difficulty. Pathfinding, the game world is a maze, and the game provides no map.

- *Borderlands 3*—Enemies and tasks/quests.

- *Tetris*—Increase in speed and blocks that do not fit well.

- *Vikings: War of Clans*—At a low level, time is the primary obstacle as progression. Timers act as a gate for every action the player can take. Early actions take as little as 30 seconds; later game actions take months of real-time to complete. At a high-level, opposition by other players becomes the primary obstacle.

- *Pokémon Go*—The difficulty of catching Pokémon, opposition of other players, limited player mobility.

- *The Witness/Myst*—Environmental and abstract logic puzzles.

- *Warcraft/World of Warcraft*—Enemies, tasks/quests, and player opposition.

- *Kingdom Death: Monster*—Enemies and random events are obstacles.

- *Journey*—Simple environmental effects and platforming puzzles.

- *Virginia*—Discovering event triggers; the obscurity of the narrative is an obstacle to understanding the plot.

- *Dear Esther*—Pathfinding could be considered an obstacle or the time required to walk through the game, but practically there are no obstacles.

- *Loneliness*—There are no "obstacles," but it is not possible to achieve your goals.

3. Is there an antagonist who is behind the obstacles? What is the relationship between the protagonist and the antagonist?

   - *Dark Souls*—The nature of the world is the primary cause of obstacles to the character. That world does not care very much for you personally. Many of the areas of the game have a boss monster that is the antagonist of that area.

   - *Borderlands 3*—Strong primary antagonists interact with the character throughout the game.

   - *Tetris*—No.

   - *Vikings: War of Clans*—At the point that you come into conflict with other players, long-term antagonistic relationships may form, but the game doesn't provide a narrative or non-player character (NPC) antagonists.

   - *Pokémon Go*—There are other teams of players and NPC enemies with a hierarchy, but those are not primary sources of opposition in the game. Because of the large player base, even the PvP conflict is relatively anonymous and doesn't generate long-term antagonistic relationships.

   - *The Witness/Myst*—Yes, there are antagonists responsible for the structure of the world and the puzzles you face. They are not primary motivators for the player to overcome the obstacles.

   - *Warcraft/World of Warcraft*—Yes, both NPC and player antagonists are a significant focus of the game.

   - *Kingdom Death: Monster*—Recurring monsters and an enemy hierarchy create potent antagonists.

   - *Journey*—No, or not in a way that the player confronts in gameplay. You realize that your society did this to themselves.

- *Virginia*—No, or not in a way that the player confronts in gameplay. "The enemy is society."

- *Dear Esther*—No, or as in *Journey*, you are narratively confronting the history of your character. "The enemy is yourself."

- *Loneliness*—There is not an antagonist, but indifference and social isolation are antagonistic forces. "The enemy is society" is the literary theme invoked here.

4. Do the obstacles gradually increase in difficulty?

- *Dark Souls*—Yes.

- *Borderlands 3*—Yes.

- *Tetris*—Yes.

- *Vikings: War of Clans*—Yes.

- *Pokémon Go*—Yes. In the PvP competition, each season starts easy and gets harder as you rise in rank.

- *The Witness/Myst*—Yes, puzzle difficulty increases. The difficulty curve in *The Witness* is more apparent and more intentional.

- *Warcraft/World of Warcraft*—Yes.

- *Kingdom Death: Monster*—Yes.

- *Journey*—No.

- *Virginia*—No, though perhaps as the game progresses, you have more narrative events to consider, so constructing a narrative out of them becomes more difficult.

- *Dear Esther*—No.

- *Loneliness*—No.

5. Are the obstacles big enough? Can they be bigger?

- *Dark Souls*—Yes, the game achieves its desired level of difficulty. No, not if the desire is for the player to be able to complete the game.

- *Borderlands 3*—Yes. Though the developers didn't intend the game to be punishingly difficult, the challenges it presents create the desired experience of character power and struggle. No. If enemies were more dangerous and quests harder to complete, the higher level of challenge would decrease the power fantasy that is core to the gameplay experience.

- *Tetris*—Yes. No.

- *Vikings: War of Clans*—No, there is very little in the way of obstacles outside of time. And although time is an effective enemy, it's not a very interesting one. Players as enemies may be challenging enough, but the game does not reveal this difficulty in a way that's understandable to most players. Having clearer goals, obstacles, and difficulty progression would improve the game for many players.

- *Pokémon Go*—No, progression through the game is quite easy, and the obstacles are mostly symbolic. The only real difficulty is in higher levels of PvP play, and that ramps up so quickly that it feels like facing an insurmountable obstacle rather than facing an interesting challenge. The NPC opponents the player faces help with this, but the core of the gameplay progression, catching and powering up creatures, does not feel integrated with the PvP-based obstacles at the end of the game. This issue is similar to that in *Vikings*.

- *The Witness/Myst*—These games are very obstacle-focused. The obstacles in *Myst* are very challenging and have little concern for the player's ability to overcome them. Those in *The Witness* may be even more difficult, but they lead the player to the understanding needed to solve them. So, *Myst* has obstacles that are too big, and the obstacles in *The Witness* are just right, even though they are bigger than those in *Myst*.

- *Warcraft/World of Warcraft*—The challenges in both games are satisfying. Those in *World of Warcraft* are perhaps too easy to overcome until high-level play (progression raiding). Then they become punishingly difficult in order to present the players with challenges that will keep them occupied until the developers produce new content, rather than remaining at levels that produce optimal gameplay. I think that this is because the primary purpose of those endgame obstacles is not to make the goal meaningful.

- *Kingdom Death: Monster*—The obstacles are very difficult. The game, similarly to *Dark Souls*, presents itself as a brutal challenge. In this case, that terrible difficulty imparts more profound meaning to the narrative events that the gameplay generates.

- *Journey*—Yes. Yes, the obstacles could easily be bigger. However, the narrative impact of the game isn't reduced by the game not being difficult to complete. The obstacles the player overcomes are just not very important to the story.

- *Virginia*—No. I think the obstacles, or lack of them, is probably something that contributes to players not feeling invested in the game. Also, the serious difficulty of the obstacle to narrative understanding makes the game less compelling. That is not to say that parts of the game are not very effective, just that this lens reveals some major flaws in the game.

- *Dear Esther*—Yes. The narrative of the game is not about overcoming challenges. The game chooses to be short and to have a flow of gameplay not interrupted by a challenge. No, adding more difficult obstacles would probably make the game less effective, even if it addressed the complaint that the game lacks sufficient gameplay to qualify as a "game" for some players.

- *Loneliness*—Yes. No. The only obstacle in the game is that the other dots move away from the player. The goal of the player is to reach the dots, and that is not possible. The game's purpose is to confront the player with the feeling of loneliness caused by failing to connect with the other dots; this obstacle succeeds. Because the player cannot overcome the obstacle, there is no way to make it "bigger."

6. Great stories often involve the protagonist transforming to overcome the obstacle. How does your protagonist transform?

- *Dark Souls*—The character gains mechanical abilities and equipment. Though they don't have a narrative character progression, the player transforms in terms of their skill level.

- *Borderlands 3*—There are relatively high levels of mechanical character development and some level of narrative character progression, though it's not a focus of the game.

- *Tetris*—There is no character protagonist, but the player gains skill.

- *Vikings: War of Clans*—There is mechanical progression, but no character progression narratively at all. There may be a social progression as the player interacts with other players and forms a community.

- *Pokémon Go*—There is a progression of the player's creature collection and each creature's power. There is no narrative character progression, however. There may be a social progression as the player interacts with other players and forms a community.

- *The Witness/Myst*—There is a progression in player understanding of the mechanics, though there is little narrative character progression.

- *Warcraft/World of Warcraft*—There are high levels of mechanical change, but low levels of narrative character transformation.

- *Kingdom Death: Monster*—The characters in the game change both mechanically, and their actions are constructed into dynamic arcs by many players.

- *Journey*—There is some mechanical progression as the character's ability to fly increases, but there is a transformative character narrative that builds through gameplay.

- *Virginia*—There is little mechanical progression, but there is a substantial narrative character transformation.

- *Dear Esther*—There is no mechanical progression, but there is character transformation as the character prepares for death.

- *Loneliness*—There is no mechanical progression, but the progression from hope to despair is the point of the game.

Step 4: For each question, consider your ten responses and look for patterns.

1. What is the relationship between the main character and the goal? Why does the character care about it?

The nature of the relationship between character and goal or player and goal should match the nature of that goal.

If the goal and motivation are abstract such as "to survive" or "to gain the most points," then the motivation should also be abstract/mechanical. You see this in games like *Tetris* or *Dark Souls*, where you achieve your goal through an intrinsically rewarding core gameplay loop.

When the goal is narrative and less connected to the core gameplay, such as "to save the kingdom" or "to open the vault," then the motivation also needs to be narrative.

The strongest games combine these techniques. In *Ori and the Will of the Wisps*, the narrative goal of finding your friend and saving the forest is motivated by empathy created through NPC interaction and cut scenes. The mechanical goal, moving through the game, is motivated by the joy of using your skills. And there are both narrative and mechanical obstacles, but the progress and challenge in both aspects of the game make the whole more meaningful.

So I would list the patterns as:

- The type of obstacles in a game should match the kind of goal the game has.

- Games with abstract goals benefit from mechanical obstacles that directly progress the player toward the goal when overcome.

- Games with narrative goals work well with plot-based obstacles, where overcoming the obstacles forms a narrative path to the goal.

- Games with multiple different types of goals and obstacles are stronger if those types support each other.

2. What are the obstacles between the character and the goal?

- Anything that the player must do between the beginning of the game and the end could be considered an obstacle. For obstacles to be meaningful, the player must be able to recognize them and to understand how overcoming them advances them toward their goals.

    A positive example of this is *Tetris*, and a negative one is *Vikings*. Though mechanically simple, existing blocks that have accumulated in *Tetris* are a clear obstacle. Completing lines makes the blocks disappear dramatically, showing the player's progress. In *Vikings*, the impact of upgrading a building or training a new skill by "overcoming" the obstacle of the time it took to complete that task may advance you incrementally toward being a dominant player. However, that progress is so abstract and incremental that the impact of overcoming any single obstacle is minimal.

This can also be seen in the difference between *Myst* and *The Witness*. In *Myst*, each puzzle you solve moves you toward the end of the game, but how or even why that's true is often not clear, and the player's experience of the game is sometimes doing things because they can be done until the world changes and they can progress. Whereas in *The Witness*, puzzles are clearly defined, and mastering a set of puzzle mechanics results in the ability to complete a larger puzzle that moves the game forward.

- The more concrete the goal, the more mechanical the obstacle can be, as seen in *Tetris* or *Dark Souls*.

- The more internal or abstract the goal, the more the obstacles need to be narrative or symbolic, as is the case in *Journey* or *Loneliness*.

3. Is there an antagonist who is behind the obstacles? What is the relationship between the protagonist and the antagonist?

- The effectiveness of having an antagonist responsible for the obstacles to a player's goals relates to whether the obstacles need narrative justification and whether the player needs narrative motivation. *Tetris* wouldn't be made stronger by having an antagonistic character responsible for the falling blocks, because the obstacles are mechanical, and the motivation for overcoming them is not narrative. But *Vikings*, which has weeks or months of build-up before you reach the core gameplay, would probably benefit from a strong antagonist and narrative framework, at least early on when the player is learning the mechanics and not yet confronting other players.

4. Do the obstacles gradually increase in difficulty?

- Change in the difficulty of obstacles creates a drive for character or player advancement or "transformation." If the goal of the game is to show this transformation, the ways that the character or player changes should be meaningful to the character or player. If the character is transforming, then there should be narrative or mechanical feedback acknowledging the shift. If the player is advancing in skill or understanding, the game should recognize that and point it out to the player.

Most of the preceding examples don't show strong character or player transformation. *The Witness* does a pretty good job by presenting a player with an obstacle they can't overcome, a set of smaller obstacles they do overcome, and then returning them to the more difficult problem with the understanding needed. Those moments of epiphany are then obvious to the player. To increase confidence in this pattern, I would need to consider other games, like *Silent Hill 2* or *Planescape: Torment,* that focus on character transformation.

5. Are the obstacles big enough? Can they be bigger?

- The intent of the game governs the scale of obstacles. If the meaning of achieving the goal relates to the struggle to attain it, then obstacles need to be large enough to challenge the player.

- Often that size is very dependent on the skill of the player, and the game must either adjust obstacle size to match player skill, or provide the space for the player to acquire the skill they need.

  A power fantasy game like *Doom Eternal* may have obstacles that seem massive, and in some modes are very difficult, but the designer intends to empower the player to crush those obstacles. A game like *Dark Souls* has tremendous obstacles, but they remain tough to overcome because the designers aim to give the player the experience of hard-won struggle. In both cases, the size of the obstacles matches the needs of the game. The epic power of The Doom Slayer would be undermined if cautious, meticulous gameplay were required to defeat enemies. And the grimdark hopelessness of the world of *Dark Souls* would be trivialized if the character could run through the game exploding every enemy with reckless abandon.

6. Great stories often involve the protagonist transforming in order to overcome the obstacle. How does your protagonist transform?

- Progression of both player skill and character ability is very common in games. If the game intends to show how that progression is transforming either the player or character, then the game must work to show that transformation to the player.

- For change to be "transformation," it must be meaningful. For character advancement to be meaningful, it must allow the character to overcome obstacles that were once difficult or impassable. For an increase in player skill to be significant, the player must achieve a sense of mastery.

Step 5: Look across all of your responses for all ten games for high-level patterns.

1. The Law of Ludonarrative Obstruction—This potential high-level pattern would state that there are two kinds of goals and obstacles in games: narrative and mechanical. Games need to present obstacles that relate to the goals they're blocking. To the degree that games have a narrative, goals can be more meaningful if they are essential to the narrative. Mechanical obstacles can support narrative goals, and narrative obstacles can support mechanical goals, but only if overcoming the obstacle is perceived to move the player or character toward the goal.

Step 6: Document each pattern using the pattern template.
I identified 14 possible patterns in steps 4 and 5 of this exercise. Another designer looking at this lens might identify an entirely different set of patterns relating to the game or design problem they were applying Lens #74 to. This step is vital, because documenting the patterns using the template will require that you articulate the design problem that the pattern solves and provide example games. For this example, I will document one of these 14 possible patterns and leave the others to interested readers.

Step 7: Consider whether your game needs to solve any of the problems that those patterns address.
The patterns, generated by applying this exercise to Lens #74, cover a lot of design ground! Not all of them will be needed to solve problems found in any one game, but at least some of them likely will. Applying those patterns would help me as a designer understand how to use the perspective of Lens #74 in my game. Beyond helping with that immediate problem, all of the patterns can be added to my Pattern Language and used in future games.

I proposed 13 potential patterns by looking at this one lens. You could document each using the pattern template, as I have done later with Just

Look at What You've Become. Working through this exercise for all 116 lenses would likely yield hundreds of patterns, perhaps as many as a 1,000! Is it necessary to perform this exercise for every lens? Probably not. Different developers will find different lenses more or less intuitive. This exercise provides a tool for exploring the lenses that present you with the most difficulty.

––––

Here is the pattern generated by the last question in the lens: For change to be "transformation," it must be meaningful. For character advancement to be meaningful, it must allow the character to overcome obstacles that were once difficult or impassable. For an increase in player skill to be meaningful, the player must achieve a sense of mastery.

Pattern

Name: Just Look at What You've Become
Confidence: 2
Image:

FIGURE 16.2 Actions that change your character can also change the game world. Seeing that can show a player how their character has transformed.

Author: Chris Barney

Design problem: Character progression systems and player skill growth are part of many games. How can those systems be made meaningful and not just the mechanical side effects of systems introduced to balance each other?

Description: Consider the statement: "For change to be 'transformation,' it must be meaningful. For character advancement to be meaningful, it must allow the character to overcome obstacles that were once difficult or impassable. For an increase in player skill to be meaningful, the player must achieve a sense of mastery." This assertion implies three levels of design. First, a game may include systems of player advancement and/or require players to increase their skill to progress. Second, those systems may be made meaningful by allowing the player to overcome obstacles and to achieve a sense of mastery. And third, when a game meets the previous two levels of conditions, a designer may give meaning to the change in the character and player.

A player can derive meaning from those changes on their own, but when the developer has given meaning to the systems, *they* then have the opportunity to ascribe meaning to the changes those systems produced.

Because the player will have participated in those systems and be part of producing that change, the meaning they ascribe to those changes can be compelling. Whether the player adopts the meaning ascribed by the developer depends on how visibly the designer communicates that meaning through systems and game narrative.

Games that use this pattern and how:

- *Planescape: Torment*—The character begins as a blank slate; the player discovers the character's history through play and decides whether to make choices in keeping with the character's pastor become a new person based on their interactions with the events of the game. The game guides the player toward making "good" choices. By the end of the game, the character has become incredibly powerful and confronts the embodiment of what they used to be. Defeating that avatar of their past evil through choices made over 30 to 100 hours of hard gameplay answers the game's tagline question: "What does it take to change the nature of a man?"
- *Spec Ops: The Line*—In this game, the player uses standard first-person shooter skills and abilities to wreak havoc across the levels of the game. At the last minute, the game reframes the actions of the "heroic soldier" character that the player controls as a descent into madness and violence. The designers intentionally hide this transformation from the player until the end of the game. The deceit increases the impact of the transformation, without concern for whether the player will be comfortable with their role in guiding the character.

- *Fable II*—In the *Fable* games, the actions the character takes physically transform them, making them look more angelic or more demonic. The dichotomy is simplistic, but the effect of seeing the character change throughout the game is dramatic. The reactions of NPCs to the character reinforce this change.
- *Infamous*—Similar to the *Fable* games, the progression system for the character features "good" or "bad" options, and the effects of the abilities reflect these designations: a good ability might heal, a bad ability might set everything on fire. By the end of the game, the character becomes a savior or destroyer depending on the player's choices. The consequences of that transformation are obvious in the gameplay.
- *Legacy of Kain*—In this game, the character is turned into a vampire early in the game. They gain vampiric powers throughout the game and become a superhuman being by the end of play. After the final boss fight, when the character has destroyed the "villain," the player can choose to "save the world" and be forgotten, or rule it from atop a literal throne of skulls. Sequels to the game canonized the choice to become the evil ruler in keeping with the character's actions in the game.

Seed: Exercise 25: Creating Patterns from Lenses—Lens #74 The Lens of the Obstacle
Related patterns:
Parent patterns:
Coercive Ludonarrative Resonance* (Confidence: 2)—Creating meaningful character transformation using Just Look at What You've Become requires the alignment of mechanics and meaning that this pattern provides.

I'm Doing It As Hard As I Can[†] (Confidence: 3)—If you want to drive character transformation, you must create a game world that demands that the character advance to overcome its challenges. Use this pattern to guide your implementation of escalating difficulty.

SUGGESTED EXERCISE

Use **Exercise 24: Theoretical Patterns** to generate a pattern based on the following theory: The Law of Ludonarrative Obstruction. There are two kinds of goals and obstacles in games: narrative and mechanical. Games need to present obstacles that relate to the goals they are blocking. To the degree that games have a narrative, goals can be more meaningful if they are important to the narrative. Mechanical obstacles can support narrative goals, and narrative obstacles can support mechanical goals, but only if overcoming the obstacle is perceived to move the player or character toward the goal.

---

* Example pattern for Exercise 14: Player Manipulation Patterns.
[†] Example pattern conversion from *Game Mechanics: Advanced Game Design* described in Chapter 16.

Child patterns:
One of These Days That's Going to Get You Killed* (Confidence: 2)—Use this pattern to introduce natural consequences to the ways that the character changes when you apply Just Look at What You've Become.

Other related patterns:

SUGGESTED EXERCISE

Use **Exercise 24: Theoretical Patterns** to document any of the 12 remaining possible patterns. You could just document the patterns, but because you are taking my theories based on the preceding exercise, you'll get more out of the process if you take the time to use Exercise 24.

For each pattern, consider how it's related to this one. Is it a parent or child? Is it additive or subtractive? Or does it just share a parent?

Keywords: Narrative, Mechanics, Meaning, Player, Character, Goals, Obstacles, *Boundaries, Contrast, Echoes*

PITFALLS OF PATTERN RELATIONSHIPS

When describing the relationship of two patterns, it's important to be clear about whether a higher-level pattern is always necessary for a lower-level pattern to function and is thus a child pattern. Sometimes one pattern makes another stronger, but is not always found in games that successfully implement the other pattern and is therefore additive without being a parent or child. Other times, a pattern is often co-present with the lower level pattern but doesn't affect the effectiveness of the lower-level pattern. In those cases, the patterns have no formal relationship, other than possibly sharing keywords.

Failing to be clear about the nature of the relationship can lead you or another developer to try to include patterns in a game to solve a problem when they're not needed, or might even interfere with the solutions that the patterns required suggest.

To help prevent this kind of confusion, you should describe the relationship between two patterns narratively in addition to assigning the relationship a confidence rating.

---

* Example pattern for Exercise 1: Basic Pattern Exercise.

COMBINING PATTERNS

When working on a Pattern Language in a group or integrating your language with other developers you'll often find that similar patterns have emerged from different members of the group. At times, these patterns will be distinct enough that it's valuable to consider them separately. But most of the time, you should assess the possibility of combining them aggressively. If you can look at both patterns and capture the nuance of both in a single pattern that's more broadly applicable than either was alone, then you should remove the duplicate patterns and replace them with a combined pattern.

You can often capture the subtle differences in two patterns by including examples of games that show the way the new pattern can create the effects of the source patterns. Generalizing one pattern to have this flexibility is preferable to including the two similar rigid patterns. Remember Alexander's original description of a pattern as a solution to a design problem with a thousand possible expressions.

When you encounter two patterns that are functional duplicates of each other, it's best to combine the two patterns by selecting the aspects of each that are most usable. You should pick the pattern name that is most evocative and memorable, include the example games that make the purpose of the pattern most clear, choose the most clearly worded pattern description, and so on.

The example patterns in this book will be good candidates for combining with the patterns you, or your students or co-workers, produce. Don't assume that a pattern in this book is superior or "official" in some way just because I included it here. While the patterns in this book are well-considered, I haven't produced a sufficient number of patterns, compared them to enough other patterns, or even designed games with enough of them to have a high level of confidence in them. They will likely become stronger over time by being combined with other patterns.

The following example shows two patterns that were created by students in different semesters of a level design course that I taught. Both sets of students created similar patterns independently. The third example here is a combined pattern that includes strong points from both student patterns.

> I have many international students who are working in English as their second or third language. I have edited the text of the patterns for clarity, so that their insight and expertise will be as evident to readers as it is to me.

Name: Dead Friend/Good Until It's Gone
Authors: Yiyi Liu and Ysabelle Coutu
Confidence: 2
Design problem: It is always a problem for designers to make players understand the emotions they want to express. Sadness is one of the emotions. How to make players feel sad as the character in the game or make them feel sad about what happened to the characters is a challenge.
Pattern description: During the game, give players some helpers and friends, which can be human beings or animals. As time goes by, show players how great the friend is, how friendly and helpful they are. Then at some point, ask players to give up the friend or let the other NPCs kill the friend to pass the level. The more players like the friend before, the more sadness and pain they will feel.

Games that use this pattern and how:

- *Brothers, a Tale of Two Sons*—The sadness in this game is around death; the death of the bird, the death of a person they met during the journey, and the death of the elder brother. The younger brother goes back home and needs to face some problems they solved before, but now he needs to do it himself, and players need to use the elder brother's side of the controller to help the little brother to go over it, it is really sad.
- *The Walking Dead*—The background of the game is a world with zombies and human beings without the resources they need to live. The enemies are not just zombies, but also other human beings, who are just bad people who enjoy the bad world. The character tries his best to survive and save his friends. But his plans always fail, and there are always things that break the peace in his life. The game has you play as a character (Lee) for the whole first season, but ends up killing him. The player must choose how this happens, heightening the impact of this moment.
- *Journey*—The game takes you on a beautiful and emotional journey across a sweeping landscape that is a joy to traverse, and can also connect you in a deep and meaningful way with a stranger. Thus, seeing your avatar (and potentially your companion) vanish into the light of the mountain is a profoundly bittersweet moment.

Seed: Exercise 6: Emotional Patterns—Sadness
Related patterns: Sadness Trigger
Parent patterns: Give Up Something for Something Else
Child patterns: None listed.
Keywords: Emotion, Immersion, Narrative, NPC, Sadness

Name: Empty Nest
Author: Nico Ulloa, Gilbert Cranton, Will Bridges, and Justin Brady
Confidence: 2
Design problem: How to make the player feel the loneliness or sadness.
Pattern description: Utilizing companion characters to create a constant in the player's experience and then removing it wholly, whether permanently or temporarily, will make the player feel incredibly lonely and acknowledge the character's loneliness.

Games that use this pattern and how:

- *Twilight Princess*—Midna, the helper character and sidekick, is temporarily incapacitated (and at risk of death). The uncommon silence, accompanied by rainy and dreary visuals and a solemn piano track, underscores the fundamental loneliness of the player and the character.
- *Death Stranding*—In one chapter, you lose your constant companion baby BB. This loss has mechanical consequences in that you are more vulnerable and weak against the threats of the world.
- *Emily is Away*—The game establishes the player's connection to Emily early in the game, but as it progresses, you get further and further apart. When Emily ultimately leaves for good, you feel that loss like you lost a real friend.

Seed: Exercise 6: An Emotional Pattern—Loneliness.
Parent patterns: None listed.
Child patterns: None listed.
Keywords: Emotion, Loneliness

The combined pattern:

Name: A Suddenly Empty Nest
Author: Chris Barney, revised from Dead Friend/Good Until It's Gone by Yiyi Liu and Ysabelle Coutu; and Empty Nest by Nico Ulloa, Gilbert Cranton, Will Bridges, and Justin Brady
Confidence: 3
Design problem: Making the player feel the loneliness or sadness experienced by a character.
Pattern description: To create empathy in the player for the loneliness or sadness felt by a character, developers may wish to use companion characters to create a constant in the player's experience and then remove them, either permanently or temporarily.

Games that use this pattern and how:

- *Twilight Princess*—Midna, the helper character and sidekick, is temporarily incapacitated and at risk of death. The uncommon silence, accompanied by rainy and dreary visuals and a solemn piano track, underscores the fundamental loneliness of the player and the character.
- *Death Stranding*—In one chapter, you lose your constant companion baby BB. This loss has mechanical consequences in that you are more vulnerable and weak against the threats of the world.
- *Emily is Away*—Establishes the player's connection to Emily early in the game, but as it progresses, you get further and further apart. When Emily ultimately leaves for good, you feel that loss like you lost a real friend.
- *Brothers, a Tale of Two Sons*—In this game, you play as two brothers. Sadness comes from death; the death of a bird, the death of a companion met during their journey, and finally, the death of the elder brother. When the younger brother goes back home and needs to face the same problems he solved with his brother, but now needs to face them alone, you need to use the elder brothers' side of the controller, emphasizing the elder brother's absence and evoking real sadness.
- *The Walking Dead*—The developers set this game in a world with zombies where humans don't have the resources they need to live. The enemies aren't just zombies, but also other humans who are bad people enjoying the bad world. The character tries to survive and to save their friends, but their plans always fail. Something always disrupts the peaceful moments in their life. The game has you play as one character (Lee) for the whole first season. But at the end of the season, he dies, and you must decide how it happens. You continue as a different character in the next season, but the sadness in the game is more meaningful because of your loss as the player.
- *Journey*—The game takes you on a beautiful and emotional journey across a sweeping landscape that is a joy to traverse, and can also connect you in a deep and meaningful way with strangers during most of the game. Thus, seeing your companion freeze on the slopes of the mountain is a profoundly tragic and isolating moment.
- *Ori and the Will of the Wisps*—The designers introduce the companion character of a baby owl in the game's tutorial section. A year passes for the characters as the player learns the basics of movement in the game. During these scenes, the player moves the character through scenes of daily life while the baby owl grows up. As the tutorial ends, the pair set out on an adventure but are immediately separated. The first act of the game is your search for your young companion. At the end of the first act, she dies. The sadness of losing her creates a sense of isolation while playing the rest of the game alone.

Seed: Exercise 6: Emotional Patterns–Loneliness
Parent patterns: Give Up Something for Something Else*
Child patterns: Sadness Trigger†
Keywords: Emotion, Sadness, Loneliness, NPC, Companion

ELIMINATING PATTERNS

You can eliminate some patterns by combining them with other similar patterns. At other times you may discover that a pattern that you observed does not function in the way that you intended. If you see that a pattern, as you have described it, has unintended side effects or does not solve the design problem as stated, you should remove it from your language.

Note that you should not discard the pattern entirely, as the design problem still exists, and your work in deriving the pattern is still valuable. You should instead return to the exercise that you used to create the pattern in the first place. Look for additional examples of games that solve the design problem in ways that are different from those of the games you first listed. Consider how you need to change the pattern to account for the additional data.

If the pattern was generating unintended side effects, then you should look for games that implement the pattern but don't suffer those effects. Consider how they differ from the game where you observed the unintended consequences. Update the pattern to reflect these changes.

As you develop a more significant number of patterns, your mastery of the process will increase, and you may find that the patterns you derived early on are incomplete or less robust versions of patterns that you developed more recently. Always be ready to discard such patterns when you become aware of their shortcomings. You may even find that patterns that seemed reasonable earlier in your process are simply poorly formed or unusable. Culling these early attempts at pattern generation from your language is a normal part of the process of developing a robust and healthy language.

---

* Pattern from the language generated by students in the course Spatial and Temporal Game Design at Northeastern University, fall 2019.
† Pattern from the language generated by students in the course Spatial and Temporal Game Design at Northeastern University, fall 2019.

The following is an example of a poorly formed student pattern that should be eliminated from their language as they become aware of its flaws. Read through this pattern, and see how many problems you can find. I will discuss the problems with the pattern, as well as point out the reasons that it is still valuable.

Name: Game Perspective
Author: Anonymous (Spatial and Temporal Game Design at Northeastern University, fall 2018)
Confidence: 2
Design problem: How do we choose the perspective of the game?
Pattern description: Games in a top-down perspective allow players to view the entire space. Most of the information is displayed on the screen. Players can see their obstacles and goals. They use their strategies and skills to overcome obstacles and win the game.

Side-view games provide less information to players than top-down games, especially in a side-scrolling view. Players should react more quickly because they don't know when the obstacles will appear. Players should be more skillful than the top-down games. The side-view game has a sense of gravity. Some games allow players to jump, climb, and fall.

Games in isometric perspective are the same as top-down games. Players can view the entire space. An isometric perspective allows the world with depth.

Players who play a first-person game are much more easily immersed in the game. Players can see more details of the environment, but they can't see the whole space. First-person games provide less information to players than top-down view games as well. Players have more difficulties in noticing the threats around them and will have a sense of dizziness.

Third-person games provide more information. Strategic games use third-person perspectives more often.

GAMES THAT USE THIS PATTERN AND HOW:

- *Pac-Man*—Top-down 2D. Players can see beyond walls to avoid enemies. By seeing the whole screen, they can know where enemies and goals are, and plan accordingly.
- *flOw*—Top-down 2D. The game displays all info on a plane, no gravity, all visual information available (nothing hidden).
- *Battleship*—Top-down 2D. Easy for all players to see information, but info to players is limited.
- *Donkey Kong*—Side view. Players can see the whole screen, but there's gravity, can see threats, sense of direction.

- *Prince of Persia/Super Mario Bros.*—Side-scrolling. Jumping/up-down movement is a core mechanic.
- *Fez*—Side-scrolling, 3rd person, 2D (kinda?). But can rotate the game world. Why? To subvert the usual platformer paradigm?
- *Cuphead*—Side-scrolling, 2D platformer. To support the aesthetic of hand-drawn animation. Also isometric map view takes you outside the gameplay.
- *Legend of Zelda: A Link to the Past*—2D isometric. Allows a world with depth (cliffs), verticality.
- *Q*bert*—Isometric. Puzzle game depending on the perspective.
- *Age of Empires*—Isometric 3D. 3D for aesthetic, viewpoint because of simulation, "god" view.
- *Wolfenstein/Doom*—1st person. Projection into character, immersion, hiding info, unlike Pac-Man.
- *Portal*—1st person 3D. Why? 3D because it focuses on physical space and moving through it, 1st person because of immersion? Aiming? Makes danger more immediate? No character development.
- *Total War: Warhammer 2*—3D movable camera. Control because it's a strategy game, see details but also the big picture, again "god" view, large map to view.

Pattern seed: Exercise 22: The First Choice—Game Perspective

First, many of the problems with this pattern are my fault as an instructor. The student wrote this pattern early in the development of the techniques I describe in this book. So the issues here are not due to any lack of skill or understanding on their part. My understanding of and ability to explain patterns has improved. I present exercises more clearly now and have improved the format of the Pattern Template in the years since the student wrote this pattern.

I'll work through the problems in order. First, the title is descriptive of the problem, but it doesn't suggest the solution it presents. The statement of the design problem is broad; a pattern about the way to make that high-level decision would be useful, though, so it's not necessarily a problem. However, it is an indicator of the problems that follow.

The pattern description isn't the description of a pattern. It's a listing of observations about how different perspectives can affect games. That is valuable information, and some of it is insightful, but that doesn't make it a pattern. Looking at the sections, I see several observations that are worth investigating further as possible patterns:

- Top-down perspectives allow high information density and low levels of hidden information.

- Side-view games often have more restricted information.

- Side-view games emphasize gravity, likely because they show the Y-axis on which gravity operates (at least in terms of most physics implementations) and because movement mechanics in side-view games are strongly affected by gravity.

- Isometric games, which are between top-down and side view, provide some of the benefits of both.

- First-person games are "more immersive."

- The restricted view in first-person games can reduce situational awareness.

- Third-person games (by which I think the author means games that have a third-person camera that is attached to the character, or which can be manipulated by the player, so games like *Gears of War* or *StarCraft II*) provide more information than first-person games. This observation fits with the fact that they are a step between isometric views and a first-person views.

For a pattern that was operating at the very high level of the stated design problem, I would probably come up with something like: "Camera perspective has a huge impact on gameplay because different perspectives enable different mechanics and design techniques for a wide variety of reasons. To choose the most effective camera perspective for a specific game, the designer should consider the purpose of the game and the core mechanics that they intend to use." That description may seem so vague as to be useless. However, providing good examples of different perspectives and how they affect the games that use them will help the reader to consider the effect of the camera perspective. This example-based understanding is better than a fixed list of effects that will inevitably be incomplete and rigid in a way that's counter to the purpose of a pattern.

The examples section doesn't provide enough description. Because of the poorly formed pattern description, any game will qualify as using the pattern. If we adopt the revised pattern description, then each example can be assessed by whether the perspective supports its core mechanics. In this case, we could revise the examples to be ones more like these:

- *Pac-Man*—The top-down 2D perspective in this game gives the player complete information on the playspace; it allows the core mechanics of pathfinding and threat avoidance.

- *flOw*—This game also uses a top-down 2D perspective, but allowing scrolling of the screen as the player moves enables the mechanics of exploration and increases tension, as unknown threats can enter the screen.

- *Donkey Kong*—This game provides complete information through its fixed side-view 2D camera. It supports its jumping and barrel-rolling mechanics by using the side view, which emphasizes gravity.

This list could be extensive, but the general practice of introducing an example that's the simplest use of a perspective and then providing one that uses a more complex perspective to support more complex mechanics is a good one. For this kind of pattern, I would probably provide more examples than in other patterns; two examples for each major camera perspective would be reasonable. Games that use the camera perspective poorly or for which you, as a designer, do not understand the reason for the use of perspective should be omitted.

Another approach that would be even better would be to provide only a few examples, perhaps three, and then to create a child pattern that explores the effects of each perspective in depth.

As you can see, the pattern that would result from addressing all of the flaws in the original pattern would be so different that it should be considered a new pattern. You might give the new pattern a title like "What You Need to See Depends on What You're Going to Do."

When considering the patterns that you've written, it is essential to remember that it's better to revise a pattern than to leave it in your language if it's unclear or misleading. You don't have to throw it away, but you should set it aside until you have the experience you need to revise it into a well-formed pattern.

CHAPTER 17

Creating New Pattern Exercises

T HE 25 EXERCISES IN this book will not cover every possible pattern you might want to derive. The general exercise at the beginning of the book is flexible. Still, if you want to assign students an exercise that will focus them in a particular area or have your team investigate an aspect of design important to a project you are beginning, it may be too blunt an instrument.

There is nothing special or sacred about the exercises in this book. They have had a little playtesting and iteration, but they are just the first steps on the path to this method of learning design. You can create new exercises of your own and tailor them to your needs.

Pattern exercises usually consist of five to ten steps that guide the developer through the process of creating the pattern. These steps break down into four sections:

1. Framing the intent of the exercise
2. Listing and describing examples
3. Analyzing the examples
4. Articulating the pattern

Often there are multiple steps within each of these areas. For example, Exercise 2: High-Order Patterns asks the designer to pick a design element, then describe the problems it solves, and then pick one of those problems as the starting point for the pattern. Those three steps are all part of the first area of the pattern exercise. To be able to construct new pattern exercises, you will need to consider each of the aforementioned four sections in detail.

FRAMING THE INTENT OF THE EXERCISE

You should only create a new exercise if you're trying to derive patterns that are in some way different from those produced by the existing exercises. Perhaps you want to look at a new area of design, find patterns that require multiple parents, or derive patterns that function independently from any other pattern. Before you begin, you should be able to state why you need the exercise and specifically what kind of pattern you intend it to produce.

LISTING AND DESCRIBING EXAMPLES

This step often takes the form of a simple list of games that are examples of the starting point aspect or technique. It is necessary to ask for at least ten example games. It can often be challenging to find a full ten examples, but trying forces the designer to consider edge cases and find games that call into question weak patterns that they might begin to pursue based on the most prominent examples. More examples are better, but asking for more than ten can make an exercise prohibitively difficult. One solution is to create an exercise that you intend to be completed by a group, and ask that each group member find ten independent examples. In the initial listing, it's important that the designer just list and describe the games. The analysis comes later, and the details that come out in the process of describing the games are often critical.

Sometimes you may not be asking for a list of games in this area. For example, Exercise 12: Embedded and Environmental Narrative Patterns starts with picking a single game, but in this section asks the user to describe ten techniques used to incorporate narrative into the game. Then it asks the designer to repeat that process multiple times for other games with a similar narrative.

In the end, the purpose of this part of the pattern exercise is to generate a reasonably large set of data points and elicit enough detail about them that the designer has the material they need to conduct their analysis in the next section.

ANALYZING THE EXAMPLES

This section is usually the hardest to complete as part of the exercise. You may simply ask the user to look at the example games they've listed and their descriptions to see if there is a visible pattern relating to your starting point. However, it's often useful to ask for a more structured and specific analysis. The particular question posed in the analysis section generally relates to the starting point and the purpose of the exercise. For example, Exercise 4: Formal Patterns is intended to create patterns about the use of formal elements in a game. It asks the designer to identify the problems that the formal element solves in each example game, and then to describe the way that each example game uses the formal element to solve those problems. Exercise 14: Player Manipulation Patterns asks the designer to consider the differences between games that create the expected effect and games that create that same effect unexpectedly.

ARTICULATING THE PATTERN

The final section of each exercise calls for the designer to consider the results of their analysis, and then to describe all of the patterns they see. Then it asks them to pick one of those patterns and articulate it using the Pattern Template. I have made a point of reminding the designer that they may want to consider writing up the remaining patterns they have noted using the Pattern Template. Not all of those observed patterns will be significant or well-formed enough to convert into a formal pattern, but considering each idea will help the designer understand the space around the patterns they have formalized.

I strongly recommend that you take the time to complete any exercise you create yourself. It's very easy to assume that an exercise will work and create the kind of patterns you intend. It's also very easy to be wrong about that! If you can complete the exercise and the result surprises you with its insightfulness, or turns out to be a clear and fundamental principle of game design in the area you intended, then it's probably worth sharing with your students or colleagues. If you struggle to complete the exercise or find the result underwhelming, try revising the exercise and attempting it again.

CHAPTER 18

Designing with a Pattern Language

A T THIS POINT, YOU should have created a body of patterns, alone or with your colleagues or classmates. You should have linked them together into a language. What now? Hopefully, the process of deriving the patterns and linking them has been useful and helped you develop a better sense of game design. That may be enough. The conceptual framework of understanding how to describe the purpose and effects of mechanics and techniques as patterns, and how different groupings of the mechanics and techniques in those patterns support each other will shape how you design games for the rest of your career. But you may want a more direct and concrete way to apply your Pattern Language. I will describe that process in the next section.

Aside from the skills and techniques used in game design, there are nearly as many ways to approach the process of designing a game as there are developers. Sometimes the shape of that process is a personal choice; sometimes it is dictated by external constraints of studio policy or a professor's whim. There are two primary ways that you can use your Pattern Language: either integrating it into existing systems of design or using it to drive the design process.

INTEGRATING PATTERN LANGUAGE USE
INTO EXISTING DESIGN PROCESSES

You can integrate your Pattern Language into existing design processes by using patterns to assess potential design choices or to validate the choices you've already made. In this case, you will look at the design decision that you're considering; perhaps you're thinking of adding a double jump mechanic to your platformer or a co-worker has asked you to take a look at their prototype of that mechanic. First, you would consider whether that mechanic is the implementation of a pattern you've created. If I were considering implementing a double jump mechanic, I might look at the example response I created at the beginning of this book for the Basic Pattern exercise (Exercise 1). In my example, I only detailed a single pattern from the seed of jumping, but I suggested several more.

Looking at those patterns, I would see that I should assess several things when considering adding jumping. If I want to use jumping to give me more options for creating platforming level designs, I should first consider how to maintain the player's level of power as I give them more autonomy in the game by increasing their abilities. But I should also note that I'm increasing the level of complexity in character movement, and so I should provide the player with the opportunity to develop mastery over the character's new abilities. I might look for patterns that suggest ways to do that or assess the ways that I intuitively solve those problems by looking for the patterns that relate to my solutions. Moving down the list of jumping patterns, I might consider how this new kind of jump will interact with my combat system. I would need to decide whether I'm trying to create an identifiable or aspirational character. If I want the player to feel like they could be the character, I might not want to use a mechanic like double jump, given that it grants the character abilities the player can never have. If I'm trying to create a power fantasy for the player, then my double jump mechanic might be the right choice.

I would then look at the parents of the patterns that I think apply to my double jump. If those parent patterns are already in the game, then my new mechanic is more likely to work as intended in the game. If they're not, then I should consider why. If those patterns have effects that go against the design intent of my game, then perhaps the double jump will not fit in as well as I thought. But if the parent patterns aren't present but do align with the design intent of the game, I may consider how the game could be implementing them.

Last, I would look to see if any of the child patterns of the patterns that relate to my double jump seem like they would fit in the game. Some might already be present, others would not match the design intent; but if I see any that look appealing, I would note them and consider using them in my design moving forward.

If I were assessing another designer's work, I would consider whether they were familiar with patterns. If they were not, then I would need to phrase my assessment without relying on the concepts of pattern theory—basically avoid using jargon that the other developer won't understand. I would probably also look for opportunities to introduce them to pattern theory, especially if they appreciated my assessment of their work. On the other hand, if they were comfortable using patterns themselves, then I would be able to refer them to the patterns that I used to analyze their application of the double jump mechanic to the game. Even if they had never seen those particular patterns, they would be able to read them and understand the design behind my assessment.

I think that this use of Pattern Language in design is the most likely to succeed soon. Until patterns are proven to be effective in shipped games, it will be tough for you to convince a team of developers to base their whole design process around a Pattern Language. And that's setting aside the need to have created a functionally complete language, which itself is a process that will take us years to generate.

When you find that you don't have the patterns you need to assess a design element you're considering, select the appropriate pattern exercise and complete it to produce the patterns you need. Over time, your language will grow. Your colleagues may adopt the use of patterns in their work, and by sharing your language, you will strengthen each other's design abilities.

PATTERN LANGUAGE AS THE BASIS OF DESIGN

The goal of using a Pattern Language as intended—to create a design from the first question to the most specific detail—is attractive, but has a high bar for entry. First, you need to have a functionally complete language, then a team that understands pattern theory well enough to use it, then a studio or publisher that will allow you to use a new process. To get to that place, you need to take a few intermediate steps.

First, use the language that you're developing, as described in the preceding section. Second, try using your language in small projects, such as a prototype or a game jam. Limit the number of patterns you're using at first to fit the scope of those smaller projects.

But eventually, you may have the opportunity to use patterns as the basis for a larger project. It's critical to get all the members of the project team familiar with pattern theory. If only you, as the lead designer, are using patterns and then handing off design specs to many developers to implement, it will result in confusion and misunderstanding, and produce a game that fails to implement the patterns as intended.

You need to understand that the Pattern Language you begin designing with is most likely still incomplete. And to the degree that the patterns you need are present, they should have low confidence ratings. The links between those patterns that you're trying to follow also likely have low confidence ratings. All of this may make it sound like a bad idea to even attempt using your language. It's not a bad idea, as long as you don't insist that your patterns are correct, infallible, and unquestionable. The patterns and your language are a tool to help you and your colleagues understand the design. The process of using your patterns and language in design is the only way to increase your confidence in your language.

If you're trying to apply a pattern to solve a design problem and it's caus-ing issues, stop and ask why. Be ready to revise your pattern or abandon it if you find it flawed. Consider the use of the pattern as the final step in any pattern-generation exercise. As you apply a pattern, consider whether your implementation of it is solving the intended problem. If it's not, then find a different implementation. If you can't think of an application of the pattern that will solve the stated problem in your specific game, note that in the pattern, then return to the exercise that you used to create it. This time, consider games that solve the problem and also share the aspects of your game that interfered with the first pattern. Derive a new pattern from those games. Then assess whether the new pattern should replace your old pattern, or be a child or sibling of it.

The process of using a Pattern Language as the primary driver of design is iterative. That is to say, you don't want to ask your first question, select a pattern to solve it, and then proceed to construct your entire design by selecting child pattern after child pattern. There are too many unknowns and new questions that will arise as you figure out how you will implement each pattern.

Instead, you should select a pattern, consider your implementation, and only look to additional patterns with each new design problem or decision you need to make. Everyone on the design team should be empowered to use the language to address their specific design concerns. As a lead designer, you may select a small number of high-level patterns as you conceptualize the game. Include those patterns in your design document. As other developers implement aspects of your design, they will be able to refer to those patterns to understand your intent in making the design decisions you've made.

Then, as they face lower-level decisions, they'll be able to consider whether the patterns they select reinforce the ones you've chosen. You'll be able to more easily and accurately understand and assess their work by referring to the patterns that they've chosen. Because patterns encapsulate not just the design solution but the problem that it solves—the how and why of a design choice—they allow both upstream and downstream communication for designers.

When your design is complete and your game is shipped, you must return to its patterns during your postmortem. Look at the game as a functioning whole, and consider its reception and effect on actual players. Look at the list of patterns that you used, and for each, determine whether it served its purpose. If a pattern performed as expected, raise its confidence level as indicated in the pattern confidence rubric. If a pattern and its parent or child worked together as intended, increase their link confidence levels as indicated in the link confidence rubric.

CHAPTER 19

Teaching Yourself or Students with Pattern Languages

One of the most important features of every pattern language is to not see it as a model, but as a platform that enables us to take the first steps in adapting specific patterns to our own particular circumstances.

(Helfrich, 2020)

I present this chapter to instructors attempting to use the ideas in this book to inform their pedagogy. However, the techniques, activities, and exercises that follow apply to individual designers or teams who are working on learning pattern theory.

One option is to have a class focus entirely on the use of Pattern Languages. In that case, simply working through the exercises in the book is a good option. It can also work well to combine the exercises with a game design survey course that is looking at different game design techniques and theories.

If you're not basing a course around this text, it's still relatively simple to include pattern exercises in your curriculum. The first requisite is teaching the Pattern Language concept to the students or becoming comfortable with it yourself. I recommend having students read at least the introduction to the book (Chapter 1) and Section III. I then recommend completing at least one pattern generation exercise as practice, without having other assignments rely on the outcome of that exercise. You should give constructive feedback on the patterns generated in this first attempt, referring to the pattern samples in this book as well as to Chapter 6, "Common Problems in the Proposed Patterns." It's common for patterns created in this first attempt to be poorly formed and unusable. Students need to know that it's normal to struggle here, and that this first practice exercise will not be graded for quality.

At this point, students should be ready for you to integrate pattern exercises with course material. In any course that requires practical game design or implementation, you can pick an exercise related to the assignment and then require that students complete it and use the resulting pattern in that design assignment. For example, in the course Spatial and Temporal Design, I give an assignment where the students must implement a scene demonstrating formal game design elements. In class, each student team completes Exercise 4: Formal Patterns from this book, and then they must use the pattern they created in the scene they build demonstrating formal elements. Adding the pattern-generation step to the design process focuses students on the effect of the elements they're using. This focus creates deeper understanding than just including elements because the textbook or lecture mentioned them. They are not, for instance, just creating a scene with platforms; they are considering the problems that platforms exist to solve, and the effect that their specific use of platforms creates in players.

You may find an exercise in this book that fits well with a particular assignment. Still, you may wish to focus the exercises further by requiring that the first step in a given exercise relate to the topic you're discussing in the class. The Basic Pattern Exercise (Exercise 1) is a good example. The first step is "name a design element." You can require that that element be related to your topic, whether that's jumping, non-player character (NPC) pathing, or narrative. Most of the other exercises can be similarly modified.

I often end courses that have made heavy use of patterns with a section on combining the patterns the class has generated into a language. More specifically, that means combining the patterns generated by identifying how they connect to all of the other patterns created in the class. Everyone needs to understand that those patterns are unlikely to be sufficient to constitute any kind of functionally complete language, but that despite that they can be useful and form the basis for an expanding language that can grow throughout the students' careers.

If you or your department are using patterns in multiple courses in your curriculum, it will be useful for students to maintain a pattern journal that they take with them between courses. Students can then use their journals to collect patterns, and use them to structure their understanding of game design throughout their course of study.

AN INSTITUTIONAL PATTERN LANGUAGE

As an instructor, you may find it useful to maintain a pattern repository created by all of your students across your courses and semesters. You will very quickly accumulate a large collection of patterns. The task of maintaining this kind of pattern library or language is formidable, and it's likely beyond the time available for an individual instructor. However, there is value in learning the techniques necessary to curate such a collection. It's possible to assign some of the required tasks to students, so long as they relate to your curriculum. Exposure to a larger body of patterns, including both good and bad student examples, can help students develop their understanding of patterns.

An example of such an assignment might be to search your institutional pattern language for an existing pattern that addresses a particular design problem before creating a pattern to solve that problem. Alternately, the assignment could be to search for similar patterns after completing a pattern exercise. The second option is more difficult, as it requires students to decide whether a similar pattern is a duplicate that they can eliminate, a refinement that should be incorporated, or a related pattern that should be connected. Both tasks are useful for a student to perform, but I would not assign the latter to students until they are comfortable with the pattern-creation process.

If you have created a significant institutional Pattern Language, it can be used as the basis for the design of student projects regardless of whether those projects directly involve creating new patterns.

DEVELOPING WITH PATTERNS

In the classes where I use patterns, I give short weekly development exercises where students have to create simple scenes using the patterns they develop. The projects should fit the kind of patterns that the students are creating. In my architecture/level design courses, I give the assignment to create a gray-boxed scene that utilizes the pattern. In my Experimental Game Design course, I give the assignment to create a paper prototype of a simple physical game. You could use similar exercises for courses focused on writing or visual arts .

The exercises must be simple enough that the students can focus on implementing the patterns they have derived, rather than being distracted by the complexities of full game development. For instance, in the level design courses, I don't allow the students to implement mechanics. If mechanics are important to the patterns, they must simply describe the mechanic and how it relates to the gray-boxed level they've produced.

Forcing students or new developers to focus on implementing the pattern is particularly important early in the process of learning to develop with patterns. I often see students attempt a project that's too large and lose sight of which aspects of their design are related to the pattern. Instead, they focus on an interesting challenge with the editor, or the imagined core gameplay loop, or the lighting, or any of a thousand things that are critically important, but unrelated to their assignment. Even as an individual experienced developer, forcing yourself to test your patterns with small, focused exercises will help you both understand the pattern and build the skill of incorporating a pattern into a design.

PROVIDING FEEDBACK

If you're an instructor or a developer driving the use of patterns at a studio, you will find yourself in the position of needing to give feedback on patterns that others are developing. This kind of feedback broadly falls into three phases.

During the initial ideation phase of pattern development, when the author(s) are working through the steps of a pattern exercise, check in with them as often as possible and ask about their answers to each question. Early on, you might ask if they are comfortable with the process, but in general, you should participate in the discussion they have, allowing them to explain their ideas. You should also provide feedback and suggestions if the authors are struggling, but you must learn to see the pattern that the students are trying to articulate, even if they are phrasing it poorly. Only then can you guide them toward creating a well-formed pattern. The students will learn far more from refining their pattern until it is clear than from receiving a poor grade for failing to get it right the first time.

In the final stages of pattern development, when the authors are translating their exercise responses into the Pattern Template, you may need to point out the places where they are having one of the common problems in proposed patterns.* Look at the students' exercise responses and suggest ways they can improve their final pattern.

The last stage where providing guidance is essential is in the integration of the pattern into a language that will be used by your group. You must help the authors understand the parent–child relationship of their pattern, and if others in your group of authors have derived similar patterns, either help them define the differences or help them combine the duplicate patterns.

Early in the process of learning to derive patterns, it's more important to become comfortable with the process than to generate useful patterns. As authors master the process, it may be helpful to have them revisit their old patterns and revise and improve them.

ASSESSING PATTERNS FROM OTHERS

Individual developers and students often feel justifiably proud of their initial pattern attempts. I've found that students and developers alike can have a hard time seeing the problems with their patterns. To develop a better sense of the problems a pattern can have, and the things that pattern authors need to change to make their patterns usable, I have students review and provide feedback on each other's patterns. Rather than pairs trading patterns, I find that this works best if they circularly review the patterns:

- Person A reviews the pattern from person B.

- Person B reviews the pattern from person C.

- Person C reviews the pattern from person A.

It is important to leave both positive and constructive feedback. Trading work can result in either each person saying only nice things or one person being critical and the other responding in kind. The circular arrangement decouples the feedback a student gets from the feedback they give.

It's convenient if the students record their patterns using a word processor where others can leave comments. After reviewing patterns, the students or developers should address the comments to improve their patterns.

---

* See Chapter 6.

Simply knowing that their peers will be looking at a pattern and trying to understand it has a significant positive effect on the quality of patterns. Being required to read and incorporate peer feedback further improves both the patterns and the students' understanding of the process, and the qualities of a good and usable pattern.

DEVELOPING WITH OTHER PEOPLE'S PATTERNS

As a follow-up to the aforementioned assessment and revision exercise, I have students use a pattern written by another student. Again, I try not to have students trade patterns, to avoid setting up rivalries or alliances. I encourage students to ask the pattern's author further questions. This interrogation is useful to both the author and the implementing developer. It helps the author understand what was missing from their pattern, and it helps the reviewer understand what unstated information they take for granted in the patterns they've written. The goal is for students to be able to write patterns that don't require developers to ask additional questions to use them.

GROUP PATTERN EXERCISES

In my classes, I predominantly assign group pattern development and implementation exercises. I think that individual exercises are a good place to start. But solo development is relatively rare, and patterns serve both as a structure for ordering design knowledge and as a clear way to communicate about design as a group.

As students develop more and more patterns over a semester or a degree program, they begin to communicate about their designs in terms of their Pattern Language. This immediate use of their language is possible because the projects they're working on are small in scope and designed around specific patterns. However, it also serves as early evidence that as developers generate larger pattern languages throughout their careers, they will be able to use them to communicate more clearly with their colleagues.

DIVIDING THE EXAMPLES

When working with groups, I have found it useful to assign each group member the task of coming up with their share of the example games from the pattern exercise. Most of the pattern exercises ask for a list of at least ten games in one of the early steps of the exercise. You may divide those among the group members.

The purpose of this is to prevent a common bad habit that can form when deriving patterns. As a developer works their way through finding and writing about the ten requested games, they often recognize one or more patterns after only a few games. It then becomes very hard not to select and analyze the subsequent games without bias toward that glimpsed pattern. Prematurely latching on to a pattern is a problem, because it prevents the developer from objectively selecting a variety of games and accurately analyzing them. This selection bias results in patterns that only apply to a more limited set of games than they claim to, and also in patterns that are not as deep or robust as they would have been in an unbiased process.

REVIEWING OTHER'S PROJECTS

I also find it useful to have students review the completed projects of other students or groups. The reviewing student examines the pattern(s) that a project claims to implement. They must discuss whether the project implements the pattern well, and whether it has the intended effect. Depending on the level of the students, I may require them to identify other patterns that are present in the design, and discuss whether those patterns support the design, are neutral to it, or subtract from it. Additionally, I may ask them to discuss whether the designers could (or should) remove unrelated or subtractive patterns from the project.

CREATING KEYWORDS

As discussed in Chapter 15, keywords are an important aspect of any pattern language. Before creating a design based on the full application of a pattern language, I give students the task of looking through all of the patterns that they've created over a semester and identifying keywords to describe them. I find that this produces better and more consistent results than asking students to create keywords as they initially develop their patterns. Waiting until students have written a significant number of patterns works better, because the purpose of the keywords is to connect the individual patterns into a network they can use as a language. At the point where students have a significant number of patterns that they've created or used, they are better able to identify keywords that apply to many patterns.

I have provided a sample set of keywords. These may be useful to developers creating patterns. However, students should use them with caution. This set of keywords isn't definitive; it arises from patterns in this book and those developed by students. There's value in requiring that students create keywords themselves. As part of the keyword generation exercise, students add each keyword they choose to a shared list. When that process is complete, the class looks at the list and eliminates duplicates, considers whether each keyword is the best descriptor, and revises the keywords field on their patterns accordingly.

It seems likely that in the long term, these lists would converge on a shared set of descriptors. However, students should understand that the particular words used are not important, so long as they're consistent across the patterns in the language and the contributing developers clearly understand them.

Even if you're working with an institutional Pattern Language, it's useful to have students select keywords independently. After they've settled on a set of keywords, they should then integrate those into the institutional collection, adjusting their own to match the words used in the institutional list or changing the master list to match their own if it increases clarity. This gradual expansion and improvement will almost certainly be preferable to simply using the list I provide.

CATEGORIZING PATTERNS

As part of the process of generating keywords for patterns, I ask students to focus on what aspects of game design their patterns address. They need to understand that the patterns they're creating, even collectively, are limited by their experience and interests. Looking at the provided lists of game design categories in Chapter 15 will help students to both understand the nature of the language they are constructing and see the gaps in it. For example, they may be able to see that they have a language rich in mechanical patterns, but that doesn't address the narrative or learning or sound-related aspects of design.

When the keyword generation for a set of patterns is complete, I ask students to take the list of categories and mark each category they've used as a keyword to describe at least one pattern in their language. This process creates a clear visual display of the scope of their language and the gaps in it.

ASSESSING A PATTERN LANGUAGE

The process of evaluating a Pattern Language and the patterns in it is vastly complicated and could easily be the subject of another book. The actual assessment of specific patterns or whole languages could be the subject of the doctoral work of a generation of scholars. Nevertheless, while a comprehensive discussion of the topic is out of the scope of this book, I do feel that these guidelines and thoughts are useful.

The development of an individual pattern or whole language may produce "bad" patterns. Some common problems with patterns are discussed in Chapter 6. The exercises generate patterns based on observation. While careful observation and analysis can suggest many useful patterns, it's essential to note that even patterns observed across many games have low confidence. That fact is acknowledged in the confidence rubric in Chapter 5. To raise confidence in these patterns, you must use them intentionally in designs over and over again. Only when you observe their success and revise them in response to their failures can you begin to validate their efficacy.

In addition to raising confidence in patterns through use, it may be possible to study their effects directly. There has not yet been academic work assessing the effectiveness of patterns in game design. There has not even been work describing how to go about assessing pattern effectiveness. However, an interesting early attempt has been made by one of my students, Ysabelle J. Coutu, in her thesis "Patterns for Environmental Narrative."

To explore the possibility of empirically validating the efficacy of a pattern, Coutu used the following methodology. She created and tested an initial build of a level without using pattern techniques in its design or implementation. She then measured the effectiveness of the level in achieving its design goals of conveying a story through the environmental narrative by observing the playtesters and taking a follow-up survey.

Having established this baseline, she then developed a set of four patterns using Exercise 12: Embedded and Environmental Narrative Patterns. She then implemented these patterns within the game, and then held a second set of playtests. In each set of playtests, she used two groups of subjects.

The first set were members of a game development community that created and supported the engine that she was using for development. This group of subjects was highly familiar with the game type and highly motivated to engage with the game. The second group of testers consisted of students within the university whom she recruited for testing. These subjects were neutral toward the game and had lower levels of experience with the game type. However, the second group of testers, for both playtests, were physically present in a usability lab. Coutu recorded eye-tracking data and other biometrics.

She coded the results by assessing whether users were able to articulate the intended narrative by the end of the playtest, and then by noting whether they had observed particular details in the environment. For the first group, she determined this through a survey, in the second group, she also used eye-tracking data.

As is common in master's thesis level of work, where part of the purpose is developing research skills, there were shortcomings in the results. The faults in research methodology and execution provided a valuable learning experience, as intended. Coutu noted that in future research it would be necessary to analyze the initial design during the second phase of the research. This analysis would allow researchers to see what patterns relating to the design intent the designer had instinctually incorporated. This recommendation recognizes that all designers are using design techniques according to internalized principles of design. Researchers will need to articulate those techniques as patterns to factor them out of the assessment of the patterns they're evaluating.

She also determined that it would be valuable to code the details in the environment that she intended to convey in the narrative before playtesting, rather than compiling this list based on the data generated by the testing.

The general results of her research indicate that the iterative process of incorporating patterns was effective at increasing the amount of narrative content that players perceived. However, the limited number of playtesters and limited scope of the work, as appropriate for a thesis, make those conclusions tentative. That said, the research explores the process for empirically validating the use of patterns and in that respect it is very encouraging.

These types of techniques should be developed and standardized by developers and academics interested in validating both the effectiveness of individual patterns and the broader validity of the approach of using patterns as the basis for game design.

The study of the application of patterns and the development of ways to empirically validate their effects is an exciting prospect, and suggests a significant way that game scholars and game designers could benefit from each other's work.

DESIGN EXERCISE USING PATTERNS

In a course that will introduce the idea of a Pattern Language, I have found it useful to have students complete the following exercise before introducing the pattern concept:

- Each student should write down one element of game design on a 3 × 5 index card. These elements should be as low level and discrete as possible. Examples might include jumping, platforms, fantasy theme, strategy genre, health meter, enemies, and combat.

- Shuffle all of the index cards and select ten randomly.

- The class should look at the selected elements together and, in an ad-hoc way, hash out a design that incorporates those elements. This process should be as rapid as possible, taking half an hour at most.

- Record the design and the elements selected.

- The class should then look at all of the design elements on the index cards again and select ten elements by consensus, either by vote or by arguing for each element to include.

- The students should form a second design that incorporates all of these elements.

- Record the elements used and the second design.

At the end of the class when a Pattern Language has been created, to the degree that it can be during one course, have the class complete the following exercise:

- Assess the designs from the beginning of the class.

- Identify the patterns produced by the class which have any of the design elements from the initial set of index cards.

- Look for patterns that are present or missing from the first design based on the element keywords that they selected for that design at the beginning of the semester.

- Look for patterns that are present or missing from the second design based on the element keywords that they selected for that design.

- Ask whether there are more patterns present in the first or second design and why.

- Write down the name of each pattern produced in the class and the keywords associated with it on a 3 × 5 index card. (This can be given as a homework assignment, asking each student to create the index cards for the patterns they generated.)

- Have the students decide on a design problem to base a game on by any method desired (e.g., submitting suggestions and arguing for or randomly selecting one).

- Select from the index cards a set of patterns to use in the design that will address that design problem.

- Take half an hour or an hour to propose a high-level design that incorporates as many patterns as the class would like from the selected index cards.

- Compare the three designs produced throughout the course and how they differ.

More than any exercise in this book, this will show the ways that using patterns can shape design for better or worse. Noting how many patterns were present even before you introduced the concept of patterns is important. Noting how using patterns that relate to and support each other improves design is also essential. Noting how overly focusing on applying patterns can limit the creativity of design is critical as well. This exercise can be an excellent opportunity to remind students that patterns should be general enough to allow creativity in their application.

Afterword

Y OU HAVE COVERED A lot of ground in this book. You've come to
understand the basics of pattern theory. You've completed exercises
examining your experience of playing and designing games and turned
that understanding into patterns that guide your design. You've taken
those patterns and connected them into a Pattern Language that lets you
know what tool to reach for when you face a design challenge, to understand why it's the right tool, and to predict how it will affect your game.
You've learned how to share all that with your fellow designers, and use it
to design together.

In short, you've gotten off to a good start.

Wait, we're in the Afterword, and I'm telling you we've made a good
start?!

Yes, all that work is just the bare beginning of learning to create and use
patterns in game design. Of course, you can now spend years creating patterns as you need them and incorporating them into an ever-richer language. But it turns out that beyond that, there's still more work to be done.

As I've put this book together, taking the ideas of Christopher Alexander
and turning them into a practical pedagogy for learning game design,
I've begun to see what we need to do next. In the most recent work by
Alexander, he talks about the need to create or discover the "generative
codes" for using patterns. These are a new, more profound, and more complicated concept, so I'm sorry, but I have to give you one more chunk of
theory.

ADVANCED PATTERN THEORY: GENERATIVE CODES

When Alexander looked at design projects that had gone wrong, even projects that used a pattern language, he discovered that the process of building, including the order that we do things in, matters very much. In his
paper "Generative Codes," he proposes the idea of rules that govern not just

design, but the entire process of creating centers (Alexander et al. 2005). He calls these meta-patterns *generative codes* and describes them as a "system of unfolding steps." He goes on to describe these steps:

> The steps are governed by rules of unfolding that are not rigid, but depend on context, and on what came before. The rules work in a way that is similar to the rules that nature follows to unfold an organism or a natural landscape, much as genetic codes unfold embryos. But these rules unfold ... from the whole, and lead to a unique result for each particular place. The rules tell you how to take specific steps, in a certain way that allows unfolding to proceed.
>
> The specifics of the rules that he details relate to the construction of architecture, but the principles behind them are broadly applicable.
>
> Like patterns (identified in *A Pattern Language*, 1975), the rules cover a great range of scales. ...
>
> The rules are ordered—sequenced—to unfold each part of the environment being created, smoothly and coherently.
>
> Also, in the generative code, each rule is specifically tied to a certain group of individuals, whose job it is to undertake that part of the unfolding together.
>
> Finally, in order to make the process succeed, the overall operation of the unfolding, which goes forward step by step, is accompanied by a general set of practical specifications for the conditions ... in which the process is being carried out.

Applying this to game design indicates that there are "rules" around the process of creating games that go beyond the creation of a design. The order in which you develop aspects of your design matters, as does the order in which you implement your designs. These rules apply not just to designers, but to everyone in the creation process, from coders to artists to project and community managers.

In his conclusion, Alexander finds that it helps to have someone in charge of the entire development process. Surprisingly, he does not suggest that the person should be the designer. He describes a project manager who is responsible to the purpose of the project. In the case of games that means a project manager whose purpose is to make sure that the game creates the intended experience for a player. That project manager should not be in charge of design, but they must understand it. They should not be responsible for the budget of the game or benefit from its profits, though they should understand and manage those constraints. Of course, Alexander recognizes the high bar that he's setting, and he's arguing for a better system rather than describing a process that exists outside of projects that he has had direct control over. However, it's interesting how well his ideas align with those of Agile project management, as described in *Agile Software Development with Scrum* (Ken and Beedle 2002). Having stated that the order of development matters, Alexander goes on to cite eight examples. Some of them seem specific to architectural construction, but I can apply seven of them to games.

1. "Diagnosis of the site is an essential early step."

   In games, we must consider many constraints before we begin to create or implement any design. For instance, we must know the target audience for a game's experience. We must decide what platform we will implement it on and in what venue players will experience it.

2. "Roads and driveways must be located and built after the pedestrian structure, not before."

   The structure of the game should reflect the way that players will experience it. That statement should be self-evident, but I can think of dozens of examples of games where designers did not consider the user experience when implementing systems. As with roads in architecture, this happens most often in the connective tissue of games, in the way players move between levels or use menus and user interface elements to access features of the game.

3. "Roads must be located and built after the houses, not before."

   The structure of the game must serve its core gameplay. As a counterexample, take an open-world game where designers scatter enjoyable encounters around a large map. This distribution often breaks up the game's pacing, because they chose the open-world design before understanding what parts of the gameplay would create the core experience for the player.

4. "When houses are designed, the garden must be placed (located) before the house volume is located, not after."

I think this analogizes to rewards, structural gameplay elements, and player motivation. Before you design the "necessary" structural elements or core gameplay loops, you should understand what parts of the game will be pleasurable or satisfying to the player, and what their motivation in playing will be. If combat is the fun part of a game, then don't design gameplay elements that keep the player from engaging in combat. If building a peaceful farm is the part the players will enjoy, don't design elements that will force the player away from that experience.

5. "Construction work must begin long before final drawings are ready, and the drawings develop, in parallel with the construction process."

This guideline has a clear reflection in pater prototyping, the Agile process, and iterative design.

6. "Windows must be placed, designed, and measured and built, after the walls or wall framing has begun, so that they reflect the real situations in the room, its light, and view."

You must consider the experience of the player and assure it throughout the development process by player testing and iterative design.

7. "According to contract, changes of design which have no effect on quantity of units built, must not be viewed as change orders, but as part of the builders' obligation, provided they stay within parameters of quantity and price."

I think this relates to player testing as well, possibly to open design practices and community feedback. You should consider the feedback of players and adjust designs to meet player needs where they align with the design intent. I don't mean that you should implement players' every whim, but you should understand player feedback, and where its purpose aligns with your design intent, you should prioritize it rather than dismissing it.

All of the preceding guidelines and theories are useful. But how do we turn them into a set of generative codes for applying our patterns to games? As I said at the start of this afterword, this question leaves us at the beginning.

As designers, we must observe when our patterns succeed and fail in games. If we see a pattern working in many games, but then watch it fail when we implement it, we must consider whether the pattern is flawed, and also whether our implementation of it caused the failure. If it was our implementation, then how did we use it, and how can we change our application next time?

When we implement a pattern successfully, we should note the specifics of our implementation. Over time we can compare our many successes and failures and look for higher-order patterns there. We can begin to understand and record the generative codes of game design.

In *The Nature of Order*, Alexander (2004) began to talk about "centers." You saw the term used in Chapter 13 when I described how his fifteen properties of wholeness applied to game design. As he examined how patterns helped to connect "things," Alexander became dissatisfied with calling buildings or roads or groups of people "things." Saying "things" made them sound like isolated entities that existed on their own. If you talked about a house as a 'thing,' you could imagine it floating in a void, you could imagine just how it should be to have the nameless quality. But houses don't exist in voids. If you took your perfect home and placed it in the world, perhaps you could put it in just the right spot to fit and continue to be "whole." But I could almost certainly pick a place for it that would be terrible. The wrong climate or the wrong culture could strip the nameless quality from the house. Putting a beautiful, functional, comfortable farmhouse into an urban setting, for example, could prevent it from being alive.

So he began to use the word "centers." If you call a house a center, then you are implying that it is the center of something else. The farmhouse is the center of a farm. Its shape and placement make the design of the farm stronger. The farm is a center in a neighborhood, one center among many working to make the center that is the town stronger; towns become centers in a region, and so on. Moving inward as well, the house is composed of centers that are its rooms. Doors, windows, tables, and beds are centers supporting the rooms. And all of the centers, up and down in scale, contain as many of the properties of wholeness as possible.

Only through cultivating this broader sense of awareness can we commit acts of design that are not just whole themselves, but also strong centers in larger designs. I have said before that what we design are not games, but the experiences that players have when they play games. Of course, we want those games and those experiences to have the *Lebendigkeit* that Alexander calls "the nameless quality." But players don't just play one game; they don't have only one experience. It's not sufficient that we create games that seem to be alive when we imagine them in a void. We must design games as they will be played in the world, to make them centers that make the larger centers of their players' lives stronger. To help those lives make the center of our world strong enough to hold.

Games Reference

THE FOLLOWING IS A reference for all of the games that I mention in this book. The secondary purpose of this list is both to give attribution to the developers of the games and to make it clear which games I'm referring to in cases where the games are unfamiliar or names are ambiguous. However, the primary purpose is to allow you to learn more about these games and to find and play them if you want to. The games that you've experienced drive the techniques that you explored in this book. This reference is not a declaration of a canon of games that you should consider when looking for patterns; it is merely the list that grew organically from the process of creating the example patterns in this book. To make this list concise and useful, I use the following conventions and format:

- **Game name:** The full game name is listed first in every entry in bold text.

- **Developer:** I always list the original developer for a game. Some games may have had many additional developers for ports and remastered versions.

- **Publisher:** I try to list the original publisher for a game. Multiple publishers may have distributed some games over many years.

- **Released:** I list the earliest available commercial release date for a game. Some games were available in "early access" or beta states before that date or rereleased in enhanced or remastered versions after that date. If I am referring to a specific edition of the game in the text, I list the date for that version here.

- **Platforms:** The purpose of this section is to tell you which platforms you can play the game on now. In some cases, a game is available for a large number of platforms. To make this reference concise, I abbreviate the platform PlayStation to PS. I list the most modern platform for the game, so PS4 for a game available on the PS2, PS3, and PS4. For games that are available across many platforms, I may generalize, for instance, saying mobile rather than listing many current and legacy mobile devices. I indicate the platform that the "Available through" reference is for in bold where I am able to supply a source for the game.

- **Game type:** This refers to the medium the game was created for, either digital or physical.

- **More information:** This is a link to the official website for the game, if available. If the game does not have an official site, it is a link to a wiki article or FAQ on the game.

- **Available through:** This lists the service that the game can be played through if it is available digitally. For physical games, it contains the distribution channel that you can purchase the game through.

- **Description:** Last, I provide a brief description of each game to help you understand how the game fits into the patterns and exercises that cite it.

GAME DESCRIPTIONS

Alice: Madness Returns

Developer: Spicy Horse	**Platforms: PC**, PS3, Xbox 360
Publisher: Electronic Arts	**Game type:** Digital game
Released: 2011	

More information: www.ea.com/games/alice/alice-madness-returns

Available through: www.origin.com/usa/en-us/store/alice/alice-madness-returns

Alice: Madness Returns is a third-person single-player platform horror game with both combat and introspective character-driven mystery elements. This is a sequel to the game *American McGee's Alice* and has enhanced graphics and movement control. The sequel also has a more sophisticated narrative that tells of Alice's emotional struggles.

American McGee's Alice

Developer: Rogue Entertainment	**Platforms: PC**, Mac, PS3, Xbox 360
Publisher: Electronic Arts	**Game type:** Digital game
Released: 2000	

More information: www.ea.com/games/alice/american-mcgees-alice

Available through: Free PC download, www.myabandonware.com/game/american-mcgee-s-alice-452

American McGee's Alice is a third-person single-player platform horror game with both combat and introspective character-driven mystery elements. It utilizes the elements and characters of the classic fantasy novels by Lewis Carroll.

Among the Sleep

Developer: Krillbite	**Platforms:** Desktop (**PC**), PS4, Switch, Xbox One
Publisher: Krillbite, Soedesco	**Game type:** Digital game
Released: 2015	

More information: https://en.wikipedia.org/wiki/Among_the_Sleep

Available through: www.gog.com/game/among_the_sleep

Among the Sleep is a single player first-person horror game. The game is unique in that it is played from the perspective of a toddler, this is reflected in a lower camera perspective and limited player abilities.

Anthem

Developer: BioWare	**Released:** 2019
Publisher: Electronic Arts	**Game type:** Digital game
Platforms: PC, PS4, Xbox One	

More information: www.ea.com/games/anthem

Available through: www.origin.com/usa/en-us/store/anthem/anthem

Anthem is a shared-world RPG action-adventure game in an open-world setting where players are encouraged to band together in PvE situations. Players can play alone, but there are systems in place that make groups advantageous in combat. Multiplayer chat and NPC dialogue options enable communication.

Apocalypse World

Developer: D. Vincent Baker, Meguey Baker	**Released:** 2010
	Game type: Pen-and-paper RPG
Publisher: Lumpley Games	

More information: www.kickstarter.com/projects/226674021/apocalypse-world-2nd-edition

Available through: http://apocalypse-world.com/

Apocalypse World is a dice RPG where the players' initial character creation and subsequent play create the post-apocalyptic world. The play focuses on relationship building and survival skills. Each game has the possibility of a radically different world based on the player's choices but is still grounded in the archetype structure of the character classes and their abilities.

Assassin's Creed

Developer: Ubisoft/Gameloft/Griptonite/ Blue Byte	**Platforms:** PC, PS3, Xbox 360
	Released: 2007
Publisher: Ubisoft	**Game type:** Digital game

More information: www.ubisoft.com/en-us/game/assassins-creed/

Available through: https://store.steampowered.com/app/15100/Assassins_Creed_Dir ectors_Cut_Edition/

Assassin's Creed (the first in a series and franchise) is an open-world stealth action-adventure game with an emphasis on environmental obstacles/advantages. Over-the-shoulder third-person perspective allows the player to explore historically accurate landscapes while playing a fictional plotline.

Assassin's Creed IV: Black Flag

Developer: Ubisoft	**Released:** 2013
Publisher: Ubisoft	**Game type:** Digital game
Platforms: PS4, Xbox 360, Wii U, PC, Xbox One, Nintendo Switch (2019)	

More information: www.ubisoft.com/en-us/game/assassins-creed-iv-black-flag/

Available through: https://store.steampowered.com/app/242050/Assassins_Creed_IV_ Black_Flag/

Assassin's Creed IV: Black Flag is a third-person open-world action-adventure. In this fourth instalment of the *Assassin's Creed* series, travel and battle via ships is available through the pirate-themed story, based in the West Indies. Hunting of land and sea animals is also available, as is limited (on land) multiplayer options. Single and multiplayer.

Asteroids

Developer: Atari	**Released:** 1979
Publisher: Atari	**Game type:** Digital game
Platforms: Arcade, Atari 2600, **iOS**	

More information: https://en.wikipedia.org/wiki/Asteroids_(video_game)

Available through: https://apps.apple.com/us/app/atari-asteroids-arcade-skills/id144 9639275

Asteroids is an early arcade game created by Lyle Rains, Ed Logg, and Dominic Walsh for Atari Inc. The game was inspired by Spacewar! and Space Invaders. It is one of the first games that recorded an instance of a player exploit and which used playtesting to inform development. The game used vector graphics and had a joystick control.

Bastion

Developer: Supergiant Games	**Released:** 2011
Publisher: Warner Brothers/ Interactive Entertainment	**Game type:** Digital game
Platforms: PC, Mac, iOS, Nintendo Switch, PS4, PS Vita, Xbox One	

More information: www.supergiantgames.com/games/bastion/

Available through: https://store.steampowered.com/app/107100/Bastion/

Bastion is an action-adventure RPG in an isometric 2D point and click third-person. It has a vibrant environment, dynamic voice-acted plot and scene specific narration. Between levels there are extra challenge sections. Only single-player mode is available.

Battle Chess

Developer: Interplay Productions/ Silicon & Synapse	**Platform: PC**, Mac, Atari
	Released: 1988
Publisher: Interplay Productions	**Game type:** Digital game

More information: https://en.wikipedia.org/wiki/Battle_Chess

Available through: https://store.steampowered.com/app/622830/Battle_Chess/

Battle Chess is an animated battle version of traditional chess. It follows the same rules as a chess game with animated creatures fighting out the moves. There is voice narration in some versions. There are both single-player and PvP options.

Beat Saber

Developer: Beat Games	**Released:** 2018
Publisher: Beat Games	**Game type:** Digital VR game
Platforms: PC (HTC Vive, Oculus Rift, Oculus Quest), PS4 VR	

More information: https://beatsaber.com/

Available through: https://store.steampowered.com/app/620980/Beat_Saber/

Beat Saber is a VR rhythm and music game that emphasizes physical coordination with rhythmic visual and musical cues. It has edit mode that enables players to adjust the speed of a song and also a custom song mode. It has both single-player mode and party mode, which ranks players.

Bejeweled

Developer: PopCap Games	Platforms: PC, Mac, Mobile (iOS), Web
Publisher: PopCap Games	Game type: Digital game
Released: 2001	

More information: https://en.wikipedia.org/wiki/Bejeweled

Available through: https://apps.apple.com/us/app/bejeweled-classic/id479536744

Bejeweled is a match-three tile game where speed and puzzle-solving is paramount. *Bejeweled* has a normal mode and time challenge. Only single-player mode is available. This is the game that popularized the "match-three" mechanic.

The Binding of Isaac

Developer: Edmund McMillen	Released: 2011
Publisher: Florian Himsl, Edmund McMillen	Game type: Digital game
Platforms: Desktop (PC)	

More information: https://bindingofisaac.com/

Available through: https://store.steampowered.com/app/113200/The_Binding_of_Isaac/

The Binding of Isaac is a dungeon crawl in a top-down view. There are two-dimensional sprites in a procedurally drawn environment. The player plays a primary character or one of eleven unlockable characters to defeat foes and survive. The play is meant to express the developer's struggle with religion within his family. Only single-player mode is available.

BioShock

Developer: 2K Games	Released: 2007
Publisher: 2K Games	Game type: Digital game
Platforms: PC, Mac, iOS*, PS4, Xbox One	

More information: https://2k.com/en-US/game/bioshock/

Available through: https://store.steampowered.com/app/7670/BioShock/

BioShock is a first-person shooter game with elements of an RPG. The stealth/survivor horror motifs enable players to make morality-based choices in an artistic and emotionally effective manner.

---

* No longer available through the iOS App Store.

Black & White

Developer: Lionhead Studios	**Released:** 2001
Publisher: Electronic Arts, Feral Interactive	**Game type:** Digital Game
Platforms: PC, Mac	

More information: https://en.wikipedia.org/wiki/Black_%26_White_(video_game)

Available through: Not currently available.

Black & White is a game in the 'God Game' genera that used a distant third person perspective and world effecting player abilities. This game was innovative in its use of an AI controlled companion that adapted to player behavior creating a sense of moral consequence.

Borderlands 3

Developer: Gearbox Software	**Released:** 2020
Publisher: 2k	**Game type:** Digital Game
Platforms: PC, PS4, Xbox One	

More information: https://en.wikipedia.org/wiki/Borderlands_3

Available through: https://store.steampowered.com/app/397540/Borderlands_3/

Borderlands 3 is the fourth game in this FPS franchise. The series stands out for its use of procedural loot generation to create a near infinite number of weapons. It is one of the games that define the 'looter shooter' genre. Strong cooperative elements and a crass sense of humor are also hallmarks of this game.

Braid

Developer: Number None	**Released:** 2008
Publisher: Microsoft Game Studios, Number None	**Game type:** Digital game
Platforms: PC, Mac, Linux, PS3, Xbox 360	

More information: http://braid-game.com/

Available through: https://store.steampowered.com/app/26800/Braid/

Braid is a side-scrolling platform puzzle game. It adds in elements of time manipulation and mutable sequentially related levels. This game may be considered a critique of the "do-over" in gaming experiences, but more closely contemplates morality and philosophy in games. Music and artwork are meticulously intertwined.

Brothers, a Tale of Two Sons

Developer: Starbreeze Studios   **Released:** 2013

Publisher: 505 Games   **Game type:** Digital games

Platforms: PC, Android, iOS, PS4, Windows Phone, Xbox One, Switch

More information: https://en.wikipedia.org/wiki/Brothers:_A_Tale_of_Two_Sons

Available through: https://store.playstation.com/en-us/product/UP4040-CUSA02297_00-BROTHERSLICENSE4

Brothers, a Tale of Two Sons is a single player third person action game. It is unique in that the player controls two characters at the same time, one with each joystick on their controller.

Call of Duty

Developer: Infinity Ward, Treyarch, et al.   **Released:** 2003

Publisher: Activision   **Game type:** Digital game

Platforms: PC, PS3, Xbox 360

More information: https://en.wikipedia.org/wiki/Call_of_Duty_(video_game)

Available through: https://store.steampowered.com/app/2620/Call_of_Duty/

Call of Duty (and its subsequent sequels, later releases and franchise) is a realistic first-person shooter. Gameplay consists of wartime infantry and combined arms strategy. There are single-player and massive multiplayer options.

Call of Duty: Advanced Warfare

Developer: Sledgehammer Games   **Released:** 2014

Publisher: Activision   **Game type:** Digital game

Platforms: PC, PS4, Xbox One

More information: https://en.wikipedia.org/wiki/Call_of_Duty:_Advanced_Warfare

Available through: https://store.steampowered.com/app/209650/Call_of_Duty_Advanced_Warfare__Gold_Edition/

In the *Call of Duty* family the 11th major game installment from the franchise, *Call of Duty: Advanced Warfare*, introduced advanced movement options. This game was under the umbrella of the *Modern Warfare* lineage of *Call of Duty*. This game includes a single-player mode, where subsequent games from the franchise do not.

Call of Duty: Modern Warfare 2 (also known as *Call of Duty 6* prior to its release)

Developer: Infinity Ward	**Released:** 2009
Publisher: Activision	**Game type:** Digital game
Platforms: PC, Mac, PS3, Xbox 360, Nintendo DS	

More information:https://en.wikipedia.org/wiki/Call_of_Duty:_Modern_Warfare_2

Available through: https://store.steampowered.com/app/10180/Call_of_Duty_Modern_Warfare_2/

This, the sixth installment of the *Call of Duty* family, was the direct sequel to *Call of Duty 4: Modern Warfare* and continues the same storyline. It contains some controversial levels of play, as well as continuing the tradition of improved movement and massive multiplayer options.

Canabalt

Developer: Adam Saltsman	**Platforms:** PC, Web, Mobile
Publisher: Semi-Secret Software, RGCD, Beatshapers, Kittehface Software	**Released:** 2009
	Game type: Digital game

More information: http://canabalt.com/

Available through: https://store.steampowered.com/app/358960/Canabalt/

Canabalt is credited as the first endless-runner platform game. The player has no options for control other than jump. The playtime continues until the player dies. Time and distance calculate "winning" and online leaderboards encourage competition for the highest score.

Candy Crush (browser version)

Developer: King	**Released:** 2011
Publisher: King	**Game type:** Digital game
Platforms: Browser	

More information: http://www.royalgames.com/games/puzzle-games/candy-crush/

Available through: http://www.royalgames.com/games/puzzle-games/candy-crush/

Candy Crush is a puzzle match-three game. Play consists of swapping candies to create groups of three or more of a kind and attempting to clear the gamespace to make room for new candies. Boost candies are available. There are many versions. This game's sequel *Candy Crush Saga* has been called the first and most successful "freemium" game. King has released three other spin-offs as well. Only single-player mode is available.

Carcassonne (board game)

Developer: Klaus-Jürgen Wrede

Publisher: MINDOK s.r.o., Devir, Hans im Glück, and more

Platforms: Tabletop board game

Released: 2000

Game type: Board game

More information: https://boardgamegeek.com/boardgame/822/carcassonne

Available through: Retail

Carcassonne and its expansions are tile-placing turn-based games for 2–5 players. The game consists of the creation of a contiguous landscape via placing tiles on the table. Players then choose to utilize the tile they place or not, and then play proceeds to the next player.

Carcassonne (digital game)

Developer: Sierra Online Seattle,

Publisher: Vivendi Games

Platforms: Xbox, Nintendo Switch, Mobile (iOS), Desktop

Released: 2007

Game type: Digital game

More information: https://carcassonneapp.com/

Available through: https://apps.apple.com/us/app/carcassonne/id375295479

Carcassonne and its expansions were adapted to digital games that mimic the same turn-based play of the board games. You may play as a single-player against AI or choose PvP mode online. There are many adaptations and expansions available on multiple platforms.

Catan Universe

Developer: Exozet Game

Publisher: Azmodee, United Soft Media

Platforms: PC, Mac, Android, iOS, Nintendo Switch

Released: 2017

Game type: Digital game

More information: https://catanuniverse.com/en/

Available through: https://store.steampowered.com/app/544730/Catan_Universe/

Catan Universe is an online game mimicking the tabletop board and card game series Catan. It includes the original board game, the expansions, and the card game as well. Up to three players can participate in a real-time game experience. The online game offers AI and single-player options. An online-only expansion is available for in-game purchase.

Catherine

Developer: Atlus	**Released:** 2011
Publisher: Atlus	**Game type:** Digital game
Platforms: PS4, Switch, PS Vita / PS3, Xbox 360, **PC**	

More information: www.catherinethegame.com/fullbody/

Available through: https://store.steampowered.com/agecheck/app/893180/

Catherine is a narratively driven platformer/puzzle game with gameplay derived from the classic arcade game *Q*bert*. It is notable for its "mature" themes that generated praise from some and were seen as sexist and misogynist by others. A new edition of the game subtitled *Full Body*, with more content/storylines, was released on modern consoles in 2019/2020.

Chess

Developer: N/A	**Game type:** Board game
Released: 15th century	

More information: www.chess.com/

Available through: Retail

Chess is an ancient two-player strategy board game. Chess is played on a checkered board with 64 squares. Each player has 16 pieces; each piece has a type of movement it can do, sometimes more than one. Play is turn-based and can be timed.

Clash Royale

Developer: Supercell	**Released:** 2016
Publisher: Supercell	**Game type:** Digital game
Platforms: iOS, Android	

More information: https://supercell.com/en/games/clashroyale/

Available through: https://apps.apple.com/app/id1053012308

Clash Royale is a real-time multiplayer strategy game. It includes elements of collectible card games, multiplayer arena style combat, and tower defense-style play. The game has a top-down view of the space, and play is conducted with "cards" that resemble physical playing cards. Players choose among their collection and compose a "deck" prior to play to use in combat.

Clicker Heroes

Developer: Playsaurus	**Released:** 2014
Publisher: Playsaurus	**Game type:** Digital game
Platforms: Browser, **PC**, Mac, Mobile, PS4, Xbox One	

More information: www.clickerheroes.com/

Available through: https://store.steampowered.com/app/363970/Clicker_Heroes/

Clicker Heroes is a simplistic idle game, in isometric view. In gameplay players only have the choice to click on an enemy. Only single-player mode is available.

Clue/Cluedo: The Classic Mystery Game

Developer: Anthony E. Pratt	**Platforms:** Board game
Publisher: Hasbro, Waddingtons, Parker Brothers, Winning Moves	Released:1949
	Game type: Board game

More information: https://boardgamegeek.com/boardgame/1294/clue

Available through: Retail

Clue is a 3–5 player mystery board game. This game is a tabletop adaptation of the traditional country house mystery parlor games played throughout the 20th century. Players choose a character and proceed to ask questions and move around the board to solve the murder mystery. The board consists of a layout of the mansion in which the murder took place. The winner is the player who discovers all the elements of the murder: who did it, with what weapon, and where it was done.

Crackdown

Developer: Realtime Worlds	**Released:** 2007
Publisher: Xbox Game Studios	**Game type:** Digital game
Platforms: Xbox 360	

More information: https://en.wikipedia.org/wiki/Crackdown_(video_game)

Available through: https://marketplace.xbox.com/en-us/Product/Crackdown/66acd000-77fe-1000-9115-d8024d5307dc

Crackdown is a third-person action-adventure shooter. The avatars are superpowered "Agents" giving the player far more enhanced movement and combat options than in previous open-world shooters. The sandbox-style gameplay allows for nonlinear gameplay and off-story adventures. Single-player and multiplayer options are available. Later sequels to Crackdown allowed for a wider range of intractable environments in a multiplayer space than had been available in a game before.

Crash Bandicoot

Developer: Naughty Dog

Publisher: Sony Computer Entertainment

Platforms: PS

Released: 1996

Game type: Digital game

More information: https://en.wikipedia.org/wiki/Crash_Bandicoot_(video_game)

Available through: N/A

Crash Bandicoot is a third-person platformer. It is the first of its series. Play is conducted by traversing levels in sequence, and avoiding or using jump or spinning attacks to combat enemies. This game was Naughty Dog's first 3D game, and special effort on the environment's natural look and organic shape was emphasized. Only single-player mode is available.

Dark Souls

Developer: FromSoftware

Publisher: Namco Bandai Games JP: FromSoftware

Platforms: PC, PS4, Xbox One, Nintendo Switch

Released: 2011

Game type: Digital game

More information: https://en.bandainamcoent.eu/dark-souls

Available through: https://store.steampowered.com/app/211420/DARK_SOULS_Prepare_To_Die_Edition/

Dark Souls is an action-adventure RPG with a strong emphasis on exploration in an openworld setting. Although communication is limited, players may choose cooperative, PvP, or single-player modes.

Dead Space

Developer: EA Redwood Shores

Publisher: Electronic Arts

Platforms: PS3, Xbox 360, **PC**

Released: 2008

Game type: Digital game

More information: www.ea.com/games/dead-space/dead-space

Available through: https://store.steampowered.com/app/17470/Dead_Space/

Dead Space is a survival/horror over-the-shoulder third-person game. Its atmospheric and close-quarters world mixed with graphic gore garnered it much attention. *Dead Space* utilized "strategic dismemberment" and monster regeneration to create a nontraditional shooter.

Dear Esther

Developer: The Chinese Room	**Platforms:** PC, Mac, PS4, Xbox One
Publisher: The Chinese Room, Curve Digital	**Released:** 2012
	Game type: Digital game

More information: http://www.thechineseroom.co.uk/games/dear-esther

Available through: https://store.steampowered.com/app/203810/Dear_Esther/

Dear Esther is an adventure/exploration game in the first-person. The atmospheric art game offers different narratives for each playthrough and has an ultimately open-ended plot resolution. The environment is highly detailed and there are no puzzle-solving events or interactions with NPCs, leaving the narrative and the environment to create a lasting impression on the player.

Death Stranding

Developer: Kojima Productions	**Released:** 2019
Publisher: Sony Interactive, 505 Games	**Game type:** Digital game
Platforms: PS4, PC	

More information: https://en.wikipedia.org/wiki/Death_Stranding

Available through: https://www.epicgames.com/store/en-US/product/death-stranding/home

Death Stranding is a third person action game by the developer Hideo Kojima. The gameplay is unusual in its focus on simulation realistic traversal of the game world.

Devil May Cry

Developer: Capcom, Ninja Theory	**Released:** 2001
Publisher: Capcom	**Game type:** Digital game
Platforms: Mobile, PC, Console	

More information: https://en.wikipedia.org/wiki/Devil_May_Cry_(video_game)

Available through: https://store.steampowered.com/app/631510/Devil_May_Cry_HD_Collection/

Devil May Cry is a hack-and-slash third-person action game. The gameplay is combat heavy, focusing on stylized string attacks and ranking players by their variety and use of those styles. There is only a single-player mode.

Diablo

Developer: Blizzard	**Released:** 1997
Publisher: Electronic Arts	**Game type:** Digital game
Platforms: PC, Mac, PS	

More information: https://en.wikipedia.org/wiki/Diablo_(video_game)

Available through: www.gog.com/game/diablo

Diablo is a hack-and-slash RPG action game in an isometric view. It includes random procedurally generated tasks and dungeon levels. Multiplayer and single-player modes are available. In the multiplayer mode players can choose between PvP and cooperative.

Don't Starve

Developer: Klei Entertainment	**Released:** 2013
Publisher: 505 Games	**Game type:** Digital game
Platforms: Mobile, Desktop (**PC**), Console	

More information: www.klei.com/games/dont-starve

Available through: https://store.steampowered.com/app/219740/Dont_Starve/

Don't Starve is an action-adventure survival game in an isometric view. Overall the game is played in a sandbox open-world, but it contains a five-level internal campaign adventure mode. Failure in the campaign returns the player to the sandbox.

Dominion

Developer: Donald X. Vaccarino	**Released:** 2008
Publisher: Rio Grande Games	**Game type:** Card game

More information: http://riograndegames.com/games.html?id=278

Available through: Retail

Dominion is a competitive turn-based strategy card game. Players each have the same deck of cards at their disposal and there is a mutual pool of cards as well. Winners have the highest score when the cards are depleted. There are 2–6 players.

Donkey Kong

Developer: Nintendo R&D1, Nintendo R&D2 (NES)	**Released:** 1981
	Game type: Arcade/ Digital game
Publisher: Nintendo	
Platforms: Arcade, Console (**Nintendo Switch**), PC, Mobile	

More information: https://en.wikipedia.org/wiki/Donkey_Kong_(video_game)

Available through: www.nintendo.com/games/detail/arcade-archives-donkey-kong-sw itch/

Donkey Kong was one of the original arcade games featuring platform-style gameplay. Innovations were introduced here with the use of characterizing graphics and cutscenes between levels to mold the storyline. Digital games allowed for multiplayer modes.

Doom

Developer: id Software	**Platforms:** Desktop (PC), Mobile, Console
Publisher: GT Interactive Software, Activision, Bethesda Softworks, Sega, Atari Corporation, SNES (North America) Williams Entertainment, Ocean Software, Nintendo	**Released:** 1993
	Game type: Digital game

More information: https://en.wikipedia.org/wiki/Doom_(1993_video_game)

Available through: https://store.steampowered.com/app/2280/Ultimate_Doom/

Doom is a first-person action shooter. Continuing the new 3D action trend it started with Wolfenstein, id Software developed this dungeon-style single player game. Minimal plot and propulsive gameplay come together to create a heavy-action playstyle that has defined the genre.

Doom 2016 (called Doom 4 prior to release)

Developer: id Software	**Released:** 2016
Publisher: Bethesda Softworks	**Game type:** Digital game
Platforms: PC, PS4, Xbox One, Nintendo Switch, Stadia	

More information: https://slayersclub.bethesda.net/en

Available through: https://store.steampowered.com/app/379720/DOOM/

Doom 2016 is a first-person shooter. While not a full reboot of the original game, it has the same core elements of play, with the same combat and movement-focused nonlinear gameplay.

Dragon Age: Inquisition

Developer: BioWare	**Released:** 2014
Publisher: Electronic Arts	**Game type:** Digital game
Platforms: PC, PlayStation 3, Xbox 360	

More information: https://en.wikipedia.org/wiki/Dragon_Age:_Inquisition

Available through: https://www.origin.com/usa/en-us/store/dragon-age/dragon-age-inquisition

Dragon Age: Inquisition is the third installment in this franchise. It is a single player third person action RPG in which the player manages a party of characters. The game features a detailed narrative and complex character interactions,

Draugen

Developer: Red Thread Games	**Released:** 2019
Publisher: Red Thread Games	**Game type:** Digital game
Platforms: PC, PS4, Xbox One	

More information: www.redthreadgames.com/draugen

Available through: https://store.steampowered.com/app/770390/Draugen/

Draugen is a first-person suspense mystery. It is designed mostly as a walking simulator that allows the player to explore the environment and solve the mystery. A highly atmospheric dynamic environment changes with the status of the character and the story points.

Dreamfall

Developer: FunCom	**Released:** 2006
Publisher: Aspyr, Empire Interactive	**Game type:** Digital game
Platforms: PC, Xbox	

More information: https://en.wikipedia.org/wiki/Dreamfall:_The_Longest_Journey

Available through: https://store.steampowered.com/app/6300/Dreamfall_The_Longest_Journey/

Dreamfall is a third person action adventure game that continues the story of the developers' previous game *The Longest Journey*. The game is known for a compelling narrative and poor combat and stealth mechanics.

Dungeons & Dragons (D&D)

Developer: Gary Gygax, Dave Arneson	**Released:** 2015
Publisher: TSR, Wizards of the Coast	**Game type:** Board game
Platforms: Originally tabletop, multiple adaptations across multiple platforms	

More information: https://dnd.wizards.com/

Available through: Retail

D&D is a fantasy tabletop RPG. It is a dungeon exploration and dice combat storytelling game for multiple players. The forefather of the tabletop RPG and still the bestseller, the D&D franchise has heavily influenced tabletop and digital games.

Dust: An Elysian Tail

Developer: Humble Hearts	**Released:** 2013
Publisher: Microsoft Games, Limited Run Games	**Game type:** Digital game
Platforms: Xbox 360, Desktop (**PC**), PS4, iOS, Nintendo Switch	

More information: https://en.wikipedia.org/wiki/Dust:_An_Elysian_Tail
Available through: https://store.steampowered.com/app/236090/Dust_An_Elysian_Tail/

Dust is an action side-scrolling RPG. Platform-adventure mechanics are Metroidvania in style (based on the mechanics of *Metroid* and *Castlevania*) containing permanent character enhancements, an open-world style of play, and the need for key items to open new spaces.

Echochrome

Developer: Game Yarouze, SCE Japan Studio	**Platforms:** PS3, PSP
	Released: 2008
Publisher: Sony Computer Entertainment	**Game type:** Digital game

More information: https://en.wikipedia.org/wiki/Echochrome
Available through: www.PS.com/en-us/games/echochrome-ps3/

Echochrome is a perspective puzzle game. Gameplay consists of manipulation of the environment through rotation and view angle rather than manipulating the character. *Echochrome* in North America is only available in single-player mode. Japan added "pair" and "others."

The Elder Scrolls III: Morrowind

Developer: Bethesda Game Studios	**Released:** 2002
Publisher: Bethesda Softworks	**Game type:** Digital game
Platforms: PC, Xbox	

More information: https://elderscrolls.bethesda.net/en/morrowind
Available through: https://store.steampowered.com/app/22320/The_Elder_Scrolls_III_Morrowind_Game_of_the_Year_Edition/

Morrowind is the third game in this series by the developer, unlike the previous two games which used procedural generation to create a huge world the open world of Morrowind was constructed entirely by hand. The setting was unique in its departure from western tropes.

The Elder Scrolls V: Oblivion

Developer: Bethesda Game Studios	**Released:** 2006
Publisher: Bethesda Softworks, 2K Games	**Game type:** Digital game
Platforms: PC, PS4, Xbox 360	

More information: https://elderscrolls.bethesda.net/en/oblivion

Available through: https://store.steampowered.com/app/22330/The_Elder_Scrolls_IV_Oblivion_Game_of_the_Year_Edition/

Elder Scrolls IV: Oblivion is the fourth installment in the *Elder Scrolls* universe. It is an action RPG in first-person. Oblivion continued the style of nonlinear narrative with a fully open world and enhanced the graphics and included fully voice-acted NPCs for this game. Only single-player mode is available.

The Elder Scrolls V: Skyrim

Developer: Bethesda Game Studios	**Released:** 2011
Publisher: Bethesda Softworks	**Game type:** Digital game
Platforms: PC, Console	

More information: https://elderscrolls.bethesda.net/en/skyrim

Available through: https://store.steampowered.com/app/489830/The_Elder_Scrolls_V_Skyrim_Special_Edition/

Elder Scrolls V: Skyrim is the fifth installment in the *Elder Scrolls* universe. It is an action RPG in either first- or third-person, set in an open world. Sandbox-style nonlinear play is exhaustive. Thousands of quests and NPC-driven mini plots are available, as well as the main storyline quests. The primary character is fully customizable and upgrades in all skills and equipment make for a very wide variety of play experiences. Only single-player mode is available.

Elder Sign

Developer: Richard Launius, Kevin Wilson	**Released:** 2011
	Game type: Board game
Publisher: Fantasy Flight Games	

More information: https://boardgamegeek.com/boardgame/100423/elder-sign
Available through: Retail

Elder Sign is a card and dice tabletop game based on the Cthulhu Mythos derived from H.P. Lovecraft's work. It is a PvE cooperative game with two- to eight-player rounds.

Elder Sign: Omens

Developer: Richard Launius, Kevin Wilson	**Platforms:** iOS, PC
	Released: 2011
Publisher: Fantasy Flight Games	**Game type:** Digital game

More information: www.fantasyflightgames.com/en/products/elder-sign-omens/
Available through: https://store.steampowered.com/app/257670/Elder_Sign_Omens/

Elder Sign: Omens is a single player adaption of the board game. Its heavy atmospheric visuals and theme deepen the timed, turn-based dice-and-card mechanics.

Emily is Away

Developer: Kyle Seeley	**Released:** 2015
Publisher: Kyle Seeley	**Game type:** Digital game
Platforms: Desktop (PC)	

More information: https://en.wikipedia.org/wiki/Emily_Is_Away
Available through: https://store.steampowered.com/app/417860/Emily_is_Away/

Emily is Away is a single player narrative adventure game presented as a mostly text interface designed to resemble early social media platforms. Players choose different conversational options that affect the course of the game. However the possible outcomes are limited and reflect the designers' desired message.

Eve Online

Developer: CCP Games,	**Released:** 2003
Publisher: Simon & Schuster, Atari (2008)	**Game type:** Digital game
Platforms: PC, Mac	

More information: www.eveonline.com/
Available through: https://store.steampowered.com/app/8500/EVE_Online/

Eve Online is a MMORPG in a sci-fi space universe in either first person or third person. It has many options for gameplay types and environments, and has PvP, PvE, and cooperative opportunities.

Fable II

Developer: Lionhead Studios	**Released:** 2008
Publisher: Microsoft Game Studios	**Game Type:** Digital game
Platforms: Xbox 360	

More Information: https://en.wikipedia.org/wiki/Fable_II

Available Through: https://www.microsoft.com/en-us/p/fable-ii/c2wkjj9f5936

Fable II is a single player third person action game. Character appearance and NPC interactions change to reflect the moral implications of the players playstyle. In the extremes the character may grow horns or develop an angelic appearance.

Fall of the Last City

Developer: Chris Barney	**Released:** 2017
Publisher: Not published	**Game type:** Tabletop

More information: http://www.fallofthelastcity.com/

Available through: Not available

Fall of the Last City is a tabletop strategy game. Play happens simultaneously each round. The game is notable for its heavy use of theming and use of player choice to create a feeling of unpredictability with a rule set that contains no randomness.

Fallout 3

Developer: Bethesda Game Studios	**Released:** 2008
Publisher: Bethesda Softworks	**Game type:** Digital game
Platforms: PC, PS3, Xbox 360	

More information: https://fallout.bethesda.net/en/games/fallout-3

Available through: https://store.steampowered.com/app/22300/Fallout_3/

Fallout 3 is a first-person or over-the-shoulder third-person action RPG. The third in the post-apocalyptic *Fallout* series, this game offers 3D graphics and real-time combat. It is single-player style, with five downloadable add-ons.

Fez

Developer: Polytron Corporation	**Released:** 2013
Publisher: Trapdoor	**Game type:** Digital game
Platforms: Desktop (**PC**), PS4, PS Vita, iOS	

More information: http://fezgame.com/

Available through: https://store.steampowered.com/app/224760/FEZ/

Fez is a single-player puzzle platform game. Perspective and alternating between 2D view and 3D view is essential to solving the puzzles and progressing the character.

Final Fantasy VIII

Developer: Square	**Released:** 1999
Publisher: Square	**Game type:** Digital game
Platforms: PC, Console	

More information: https://ffviiipc.square-enix-games.com/en

Available through: https://store.steampowered.com/app/39150/FINAL_FANTASY_VIII/

Final Fantasy VIII is the eighth installment in the *Final Fantasy* series. The RPG has a third-person view of the party of characters and the 3D landscape is navigable through three maps choices. This game includes motion capture technology and realistically proportioned characters among other changes to make the game more realistic looking. Only single-player mode is available.

Final Fantasy XIII

Developer: Square Enix 1st Production Department	**Released:** 2014
	Game type: Digital game
Publisher: Square Enix	
Platforms: PS3, Xbox 360, **PC**, Mobile	

More information: https://square-enix-games.com/en_GB/games/final-fantasy-xiii/

Available through: https://store.steampowered.com/app/292120/FINAL_FANTASY_XIII/

Final Fantasy XIII is a third-person, single-player action RPG. With a 360° view, the proportional environment is new to this 13th installment of the series. When combat is initiated a new screen appears with the combat progress. Players may choose to use the automated combat system or choose their own moves, but only one character is operable by the player in a party of characters.

The Flame and the Flood

Developer: The Molasses Flood	**Game type:** Digital game
Publisher: Curve Digital	
Platforms: PC, Mac, Nintendo Switch	
Released: 2016	

More information: http://www.themolassesflood.com/

Available through: https://store.steampowered.com/app/318600/The_Flame_in_the_Flood/

This third-person "roguelike: survival game is heavily themed with a "post societal: setting reflected in its art and haunting alt-country soundtrack. The procedurally generated gameplay is very difficult and reflects the theme.

Flashback: Remastered Edition (Mobile)

Developer: Delphine Software International, Tiertex, Chui	**Released:** 2019
Publisher: U.S. Gold, JoshProd, Microïds	**Game type:** Digital game
Platforms: PC, PS4, Mobile, Nintendo Switch	

More information:

Available through: https://store.steampowered.com/app/961620/Flashback/

Flashback: Remastered Edition is the same as the classic puzzle-platformer sci-fi game of the same name, with updated graphics. It intermingles elements of previous releases such as cutscenes that were available with a macOS release and the original music score from the first Amiga release. The character is challenged with levels of platforming nonscrolling environments that scale in difficulty.

Fortnight

Developer: Epic Games	**Platforms:** Desktop (**PC**), Console, Mobile
Publisher: Epic Games, Warner Bros. Interactive Entertainment	**Released:** 2017
	Game type: Digital game

More information: www.epicgames.com/fortnite/en-US/home

Available through: www.epicgames.com/store/en-US/product/fortnite/home

Fortnight has three modes all using the same gameplay and engine in third-person. Available in sandbox open-world creation mode, PvP mode, and a team cooperative survival/shooter mode. Multiplayer.

Gears of War

Developer: Epic Games, People Can Fly, The Coalition, Mediatonic, Splash Damage	**Released:** 2006
	Game type: Digital game
Publisher: Xbox Game Studios	
Platforms: Mobile, **PC**, Xbox One	

More information: https://en.wikipedia.org/wiki/Gears_of_War_(video_game)

Available through: https://gearsofwar.com/games/gears-of-war

Gears of War is a third-person action shooter game. Emphasis on cover and avoidance of damage by strategic positioning has been a hallmark of this game and subsequent franchise. Single-player and multiplayer modes are available.

Gloomhaven

Developer: Isaac Childres	**Released:** 2017
Publisher: Cephalofair Games	**Game type:** Board game

More information: http://www.cephalofair.com/gloomhaven

Available through: https://steamcommunity.com/sharedfiles/filedetails/?id=1340508741*

Gloomhaven is a strategy tile and card game for 1–4 players in a dungeon-crawl style. The branching narrative storyline is very large for a board game. This is a "legacy"-style board game where the game is changed in a permanent way every time it is played, creating an evolving campaign world.

God of War

Developer: SIE Santa Monica Studio	**Platforms:** PS3, PS Vita
Publisher: Sony Computer Entertainment, Capcom	**Released:** 2005
	Game type: Digital game

More information: https://en.wikipedia.org/wiki/God_of_War_(2005_video_game)

Available through: https://store.playstation.com/en-us/product/UP9000-NPUA80490_00-GODOFWARHDUS0000

God of War, the first game of the franchise, is a third-person action-adventure. It is single-player and offers puzzle and platforming gameplay as well as combat. The introduction of dramatic action setpieces in which control of the character is abstracted to arbitrary sequences of prompted button presses was innovative at the time and is commonly referred to as 'Quick Time Events'.

God of War

Developer: SCE Santa Monica Studio	**Released:** 2018
Publisher: Sony Computer Entertainment	**Game type:** Digital game
Platforms: PS4	

---

* This is a board game, but a digital simulation is available through the Tabletop Simulator. Additionally there is a digital adaptation that is in early access, but that should be considered a distinct game. The physical game is available through retail channels.

More information: https://en.wikipedia.org/wiki/God_of_War_(2018_video_game)

Available through: http://store.playstation.com/en-us/product/UP9000-CUSA07408_00-00000000GODOFWAR

This edition of *God of War* is a reimagining of the franchise set later in the protagonist's life. The gameplay of this version is similar to the previous games but its tone is much more mature and thoughtful. The introduction of the character's son requires the player to consider the NPC in their strategy.

Gone Home

Developer: The Fullbright Company, BlitWorks (Switch)	**Platforms:** Desktop (**PC**), Console, iOS
	Released: 2013
Publisher: The Fullbright Company, Majesco Entertainment, Annapurna Interactive	**Game type:** Digital game

More information: https://gonehome.game/

Available through: https://store.steampowered.com/app/232430/Gone_Home/

Gone Home is a highly interactive first-person exploration game. It has narration-driven nonlinear gameplay in a mode that is nonstandard and often called a walking simulator.

Gradius

Developer: Konami	**Released:** 1986
Publisher: Konami	**Game type:** Digital game
Platforms: Arcade, PC, Console (**PS4**)	

More information: https://en.wikipedia.org/wiki/Gradius_(video_game)

Available through: https://store.PS.com/en-us/product/UP0571-CUSA02307_00-HAMPRDC000000001?emcid=se-pi-239770

Gradius is a side-scrolling shooter game. It is the first in its series, originally released for arcade and other versions were made later for other platforms. The player controls a single spaceship, Vic the Viper, and must fight squads of invading ships, often containing a boss ship with a "core" that must be destroyed. 1–4 players depending on platform.

Grand Theft Auto IV

Developer: Rockstar North, Rockstar Toronto	**Platforms:** PC, PS3, Xbox One
	Released: 2008
Publisher: Rockstar Games	**Game type:** Digital game

More information: www.rockstargames.com/gta/

Available through: https://store.steampowered.com/app/12210/Grand_Theft_Auto_IV_The_Complete_Edition/

Grand Theft Auto is an action-adventure third-person game in an open-world setting. There are a variety of play options including driving, racing, shooting, melee, stealth, and some role-playing.

Gravity Rush

Developer: Team Gravity	**Released:** 2012
Publisher: Sony Computer Entertainment	**Game type:** Digital game
Platforms: PS Vita, **PS4**	

More information: https://en.wikipedia.org/wiki/Gravity_Rush

Available through: www.PS.com/en-us/games/gravity-rush-remastered-ps4/

Gravity Rush is a third-person open-world action-adventure where the player manipulates gravity via the character's special powers to traverse the world, interact with objects, and avoid enemies. There is only a single-player mode. Moving the screen around as you shift gravity was a major gameplay feature in the mobile version.

Gris

Developer: Nomada Studio	**Released:** 2018
Publisher: Devolver Digital	**Game type:** Digital game
Platforms: Mac, **PC**, Nintendo Switch, PS4, Mobile	

More information: https://devolverdigital.com/games/gris

Available through: https://store.steampowered.com/app/683320/GRIS/

Gris is a platform adventure game in the third-person. The lush soundtrack is highly integrated into play and the environment.

Guild Wars 2

Developer: ArenaNet	**Released:** 2012
Publisher: NCSOFT	**Game type:** Digital game
Platforms: **PC**, Mac	

More information: www.guildwars2.com/en/the-game/

Available through: www.guildwars2.com/en/

Guild Wars 2 is a MMORPG with nonstandard responsive narrative that integrates player actions into an overall persistent open-world. Rather than using quests, *Guild Wars 2* incorporated instanced events and environments in real-time 3D to further the ripple-effect narration of the game. Initially only in third-person view, a first-person option was added later.

Half-Life

Developer: Valve	**Released:** 1998
Publisher: Sierra Studios	**Game type:** Digital game
Platforms: PC, Mac, PS2	

More information: https://en.wikipedia.org/wiki/Half-Life_(video_game)

Available through: https://store.steampowered.com/app/70/HalfLife/

This story-focused first-person shooter represented a major shift from games solely focused on action to action mechanics being used to tell a story. It also launched Valve software and its success positioned the company to assume its current dominant position in the industry.

Halo: Combat Evolved

Developer: Bungie, Gearbox Software (PC), Westlake Interactive (Mac)	**Platforms:** Xbox, Mac, PC
	Released: 2001
Publisher: Microsoft Game Studios, MacSoft (Mac)	**Game type:** Digital game

More information: https://en.wikipedia.org/wiki/Halo:_Combat_Evolved

Available through: https://store.steampowered.com/app/1064221/Halo_Combat_Evolved_Anniversary/

Halo: Combat Evolved is a sci-fi first-person shooter in a 3D world. Drivable vehicles maintain the third-person view from earlier *Halo* games. Single-player and multiplayer (both competitive and cooperative) modes are available.

Hellblade: Senua's Sacrifice

Developer: Ninja Theory	**Released:** 2017
Publisher: Ninja Theory	**Game type:** Digital game
Platforms: PC, PS4, Xbox One, Nintendo Switch	

More information: www.hellblade.com/

Available through: https://store.steampowered.com/app/414340/Hellblade_Senuas_Sacrifice/

Hellblade is an over-the-shoulder third-person action adventure, with a highly integrated mental-health theme of psychosis. Gameplay reflects the character's condition in a variety of ways. This is a single-player game that integrates puzzles and combat, cutscenes, and voice acting.

Horizon Zero Dawn

Developer: Guerrilla Games	**Released:** 2017
Publisher: Sony Interactive Entertainment	**Game type:** Digital game
Platforms: PS4, PC	

More information: www.guerrilla-games.com/play/horizon

Available through: https://store.steampowered.com/app/1151640/Horizon_Zero_Dawn_Complete_Edition/

Horizon Zero Dawn is an open-world third-person action-adventure RPG. Single-player story-based quests and dynamic environments add to the discovery elements of the open world. Combat is real-time and multiple options exist for strategy and varied styles of play.

Illimat

Developer: Keith Baker, Jennifer Ellis, Carson Ellis,	**Released:** 2017
	Game type: Board game
Publisher: Twogether Studios	

More information: https://boardgamegeek.com/boardgame/210040/illimat

Available through: www.illimat.com/

Illimat is a 2–4 player rounds-based strategy card game. Rules for play change based on the "season" represented by the game's box orientation in the center of the table. Changing the season is a strategy in the game.

Journey

Developer: Thatgamecompany	**Platforms:** PS3, PS4, PC, iOS
Publisher: Sony Computer Entertainment, Annapurna Interactive	**Released:** 2012
	Game type: Digital game

More information: https://thatgamecompany.com/journey/

Available through: www.epicgames.com/store/en-US/product/journey/home

Journey is an adventure platformer game in the third-person. It has nonlinguistic narrative-driven gameplay. Its environments are sparse but beautiful, as are the music and gameplay. Everything contributes to the atmosphere of the game. Very limited random multiplayer interaction may occur, and others are intended to feel like random strangers met on your journey.

Jumpman

Developer: Epyx

Publisher: (Automated Simulations) Epyx

Platforms: Atari 8-bit, Commodore 64, Apple II, ColecoVision, PC

Released: 1983

Game type: Digital game

More information: https://en.wikipedia.org/wiki/Jumpman_(video_game)

Available through: www.myabandonware.com/game/jumpman-2f/play-2f

Jumpman is a side-scrolling platformer game. Play is accomplished by both avoidance of bullets, successful diffusion of bombs, and traversal of platforms. New levels scroll up. It is single-player.

Kingdom Death: Monster

Developer: Adam Poots

Publisher: Kickstarter by Adam Poots

Released: 2015

Game type: Board game

More information: https://boardgamegeek.com/boardgame/55690/kingdom-death -monster

Available through: https://shop.kingdomdeath.com/products/kingdom-death-monster -1-5

Kingdom Death: Monster is a cooperative strategy figurines game for four players. The game is rounds based with extensive narrative elements. Each round, or "lantern year," is made up of three phases and players can record their progress at the end of play. There are approximately 30 lantern years. This progression enables long-term play over many sessions.

Labyrinth

Developer: Max Kobbert

Publisher: Ravensburger

Released: 1986

Game type: Board game

More information: https://boardgamegeek.com/boardgame/1219/labyrinth

Available through: www.ravensburger.org/uk/discover/labyrinth/index.html

Labyrinth is a 2–4 player competitive strategy card and board game. Players move sections of the labyrinth to thwart their opponents while progressing their own piece within the board.

The Last Blade

Developer: SNK	**Released:** 1997
Publisher: SNK	**Game type:** Digital game
Platforms: Arcade, Neo-Geo CD, NGPC, **PC**	

More information: https://en.wikipedia.org/wiki/The_Last_Blade
Available through: https://store.steampowered.com/app/465840/THE_LAST_BLADE/
The Last Blade is a hack-and-slash 2D fighter game in an arcade style. Players can select from 12 characters to defeat 10 opponents. Two-player competitive mode is available.

The Last of Us

Developer: Naughty Dog	**Released:** 2013
Publisher: Sony Computer Entertainment	**Game type:** Digital game
Platforms: PS4	

More information: https://en.wikipedia.org/wiki/The_Last_of_Us
Available through: www.PS.com/en-us/games/the-last-of-us-remastered-ps4/
The Last of Us is a third-person survival action game. This is a story-driven adventure in a post-apocalyptic landscape. The player controls Joel who must escort an NPC named Ellie through all but one of the chapters. Ellie is active in combat and problem-solving. The player controls Ellie during one chapter of the game. If Ellie dies the game ends. Single-player and multiplayer modes, both cooperative and competitive, are available.

The Legend of Zelda

Developer: Nintendo EAD	**Released:** 1986
Publisher: Nintendo	**Game type:** Digital game
Platforms: Famicom Disk System, Nintendo Entertainment System	

More information: https://en.wikipedia.org/wiki/The_Legend_of_Zelda_(video_game)

The Legend of Zelda is an overhead-view action-adventure RPG. Players control the character Link through an open environment containing dungeon instances. The nonlinear play encourages exploration but there are ranked instances that must be completed and items to collect in order to unlock the final boss. Only single-player mode is available.

The Legend of Zelda: Breath of the Wild

Developer: Nintendo

Publisher: Nintendo

Platforms: Nintendo Switch, Wii U

Released: 2017

Game type: Digital game

More information: https://en.wikipedia.org/wiki/The_Legend_of_Zelda:_Breath_of_the_Wild

Available through: www.nintendo.com/games/detail/the-legend-of-zelda-breath-of-the-wild-switch/

The Legend of Zelda: Breath of the Wild is a third-person action-adventure RPG. It is the 19th in the *Zelda* series. The play is open-ended to encourage exploration and side quests. The open-world setting is created with high-definition visuals and detailed physics. Only single-player mode is available.

The Legend of Zelda: Twilight Princess

Developer: Nintendo

Publisher: Nintendo

Platforms: Wii U, Nvidia Shield TV

Released: 2006

Game type: Digital game

More information: https://strategywiki.org/wiki/The_Legend_of_Zelda:_Twilight_Princess

Available through: https://www.nintendo.com/games/detail/the-legend-of-zelda-twilight-princess-hd-digital-version-wii-u/

The Legend of Zelda: Twilight Princess is the thirteenth game in the Legend of Zelda franchise. Its primary differences from previous versions are the use of motion controls, shifting between two character forms, and a darker narrative tone.

League of Legends

Developer: Riot Games

Publisher: Riot Games

Platforms: PC, Mac

Released: 2009

Game type: Digital game

More information: https://play.na.leagueoflegends.com/en_US

Available through: https://play.na.leagueoflegends.com/en_US

League of Legends is a MOBA strategy game. It has an isometric perspective and offers NPC enemies to fight as well as the overall team co-op vs. AI and matchmaking.

Left 4 Dead

Developer: Valve South	**Released:** 2008
Publisher: Valve	**Game type:** Digital game
Platforms: PC, Xbox 360, Mac	

More information: https://en.wikipedia.org/wiki/Left_4_Dead

Available through: https://store.steampowered.com/app/500/Left_4_Dead/

Left 4 Dead is a multiplayer survival/shooter horror game in the first-person. There are four game modes including group competitive (8 players), group cooperative (4 players), single player, and group survival (4 players). The game encourages cooperative play to the point that movement choices, voice acting and visuals, and respawn criteria are built in specifically to aid in the coordination of teams. Both single-player and multiplayer modes are available.

Legacy of Kain: Soul Reaver

Developer: Crystal Dynamics, Nixxes Software BV	**Platforms:** PS, Dreamcast, **PC**
	Released: 1999
Publisher: Eidos Interactive	**Game type:** Digital game

More information: https://en.wikipedia.org/wiki/Legacy_of_Kain:_Soul_Reaver

Available through: https://store.steampowered.com/app/224920/Legacy_of_Kain_Sou l_Reaver/

Legacy of Kain: Soul Reaver is a third-person action adventure. Gameplay includes platforming, block puzzles, timed puzzle-solving and hack-and-slash combat.

Life is Strange

Developer: Dontnod Entertainment	**Released:** 2015
Publisher: Square Enix, Feral Interactive, Black Wing Foundation	**Game type:** Digital game
Platforms: Mobile, Desktop (**PC**), Console	

More information: https://lifeisstrange.square-enix-games.com/en-us

Available through: https://store.steampowered.com/app/319630/Life_is_Strange__E pisode_1/

Life is Strange is a narrative-driven third-person adventure game. Players can interact with the environment, and branching NPC conversations and the ability to "rewind time" enables further puzzle-solving options.

Loneliness

Developer: Jordan Magnuson	**Released:** 2010
Publisher: N/A NecessaryGames.com	**Game type:** Digital game
Platforms: Browser with Flash	

More information: www.gametrekking.com/the-games/korea/loneliness

Available through: www.necessarygames.com/my-games/loneliness/flash

Loneliness is a micro-game in which play consists of playing a dot and attempting to interact with other dots. It has a highly metaphoric and atmospheric nonlinguistic narrative. Only single-player mode is available.

The Long Dark

Developer: Hinterland Studio	**Released:** 2017
Publisher: Hinterland Studio	**Game type:** Digital game
Platforms: Desktop (**PC**), Xbox One, PS4	

More information: www.thelongdark.com/about/

Available through: https://store.steampowered.com/app/305620/The_Long_Dark/

The Long Dark is a first-person survival game. There are two play modes, survival and story. The story mode has gone through many versions. Survival mode is PvE, a simulation of wilderness survival, containing randomly spawned items, wildlife, and weather patterns. Only single-player mode is available.

Magic: The Gathering

Developer: Richard Garfield	**Released:** 1993
Publisher: Wizards of the Coast	**Game type:** Collectible card game

More information: https://magic.wizards.com/en

Available through: Retail

Magic: The Gathering is a collectible card game for 2 or more players. Players assemble a deck of cards prior to play and use in turn-based play to attack opponents and defend themselves. Players may choose to cooperate temporarily to eliminate other opponents, but there is only one winner.

Magic: The Gathering Arena

Developer: Wizards Digital games Studio	**Released:** 2018
Publisher: Wizards of the Coast	**Game type:** Digital game
Platforms: PC, Mac	

More information: https://magic.wizards.com/en/mtgarena

Available through: https://magic.wizards.com/en/mtgarena?source=MX_Nav2020

The original Magic: The Gathering was again ported to digital media (after *Magic: The Gathering Online*) and play is conducted with the same rules as the analog game. Gameplay is free with micro-purchasing available. Deck building is available in both Constructed (player chosen from library of cards) and Draft (randomized deck building with free library of cards) with corresponding rules for winning new cards. Players may not trade cards amongst themselves. No redemption from digital to paper is available.

Magic: The Gathering—Duels of the Planeswalkers

Developer: Stainless Games	**Released:** 2009
Publisher: Wizards of the Coast	**Game type:** Digital game
Platforms: PC, Xbox 360, **PS3**	

More information: https://en.wikipedia.org/wiki/Magic:_The_Gathering_-_Duels_of_the_Planeswalkers

Available through: www.PS.com/en-us/games/magic-the-gathering-duels-of-the-planeswalkers-ps3/

Magic: The Gathering—Duels of the Planeswalkers is a simplified version of the original game. Cards are not monetized. Decks are prebuilt and gameplay may award new cards and open new decks, but choice is limited. Players play against AI opponents, other players, or team up against AI opponents.

Magic: The Gathering Online

Developer: Leaping Lizard Software, Wizards of the Coast	**Platforms: PC**
	Released: 2002
Publisher: Wizards of the Coast	**Game type:** Digital game

More information: https://magic.wizards.com/en/mtgo/gameguide

Available through: https://magic.wizards.com/en/mtgo?source=MX_Nav2020

Magic: The Gathering Online was ported from the original game and consisted of all the same cards and expansions after Mirage. Mirage is the oldest set that online supports.

Players must purchase the digital cards at the same MSRP as paper cards. Play consists of choosing a room (leveled by difficulty and deck choice) and playing with up to 8 opponents. Tournaments are offered and cash prizes. Players may trade cards amongst themselves in digital form. Digital decks and booster packs are monetized. Wizards of the Coast has allowed redemption (for a fee) from digital to paper cards (full sets only) and has entertained the idea of redemption from paper to digital cards.

Mass Effect

Developer: BioWare

Released: 2007

Publisher: Microsoft Game Studios

Game type: Digital game

Platforms: Xbox 360, **PC**, PS3

More information: www.ea.com/games/mass-effect/mass-effect

Available through: https://store.steampowered.com/app/17460/Mass_Effect/

Mass Effect is a third-person sci-fi shooter RPG. This is the first installment in a trilogy. Play is accomplished in a quest-based single-player format. There are six classes for the player to choose from before beginning the game.

Max Payne

Developer: Remedy Entertainment

Released: 2001

Publisher: Gathering of Developers

Game type: Digital game

Platforms: PC, PS2, Xbox, Mac, Game Boy Advance, iOS, Android

More information: www.rockstargames.com/maxpayne/index.html

Available through: https://store.steampowered.com/app/12140/Max_Payne/

Max Payne is a third-person neo-noir shooter. Gameplay features slow-motion abilities that allow the player to view attacks advantageously, reposition the reticle, and then play forward in real-time. Camera shots of the slow-motion bullets picked up the term "bullet time" from *The Matrix* movie series. Only single-player mode is available.

Metro 2033

Developer: 4A Games

Released: 2010

Publisher: THQ, Deep Silver

Game type: Digital game

Platforms: Desktop (**PC**), Console

More information: http://www.metrothegame.com/en-gb/

Available through: https://store.steampowered.com/app/286690/Metro_2033_Redux/

Metro is a horror first-person shooter in a post-apocalyptic setting. Throughout the game the character encounters humans and mutants, and is given subtle choices that affect the cutscenes at the end of the game. Limited ammo and supplies encourage stealth and influence the choices the player faces.

Metroid

Developer: Nintendo R&D1, Intelligent Systems	**Released:** 1986
	Game type: Digital game
Publisher: Nintendo	
Platforms: Console, Arcade, **Nintendo 3DS**	

More information: www.nintendo.co.uk/Games/NES/Metroid--275726.html

Available through: www.nintendo.com/games/detail/metroid-3ds/

Metroid is a single-player platformer with a 2D side-scrolling camera perspective. The game often requires players to scroll backward to retrace their steps in a nonlinear storyline. At the end of the game the character is revealed to be a female in spite of English-language manuals using the "he" pronoun.

MidiMaze

Developer: Xanth Software F/X	**Released:** 1987
Publisher: Hybrid Arts, Bulletproof Software	**Game type:** Digital game
Platforms: Atari ST, Game Boy, Game Gear, SNES, PC-Engine CD-ROM	

More information: www.atariprotos.com/8bit/software/midimaze/midimaze.htm

Available through: Not available

MidiMaze is a multiplayer maze first-person game. Gameplay offers a 360° turning ability in a 3D maze. Players fire bullets at each other while traversing the maze. Up to 16 computers could be networked together via MIDI ports, thus creating the first deathmatch multiplayer.

Mirror's Edge

Developer: EA DICE	**Released:** 2009
Publisher: Electronic Arts	**Game type:** Digital game
Platforms: PS3, Xbox 360, **PC**, iOS, Windows Phone	

More information: www.ea.com/games/mirrors-edge/mirrors-edge

Available through: https://store.steampowered.com/app/17410/Mirrors_Edge/

Mirror's Edge is an action-adventure platformer in first person. Dynamic camera and movement elements including momentum play a prominent role in the traversal play. This is a single player game but a mode to download "ghosts" of other players to compete against is available, as are additional short-timed maps.

Monument Valley

Developer: Ustwo Games	**Released:** 2014
Publisher: Ustwo Games	**Game type:** Digital game
Platforms: iOS, Android, Windows Phone	

More information: www.monumentvalleygame.com/mv1

Available through: https://apps.apple.com/us/app/monument-valley/id728293409

Monument Valley is a nonlinguistic single-player puzzle game in an isometric view. Gameplay consists of manipulating the environment to solve the puzzles, which include visual illusions and impossible objects.

Myst

Developer: Cyan Inc.	**Released:** 1993
Publisher: Brøderbund	**Game type:** Digital game
Platforms: Desktop (**PC**), Console, Mobile	

More information: https://cyan.com/games/myst/

Available through: https://store.steampowered.com/app/63660/Myst_Masterpiece_Edition/

Myst is a first-person single-player puzzle adventure game. The environment is interactive and the play open-ended to encourage discovery and revisitation of areas of discovery. Gameplay is entirely puzzle and discovery based, with no NPC enemies and no combat. Characters cannot die.

NieR: Automata

Developer: PlatinumGames	**Released:** 2017
Publisher: Square Enix	**Game type:** Digital game
Platforms: PS4, PC, Xbox One	

More information: https://en.wikipedia.org/wiki/Nier:_Automata

Available through: https://store.steampowered.com/app/524220/NieRAutomata/

Nier: Automata is a single-player open-world third-person action game that breaks many gaming conventions. The perspective of the game shifts from close third person to top-down isometric or side scrolling depending on the needs of the narrative and gameplay. The narrative structure is also unusual in that the game is intended to be played multiple times and changes radically with each playthrough.

Night in the Woods

Developer: Infinite Fall	**Released:** 2017
Publisher: Finji	**Game type:** Digital game
Platforms: Desktop (**PC**), Console	

More information: http://www.nightinthewoods.com/

Available through: https://store.steampowered.com/app/481510/Night_in_the_Woods/

Night in the Woods is a single-player adventure discovery game. It is third-person and narrative-driven with themes of mental health and small-town socioeconomic collapse.

Ninja Pizza Girl

Developer: Disparity Games	**Released:** 2015
Publisher: Disparity Games	**Game type:** Digital game
Platforms: Desktop (**PC**)	

More information: https://www.disparitygames.com/ninja-pizza-girl/

Available through: store.steampowered.com/app/319470/Ninja_Pizza_Girl/

Ninja Pizza Girl is a game about ninjas delivering pizza, but is also a serious game about bullying and the emotional experience of being a teenage girl. The game features traditional action platforming but replaces combat with a system reflecting the emotional state of the character.

Noita

Developer: Nolla Games	**Released:** 2019
Publisher: Nolla Games	**Game type:** Digital game
Platforms: PC	

More information: https://noitagame.com/

Available through: https://store.steampowered.com/app/881100/Noita/

Noita is a side-scrolling action-adventure game in a 2D open-world that is procedurally generated. Each pixel in the game is interactable and has expressed physics. Only single-player mode is available.

Ori and the Blind Forest

Developer: Moon Studios

Publisher: Microsoft Studios

Platforms: PC, Xbox One, Nintendo Switch

Released: 2015

Game type: Digital game

More information: www.orithegame.com/blind-forest/

Available through: https://store.steampowered.com/app/261570/Ori_and_the_Blind_Forest/

Ori and the Blind Forest is an action-adventure platformer in 2D. Play includes puzzles and skills progression in a Metroidvania manner. In order to save the game players must collect energy cells, which are not abundant, making the player choose carefully where and when to save the game. The environment contains no repeated objects.

Ori and the Will of the Wisps

Developer: Moon Studios

Publisher: Xbox Game Studios

Platforms: PC, Xbox One

Released: 2020

Game type: Digital game

More information: www.orithegame.com/

Available through: https://store.steampowered.com/app/1057090/Ori_and_the_Will_of_the_Wisps/

Ori and the Will of the Wisps is a direct sequel to the first *Ori* game. Platforms and puzzles are predominant with a strong narrative. The save element was changed to auto in this second game and the "shard" system has replaced the sequential skill-building.

Papers, Please

Developer: 3909 LLC

Publisher: 3909 LLC

Platforms: Desktop (**PC**), iOS, PS Vita

Released: 2013

Game type: Digital game

More information: https://papersplea.se/

Available through: https://store.steampowered.com/app/239030/Papers_Please/

Papers, Please is a puzzle simulation empathy game. Players take on the role of an immigration officer in a fictitious postwar state and have to evaluate each immigrant as they apply for passage. It is single-player and gameplay is conducted through a single-screen interface, showing current paperwork, the current applicant, and an overall view of the line forming in wait.

Phantasy Star IV

Developer: Sega	**Released:** 2012
Publisher: Sega	**Game type:** Digital game
Platforms: Sega Genesis, **PC**	

More information: https://en.wikipedia.org/wiki/Phantasy_Star_IV

Available through: https://store.steampowered.com/app/211205/Phantasy_Star_IV_The_End_of_the_Millennium/

Phantasy Star IV is a party adventure RPG in an isometric view. It includes turn-based combat, overworld maps, exploration, and dungeon areas. It is single-player.

Planescape: Torment

Developer: Black Isle Studios, Beamdog, IdeaSpark Labs Inc.	**Released:** 1999
	Game Type: Digital game
Publisher: Interplay Entertainment	
Platforms: PC, Linux, Mac, Android, iOS, Nintendo Switch, PS4, Xbox One	

More Information: https://en.wikipedia.org/wiki/Planescape:_Torment

Available Through: https://planescape.com/

Planescape: Torment is an isometric role playing game. The narrative of the game was more complex and nuanced than was common at the time of its release. The game features a large amount of text in the form of dialogue, item descriptions and diegetic writing.

Pokémon Go

Developer: Niantic	**Released:** 2016
Publisher: Niantic	**Game type:** Digital game
Platforms: iOS, Android	

More information: www.pokemongo.com/en-us/

Available through: https://apps.apple.com/us/app/pok%C3%A9mon-go/id1094591345

Pokémon Go is an augmented reality mobile game using the Pokémon collectibles from the franchise. It is location-based, and play consists of physically traversing the real world and viewing it on your map interface with either an AR background or a virtually rendered background and finding the Pokémon on the map. PvP is available, as well as cooperative battles and captures.

Pokémon: Sword / Pokémon: Shield

Developer: Game Freak	**Platforms:** Switch
Publisher: Nintendo, The Pokémon Company	**Released:** 2019
	Game Type: Digital game

More information: https://swordshield.pokemon.com/en-us/

Available through: https://swordshield.pokemon.com/en-us/

Pokémon: Sword and *Pokémon: Shield* are the 2020 editions of this franchise. They largely follow the exploration, collection and combat formula of the previous versions, while introducing open world elements and online play for small groups of players.

Poker

Game type: Card game

More information: https://bicyclecards.com/how-to-play/basics-of-poker/

Poker is a family of strategy card games played by 2 or more. It involves several sets of rules for differences in play, but consistently includes betting and elimination of players. It is turn-based and consists of collecting prescribed sets of cards (three-of-a-kind, full house, etc.) and placing bets into the pot based on the confidence level of the influence of the sets. Players do not reveal their sets to each other until a full round of betting has been completed. Winning a round is having the highest set value; winners take the pot.

Poptropica

Developer: Jeff Kinney Group, StoryArc Media	**Platforms:** iOS
	Released: 2007
Publisher: Pearson Education, Sandbox Networks	**Game type:** Digital game

More information: www.poptropica.com/

Available through: https://apps.apple.com/us/app/poptropica/id818709874

Poptropica is a 2D adventure platformer game with social multiplayer elements. More than 50 standalone adventures were produced for the game as well as multiplayer minigames and procedurally generated worlds that players could modify to create their own levels to share with other players.

Portal

Developer: Valve	**Released:** 2007
Publisher: Valve	**Game type:** Digital game
Platforms: PC, PS3, Xbox 360, Mac, Linux, Android	

More information: https://en.wikipedia.org/wiki/Portal_(video_game)

Available through: https://store.steampowered.com/app/400/Portal/

Portal is a puzzle-platform single-player game in first-person. Interspatial portals are projectable via a portal gun device and the character can then pass through the portal. Play is predominantly teleporting through these portals to solve the puzzles. There is no combat in *Portal*.

Prince of Persia

Developer: Broderbund	**Released:** 1989
Publisher: Broderbund	**Game type:** Digital game
Platforms: Desktop (**PC**), Console, Mobile	

More information: https://en.wikipedia.org/wiki/Prince_of_Persia_(1989_video_game)

Available through: www.microsoft.com/en-us/p/prince-of-persia-pc/9nblggh35r2n

Prince of Persia is a side-scrolling action game emphasizing jumping. The use of rotoscoping to capture realistic movement made this game an important milestone.

Prince of Persia (2008)

Developer: Ubisoft Montreal	**Released:** 2008
Publisher: Ubisoft Montreal	**Game type:** Digital game
Platforms: PS3, Xbox 360, Desktop (**PC**)	

More information: https://en.wikipedia.org/wiki/Prince_of_Persia_(2008_video_game)

Available through: https://store.steampowered.com/app/19980/Prince_of_Persia/

Prince of Persia (the reboot 2008) is an action-adventure platformer with hack-and-slash combat. The game features an open-world to encourage exploration of the nonlinear plot. Play is third-person. The combat and open-world elements differ strongly from the original *Prince of Persia* (1989) and also vary from the many sequels that followed that original.

Prototype

Developer: Radical Entertainment	**Released:** 2009
Publisher: Activision	**Game type:** Digital game
Platforms: PC, PS4, Xbox One	

More information: https://en.wikipedia.org/wiki/Prototype_(video_game)

Available through: https://store.steampowered.com/app/10150/Prototype/

Prototype is an action-adventure in a sandbox-style but with a strong narrative. The character is a shapeshifter, which enables assorted combat styles. This is a single-player game in a third-person.

Q*bert

Developer: Gottlieb	Intellivision, NES, Odyssey, Mobile, SG-1000, Standalone tabletop, TI-99/4A, PS3-4, ZX Spectrum
Publisher: Gottlieb	
Platforms: Arcade, Atari 2600, Atari 5200, Atari 8-bit, ColecoVision, Commodore 64, Game Boy Color, MSX, VIC-20,	
	Released: October, 1982
	Game type: Digital game

More information: https://en.wikipedia.org/wiki/Q*bert

Available through: www.sonypictures.com/games/qbert

*Q*bert* is an action/puzzle arcade game in an isometric view. Play consists of hopping on cubes while avoiding obstacles and enemies. It is a one- to two-player game.

Quake

Developer: id Software	**Released:** 1996
Publisher: GT Interactive	**Game type:** Digital game
Platforms: Desktop (PC), Console	

More information: https://en.wikipedia.org/wiki/Quake_(video_game)

Available through: https://store.steampowered.com/app/2310/QUAKE/

Quake is a first-person shooter. The environment is a 3D dungeon crawl with medieval/Gothicesque architecture. *Quake* has both single-player and multiplayer deathmatch modes. Mods and add-ons exist to further the multiplayer options.

Red Dead Redemption

Developer: Rockstar San Diego	**Released:** 2010
Publisher: Rockstar Games	**Game type:** Digital game
Platforms: PS3, Xbox 360	

More information: www.rockstargames.com/reddeadredemption/

Available through: https://store.playstation.com/en-us/product/UP1004-NPUB30638_00-PSNREDDEAD2V0004

Red Dead Redemption is a third-person action-adventure in an expansive open-world. The setting is a fictionalized American Old West in 1911, and horseback riding and gun-fighting combat are prominent. Throughout the narrative the character is forced to make morality choices that influence their status in the game. Single-player and multiplayer are available, and there are cooperative and competitive modes for multiplayer.

Red Dead Redemption 2

Developer: Rockstar Studios	**Released:** 2019
Publisher: Rockstar Games	**Game type:** Digital game
Platforms: PS4, Xbox One, **PC**, Stadia	

More information: www.rockstargames.com/reddeadredemption2/

Available through: https://store.steampowered.com/app/1174180/Red_Dead_Redemption_2/

Red Dead Redemption 2 is a prequel to *Red Dead Redemption* and takes place in the same expansive open-world setting. This game adds hunting and swimming, dual-weapon wielding, dynamic NPC interactions, and the ability to use a bow. The high level of detail for actions and adventures was well received. Single-player and multiplayer are available.

Resident Evil 7: Biohazard

Developer: Capcom	**Released:** 2017
Publisher: Capcom	**Game type:** Digital game
Platforms: PC, Console	

More information: http://www.residentevil7.com/us/#_top

Available through: https://store.steampowered.com/app/418370/RESIDENT_EVIL_7_biohazard__BIOHAZARD_7_resident_evil/

Resident Evil 7: Biohazard is a first-person survival horror game. Unlike the rest of the franchise, which focused on action, this game focuses on survival and exploration. It is also the first of the franchise to use a first-person perspective. This is a single-player game; VR is available on PS4.

Rock Band

Developer: Harmonix, Pi Studios	**Released:** 2007
Publisher: MTV Games	**Game type:** Digital game
Platforms: Xbox 360, PS3, Wii	

More information: https://en.wikipedia.org/wiki/Rock_Band_(video_game)

Available through: https://marketplace.xbox.com/en-US/Product/Rock-Band/66acd000-77fe-1000-9115-d80245410829

Rock Band is a rhythm game where 1–4 players use peripherals to mimic the musical "notes" on their interface. There are four different peripherals: vocal, lead guitar, bass guitar, and drums. Players can choose a character who will be locked into one type of musical instrument. Single-player and multiplayer is available. Multiplayer is cooperative.

Roulette

Game type: Casino table game

More information: www.wikihow.com/Play-Roulette

Roulette is a betting game on a numbered wheel with two sections. The croupier (dealer) spins the wheel of numbers in alternating colors (usually red and black) in one direction, while inside the wheel they spin a ball in the opposite direction, when momentum stops the ball drops onto one of the numbers. Bets are placed before the spin in four types: what color, what number, odd or even number, or low or high number. French/European roulette has 37 numbers and American roulette has 38 (double zero).

Spacewar!

Developer: Steve Russell	**Released:** 1962
Platforms: PDP-1, **PC** (emulator)	**Game type:** Digital game

More information: https://en.wikipedia.org/wiki/Spacewar!

Available through: https://www.masswerk.at/spacewar/

In this, the first video game, two players control simple two-dimensional representations of space ships in the gravity well of a star. They can maneuver and fire at each other. The game was developed as a hardware demonstration by Steve Russell, Martin Graetz, Wayne Wiitanen, Bob Saunders, and Steve Piner among others.

Scrabble

Developer: Alfred Mosher Butts	**Released:** 1948
Publisher: Mattel, Hasbro	**Game type:** Board game

More information: https://boardgamegeek.com/boardgame/320/scrabble

Scrabble is a tile-placing word game for two to four players. Play is turn-based. The game board is a 15-by-15 grid of squares. The squares all have varied values. The tiles each also have a value. Players place whole words consisting of tiles with a letter each on the gameboard (utilizing other players tiles if they want) in a crossword-like manner. When the tile pool is exhausted the player with the highest score on the board wins.

The Secret World

Developer: Funcom	**Released:** 2012
Publisher: Electronic Arts	**Game type:** Digital game
Platforms: PC	

More information: www.secretworldlegends.com/

Available through: https://store.steampowered.com/app/215280/Secret_World_Legends/

The *Secret World* is a MMORPG with strong horror and dark-fantasy elements. Players may choose either first-person or third-person and interact with both NPC and other player characters. The regions of the game are difficulty-based but the setting is open world. This game differs from other MMORPGs by making on-the-fly reconfiguration of abilities available at any time in the game. Multiplayer except for a novice introduction section.

Sekiro: Shadows Die Twice

Developer: FromSoftware	**Released:** March 21, 2019
Publisher: Activision, FromSoftware	**Game type:** Digital game
Platforms: PC, PS4, Xbox One	

More information: www.sekirothegame.com/

Available through: https://store.steampowered.com/app/814380/Sekiro_Shadows_Die _Twice/

Sekiro: Shadows Die Twice is a third-person stealth/action-adventure. Combat is focused on unbalancing the enemy or breaking their poster to create an opening for a killing blow. There is limited gear enhancement and a skill tree, but no large-scale investing mechanism of improvements for character building. Only single-player mode is available.

Settlers of Catan

Developer: Klaus Teuber	**Released:** 1995
Publisher: Kosmos, Catan Studio, and many others	**Game type:** Board game

More information: www.catan.com/#start

Available through: www.catan.com/game/catan

Settlers of Catan is a multiplayer strategy board game. Game play is the accumulation and use of the resources as represented on the board, randomized with dice and enhanced with bonus cards. Players may negotiate with each other and trade resources within their turn. There are many expansions and adaptations to the main game. The winner is the first player to get to ten Victory Points. Three to four players, or up to six with expansions.

Silent Hill

Developer: Konami Computer Entertainment Tokyo (Team Silent)	**Platforms:** PS, **PSP, PS3**
	Released: 1999
Publisher: Konami	**Game type:** Digital game

More information: https://en.wikipedia.org/wiki/Silent_Hill_(video_game)

Available through: https://store.PS.com/en-us/product/UP9000-NPUJ00707_00-0000000000000001

Silent Hill is a single-player survival-horror game in third-person. It uses 3D real-time rendered environments made possible through limiting visibility with fog and darkness. The atmospheric and psychological elements of the horror motif are put into sharp relief by the "everyman" character who is not skilled in combat. There are five possible endings.

Silent Hill 2

Developer: Konami Computer Entertainment Tokyo (Team Silent)	**Platforms:** PS3, **Xbox**, PC
	Released: 2001
Publisher: Konami	**Game type:** Digital game

More information: https://en.wikipedia.org/wiki/Silent_Hill_2

Available through: https://marketplace.xbox.com/en-us/Product/Silent-Hill-HD-Collection/66acd000-77fe-1000-9115-d8024b4e0845

Silent Hill 2 is the second installment in the *Silent Hill* series. Although the plot is unrelated, the main world mythos is the same and ^2 takes place in the same town (named Silent Hill) as the first game. While maintaining the same psychological and atmospheric survival/horror mode as its predecessor, *Silent Hill 2* focuses closely on navigation, puzzle-solving, and avoidance of combat. The game has six alternative endings. It is single-player.

Silent Hill: Shattered Memories

Developer: Climax Studios	**Released:** 2009
Publisher: Konami Digital Entertainment	**Game type:** Digital game
Platforms: Wii, PS2, **PSP**	

More information: https://en.wikipedia.org/wiki/Silent_Hill:_Shattered_Memories

Available through: www.PS.com/en-us/games/silent-hill-shattered-memories-psp/

Silent Hill: Shattered Memories is a reimagining and reframing of the first *Silent Hill*. Using the same premise and many of the same characters, this game places the plot in a different fictional universe and includes new characters. Play is framed in two parts, the first being the creation of the character and scenario via the means of an interview format that is also part of the plot. The second part is the character's quest. Unlike the first game of *Silent Hill*, there is no option for combat. Stealth, puzzles, strategy, and navigation are prominent. There are four alternative endings. It is single-player.

The Sinking City

Developer: Frogwares	**Released:** 2019
Publisher: Bigben Interactive	**Game type:** Digital game
Platforms: PC, Console	

More information: http://frogwares.com/games/

Available through: https://store.steampowered.com/app/750130/The_Sinking_City/

Sinking City is a horror action-adventure game in third-person. The play is an open-world exploration and mystery-detective style. The plot and themes are rooted in the H.P. Lovecraft horror mythos. Only single-player mode is available.

Snatcher

Developer: Konami	**Released: 1988**
Publisher: Konami	**Game type:** Digital game
Platforms: PC, Sega CD, PS, Sega Saturn	

More information: https://en.wikipedia.org/wiki/Snatcher_(video_game)

Available through: Not available

Snatcher is a mystery puzzle adventure game. Cinematic and narrative-driven play is conducted in a semi-open world, with a static/animated display and tab menu options. Only single-player mode is available.

Sonic The Hedgehog (8-bit)

Developer: Ancient	**Released:** 1991
Publisher: Sega	**Game type:** Digital game
Platforms: Desktop (**PC**), Mobile, Console	

More information: https://en.wikipedia.org/wiki/Sonic_the_Hedgehog_(1991_video_game)

Available through: www.sega.com/games/sonic-hedgehog

Sonic The Hedgehog is a platformer with a side-scrolling playfield. The 8-bit was developed for mobile devices and has all the same characteristics of the 16-bit version with less complexity. There are more exploration elements in the slightly slower 8-bit version. It is single-player.

Soulcalibur

Developer: Project Soul

Released: 1998

Publisher: Bandai Namco Entertainment

Game type: Digital game

Platforms: Arcade, Dreamcast, iOS, **Xbox 360**, Android

More information: https://en.wikipedia.org/wiki/Soulcalibur_(video_game)

Available through: www.microsoft.com/en-us/p/soulcalibur/c27k7xx3dtrd

The second *Soul* game in the series, this arcade-style hack-and-slash was ported to many other consoles, including upgrades and multiple small differences for each. This game featured an overall improved movement system over its predecessor and favorable buffering for combat moves. There are 19 characters to choose from: 9 from the first *Soul* game and 10 new ones. Third-person. 1–2 players.

Space Invaders

Developer: Taito

Released: 1978

Publisher: Taito, Atari, Inc. and others

Game type: Digital game

Platforms: Arcade, Atari, Desktop, **Android**

More information: https://en.wikipedia.org/wiki/Space_Invaders

Available through: https://play.google.com/store/apps/details?id=jp.co.taito.am.spaceinvaders&hl=en_US

Space Invaders is an arcade fixed-shooter game. One to two players must shoot down a barrage of enemies as quickly and accurately as possible with a fixed weapon that can only move horizontally. Enemies scroll down from the top of the screen in rows.

Spec Ops: The Line

Developer: Yager Development

Released: 2012

Publisher: 2K Games

Game type: Digital game

Platforms: Desktop (**PC**), PS3, Xbox 360

More information: www.2k.com/en-US/game/spec-ops-the-line/

Available through: https://store.steampowered.com/app/50300/Spec_Ops_The_Line/

Spec Ops: The Line is a third-person shooter. Play consists of multiple war scenarios including squad tactics and environmental hazards and advantages. The plot challenges the player to make morally ambiguous choices and confronts them with the ethical and moral questions that war itself poses, while also calling into question the role of war games as entertainment. Single and multiplayer modes are available, and multiplayer is both cooperative or competitive.

'Splosion Man

Developer: Twisted Pixel Games

Released: 2009

Publisher: Microsoft Games Studios

Game type: Digital game

Platforms: Xbox 360

More information: http://www.splosionman.com/

Available through: https://marketplace.xbox.com/en-us/Product/Splosion-Man/66ac d000-77fe-1000-9115-d8025841098f

'Splosion Man is an action platform 3D game, in a side view. In this level-heavy game the character's only asset is his ability to explode. Obstacles, enemies, walls, and other explosives can be triggered/exploded by using this skill, as well as events and the ability to jump. Single-player and multiplayer modes are available.

StarCraft

Developer: Blizzard Entertainment

Released: 1998

Publisher: Blizzard Entertainment

Game type: Digital game

Platforms: PC, Mac, Nintendo 64

More information: https://starcraft.com/en-us/

Available through: https://us.shop.battle.net/en-us/product/starcraft

StarCraft is a real-time sci-fi strategy game in an isometric view. There are three races to play, and each have their own set of military strategies and support economics. There are single-player and multiplayer modes. Multiplayer is up to 8 players.

StarCraft II: Wings of Liberty

Developer: Blizzard Entertainment

Released: 2010

Publisher: Blizzard Entertainment

Game type: Digital game

Platforms: PC, Mac

More information: https://starcraft2.com/en-us/game

Available through: https://starcraft2.com/en-us/

StarCraft II was released as a trilogy, beginning with *StarCraft II: Wings of Liberty*. Each game/expansion concentrates on one of the races from StarCraft. *Wings of Liberty* focuses on the Terrans. The expansions *Heart of the Swarm* and *Legacy of the Void* complete the trilogy. These games incorporate the same characters, story, and gameplay as *StarCraft*, while introducing new elements and expanding the storyline. Single-player and multi-player modes are available.

Stardew Valley

Developer: Eric Barone, Sickhead Games

Publisher: Concerned Ape, Chucklefish

Platforms: PC, Mac, Linux, PS4, Xbox One, Nintendo Switch, PS Vita, IoS, Android

Released: 2016

Game type: Digital game

More information: www.stardewvalley.net/

Available through: www.stardewvalley.net/

Stardew Valley is an isometric farming simulator with secondary crafting and combat and social mechanics. The game uses simple pixel-art style visuals and repetitive time management gameplay. Some cooperative multiplayer elements have been added to the game post release.

Starsiege: Tribes

Developer: Dynamix

Publisher: Sierra On-Line

Platforms: PC

Released: 1998

Game type: Digital game

More information: https://en.wikipedia.org/wiki/Starsiege:_Tribes

Available through: www.tribesuniverse.com/

Starsiege: Tribes is a first-person squad-based MMO shooter game and the first in its series. There are five basic play types, and three character classes. Multiplayer.

Star Wars Roleplaying Game

Developer: Wizards of the Coast

Publisher: Wizards of the Coast

Platforms: Tabletop

Released: 2000

Game type: Physical game

More information:

This tabletop RPG is set in the Star Wars universe and id unique in that it introduced mechanics around the light and dark sides of the force. This game was produced between 2000 and 2010. Previous and subsequent Star Wars tabletop RPG's use entirely different systems and were developed independently.

Street Fighter

Developer: Capcom	**Released:** 1987
Publisher: Capcom	**Game type:** Digital game
Platforms: Arcade, Desktop, Console (**Xbox One**)	

More information: https://en.wikipedia.org/wiki/Street_Fighter_(video_game)

Available through: www.microsoft.com/en-us/p/street-fighter-30th-anniversary-collect ion/c24t2mrdbb3w

Street Fighter is a competitive third-person fighter arcade game. Pressure sensitive controls in the deluxe edition add physicality to the combat, and play is up to two people. The game has two characters: a primary and a secondary for an additional player. There are single-player and competitive play modes. Fluidity between modes exists. There are ten AI opponents.

Summer Games

Developer: Epyx	**Released:** 1984
Publisher: U.S. Gold	**Game type:** Digital game
Platforms: Legacy Console, Legacy Desktop, **PC**	

More information: https://en.wikipedia.org/wiki/Summer_Games_(video_game)

Available through: https://classicreload.com/c64-summer-games.html

Summer Game is a sports simulator in the vein of the Olympics. There are several games to compete in, which vary from platform to platform. Players choose a country to represent and compete in the games against AI or other players to win medals. Play is conducted in third-person side view. Single and multiplayer modes are available.

Super Mario Bros.

Developer: Nintendo EAD	**Released:** September 13, 1985
Publisher: Nintendo	**Game type:** Digital game
Platforms: NES, **Nintendo 3DS**	

More information: https://mario.nintendo.com/history/

Available through: www.nintendo.com/games/detail/super-mario-bros-3ds/

Super Mario Bros. is a side-scrolling platformer. It is the successor to the arcade game *Mario Bros.* Jumping is the primary combat move. The game has eight "worlds" and each world has four levels. Single-play and multiplayer cooperative modes are available.

Super Mario Kart

Developer: Nintendo	**Released:** 1992
Publisher: Nintendo	**Game type:** Digital game
Platforms: SNES, **Nintendo 3DS**	

More information: https://en.wikipedia.org/wiki/Super_Mario_Kart

Available through: www.nintendo.com/games/detail/super-mario-kart-3ds/

Super Mario Kart is a go-kart racing game in the third-person perspective 3D. This is the first in the *Mario Kart* series in the *Mario* world. Often considered the creator of the kart genre, this game departed from the earlier platformers in the *Mario* world. There are eight Mario Bros. characters to choose from and several modes of play including timed and competitive. Single player and multiplayer modes available.

Super Mario World

Developer: Nintendo EAD	**Released:** 1990
Publisher: Nintendo	**Game type:** Digital game
Platforms: Arcade, SNES, Game Boy Advance, **Nintendo 3DS**	

More information: www.nintendo.co.uk/Games/Super-Nintendo/Super-Mario-World-752133.html

Available through: www.nintendo.com/games/detail/super-mario-world-vc-snes-3ds/

Super Mario World is a side-scrolling platformer. It is the fifth in the *Mario* world. This game introduced the character Yoshi and added the ability to float or fly. The navigation is managed through both the side-scrolling field and an overworld map view. There are seven "worlds." Single-player and multiplayer cooperative are available.

Super Meat Boy

Developer: Team Meat	**Released:** November 30, 2010
Publisher: Team Meat	**Game type:** Digital game
Platforms: Xbox 360, PC, Mac, Linux, PS4, PS Vita, Wii U, Nintendo Switch	

More information: https://en.wikipedia.org/wiki/Super_Meat_Boy

Available through: https://store.steampowered.com/app/40800/Super_Meat_Boy/

Super Meat Boy is a single-player platformer. It is the sequel to *Meat Boy*. Game play is side-viewed, and timing and fine control are essential. There are unlockable alternate characters, and hidden or unlockable levels.

Tag

Game type: Physical/athletic

More information: www.wikihow.com/Play-Tag

Tag is a backyard or playground game consisting of two or more players. The player who is "it" must run and touch another player to "tag them out." The tagged player is then "out" or becomes another "it" depending on the variation. There are many variations on the game.

Teenage Mutant Ninja Turtles: The Arcade Game

Developer: Konami   **Released:** 1989

Publisher: Konami, Ultra Games,   **Game type:** Digital game

Platforms: Arcade, **PC,** Xbox 360, PS2, Game Cube

More information: https://en.wikipedia.org/wiki/Teenage_Mutant_Ninja_Turtles_(arcade_game)

Available through: http://www.abandonia.com/en/games/31368/Teenage+Mutant+Ninja+Turtles+-+The+Arcade+Game.html

Teenage Mutant Ninja Turtles: The Arcade Game is a "beat-'em-up" combat game. This arcade is based on the animated series of the same name. Players can choose one of the four turtles from the series to play. One to four players (depending on platform) in a side-scrolling 2D world. This game was released for other console platforms later.

Tetris

Developer: AcademySoft   **Released:** 1984

Publisher: AcademySoft   **Game type:** Digital game

Platforms: Desktop **(PC),** Console, Mobile

More information: https://tetris.com/about-us

Available through: https://tetris.com/play-tetris

Tetris is a tile-matching vertical field game. Players must match and combine falling tiles in speed-based play. Players may only rotate, move, or speed up the falling pieces. Scoring is based on combinations of stacked tiles and time. The game is unending. Single-player and multiplayer modes are available.

Tetris Effect

Developer: Monstars Resonair   **Released:** 2018

Publisher: Enhance Games   **Game type:** Digital game

Platforms: PS4, PC

More information: www.tetriseffect.game/

Available through: www.epicgames.com/store/en-US/product/tetris-effect/home

Tetris Effect is a tile-matching vertical field game much like its predecessor *Tetris*. *Tetris Effects* has added few additional play features, including a zone feature to clear sections of tiles. This game has enhanced themes, background graphics, music, and a variety of play-style choices. The music element is pivotal to the timing in this version. Single-player and multiplayer modes are available.

They Are Billions

Developer: Numantian Games	**Released:** 2019
Publisher: Numantian Games, BlitWorks	**Game type:** Digital game
Platforms: PC, PS4, Xbox One	

More information: http://www.numantiangames.com/theyarebillions/

Available through: https://store.steampowered.com/app/644930/They_Are_Billions/

They Are Billions is a real-time survival strategy game in an isometric view. Players must manage resources, plan developments, and fight off invasions of enemy zombies. Only single-player mode is available.

This War of Mine

Developer: 11 bit studios, War Child	**Released:** 2014
Publisher: 11 bit studios	**Game type:** Digital game
Platforms: Desktop **(PC)**, Console, Mobile	

More information: http://www.thiswarofmine.com/#stories

Available through: https://store.steampowered.com/app/282070/This_War_of_Mine/

This War of Mine is a survival war strategy game. It's a side-scrolling 3D landscape of a war-torn city. The player is responsible for a party of "Survivors" ranging from 1 to 4 and must manage resources to keep everyone alive until a "ceasefire." With point-and-click the player chooses characters to do tasks. Gameplay duration is randomly generated. Some playthroughs take only several "weeks" to complete, while other playthroughs might take "months." Usable items in the gamespace are also randomly generated so no two playthroughs are ever the same. Only single-player mode is available.

Ticket to Ride

Developer: Alan R. Moon	**Released:** 2004
Publisher: Days of Wonder	**Game type:** Board game

More information: https://boardgamegeek.com/boardgame/9209/ticket-ride

Ticket to Ride is a railway-building turn-based strategy board game for two to five players. Cards are used to purchase game tokens. Players are given a choice of destinations to connect (pairs of cities) at the beginning of play. They then have a hand of cards and an additional pool to pick from to build railway connections between these chosen cities. Players who connect their destinations get points. During play, additional destination cards can be purchased. Destinations that are not connected count against player's points at the end of the game.

Tomb Raider

Developer: Core Design	**Released:** 1996
Publisher: Eidos Interactive	**Game type:** Digital game
Platforms: Legacy Console, Desktop (**PC**), Mobile	

More information: https://en.wikipedia.org/wiki/Tomb_Raider_(1996_video_game)

Available through: https://store.steampowered.com/app/224960/Tomb_Raider_I/

Tomb Raider is an action-adventure in an over-the-shoulder third-person perspective. There are many puzzles and platforming in the 3D world, encouraging player exploration. Minimal combat, mostly with wild animals, adds to the adventure. Only single-player mode is available.

Tomb Raider (2013 reboot)

Developer: Crystal Dynamics	**Released:** 2013
Publisher: Square Enix	**Game type:** Digital game
Platforms: Desktop (**PC**), PS4, Xbox One, Stadia	

More information: https://en.wikipedia.org/wiki/Tomb_Raider_(2013_video_game)

Available through: https://store.steampowered.com/app/203160/Tomb_Raider/

Tomb Raider, the 2013 reboot, is an action-adventure over-the-shoulder third-person game. Much of the style of the gameplay is the same, but in this reboot the survival narrative is the goal rather than mystery-solving or finding objects. More combat and stealth oriented than the earlier games in the series. Single-player and multiplayer modes are available.

Torment: Tides of Numenera

Developer: inXile Entertainment	**Released:** 2016
Publisher: Techland Publishing[	**Game type:** Digital game
Platforms: Desktop (**PC**), PS4, Xbox One	

More information: https://tormentgame.com/

Available through: https://store.steampowered.com/app/272270/Torment_Tides_of_N umenera/

Torment: Tides of Numenera is a third-person isometric perspective RPG in pre-rendered 3D. This narrative-driven game has complex character interaction with NPC and a highly personalizable character-creation process. Only single-player mode is available.

Total War: Warhammer 2

Developer: Creative Assembly	**Released:** 2017
Publisher: Sega	**Game type:** Digital game
Platforms: Desktop (PC)	

More information: www.totalwar.com/games/warhammer-ii/

Available through: https://store.steampowered.com/app/594570/Total_War_WAR HAMMER_II/

Total War: Warhammer 2 is a real-time strategy game with a detailed isometric view. Players must manage resources and armies. There is a strong narrative, and players who have both the first *Warhammer* game and this second one unlock a special multiplayer option. Both single-player and multiplayer options are available.

Train

Developer: Brenda Romero	**Game type:** Board game
Released: 2009	

More information: http://brenda.games/train

Train is a one-of-a-kind (only one copy exists) board game using a dice/card system to depict the transportation of Jews to concentration camps. Players are not told what the tokens represent or where the trains are going at the beginning of play. Play is turn-based and players have to load tokens into their trains and move the trains toward their destinations. Generally play changes dramatically when the first destination card is revealed at arrival. Outcomes vary, winning is ambiguous, and rules are left intentionally vague. The intent of the game concerns complicity and the players' feelings toward it.

Trespasser

Developer: DreamWorks Interactive	**Released:** 1998
Publisher: Electronic Arts	**Game type:** Digital game
Platforms: PC	

More information: https://en.wikipedia.org/wiki/Trespasser_(video_game)

Available through: https://gamefabrique.com/games/jurassic-park-trespasser/

Trespasser is an action-adventure game set in the *Jurassic Park* universe. Play is first-person. *Trespasser* was ahead of its time in many design and engine implementations, creating issues with the computers at the time that could not render and run the game fast enough. The rushed development of the game compounded these issues, resulting in less than satisfactory movement and graphics despite their cutting-edge intent. Only single-player mode is available.

Trials HD

Developer: RedLynx	**Released:** 2009
Publisher: Microsoft Game Studios	**Game type:** Digital game
Platforms: Xbox 360	

More information: https://en.wikipedia.org/wiki/Trials_HD

Available through: www.microsoft.com/en-us/p/trials-hd/c0pk4504xscn?activetab=pivot:overviewtab

Trials HD is a motorcycle racing game. It is the third in the *Trials* series. This game includes 2.5D-enhanced graphics courses, an improvement on the graphics of previous *Trials*. It also includes modifications to the management of physics, and although the physics is almost realistic, it has been tweaked to create a slightly enhanced feel. *Trials HD* also includes a level editor where players can create and share their own courses. Only single-player mode is available.

Vikings: War of Clans

Developer: Plarium	**Released:** 2015
Publisher: Plarium	**Game type:** Digital game
Platforms: Browser, iOS, Android	

More information: https://plarium.com/en/strategy-games/vikings-war-of-clans/

Available through: https://plarium.com/en/strategy-games/vikings-war-of-clans/

Vikings: War of Clans is an MMO strategy game. Play consists of resource management and competitive strategy. While groups of players are encouraged to create and participate in Clans through rewards and cooperative elements, both voluntary and game-managed, it is not necessary to be a member of a Clan. Multiplayer.

Virginia

Developer: Variable State	**Released:** September 22, 2016
Publisher: 505 Games	**Game type:** Digital game
Platforms: PC, Mac, PS4, Xbox One	

More information: https://505games.com/games/virginia/

Available through: https://store.steampowered.com/app/374030/Virginia/

Virginia is a first-person mystery game. Cinematic editing and minimalistic interactive objects draw focus toward a narrative-driven story. Only single-player mode is available.

VVVVVV

Developer: Terry Cavanagh	**Released:** September 7, 2010
Publisher: Nicalis	**Game type:** Digital game
Platforms: PC, Nintendo Switch, Mac, Linux, Nintendo 3DS, PS Vita, PS4, iOS, Android, Ouya, Commodore 64, Pandora	

More information: https://en.wikipedia.org/wiki/VVVVVV

Available through: https://store.steampowered.com/app/70300/VVVVVV/

VVVVVV is a puzzle platformer in a side-view, side-scrolling 2D game. Unlike other platformers this game utilizes the manipulation of gravity rather than the option to jump. Only single-player mode is available.

The Walking Dead

Developer: Telltale Games, Skybound Games	**Released:** 2012
Publisher: Telltale Games	**Game type:** Digital game
Platforms: Desktop (**PC**), Console, Mobile	

More information: https://en.wikipedia.org/wiki/The_Walking_Dead_(video_game_series)

Available through: https://store.steampowered.com/app/207610/The_Walking_Dead/

The *Walking Dead* is an episodic, third-person, story-driven game. In this graphic adventure style, players' choices both in action and in dialogue trees manipulate the actions and reactions of NPCs. The game allows players to compare their choices with others who have played the game, as well as "rewinds" to explore other choice options. Only single-player mode is available.

Warcraft: Orcs & Humans

Developer: Blizzard Entertainment	**Released:** November 23, 1994
Publisher: Blizzard Entertainment	**Game type:** Digital game
Platforms: MS-DOS, Classic Mac OS	

More information: www.blizzard.com/en-us/games/legacy/

Available through: www.gog.com/game/warcraft_orcs_and_humans

Warcraft: Orcs & Humans is a real-time strategy game in a top-down view. This is the first game in the *Warcraft* universe and departed from the usual RTS games by including new types of quests and missions that varied play from the norm. Single-player and multiplayer modes are available.

Warhammer 40,000 (eighth edition)

Developer: Games Workshop, Citadel Miniatures, Forge World	**Released:** 1983
	Game type: Board game
Publisher: Games Workshop	

More information: https://warhammer40000.com/

Warhammer 40,000 is a miniatures wargame. Play is conducted on a tabletop "battlefield" with players each presenting their models of troops and vehicles on either end. In turn players move their models into battle formations and wins are decided with math and dice rolls. All models are predetermined in the rulebook, but must be assembled and painted by the players. The eighth edition updated the rules to offer a simplified beginner-friendly approach. Two or more players.

Warhammer Quest 2: The End of Times

Developer: Perchang	**Released:** January 31, 2019
Publisher: Perchang, Chilled Mouse	**Game type:** Digital game
Platforms: PC, Mac, Nintendo Switch, Mobile	

More information: https://boardgamegeek.com/videogame/228149/warhammer-quest-2-end-times

Available through: https://store.steampowered.com/app/910450/Warhammer_Quest_2_The_End_Times/

Warhammer Quest 2 is a tactical strategy RPG game in 3D with a rotational view. It is the second of the Warhammer Quest digital games and based off of the Warhammer Quest board game in the Warhammer Series. It has turn-based combat and mimics the board game. Only Single Player is available.

Werewolf (Mafia)

Developer: Dimitry Davidoff	**Game type:** Board game
Released: 1986	

More information: www.playwerewolf.co/rules

Available through: www.playwerewolf.co/buy-werewolf

This game designed by Dimitry Davidoff created the social deduction genre and has gone on to be adapted into various forms. It has been released commercially with different themes, the most successful versions are Werewolf, Ultimate Werewolf, and WitchHunt. The game provides very little information to players and creates a situation of distrust to drive social gameplay.

White Death

Developer: Nina Runa Essendrop

Game type: Live-action role-playing game

Released: 2012

More information: http://www.ninaessendrop.com/white-death/

White Death is a nonverbal live-action RPG. Restricted player movement and emotional direction create an intense emotional experience. Also notable is the use of light to define the playspace and music to denote the progression of time.

The Witness

Developer: Thekla, Inc.

Released: 2016

Publisher: Thekla, Inc.

Game type: Digital game

Platforms: PC, Mac, PS4, Xbox One, iOS

More information: http://the-witness.net/news/media/

Available through: https://store.steampowered.com/app/210970/The_Witness/

The Witness is a first-person puzzle game in an open-world environment. Play is conducted by solving puzzles as the player moves toward the center of the island. Rules and instructions are given to the player in the form of the puzzles themselves, adding complexity as the player progresses. Keen observation of the environment also plays a role. Only single-player mode is available.

Words With Friends

Developer: Zynga, Newtoy

Released: 2009

Publisher: Zynga

Game type: Digital game

Platforms: Android, **iOS**, Facebook, Kindle Fire, Nook Tablet, Windows Phone, Windows

More information: www.zynga.com/games/words-with-friends-2/

Available through: https://apps.apple.com/us/app/words-with-friends-classic/id321916506

Words With Friends is a tile-placing crossword-like word game. Players have a selection of tiles with letters on each tile. Each tile has a value. In turn-based play, players create words with their tiles and place them on a board. The winner is the player with the highest score when all the tiles are used. Multiplayer.

World of Warcraft

Developer: Blizzard Entertainment	**Released:** 2004
Publisher: Blizzard Entertainment	**Game type:** Digital game
Platforms: PC, Mac	

More information: https://worldofwarcraft.com/en-us/

Available through: https://us.shop.battle.net/en-us/family/world-of-warcraft

World of Warcraft is an MMORPG set in the Warcraft universe and is the fourth game in the series. Play is either over-the-shoulder third- or first-person in a 3D open-world.

References

Adams, Ernest, and Joris Dormans. *Game Mechanics: Advanced Game Design.* Berkeley, CA: New Riders Games, 2012.

Alexander, Christopher, Sara Ishikawa, Murray Silverstein, Max Jacobson, Ingrid Fiksdahl-King, and Shlomo Angel. *A Pattern Language: Towns, Buildings, Construction.* New York: Oxford University Press, 1977.

Alexander, Christopher. *The Timeless Way of Building.* New York: Oxford University Press, 1979.

Alexander, Christopher. *The Nature of Order: An Essay on the Art of Building and the Nature of the Universe, Book 1: The Phenomenon of Life.* Vol. 9. Berkeley, CA: Center for Environmental Structure, 2004.

Alexander, Christopher, Randy Schmidt, Maggie Moore Alexander, Brian Hanson, and Michael Mehaffy. "Generative Codes: The Path to Building Welcoming, Beautiful, Sustainable Neighborhoods." *Living Neighborhoods.* Center for Environmental Structure, November 2005. www.livingneighborhoods.org/library/generativecodesv10.pdf.

Alves, Valter, and Licinio Roque. "Imminent Death." *Sound Design in Games,* July 19, 2012. www.soundingames.com/index.php?title=Imminent_Death.

Alves, Valter, and Licinio Roque. "Design Patterns in Games: The Case for Sound Design." *Chania,* 2013. www.fdg2013.org/program/workshops/papers/DPG2013/b1-alves.pdf.

Auerbach, David. "Was This the Most Sexist Video Game of All Time?" *Slate Magazine.* Slate, July 24, 2014. https://slate.com/technology/2014/07/catherine-video-game-the-most-sexist-platformer-of-all-time.html.

Björk, Staffan, Jussi Holopainen, and Sus Lundgren. "Game Design Patterns." 2003. www.researchgate.net/publication/221217599_Game_Design_Patterns.

Björk, Staffan, and Jussi Holopainen. *Patterns in Game Design.* Boston, MA: Charles River Media, 2006.

Björk, Staffan. "Gameplay Design Patterns." Gameplay Design Patterns Collection, August 8, 2019. http://virt10.itu.chalmers.se/index.php/Main_Page.

Butler, Tom. "The Rise of the Jump." Polygon, January 20, 2014. www.polygon.com/features/2014/1/20/5227582/the-rise-of-the-jump.

Coutu, Ysabelle. "Patterns for Environmental Narrative." Thesis, Northeastern University, 2020.

Dawes, Michael J. "Christopher Alexander's a Pattern Language: Analysing, Mapping and Classifying the Critical Response." *City, Territory and Architecture*, 4(1) (2017). doi: 10.1186/s40410-017-0073-1.

de Rochefort, Simone. "Catherine Is Unflinching, Messy and Uplifting - Just like Real Life." Polygon, February 21, 2017. www.polygon.com/2017/2/21/14686992/sex-death-redemption-catherine-atlus.

Fogel, David B. *Blondie24: Playing at the Edge of AI*. 1st ed. San Francisco: Morgan Kaufmann, 2001.

Gabriel, Richard P. *Patterns of Software: Tales from the Software Community*. New York: Oxford University Press, 1998.

GameFAQs. "What Game Do You Think Has Perfect Jumping Mechanics?" February 2, 2018. https://gamefaqs.gamespot.com/boards/204-classic-gaming/76251195.

Gamma, Erich, Richard Helm, Ralph E. Johnson, and John Vlissides. *Design Patterns: Elements of Reusable Object-Oriented Software*. New Dehli: Pearson Education, 1994.

Helfrich, Silke. "Patterns of Commoning: How We Can Bring About a Language of Commoning." *Patterns of Commoning*. The Commons Strategies Group, 2015. Accessed April 20, 2020. http://patternsofcommoning.org/patterns-of-commoning-how-we-can-bring-about-a-language-of-commoning/.

Iba, Takashi, Mami Sakamoto, and Toko Miyake. "How to Write Tacit Knowledge as a Pattern Language: Media Design for Spontaneous and Collaborative Communities." *Procedia - Social and Behavioral Sciences* 26 (2011): 46–54. doi: 10.1016/j.sbspro.2011.10.561.

Kreimeier, Bernd. "The Case for Game Design Patterns." Gamasutra, March 13, 2002. www.gamasutra.com/view/feature/132649/the_case_for_game_design_patterns.php.

Kubala, Tom. "The Fifteen Properties." The Kubala Washatko Architects. Accessed April 20, 2020. www.tkwa.com/fifteen-properties/.

Leitner, Helmut. "Working with Patterns: An Introduction." *Patterns of Commoning*. The Commons Strategies Group, 2015. Accessed April 19, 2020. http://patternsofcommoning.org/working-with-patterns-an-introduction/.

Leitner, Helmut. *Pattern Theory: Introduction and Perspectives on the Tracks of Christopher Alexander*. Vol. 1. Graz: Helmut Leitner, HLS Software, 2015.

Lemay, Philippe. "Developing a Pattern Language for Flow Experiences in Video Games." DIGRA, 2007. www.digra.org/wp-content/uploads/digital-library/07311.53582.pdf.

Li, J., and Jason Morningstar. "A Pattern Language for Larp Design." Accessed April 20, 2020. www.larppatterns.org/.

Martin, Fasterholdt, Pichlmair Martin, and Holmgård Christoffer. "You Say Jump, I Say How High? Operationalising the Game Feel of Jumping." *DiGRA*, January 1, 1970. www.digra.org/digital-library/publications/you-say-jump-i-say-how-high-operationalising-the-game-feel-of-jumping/.

McGee, Kevin. "Patterns and Computer Game Design Innovation." 2007. Accessed April 20, 2020. http://citeseerx.ist.psu.edu/viewdoc/download? doi=10.1.1.90.29&rep=rep1&type=pdf.

Ott, Michela, Alessandro ADe Gloria, Sylvester Arnab, Francesco Bellotti, Kristian Kiili, Sara De Freitas, and Riccardo Berta. "Designing Serious Games for Education: From Pedagogical Principles to Game Mechanisms." *Proceedings of the European Conference on Games-Based Learning*, 2011. www.researchgate.net/profile/Michela_Ott/publication/257022186_ Designing_serious_games_for_education_From_pedagogical_principles_ to_game_mechanisms/links/0046352433678d8895000000/Designing- serious-games-for-education-From-pedagogical-principles-to-game- mechanisms.

reddit. "What Was the First Game with a Double Jump and Why Was It Implemented?" 2016. www.reddit.com/r/truegaming/comments/4266et/ what_was_the_first_game_with_a_double_jump_and/.

Sarkeesian, Anita. "Damsel in Distress (Part 1) Tropes vs Women in Video Games." Feminist Frequency, August 26, 2016a. https://feministfrequency. com/video/damsel-in-distress-part-1/.

Sarkeesian, Anita. "Tropes vs. Women: #2 Women in Refrigerators." Feminist Frequency, August 9, 2016b. https://feministfrequency.com/video/tropes-vs- women-2-women-in-refrigerators/.

Schell, Jesse. "The Nature of Order in Game Narrative." 2018. www.gdcvault. com/play/1025006/The-Nature-of-Order-in.

Schell, Jesse. *The Art of Game Design: A Book of Lenses*. Boca Raton, FL: CRC Press/Taylor & Francis Group, 2020.

Schwaber, Ken, and Mike Beedle. *Agile Software Development with Scrum*. Upper Saddle River, NJ: Pearson Education, 2002.

Shalev, Isaac. "Patterns in Game Design." Kind Fortress. Accessed April 20, 2020. www.kindfortress.com/category/patterns-in-game-design/.

Symonds, Shannon. "Brenda Romero: 'The Mechanic is the Message.'" The Strong, June 25, 2013. www.museumofplay.org/blog/chegheads/2013/06/ brenda-romero-"the-mechanic-is-the-message".

TV Tropes. "Checkpoint." Accessed April 19, 2020a. https://tvtropes.org/pmwiki/ pmwiki.php/Main/CheckPoint.

TV Tropes. "Mighty Whitey." Accessed April 25, 2020b. https://tvtropes.org/ pmwiki/pmwiki.php/Main/MightyWhitey.

TV Tropes. "Urban Ruins." Accessed April 19, 2020c. https://tvtropes.org/pmwiki/ pmwiki.php/Main/UrbanRuins.

Twain, Mark. *The Adventures of Huckleberry Finn*. Harlow: Pearson Education, 2008.

Wikipedia. "Robert Plutchik." Accessed May 4, 2020. https://en.wikipedia.org/ wiki/Robert_Plutchik. Last modified September 13, 2020.

Index